Writing Sci-Fi, Fantasy, & Horror

by Rick Dakan and
Ryan G. Van Cleave, PhD

FOREWORD BY Ann VanderMeer

A Wiley Brand

Contents at a Glance

Table of Contents

Foreword

You can discover many available books on the craft of writing, including specialty writing books that focus on works of science fiction, fantasy, and/ or horror. Some of those books pick one of these genres, and many of these books are excellent. So why would anyone feel the need to buy and read yet another one? Well, let me tell you why. *Writing Sci-Fi, Fantasy, & Horror For Dummies* is different from all the rest in a few different ways:

Firstly, this book tackles all these genres at once. Oftentimes there is a crossover or melding of these genres, and so having a book that directly speaks to each of these genres individually as well as collectively can only benefit you, the writer.

Secondly, this book explores many other ways of creating beyond short stories and novels. Here you can find out more about writing a screenplay, collaborating on graphic novels, designing video games and/or tabletop games, and even creating a real physical haunted house. You can express science fiction, fantasy, and horror in many ways, and this book takes you on all these journeys.

Furthermore, this book provides brilliant examples in all these genres when exploring characterization, plotting, setting, and worldbuilding. Included are discussions on how to imagine monsters, aliens, other worlds and magic systems. Clear and precise examples help illustrate how you can do it effectively. Indeed, the examples are clever and imaginative and very entertaining!

You receive advice on seeking and receiving feedback and the editing process as well as the best use of subject experts and sensitivity readers. The book also offers information on the business of writing and creating, including how to submit your work, how to pitch a story idea, and the what the pros and cons of self-publishing are. Sections throughout deal with methods to overcome writer's block and how to jump-start the creative process.

In addition, you have the benefit of all of the real-world experiences of Ryan Van Cleave and Rick Dakan, who have spent years helping writers navigate the waters of creativity. They also have plenty of writing credits, so they clearly know what they're talking about.

I first became acquainted with Ryan and Rick when I was asked to speak at a Visiting Writers Forum virtual event with the creative writing department at Ringling College of Art and Design in Florida. I was honored to be asked and immediately said yes. This invitation came to me in 2020, when we were all staying home during the pandemic but still trying to move forward artistically and keep our sanity and sense of humor.

I had a blast during this event. Typically, these programs feature a writer, so as an editor, I was doubly honored to be asked. Presenting the editor's point of view to up-and-coming writers was important because too often they haven't had much experience with the editorial or publishing process. Ryan and Rick asked thoughtful and engaging questions, and I was struck by the depth of their knowledge, not just for my own books, but for the wide range of interest they have all over the writing spectrum. You can tell they have a pure love for all speculative genres, but more importantly, they're knowledgeable about things outside of genre as well. And clearly, they're passionate about sharing their knowledge and nurturing other writers. This only serves to improve the guidance they present in this book. More importantly, although the business of writing is serious, Ryan and Rick approach it from a more playful place, which makes this book such a pleasure to read and enjoy.

— Ann VanderMeer

Introduction

Writing a successful fantasy story is far more than just whipping up a regular story and dropping in an elf on page 13. It often requires comprehensive worldbuilding, cool magical beings, and other wonder-making efforts that, taken together, propel readers into an exciting realm that's never been imagined before.

That's true for science fiction and horror as well. Readers want stories that are informed by the time-honored conventions of those genres, but manage to avoid the boring tropes, stereotypical characters, and super-familiar plots.

If that sounds intimidating, it is . . . or at least it would be if you didn't have a book like this in your hands!

About This Book

Writing Sci-Fi, Fantasy, & Horror For Dummies is equally about demystifying the writing process and revealing exactly what it takes to create successful genre stories. Everything we share in this book is informed by decades of college-level teaching, writing, editing, and — perhaps more important — reading.

Our goal with this book is to give you a strong foundation that prepares you to write genre stories that stand out from the crowd. And along the way, we share advice and tips on the publishing industry so you know what to do with those stories after they're ready for audiences.

We envision that you'll use the ideas and techniques in this book to deliver story in one of three main ways:

>> Prose (novels and short stories)

>> Scripts (film, TV, comics, and graphic novels)

>> Interactive (video games, roleplaying games, and other immersive experiences)

To keep things simple, we refer to the story's "audience" throughout this book, but by that, we mean reader, viewer, gamer, and so on as the case may be for the medium you choose. Just remember: Each medium has its own inherent strengths, so when writing fiction, for example, really embrace the world of a character's interiority. With a film script, forget dialogue tags and lovely descriptions and instead focus on external action, sound, and dialogue. With a video game, you need to build amazing worlds that are ripe for conflict so a character — the player! — can have agency over the story's plot.

Here's good news: At the center of these modes of experiencing stories is the same core set of fundamental principles and reader expectations. As soon as you familiarize yourself with those, you can apply them to any storymaking enterprise that you see fit.

Foolish Assumptions

With 30-plus combined years of college-level teaching and running workshops at writing conferences, we've found that students of all ages often believe one or more of the following:

>> You're either born a writer, or you're not.

>> Writing comes easily to everyone but me.

>> I should wait for inspiration to strike before writing.

>> Good writers don't have to revise.

>> Writers need to work in solitude.

>> Getting published is more about who you know than what you write.

>> Editors will fix the "little stuff" (like spelling and grammar) for me.

>> I don't have enough time to write a novel/film script/TV series.

Plain and simple, each of these is false. We won't address why here because we cover all of these topics within the following chapters, but trust us to tell you the truth and make the appropriate arguments when it's time.

We do our best to reward your trust on every page. We promise.

We confess that we're making a few assumptions of our own about you as well, dear writing friend. In no particular order, they are as follows:

>> Whether you're new to writing or a lifelong scribbler, you want to improve at writing.

>> You really like genre stories, especially science fiction, fantasy, and horror.

>> You want to write original stories that resonate with readers.

>> You want to be on the pathway to publication.

If any of these sound like you, then the information in this book is specifically designed for you.

One more thing: We don't expect everyone to know every single story ever created or every author who ever wrote. We certainly don't know them all! So, we avoid referencing specific stories and authors in general, yet from time to time, we couldn't help ourselves. We're teachers, after all.

If you don't know a reference that we mention, that's fine. Ogres aren't going to bust down your door and pummel you with French dictionaries or anything. We swear. Just consider adding these stories and authors to your might-check-out-someday list because they have a lot to offer.

Icons Used in This Book

Books in the For Dummies series include helpful icons to ensure that key aspects, elements, and ideas get special attention. Without further ado, we use the following icons:

TIP

This icon notes the kind of thing that frequently produces an "Aha!" moments for writers. If you're looking for actionable ways to improve your writing, put these to work right away.

REMEMBER

This icon alerts you to something worthy of extra consideration. If you're skimming, make sure to slow down and really dig in when you see this alert.

TECHNICAL STUFF

This icon highlights bonus in-depth things that you can skip and still be fine. But if you're serious about writing, this insider information can help.

WARNING

This icon helps you steer clear of problem areas. The last things we want are for you to waste time, get frustrated, or smash face-first into a dead end.

EXERCISE

This icon points out hands-on activities you can try to spark your inspiration and start working on different elements of your written work.

Beyond the Book

For most readers, this book has all you need to succeed. But if you find yourself yearning for more ideas, insight, and inspiration, we have you covered!

Here are three additional resources beyond this book:

>> **Cheat Sheet:** Go to www.dummies.com and search for "Writing Sci-Fi, Fantasy, & Horror For Dummies Cheat Sheet" to locate a handy reference guide for all three genres included in this book.

>> **Double down with Dummies:** Couple this book with *Writing Fiction For Dummies* by Peter Economy and Randall Ingermanson and *Writing Young Adult Fiction For Dummies* by Deborah Halverson, or any other For Dummies title that grabs your interest. We won't be offended! The tips, tricks, and advice from our writing colleagues who've created other For Dummies books can absolutely support your journey to writing success.

>> **Work with us:** Both of us teach, present at writing conferences, and do a bit of freelance writing, editing, and coaching. Visit us at www.rickdakan.com or www.ryangvancleave.com to see if any of those options work for you!

Where to Go from Here

If you're totally new to writing, we suggest you begin with the basics of story construction (Part 1). Part 2 on worldbuilding contains valuable advice that informs all three genres — you're more than welcome to go right into whichever specific genre or craft concerns that you most. Or if you're not sure where to start, scan the Table of Contents or flip through the index, find a topic that piques your interest, and turn to that chapter.

Remember, Dummies books are modular, so you can read any chapter in any order. Ultimately, this book is set up to reward you whether you dive in at Chapter 1 and read straight through, or you skip around as you see fit. Treat this book like a reference. Use it when needed, but be open to putting it aside and doing what writers want to do most — *write*.

1
Getting Started: The Basics of Story

Build interesting, three-dimensional characters that genre-loving audiences will hope and fear for.

Select the best point of view to showcase the conflicts and themes in your story.

Plot your story with a focus on dramatic action and character arcs.

Create a seamless narrative by linking scenes through cause and effect.

Use high-powered story tension to keep audiences hooked.

Discover the best medium for your stories and use its inherent strengths to your advantage.

Chapter 1

Taking Journeys into the Imagination

This is a book designed to help writers tell stories better.

It's as simple and as complex as that.

Teachers, librarians, parents, and other fans of sci-fi, fantasy, and horror may get a lot from this book, too, but our goal is first and foremost to help writers tell their stories. Our areas of focus are the craft aspects and foundational considerations that increase a writer's ability to create sci-fi, fantasy, and horror stories that matter.

Because good stories matter — we firmly believe that.

Every well-told story is a wondrous journey into the human imagination. Stories are a shared enterprise that brings joy to authors and audiences. A symbiotic experience, we might suggest.

This chapter serves as your portal to the world of sci-fi, fantasy, and horror stories. If you want to create written works of these three genres, then you've come to the right place.

Looking Closer at the Big Three Genres

Three of the most popular creative writing classes we teach are Writing Science Fiction, Writing Fantasy, and Writing Horror. And in the other classes we offer, we frequently attract students who are looking to write and talk about stories with dark elf thieves, robot assassins, or hooded axe-wielding maniacs. Sometimes all in the same story!

TECHNICAL STUFF

Some people choose to group these three genres under one far larger umbrella called *speculative fiction,* which is a type of story that could've been generated from a "what if?" question because these stories include elements and aspects that don't exist in *consensus reality* (the things people generally agree on about how the world works). That's a fairly basic definition, but the term itself is slippery. Plenty of writers don't fully agree on what it means, which is one reason we don't use it in this book.

Even though other authors may be satisfied to lump sci-fi, fantasy, and horror together, we find it more useful to examine, understand, and appreciate the differences in each as a way to improve your ability to write effective stories. The lines between these genres do blur and overlap, but that's okay — we handle them separately in this book to keep things clear for you.

REMEMBER

And although the three genres do have clear distinctive characteristics, some of those characteristics can overlap in lots of interesting ways. Visit Chapter 27 for more ways to mix, match, and blend story elements to good effect.

One thing all these genres share is an emphasis on the art and craft of worldbuilding, which we cover in detail in Part 2. Chapter 5 explores the idea of creating a very specific world for your story. Chapter 6 combines research with imagination, and shares secret worldbuilding advice from Kenneth Hite, a top gamemaker. Chapter 7 helps you find ways to engage audiences on multiple levels versus sticking to a formula. Worlds can be so rich and robust that they're practically a character, too. That's the idea behind Chapter 8, which explains how worlds actively want something.

The following sections take a closer look at the three genres.

Imagining possible worlds — Sci-fi

Sci-fi stories offer audiences possible other worlds. It's based in or at least inspired by scientific reality as people know it at the time of the writing. The genre goes beyond that, however, to ask "what if?" questions about the future, new technologies, and humanity's place in the universe.

Before writing your sci-fi story, answer the following questions:

>> **What's the Big New Thing?** At the heart of a great sci-fi story is a science-based development that's vital to the narrative (that's your *Big New Thing*). What ideas do you have for a cool Big New Thing?

>> **How would it change the story world?** Whether it's new tech or a scientific breakthrough, the world should be affected by its creation or use. If not, your Big New Thing probably isn't big enough to carry your story.

>> **Who would care?** At least some people can't ignore the Big New Thing. They should be in awe, be fearful, or have some other significant reactions that will drive them to action.

>> **What conflicts emerge?** Someone wants to corner the market, change the world, oppress those who need oppressing, or just make a quick buck. If someone wants something, someone else is going to try to stop them from getting it, and the Big New Thing should be central to resolving that conflict.

To blast straight into writing sci-fi, visit Part 3, which explores the other possible worlds of science fiction. From the huge "what if?" at the center of every sci-fi story (see Chapter 9) to spaceships and space travel (refer to Chapter 10) to aliens and every type of artificial life (flip to Chapters 11 and 12), it's all here. We even investigate ways to create other planets in general and other Earths in particular — that's Chapter 13. We also get into the idea of dystopias and utopias, two possible futures that audiences like to see come alive through stories.

Imagining wondrous worlds — Fantasy

Fantasy stories give audiences impossible other worlds. In the wondrous worlds of fantasy, consensus reality is shattered to exciting and entertaining ends, which makes room for magic spells, ancient artifacts, and fantastic creatures.

Here we explore a few questions to help you write fantastic fantasy stories:

>> **What's the impossible thing?** One of the things that makes your story fantasy is the inclusion of something that's impossible for the real world. Unicorns exist. Lightning bolts can be triggered from wands. All brown-eyed people can read minds. Start with one impossible thing and build from there.

>> **What rules does it break and follow?** Thanks to being impossible, it can break all sorts of real-world rules, like physics or the need for sleep. But it can and should have its own rules. What cost does casting a spell require? What weak spot does the otherwise invulnerable dragon have? Limits make the impossible more interesting and dramatic.

- » **How does your main character encounter it?** How the impossible thing manifests needs to matter. Does your character move from a mundane world into one rich with wonder? Is the wondrous all around from page one? Or does the wonder come barreling into the character's normal world, which really mucks things up?

- » **How does the impossible thing relate to your antagonist?** If it's powerful, an antagonist surely wants it. Or maybe it's something that was simply theirs, and they want it back. In any event, wonderous, impossible things should only be included if they have meaning to characters and the story world. They shouldn't just be flavor text or props.

To transport audiences to carefully built worlds populated with rich characters and potential conflicts, fly on over to Part 4 where we peer into the wondrous world of fantasy. How do you get to the fantastic? Portals, intrusions, and immersions (see Chapter 14). How the @!#$! do you create a magic system? Think in terms of rules and costs (go to Chapter 15). Those fantasy worlds are intimidating, so how do you create a good one? The key is to think of what makes a story-rich world (refer to Chapter 16). What about those wild monsters and creatures they have? We cover those brutes in Chapter 17.

Imagining fearful worlds — Horror

Horror stories offer audiences terrifying worlds. Sometimes the scary stuff in a horror story could indeed happen (serial killers, plagues, cults, and ruthless corporations), whereas in some horror stories, it couldn't (demons, ghosts, zombies, and witches). Regardless of the pathway to terror a writer chooses, a quality horror story will make audiences quake with fear and plead to keep the lights on at night. Just in case.

REMEMBER

Here are some questions to get you thinking about a prevalent horror story type — the discovery plot:

- » **What's the mystery that launches the story?** The key discovery of this mystery (a missing child? a murder? a stolen artifact?) launches the characters into a larger story where they need to confront and survive a horrible truth they've uncovered.

- » **How does the mystery connect to your character's core want?** An easy way to do this is to make it personal — the missing child is their niece. Or the murder happened on their property. Or the artifact is their family heirloom. Regardless of your specific choices, the character should only be able to ignore it at great personal cost.

>> **How do clues and discoveries create a sense of dread?** The deeper your characters go into the story, the more foreboding and menace they should encounter. Really amp up the fear. Audiences know the protagonists have no choice but to plunge ahead (thanks to that core want driving them along).

>> **What terrible thing happens?** It's a horror story, after all, so audiences expect something terrible. A death cult wreaks havoc on a seaside community. A demon is summoned from beneath the museum of antiquities. What do your characters do in response?

To find out more about crafting hair-raising stories, we dare you to step into Part 5 that introduces you to the world of horror. We start with core audience reactions — dread, fear, and terror (see Chapter 18). We then focus on the emotional sources of fear, which includes a look at the cathartic effect of being scared (refer to Chapter 19). We face menacing monsters and equally menacing human horrors (head to Chapter 20). We investigate the many environments where unsuspecting folks may encounter horror, from haunted houses to vampire lairs to abandoned moon colonies to Himalayan mountain caves to the weird house three down from yours in Chapter 21.

Creating Characters

What people tend to remember most about stories are the characters they love. Chapter 2 reveals all you need to know to create characters worthy of great stories. *Minor spoiler:* Characters need to have a goal they're willing to work hard for, and they need to be flawed. No one's that interested in reading about perfect people who've got their act together.

REMEMBER

What audiences want is to follow along with a character who's relatable and who's doing things that matter. They want engaging characters they can hope and fear for all the way to the end. That only happens when characters are interesting. Chapter 2 also offers advice on picking the best point of view, using telling details, and crafting strong dialogue. It's a one-stop shop for all your character-making needs.

Great characters need great conflicts. And conflicts are the engine of story — making those is what Chapter 3 is all about. We examine the DNA of story conflict, showcase effective pre-existing story structures, and make an argument for the importance of character arcs. We also share our best tips for pacing, explain the various types of scenes, and look at beginnings, middles, and ends (and how to create them, of course).

Pursuing Writerly Success

We want more for you than just helping you become far more knowledgeable about sci-fi, fantasy, and horror. That's worthwhile, of course, but to be a successful writer means you regularly do things that professional writers do. That's where Part 6 of this book comes into play.

These sections give you an overview of what you can do to be a better writer.

Revising your words

No one's perfect, and you shouldn't have that level of expectation for yourself on a first or even an early draft. But when it's time to get those words under control, we recommend that you do the following:

>> **Read your work aloud.** Whether you're doing the reading or someone else is, your ears will catch things your eyes somehow miss.

>> **Take notes.** When rereading your work, make a to-do list of things to work on later versus fixing issues as you find them. Trying to fix it all as you go is too overwhelming.

>> **Track themes.** Use highlighters, sticky notes, or a color-coded spreadsheet to keep track of your themes. Do they really say what you intended to? Are there places for them to be elevated and enhanced?

>> **Revisit characterization.** Make sure that every character is consistent and believable. Are the descriptions effective? Do they have their own way of speaking, acting, and thinking?

>> **Know when to stop revising.** There's a point where you've done all you can, and further work isn't making things better — just different.

Chapter 22 shows you how to revise and edit like a pro. Doing that is a must if you want your work to be published or presented to an audience. We discuss revision plans, revising for theme, editing your scenes, sentences, and words, and much more.

Turning to pros for help

Although doing everything on your own may seem important or even glamorous, that's not how most stories are made. Writers are definitely expected to do a lot, yes, but they should know when it's appropriate to bring in outside help.

Here are just some of the types of pros they turn to for expert guidance and input:

>> **Developmental editor:** These story gurus specialize in improving the structure and content of your story. They also have marketplace insight and use that to ensure you're able to make the best story possible.

>> **Proofreader:** These folks go way beyond your software's spellcheck features and ensure your writing is free of typographical, grammatical, spelling, syntax, and formatting errors.

>> **Sensitivity reader:** If you're writing about members of any marginalized group, a sensitivity reader can scrutinize your story for insensitive, incorrect, offensive, or out-of-date portrayals. Even if you're a member of that group, a fresh perspective can still be quite useful.

>> **Subject-area experts:** These people do and know things few others can appreciate . . . until you need that information for a story. Think NASA astrobiologists, forensic anthropologists, and prosthetists.

>> **University researchers:** Even though these experts may not be in the field, they know as much — or more! — than those doing so. And they love to talk about what they're researching, teaching, and writing about.

Getting quality outside assistance and guidance is often invaluable in helping you get your work to its highest level. Turn to Chapter 23 for more details.

Focusing on the three Ps

The three Ps are important parts of your writing journey. In no particular order, they are as follows:

>> **Pitching:** A *pitch* is the bite-sized, most compelling version of your story in verbal or written form. It's often called an *elevator pitch* because you should be able to deliver it in 30 seconds or less (about the duration of a normal elevator ride).

>> **Publication:** This is your goal with writing stories, whether publication is book form, live performance, audio production, or any of the other main delivery options to get your work before audiences.

>> **Promotion:** Selling yourself as a writer and your work as worthwhile is a skill all on its own. Those who develop this gift really reap the rewards.

Chapter 24 explains the three Ps in much greater detail. We're really getting into industry stuff here, which is something you don't need to worry about much until you've got a complete draft of a manuscript that you're extremely proud of, and you want to get it out in the world. Until then, agents and publishing house editors aren't something in which you should invest much time.

Setting the right goals for you

Your success as a writer is going to be different than that of another writer. You may share a few common goals with others, but some specific goals are uniquely theirs. Set your own goals and figure out what you want to do with your stories. To help get a handle on your relationship with writing, consider the following questions:

>> Why do you want to write?

>> What can you write that nobody else can?

>> What type of writing do you find most rewarding?

>> Does it matter who — or how many people — connect with your writing?

>> Is writing a hobby, a part-time thing, or something you want to do as a full-time career?

>> If people read your stories, does it matter if your writing makes money?

WARNING

One mistake we see students and early-career writers make is solely thinking about big picture success, like writing a blockbuster movie, penning a bestselling book, or creating the next Netflix hit series. We hope those outcomes are in your future, but for most, they're still a long way off. If that's your benchmark of success, you may feel like a failure because you may feel as if you're making little to no progress because the target remains so far away.

Instead, we suggest you create a series of goals that are organized by the amount of time and energy they require, such as:

>> **Short-term goals:** Finish reading this book. Practice 30 minutes of morning journaling for a week. Come up with five story ideas. Select one idea and create an outline for the entire story. For five days straight, write 300 words of that story each day.

>> **Medium-term goals:** Revise, deepen, and enhance the story outline. Write 300 words of that story each day for a month. Repeat for the next month. And the next. And then the next one after that.

>> **Long-term goals:** Complete the entire first draft. Enlist two smart readers to give thoughtful feedback on your story. Revise the story draft in response to their comments, with the goal of cutting 10 percent of the total word count.

Having a series of measurable goals like these — that you celebrate when you achieve! — helps you avoid burnout, create accountability, and track your progress. Add in your own motivation and passion, and you should be well on your way toward making writing stories a meaningful part of your life, whatever that looks like.

THREE TYPES OF SUCCESSFUL STORIES

The incredibly prolific children's author Jane Yolen — who also writes a lot of science fiction and fantasy stories — talks about the three different types of books she writes:

- **Head books:** She creatively chews on a problem or idea that interests her.
- **Heart books:** She engages with something she's deeply passionate about.
- **Pocket books:** These are books she knows will be highly commercial.

If you wrote a head story but made little or no money on it, would that be okay? What if a heart story also brought you little or no money? Is there a way for you to write a head or heart story and have it be a pocket story?

The only good answers are the honest ones you tell yourself. Make sure you create a bull's-eye that's right for you as a writer. Then keep it in sight as you work on your craft and write the best stories you can. If your goals ever change, that's fine. Adjust as needed, and then keep writing. It's also smart to review your goals at least twice a year, if not more.

There are many ways to be successful, and we want you to pursue the ones that make sense for you and you alone. That's the correct route to take.

REMEMBER

When creating goals, think about the acronym SMART: Each goal should be specific, measurable, attainable, relevant, and timely. Do that, and you're well on your way of generating ideas, writing stories, and hitting deadlines.

Making the Most of This Book

We spent a lot of time contemplating how to ensure this book is useful from the first to the final page. Our goal was to create a fluff-less writing how-to book. We think this is it.

One way to engage with this book is to read it cover to cover, from start to finish. We'd be more than pleased if you did exactly that. There's a lot packed into here that can help new, intermediate, and advanced writers. In one big bite or many smaller meals, devour it all if you will.

But we also realize you may wish to focus on certain things first. That's a fine option, as well. Feel free to review the table of contents and plunge into the parts you need on a case-by-case basis.

You can also mix and match parts of this book to tailor-make a learning situation to suit a specific goal. For example, if you want to write your own urban fantasy (a story where supernatural/magical elements occur in a real-world city setting), you can build a reading list like this:

>> **Chapter 2:** How do you create a main character who goes where she shouldn't and engages in activities others quite reasonably avoid? Give her a powerful reason to seek an audience with a fairy criminal underboss.

>> **Chapter 7:** What's the best way to show how dangerous these fairies are? Put them in some kind of violent altercation so the main character — and the audience — can witness it and say, "Wow, those fairies are bad*ss!"

>> **Chapter 10:** What type of society do the fairies have? Let the interpersonal dynamic options of a spaceship's crew offer suggestions for how fairies might interact in close quarters with each other as they stay out of sight of normal humans.

>> **Chapter 16:** How does fairy magic work in a modern world? For a story where magic is quite rare, develop a magic system that has dramatic, interesting costs that justifies why magic isn't more prevalent.

>> **Chapter 20:** How can the fairy court be as unnerving as possible? Let them personify and fully embody a societal flaw.

If you're more inclined to try your hand at creating an untraditional haunted house story, such as an abandoned spaceship recently discovered in orbit around the third moon of Saturn, the following is an ideal reading agenda:

>> **Chapter 2:** No one travels way out in space alone, so who should accompany the main character? Provide companions to support, protect, and serve as confidantes as things get weird way out there in space.

>> **Chapter 6:** How can the derelict ship itself be uniquely interesting? Make it like every other spaceship that audiences know of, yet change one big thing that fits the mood and themes of this story.

>> **Chapter 10:** In what way can the ship be inhospitable and unwelcoming? Take away the comforts most ships offer, such as artificial gravity and a functioning life support system.

>> **Chapter 17:** What role might the monsters — whatever they are — play on this abandoned ship? The monsters may serve as obstacles to answering the larger more deadly question of what happened to the crew.

>> **Chapter 21:** How may the ship itself be a fear-generating environment? Use shifting structures to keep the main character (and whomever is still alive at this point) unsettled.

Our intention is for this book to have what you need for you to write great sci-fi, fantasy, and horror stories. Taken as a whole, the book is a comprehensive take on exactly that, but the individual parts are versatile and can work together to troubleshoot a specific problem or create a particular type of story or story effect.

IN THIS CHAPTER

» Allowing desire to drive the story

» Casting the right characters for the job

» Making point of view matter

» Crafting a character detail by detail

» Cooking up red-hot dialogue

Chapter **2**

Creating Characters

I f you think about your favorite movies and books, chances are that although you may be fuzzy on some of the specific details about what happened, the main characters remain crystal clear. That's not a surprise. Characters are what make stories linger in your head because audiences connect with them. They worry about them. They root for them. They imagine what it's like to live in their shoes . . . or space boots . . . or winged sandals!

Compelling characters are the reason people reread books and rewatch movies. Audiences want to spend more time with characters they've come to care about. Those audiences don't believe or care about? There's simply no need to revisit their lives.

On the one hand, audiences know that fiction is a form of make-believe. As much as they may wish it to be otherwise, the heroes from a beloved space opera or fantasy epic aren't real. But on the other hand, audiences enter a new story like people on a first date. They're hopeful. They're eager. They *want* to make a meaningful connection.

As a writer, your goal is to make that literary love happen by creating characters who are worthy of your audience's time and attention. This chapter gives you the basics on how to do exactly that.

TIP

Characters are meant to look, feel, act, talk, and even smell real. That means you can do a lot of firsthand research all on your own by carefully paying attention to your own life and the lives of those around you. Pro writers do this all time. Jot down things you notice and consider incorporating some of those real-world details to make your characters appear more believable.

Focusing on Your Characters' Wants

Human beings want things: A pair of shoes. A college degree in marketing. A chance to meet their birth mother. To be the first person to step foot on Mars. To win a reality TV contest.

Some desires are far less important to a story than others. Getting hold of a new spiked club, for example, doesn't mean much to a barroom brawler who already has an entire arsenal in the attic above the bar that they call home. But for a homeless elf who dreams of finding a way to stop the town bullies from stealing his food?

In the first case, no one cares that much whether that brawler gets their 20th lethal weapon or not. Honestly, the brawler likely doesn't care much either. But that poor elf is yearning for something meaningful. Getting a sword so he can finally defend himself might mean the difference between survival and starvation.

After you know what your characters really want, figuring out how they're going to respond to story events is much easier. The following sections on goals, needs, and desires reveal a lot about your character's key wants.

REMEMBER

People are complex; they often have conflicting desires that battle within themselves. For example, an undead hunter's No. 1 guiding principle may be to slay vampires. In certain cases, though — perhaps as this character develops and grows throughout the course of a story — she may be in situation where saving the life of the innkeeper's shrewish wife is more important than ramming a stake through the cold, black heart of a fanged monster that's been decimating the town's vital sheep population.

Give your characters room to experience inner turmoil. Put them in a tough spot and see how they reveal their true inner character. Situations and context can also have a profound effect on what a character ultimately chooses to do, as well.

TIP

Here's another fun wrinkle related to desire. What a character wants doesn't always make them happy. Sometimes people want something that's downright bad for them, like another drink or more dark magic. Consider how that idea manifests in real life, and then see how much mileage you can get out of this concept in your story. Another way of saying this is that old chestnut: "Beware what you wish for — you just might get it!"

Looking outside — External goals

The most obvious kind of story desire is purely external. *External goals* are things your character want from the world. These are popular choices for writers to include because it's just so clear to audiences what the prize is and how close the character is — or isn't! — to getting it.

REMEMBER

External goals should be clear and specific. They should have intrinsic value, too, even if it's only valuable to the main character, like one's sentimentality for a broken shotgun given to them by their grandfather. Getting that back may be as important to this specific character as stopping the zombie apocalypse, or nearly so.

Here are a few examples of external goals:

>> I want to retrieve the Sword of Zyzzyz from the goblin king's hoard.

>> I want to earn enough space bucks to buy a C-581 deep-space mining ship.

>> I want to stop the zombie apocalypse plaguing Ecuador.

Reflecting inward — Internal needs

Internal needs may well be less obvious than external ones, but that doesn't mean they don't matter. *Internal needs* are basically a character's hopes, dreams, and fears. They may be less tangible than outdueling a former teacher or a pilfering from a lich's treasure mound, but they can be extremely potent motivators that push your character into action.

TIP

To give characters depth, make sure they have one or more external and internal goals. This prevents them from being too one-note, which helps keep your audience engaged. No one likes boring, obvious people.

Consider these examples:

>> What might a fallen priest do in order to reclaim their once-sterling reputation?

>> How far will a swordswoman go to prove her worth in her disapproving adventurer boyfriend's eyes?

Looking a bit deeper — Hidden desires

Even though a character has external goals that are clear to the audience and internal needs that are perhaps less overt, many of the most interesting characters have a desire or drive that's hidden to everyone, including themselves. *Hidden desires* are the type of things most characters wouldn't know about themselves without $20,000 of therapy . . . or a story like yours to force them to these key realizations.

For example, perhaps a tough childhood left the city's exorcist with a terrible sense of self-worth. The little voice in her head constantly whispers, "You're not good enough, you'll never be good enough." So, she dates losers and drinks to excess no matter how much she insists to the few people left in her life that she truly just wants to be happy.

That poor exorcist can't figure out what their problem is. She likely blames others or bad luck. Yet the truth is buried behind layers of psychological angst, denial, and misdirection. But the story happenings will reveal it to them, often in or around the story's climax. Chapter 3 on plot gives you what you need to make your story's climax memorable.

Introducing the Cast of Characters

With characters in stories, your audience gets to know some far more intimately than others, and that's okay. In fact, that's almost always the best way to go. By design, not all characters are created equal.

REMEMBER

The word "create" is key here. You're not ordering them out of some wholesale writer catalogue or using a mystic summoning circle to whisk them from the Land of 10,000 Dreams. You're building them, top to bottom, through a series of creative choices that you're deliberately making.

Tailor-making them to be *exactly* who you need for the story you want to tell only makes sense. Think about major conflicts and scenes in your story, and, if you know them, the climax and story ending. What type of character is required to make those story moments work? Well, that's who you should create. Don't settle for anything else, no matter how cool or interesting those others seem. Save them for another story — or a different story role — best suited for them.

You may not know enough plot details yet to engineer the perfect character. That's okay. Until the story is published, it's a work in progress. Let the revision process — we cover it in Chapter 22 — help you revise your character to ensure they're the right person for the job.

In the following sections we explore the key character roles in stories, including the seemingly less-vital ones that often elevate a story from the mundane into something truly special.

Leading the way — Protagonists

Whether you call them the *leads, heroes, main characters, principals, central figures,* or *protagonists,* they're pretty much same thing — they're the stars of your story. The story revolves around them. It's their actions that drive the plot forward. Just like how some real-world celebrities feel the world revolves around them, the world of the story does revolve to a large extent around your protagonist.

The idea of a true hero doesn't feel believable today in the same way that it did decades or centuries ago. One manifestation of this is how so many of today's superhero stories feature gritty, flawed figures who are markedly different than the larger-than-life, shiny, perfect superheroes of the past. That's not necessarily a bad thing — it certainly makes the character more fleshed out!

Here we examine what makes a protagonist really work on the page.

Sharing what makes your protagonist tick

Because audiences spend more time with your main characters than any other person in the story, audiences need to connect with them at the highest level. Plenty of writers believe that audiences get to know protagonists even better than they know their dearest friends.

What kinds of things do audiences want to know? The list is potentially massive, but thinking about first-date or job interview questions — with a heavy dose of psychological sharing — is a good way to start. Beyond the basics of age, name, height, weight, current home, current job, marital status, and the like, asking the following questions about your character can help them grow into the job of Main Character of Your Story:

>> **What do they want?** Note that the question is "What do they want?" and not "What do they need?" because the answers are almost always different. The gap between those answers is rich story material, though it's the *want* that motivates what the character does for most, if not all, of the story. No want equals no story. Make their want profoundly important to them, and then watch how hard they go after it.

>> **What's their moral code?** What will it allow them to do (and not do) in order to get what they want? Whether stated aloud or not, everyone has hard limits. It only makes sense that your characters do, too. So, give them a hard limit, whether it's "I never lie!" or "Killing is only justified in self-defense." If you

challenge yourself by limiting what a character can or will do, the results can be terrifically original and interesting.

>> **What is more important than what they want?** For some characters, the answer is nothing. For dramatic reasons, however, it's usually more useful for them to believe in and value something(s) more important than themselves, whether it's religion, country, family, duty, or something along those lines. The tension between their own wants and the obligations of a belief system or institution make for wonderful story conflict.

REMEMBER

Ultimately, audiences need protagonists they're interested in and care about enough to spend lots of time with them because that's what a story asks audiences to do. Discover what's interesting, special, or unique about your characters and share it. Give them complexity and depth. If you do that effectively, audiences will come along for the ride, even if a character has a fairly noticeable flaw or two.

Looking for growth

The idea of growth is key. Stories are about characters who experience meaningful conflict and end up changing as a result. Determine what kind of changes your character will undergo.

Consider the following types of character growth:

>> **Change/transformation arc:** A regular person grows into a true hero, savior, or Chosen One.

>> **Maturation arc:** Someone becomes a better version of themselves through physical, spiritual, or emotional improvement, though with less of a complete overhaul as the transformation arc requires.

>> **Tragic arc:** A person makes choices that ultimately doom them, and, perhaps, others.

>> **Redemption arc:** A not-so-great character learns the error of their ways and commits to living a better life while they make amends for all the damage they've done, as best they can.

REMEMBER

Other options exist, but *key to all character arcs is change*, even if you subvert things along the way with a dose of irony or satire. Change is good. Few audiences want stories that are static or flat. They want to witness characters face the impactful consequences of their actions. That's what brings people to stories.

TECHNICAL STUFF

You may be inclined to argue that some iconic characters — such as certain super-heroes or a detective hero — don't change. You're sort of right. That type of figure is roughly the same at the end of the story as they are at the beginning, save for fresh bruises and thumps, perhaps. But change still happens — it's just shifted from internal character change to external change.

These iconic heroes enact change upon the world around them, restoring order as they solve a mystery, lock up a bad guy, or right some horrid wrong.

All other main characters in stories, however, do undergo meaningful personal change as a result of facing and overcoming all the conflicts and forces of opposition the story throws in their way. How could they not be affected by such momentous things?

If you're intrigued by this idea of iconic characters, check out Robin D. Laws' *Beating the Story: How to Map, Understand, and Elevate Any Narrative* (Gameplaywright), which explains the concept in great detail.

Standing in the way — Antagonists

Your story needs someone — or something — to thwart the desires of and oppose your protagonist. Enter the antagonist — perhaps more than one. Here we take a closer look at what antagonists are, what they're up to, and what makes them awesome.

Appreciating the range of adversaries

Whether it's a mighty ogress rampaging through the countryside, a group of bandits stealing priceless paintings from a monastery, a malicious space empire bent on destroying every asteroid mining company that doesn't join with them, an apocalyptic global snowstorm, a magic curse targeting an entire family tree, or a shadowy alien entity with a thirst for your specific DNA, the story needs an adversarial force to get in the way of the protagonist and their goals. Again and again and again.

Note that we didn't say villain. Even though a pure-evil villain can serve as a perfectly acceptable antagonist, many stories do quite well without pitting a protagonist (The Good Guy!) versus a classic villain (The Bad Guy!). An antagonist can just as easily be a relatively good person whose goals are simply in opposition to those of the protagonist. And it can also be something other than a person, such as a comet blasting toward earth, a nefarious organization, or an alien.

Motivating an antagonist

Most villains don't see themselves as villains. They don't believe they're evil. From their perspective, they're doing the right thing and likely think the protagonist is the actual "Bad Guy." Although these villains actively oppose and undermine the protagonist, in their eyes they're doing it for defensibly good reasons.

Regardless of what type of antagonist you use, give them the same level of development expected for a protagonist. If you skimp, you run the risk of letting your antagonist become a one-dimensional caricature. Use the same set of questions we present in the section, "Sharing what makes your protagonist tick," earlier in this chapter to help uncover more relevant aspects to your antagonist.

Even more than a protagonist, your antagonist needs a clear moral code to limit their mayhem, murdering, and madness. Perhaps the serial killer clown only sneaks into bedrooms at night to slit the throats of philandering husbands — she always lets the wives, children, bystanders, and faithful husbands live. This kind of framework helps make the antagonist more sympathetic. If you can find a way to make audiences love or root for antagonists, go for it. Give them a flash of their humanity, pain, or complexity.

The most effective antagonists undergo their own character arc and should be formidable in terms of power, capability, and drive. In fact, antagonists should be the strongest force in the story, which makes audiences question whether the protagonist will ever be able to win. Antagonists should also have a knack for attacking the protagonist's weak spot, whatever that is. They know just how to bring the pain.

Confronting an antagonist

If you're inclined to use an antagonistic force that's more abstract, such as a curse, the supernatural, nature, or a physical condition, try to embody it within an actual character to allow for direct confrontation. Don't just give audiences an anonymous wasting curse; give them the three-eyed cave witch who cast it because she was snubbed for the job of the General's Mystic Counsel. Don't just give audiences a category 5 storm tearing up Miami. Give them the people who are hoarding supplies to sell at a huge markup in the aftermath. Give them the jerks who sit on rooftops off Interstate 95, mocking the fools in gridlock as they try to flee to Jacksonville. (Read more about world — and nature — being its own character in Chapter 8.)

The more direct and concrete a conflict is, the easier audiences can engage with it. Putting a face on a problem makes it more real. But if it's not something you can reason with, characters will have to find another way to triumph.

Introducing supporting characters

Your story has some — if not a lot — of other characters who get their fair share of time on the page or stage. These are supporting characters. Note the key word "support." They have a function in the story, and that's to *support* and complement the more important characters — the protagonist and antagonist. If that's not happening, demote these characters to minor roles or give them the editorial boot entirely. If you can't easily create a relationship diagram that includes them, out they must go!

The best supporting characters have their own medium-level *backstory* (information about their life prior to the launch of this particular story). They're three-dimensional, having genuine strengths, weakness, motives, dreams, and flaws. Perhaps more important, they need a clear reason to be there, whether it's relating to the main plot or a subplot. That means they're providing yet another opportunity for story conflict. Hooray. It's almost impossible to have enough conflict (see Chapter 3 for more on conflict). In simple terms, think of supporting characters as falling in one (or more!) of three camps:

>> Those that help

>> Those that antagonize

>> Those that inform

The following examines some of the main ways supporting characters can earn their place in your story.

Representing a theme

Some writers like to use supporting characters as metaphorical representations of story themes, such as the barbarian chieftain's thieving brother who represents a refusal of family obligation and honor, or the cybernetic Megacorp CEO's bodyguard whose actions show her struggling with the question "Can I have honor while serving a tyrant?"

If this kind of thematic move intrigues you, layer that in. Just do it with subtlety versus hanging a flashing neon *This Is A Symbol* sign around their neck. Audiences are smart. They'll figure it out.

Acting as the BFF — The companion

The *companion* is an often-necessary supporting character who can serve the role of friend, guard, sidekick, confidante, or even love interest. Having companions play multiple roles such as the talented sorcerer's apprentice who acts as a sounding board for his master who likes to bounce a lot of ideas around before committing to any action is efficient. That apprentice can also be a protector, fiercely loyal to the point that things come to magical blows if anyone disparages the master's magic or motivations. Perhaps your story has a trustworthy squire who knows and keeps the protagonist's deepest, darkest secret while also acting as their moral compass. Maybe your story needs a companion who serves a necessary supporting character role right up until they die, giving extra oomph to the hero's desire to defeat their nemesis.

Contrasting with another character — A foil

A *foil* is another key type of supporting character — a person who puts a spotlight on the attributes of another character through opposing traits. This character may be a friend, like a fireball-chucking frenemy who handles everything with magic overkill whereas the protagonist may save their magic and use it judiciously in small, clever ways. Or the foil can be the antagonist, whose motto might be "I can never have enough magic because there's always more of it." The differing viewpoints or approaches create an interesting contrast that deepens both characters.

Providing guidance — A mentor

A *mentor* figure makes fine supporting characters because they're so good at helping and informing. The galactic sheriff who shares his hard-won knowledge with anyone who'll listen. An ancient dwarven librarian who always knows the right book to recommend. A mentor can also serve as a barometer for the protagonist's growth. What better way to dramatize change than a student who no longer needs the mentor, or at least they don't need them in the same dependent manner they once did?

Standing in direct opposition — The rival

Although not a proper villain, a *rival* is one of the forces of opposition working against the protagonist because their goals are mutually exclusive. Perhaps your protagonist yearns to become the leader of a suborbital strike team and another equally qualified soldier has the same goal. In this world, suborbital strike teams only have one leader, so one of these two isn't going to get what they want.

The story may also have a true villain antagonist who is secretly trying to kill off the protagonist for other reasons. That's yet another force of opposition that's far different than the rival, who simply wants to follow their own dreams. The rival can easily be a very likable, honorable person who still represents a more immediate and significant problem for the protagonist than the murderous villain lurking in the shadows.

Being at cross purposes — The adversary

One of our favorites, the *adversary* is someone who, like the rival, isn't a villain, but somehow manages to get in the protagonist's way over and over again. Consider an overprotective demigod mother, a snoopy, rule-following robot butler, an ogre who's smitten with the protagonist and won't leave his side, though his brutish size and fangy frown has every sheriff and all the townsfolk on edge. This type of character has oodles of comic possibilities, if you want to go that route.

Managing your supporting cast — Tips and tricks

Creating three-dimensional supporting characters is a great way to give your story a sense of reality. If you're successful, then these characters can complete your story world. If not, they can cause your story to crash and burn. Here are some other pointers to remember when assembling your supporting cast:

>> **Consider using supporting characters who are the yin to your main character's yang.** Opposites often attract. The contrast can be interesting, believable, and effective in terms of showcasing facets of both characters.

WARNING

>> **Avoid the temptation of populating your story with as many characters as you can dream up.** You want exactly as many characters as the story requires, and not one more. Combine them. Cut them. Do what you have to in order to end up with a modest-sized cast that audiences — and you! — can keep track of. It's more than twice as hard to care about a dozen characters as it is to care about six.

REMEMBER

The world of your story is going to be filled with minor characters who don't even get their full 15 minutes of fame. These folks look up at the supporting characters with envy. That's okay. It's just their lot in (story) life.

>> **Make your supporting characters realistic.** Even though minor characters come and go fairly quickly, they still need to have some personality and description beyond the cliché. The bearded old wizard doesn't have to be a doddering, forgetful fool. The mad scientist doesn't have to be obsessed with playing God. The nameless woman trying to flee from a monster doesn't have to keep tripping over her own feet.

Don't go overboard, but it's better to err on the side of development than to surrender to clichés, stereotypes, and tropes.

From Whose Eyes? Choosing Point of View

Point of view (POV) is the perspective through which the events of the story are presented to the audience. This typically happens through a narrator who may be a participant in the story, but they can just as easily be a distant observer or even someone far removed from the events. A narrator like the grandfather in *The Princess Bride* has a clear opinion about the story he's telling. Other narrators are nearly invisible, and they may be sharing the story with a calm, almost journalistic detachment.

Regardless of what type of narrator you choose for your story, the following sections are the main forms of POV available to you.

First person

If you want your main character to be a huge part of the narrative action, choose *first person*. Audiences get an incredible sense of immediacy and intimacy because the story is entirely filtered through the narrator's mind in the form of "I." What better way to create audience connection with a character than this, right? Hearing from someone directly makes the story seem credible. First person also easily allows the character's opinions to influence the story in a subtle and powerful way.

REMEMBER

First person limits the audience to only knowing what the narrator thinks, feels, says, knows, and does. If something cool is happening a few blocks away, oh well, the audience can't witness it. Not unless the first-person narrator does.

For a story with mystery, first person is a great way to keep audiences in the dark until the big reveal happens. So long as the narrator doesn't know something, it's fair game for audiences not to know it, too.

Third-person limited

Third-person limited — which uses he/she/they or the character's name — has a lot in common with first person. Because *third-person limited* sticks tightly with one person, it mirrors the intimacy created by using first person. Often it's so linked to a person that it feels almost like first person.

We sometimes think of third-person limited as having a portable camera strapped to a character's head. The audience sees things from their perspective and gets a pretty good sense of their thoughts and feelings, too.

Where third-person limited shines is its ability to back away from the focus character and give a wider perspective. In properly handled first person, audiences never get outside the character's head. They're stuck in there. With third-person limited, you can employ that useful distance to reveal biases, mistaken assumptions, or the character's unreliability. You can also shift POV from one person to another person as needed — often at section or chapter breaks.

An added benefit is that you really can't have a first-person narrator tell a story in which they die. With third person, you absolutely can!

Third-person omniscient

Writers appreciate *third-person omniscient* because it allows Godlike access to any aspect of your story. Need to follow a villain engaged in dark sorcery rituals in Venezuela? You can be there. And in the following chapter, you can instantly follow the President and her mystical entourage in Air Force One flying high over the Arctic moments before they greenlight an assault upon an alien strike team. Want to sneak in some foreshadowing about a murderous cult preparing to take over the Capitol building in that same scene? Can do.

Third-person omniscient gives you two benefits:

>> Because you know everything, you can deliver information to audiences without filtering it through any character's perspective. This POV allows you to create *dramatic irony* — the tension that comes from audiences knowing things that characters in the story are ignorant of.

>> You're using your own narrative voice versus that of a character, which adds another potential layer to the story. You can now comment directly on things, perhaps to comic effect.

Third-person omniscient works quite well for stories with a lot of characters and/or a complicated plot. It's also a fine match for stories that span worlds or cover large periods of time.

WARNING

Don't let omniscience go to your head! Yes, you can be in anywhere at any time, but don't give audiences whiplash. Moving around too much leaves audiences feeling like they've been subjected to hours of those super jerky, shaky home movies. It can leave one feeling queasy and confused.

Third-person objective

If you want to have a true fly-on-the-wall perspective to your story's events, *third-person objective* is an option. The key word here is objective: You can observe all you want, but you can't get into the head of anyone. Their thoughts and feelings are entirely off limits. With this option, the narrator can't tell the audience anything. They have to show it and trust audiences to make their own interpretations.

Some call third-person objective *dramatic point of view* because it's constant action. With this choice, you don't need to spend time trying to create character interiority because your audience doesn't have access to it. The problem with it, though, is that it works against one of the main reasons people come to fiction — to deeply inhabit the lives of others. Keeping the audience at a distance like this makes connecting with characters extremely challenging.

TECHNICAL STUFF

Films typically offer a form of third-person objective. Audiences looking at screens are kept external to the characters they see on those screens. They don't have access to character thoughts and feelings beyond what can be inferred from their words, actions, and nonverbals, or what characters reveal in dialogue. Writers who don't figure out how to overcome this challenge find themselves on the receiving end of a top-three reason for rejection from Hollywood script readers — "I don't care." That's code for "I'm not emotionally invested enough." And that's largely a point-of-view issue.

Successful screenwriters argue that scripts should try to be more subjective, meaning they follow the main character often and closely enough that audiences are squarely within their emotional perspective. If you're looking down on characters from above, you feel the awkwardness of that distance. To fix that problem, get in tight. Stay close. Emotional connection, and caring, will follow.

PRESENT OR PAST TENSE? THAT'S THE QUESTION. . .

Another important choice writers make in addition to choosing point of view is selecting the when of the story. Are you going to use present or past tense?

Compare these two versions:

- **Present tense:** Cohn eases into the back of the hearse. He smells the stink of grave dirt on the driver's breath.

  "Just drive," he whispers to the leering ghoul behind the steering wheel.

- **Past tense:** Cohn eased into the back of the hearse. He smelled the stink of grave dirt on the driver's breath.

  "Just drive," he whispered to the leering ghoul behind the steering wheel.

Most audiences argue that present tense creates more immediacy, as if the actions are unfolding right in front of the audience's eyes. There's an elegant simplicity to it. Some people think it's also more cinematic.

However, most stories are written in past tense, and it's been the more popular option for centuries. Hence, audiences are so familiar with it that they might find it easier to read.

Present tense also has a logical hiccup. The story proposes that things are literally happening now, but audiences know that's not the case because the events have to all be completed already for the book about them to have been written. For some, that's a real sticking point.

Regardless, you're going to be okay no matter which you choose. We recommend you try a few pages in each and see which feels and sounds right for your story. Just be consistent — some writers slip between the two, and it's very jarring to encounter that.

Telling "Telling Details"

Because audiences want to know characters well, writers have to deliver that information. You want to create characters that audiences can root and fear for and that they'll care about enough to invest their time and energy into the story's journey.

Use the following different methods of characterization to let audiences know more than the surface details. Just be sure not to halt the story's progress to do so. Find ways to insert this welcome information into the ongoing action.

Zeroing in on appearance

Maybe not, but looks *do* matter in the world of stories. They tell audiences a lot about a person's age, health, socioeconomic status, and much more. Are they well-groomed or slovenly? Muscley or wiry? Do they have distinguishing marks on their body such as scars, tattoos, or birthmarks? Do they spend more on custom tailoring each month than most do in a lifetime? Audiences will read a lot into what they literally see, so choose visual character details carefully.

TIP

Give your character a definitive feature or two to help them stand out as individuals. The android training to be the Oracle of Kermos' replacement? She practices talking about herself in the third person to disassociate her consciousness from her bodily form. The disgraced space pirate who used to be the Starlord's champion? His hair turned white as spider's silk after that tangle with the warp worms that also cost the Starlord's nephew his life.

The larger your cast of characters, the more important you want to help audiences remember who's who with a gentle visual cue. Audiences don't need all the information you'd pack into an online profile — just pick the things that are most relevant or distinctive.

WARNING

This sounds simple, but it's worth saying plainly — character names are one of the most effective ways to cue audiences about which character is which. Yet too often, writers don't bother to create distinguishable names. No Jan, Jen and Jill, please! Don't overcompensate here, but at least don't let them rhyme and don't start with the same initial letter or letters, if you can help it.

Digging into a character's psychology

Everyone has hopes and fears. Your characters should, too. You don't need to imagine the answers to a Myers-Briggs test for each for your characters, but definitely think about basic psychological traits. Are they fundamentally honest or not? Moody or easy going? Do they prefer solitude or being around people? Are they careful and conscientious or sloppy and aloof? Do they have anything noteworthy about how they speak, such as an accent, a specific tempo, a noticeable pitch, or pet phrases?

The way a character handles conflict can tell a lot about them. Figure out how they respond when they're uncomfortable. Do they squirm away from the slightest resistance, or will fists fly at the first sign of opposition? What does that little voice in their head say when things get truly dangerous?

We find these questions particularly useful in terms of really getting to know your character:

>> What is your deepest secret?

>> What is your greatest fear?

>> What is your deepest regret?

>> On what occasions will you lie?

>> What is your most treasured possession?

>> How would you describe yourself in one sentence?

>> How would a friend describe you?

>> How would a someone who doesn't like you describe you?

>> How would someone you just met describe you?

After you know who your character is — that is, you know what motivates them and why they do the things they do — you've got what the vital information required to keep their actions, beliefs, and voice consistent. For example, if you've got a ghost hunter who's learned the hard way not to try to fit in because they'll never belong anywhere, it makes perfect sense that they violently resist joining the increasingly strong advances of the city's new undead hunter's guild. If the hunter's deepest secret is that they were once possessed by a ghost, well, that's yet another reason for them to keep turning down offers of help even when the ghost they're chasing is maybe too much for any single hunter to handle.

Trusting an inner circle

The people that your characters choose to surround themselves with reveals something about them. Sometimes like seeks like — hence the cliques in high school. Sometimes people create a group that delivers what they psychologically need — often acceptance, deference, or admiration. Sometimes the group's makeup reveals other useful things about its members.

From family to friends to classmates to club members — who your characters associate with is yet another way to help reveal more about them without having to come out and tell audiences those things directly. They'll see it for themselves and make their own judgments.

If your story has an intergalactic bounty hunter with an inferiority complex, odds are that they choose weaker, less capable shipmates so as to always remain the most dangerous person in the room. Now that may be an issue for them if they encounter real trouble because the team isn't as strong as it might be, but on a day-to-day basis, the bounty hunter is probably pretty happy with the status quo because there's no doubt about who's in charge.

You Don't Say? Using Dialogue

Dialogue is far more than just a transcription of what a character says. Done well, it reveals that character's character, creates conflict, advances the plot, and gives useful information — sometimes all four at once! Aspire to accomplish at least two of those tasks with every line of dialogue.

REMEMBER

Dialogue is *never* a transcription of what people say in real life. Why not? Because people are inefficient in how they speak. The "umms" and "errs" and "you knows" alone would be infuriating to read on the page. That doesn't even take into account the nothings people say to each other about the weather, sports, and equally vacuous things.

Here are some things to consider when writing dialogue for your story.

Recognizing the types of dialogue

You have four types of dialogue, which we discuss in the following sections, when you're writing text. The question isn't which one you use, but rather why some writers use only one type over and over again? Our guess: They didn't have a top-level writing teacher or read a book like this one!

Giving the full story — Direct dialogue

Direct dialogue is the one you're sure to know. In fact, we see plenty of student stories where 100 percent of the dialogue is direct dialogue. Direct dialogue is offering audiences exactly what's been said.

Here is an example of this type:

> Zerbit said, "Take the loot and scram. I'm done with you."

You're essentially in the room with Zerbit as he tells off Mugmug once and for all. You're witnessing it unfolding through your eyes and ears. That's a terrific tactic to create a sense of story happening on the page.

The drawback? You're hearing every single word. Sometimes characters — or real-world people! — go on and on and on and don't really say anything important. Audiences don't have time to listen to all that. They only want to know what's important to the story.

REMEMBER

Use direct dialogue as you see fit, but if things get long/speechy/boring, employ other dialogue types as needed. Audiences will thank you for it!

Boiling it down — Summary dialogue

If you want to share what someone says in the style of a brief report to the audience, *summary dialogue* is a fantastic choice. This tactic is really efficient and keeps things moving.

Check out this example:

> Zerbit told Mugmug that their adventuring days together were now over.

The limitation of summary dialogue is that audiences don't hear any actual words that were uttered by Zerbit. That means they don't really get a sense of flavor, texture, or voice. They also can't judge diction because the spoken words are absent. Is Zerbit a low-brow dock worker or a fancy magic researcher who loves intimidatingly large words? Audiences can't tell.

Wait to use summary dialogue until audiences know the characters and have heard them talk a bit. After that's happened, they know them, and they know their voice. That helps make any subsequent summary dialogue richer and more effective.

Offering the gist — Indirect dialogue

Indirect dialogue falls right between summary and direct dialogue. With *indirect dialogue*, there's more of a sense and feel of what's been said, but it's not offering up every single word verbatim.

Witness it in action:

> Zerbit said he couldn't stand Mugmug's greediness, that he was just a selfish ogre, that he'd always been a selfish ogre, and not just because he never once asked if Zerbit wanted first pick of the magic wands they looted from the bodies of all those dead magicians.

See the difference? Indirect dialogue doesn't give audiences actual spoken words, but they have a far more robust sense of what Zerbit thinks and feels. We've got enough information to infer Zerbit's tone. There's even a strong sense of texture here.

Using all your options — Mixed dialogue

Mixed dialogue isn't so much a distinct type of dialogue, but rather a combination of the three options used together to control the pace of the scene.

Consider this example:

> Zerbit listed Mugmug's faults — all of them. "Plus, you couldn't skewer a goblin with a twenty-foot spear without me to tell you where to aim."
>
> Zerbit whipped out the Party Dissolution document the monks from the Red Tower had drawn up, and he read all twenty-two clauses aloud since Mugmug wasn't able to read it for himself.

Imagine if this were all rendered in direct dialogue, and audiences had to actually hear all that monk legal mumbo-jumbo. No thanks!

Keeping track of dialogue tags

In scripts and games, you don't have to worry about dialogue tags. In fiction, dialogue tags are vitally important because they alert audiences about who says what.

> "That is the worst fireball I've ever seen."

Who said that? Audiences have no idea. They're forced to skim back over what they just read and try to find a character's name, and then hope that's who voiced this complaint. Adding a dialogue tag clarifies things so they can keep reading ahead.

Here are three common ways to use dialogue tags. (Note where the punctuation goes! That's an issue many writers run into.)

» **Put a dialogue tag at the end.** "That is the worst fireball I've ever seen," said Urbok the Great.

» **Put a dialogue tag at the beginning.** Urbok the Great said, "That is the worst fireball I've ever seen."

» **Put a dialogue tag in the middle.** "That," said Urbok the Great, "is the worst fireball I've ever seen."

If a scene only has two characters in the scene and it's evident who's talking, you may drop the dialogue tags because your audience can easily figure out how an A/B conversation goes. However, if there's any doubt about who's speaking, go ahead and utilize those dialogue tags.

If you're inclined to get fancy with the verb in the dialogue tag, don't. Sure, you can "reply," "note," "explain," "yell," or "accuse." The default, though, is "said." If you're concerned about overusing "said," don't be. It's the default for a good reason.

Audiences learn to almost ignore the word "said" — it sort of fades away. But they surely notice when someone "declaims," "vociferates," or "asseverates" their words. And audiences laugh. Rightly so!

Stay away from sticking adverbs onto dialogue tags. For instance

"I had a great day!" Zerbit happily said.

"This makes me so mad!" Zerbit said angrily.

If you're worried audiences won't get the meaning, pick better words for the dialogue part. Skip the modifier. To paraphrase Stephen King, the road to hell might indeed be paved with adverbs.

Writing script dialogue

The dialogue options we mention in the section "Recognizing the types of dialogue," earlier in this chapter, is effective choices for fiction. However, for scripts, you have one choice — direct dialogue. And the direct dialogue is always written without dialogue tags, too. Sure, you can put in notes to direct how an actor should conveys the lines, but that's not the same thing as including all that handy exposition and nifty action around the words within quotation marks.

Don't assume that writing script dialogue is any easier or harder than fiction dialogue, however. It's just different. You simply have to invest more time into making sure that the dialogue words themselves do all they can to reveal a character's character, create conflict, advance the plot, and give useful information. If you can do more than one of those things at the time, so much the better! In scripts, dialogue needs to carry as much weight of the story as does the action.

Here are some good ways to get better at writing dialogue for scripts, though these tips can also help with fiction dialogue:

>> **Less is more.** Pare things down to only what matters. If you can't immediately find two reasons for what's being said, cut, cut, cut. With film, a lot can be done by sound, image, or action. Use those, if you can.

>> **Use subtext.** People rarely say exactly what they're thinking and feeling. Let people be evasive, contradictory, or passive aggressive. On-the-nose dialogue

is boring and feels fake. Trust that professional actors will know how to make the complexities of subtext come alive.

>> **Skip what's known.** If anyone ever says, "As you know . . ." what comes next is 100 percent unnecessary because everyone already knows it.

>> **Break it up.** In real life, people aren't grammatically sound. They don't always finish sentences because . . . Sometimes they answer the wrong question. And people interrupt. A lot. Employ just enough of that to make your film dialogue feel real.

>> **Sound natural.** Nearly everyone uses contractions, so it's odd when dialogue doesn't. "It is such a beautiful morning. Do not be afraid to enjoy it." Weird, right? Unless the speaker is a snooty professor-bot or bowtie-wearing wizard with a formal air to all they do, text without contractions comes across as inauthentic and clunky.

>> **Avoid dialect.** Using dialect without sounding absurd or offensive (see Chapter 23 on appropriateness and representation in stories) is really quite difficult. If suggesting an accent is vital, avoid the "Is 'zis 'appening?" strategy or spelling things phonetically. Instead, try strategic word choices and syntax. Sentence fragments can help, as can simply saying, "Her accent was thick as Xandatorian cheese."

>> **Don't speechify.** Lots of films have a great monologue or speech, but those instances should be rare. Keep things moving in all the other moments.

>> **Remember that silence matters.** Strategically placed silence can be as powerful — or even more so — than words.

>> **Read aloud any dialogue your write.** Even better, enlist some friends to do it while you shut your eyes and carefully listen. It'll quickly become apparent whether the dialogue is working or not.

REMEMBER

The late Oscar-winner Mike Nichols once said there were three types of scenes: a fight, a seduction, and a negotiation. Even though we can think of other types of scenes (see Chapter 3 to read all about scenes), his three categories do a very good job of summing up the bulk of dialogue exchanges. What his ideas have in common is that people want something. Get clear about that, and let the dialogue work toward that goal, whether it's yelling, smooth-talking, or arguing with logic.

Chapter **3**

Laying the Foundation — The Power of Plot

With characters your audience cares about in hand, you're ready to put them into action. That means plot, which is the framework of a story. And it also means scenes, which are the fundamental building blocks of plot. Here's a quick definition of both you can refer to again and again as you read this chapter:

» **Plot:** At a basic level, it's what happens in your story. However, plot is a good bit more than that because the what-happens occurs in a specific way — it's a dynamic chain of causes and effects. One thing leads to something else, and then that leads into something else. Nothing is random, coincidental, or without story purpose.

REMEMBER

We frequently return to this clearer definition: *Plot* is a series of story events that are deliberately arranged so as to fully reveal their dramatic, thematic, and emotional significance. To create a plot is to decide what to put in a story as well as what to leave out.

>> **Scene:** As for *scenes,* they're the building blocks of those plots. Scenes are meaningful moments of dramatized action that move a story forward. Think of them as miniature plots because, like plots, scenes take place in a specific time and location, they have both a conflict and a resolution, and they include a clear beginning, middle, and end.

Scenes, like plots, are causally connected to the scene before and after. In a good story, nothing happens in isolation.

This chapter helps you discover plot and scene techniques that successful writers use to create a well-structured story that engages audiences from page one to The End.

REMEMBER

Many people use the term "story" and "plot" interchangeably. That's fine in the same way that the world doesn't end when you say a bumblebee is a "bug" when it's actually an "insect." Still, you should be aware of the difference between story and plot. *Story* is the overall experience. It's the sum total of character, setting, action, emotion, and everything else that an audience takes away from the narrative experience. *Plot* is a machine — a purpose-built structure — that creates this powerful narrative experience.

Engineering Great Drama

Whether you call it the dramatic question or the story question, every story fundamentally asks this question: Will the protagonist do X or not?

That's it. Laid out bare, that's what people want to know from a story. Will the hero solve the mystery of the bizarre interstellar signal? Will the hero survive the deadly meteor swarm? Will the hero overcome their inner demons to become the much-needed Chosen One?

In our teaching, we rely on this sentence to get students thinking about dramatic questions and their built-in conflicts:

In a world where _____ wants _____, they can't get it because of _____.

That setup has built-in drama, and those tantalizing blanks just ache to be filled in with creative answers.

FRAMING YOUR STORY IN ANOTHER WAY

You can use other ways to frame important story questions that get at the possibilities of drama. The late beloved writing teacher Gary Provost used a popular four-sentence prompt to help students uncover the dramatic possibilities tucked away in their story ideas.

"Once upon a time, in a world where things just felt wrong, something happened to someone, and she decided she would pursue a goal. So, she devised a plan of action, and even though there were forces trying to stop her and she'd made other plans for her life, she moved forward with the help of a companion, because there was a lot at stake — both for her and for her world. And just as things seemed as bad as they could get, she lost something precious to her, she realized something important, and that understanding led to her triumph. But when offered the prize she had fought so hard to gain, she had to decide whether or not to take it, and in making that decision, she satisfied a need that had been created by something in the past."

Wow, those vague story elements just beg to be made concrete, don't they? How many stories that you love and admire fit terrifically well into this dramatic mini-questionnaire? How well does *your* story idea fit into this?

Provost's prompt addresses what audiences desire from stories, and it lays out the key story moments in a cause-and-effect setup called plot. He's not breaking new ground here. He's just reminding you of plot fundamentals and inviting you to bring your own characters, settings, actions, and ideas to make the story uniquely yours.

TIP

To engineer great drama, feel free to go beyond the main dramatic question because audiences ask all manner of less-vital-but-still-worthwhile story questions all the time. For example, "If the Chupacabra King knows that the scientists from Los Alamos are stealing Chupacabra eggs for terrible medical experiments, why doesn't it just smash through the walls of the research facility and gobble up every nerd in a lab coat?"

Great question! So, make sure your story offers an answer that satisfactorily explains why the Chupacabra King doesn't go bonkers on Los Alamos. Uncovering answers to reasonable questions will help you write and revise the story, plus they might open up even more possibilities for drama, conflict, and audience enjoyment.

Here we take a good look at how to create great drama through the use of structure, pattern, and values.

Examining values

Another good way to think about stories is how they put core human values in conflict. Love versus hate. Knowledge versus ignorance. Justice versus injustice. A dramatic question may be "Will the two merfolk ever get together?" The key conflicts in this story then would challenge the value of love. Is love worth it? Are they a good match? Can anyone truly give themselves unconditionally to another?

Depending on what actually happens in the story, writers may run across other vital questions about love. Does a mother's love have limits? Does love trump greed? Is love more important than duty?

Whichever way this merfolk story goes, the climax and subsequent resolution becomes a commentary on the value of love as dramatized in the story. Even though this comment on love may not be true for all love in all places and all times, it's absolutely true for *these* characters in *this* story.

Quality dramatic questions highlight values that inform the lives of audiences. Good genre stories are so much more than snarky dialogue, interplanetary warfare, and magic rings. Yes, genre stories should be exciting, but for them to have lasting impact on an audience, they need to engage with things that matter more than pyrotechnics and CGI. That boils down to values, those things people believe are vital to the way they live.

Creating compelling conflict

At the heart of every plot is conflict. Some writers find it hard to write conflict and it's easy to see why. All their lives, they're told at home, at school, and at work to avoid conflict. Don't yell! Don't argue! Don't fight! And now here we are, saying to go against years of constant messaging that conflict is bad.

SETTING THE STANDARD WITH SCENES

At some point in the writing process, you need to make sure that every scene contributes to the story in a meaningful manner. That means you'll likely have to throw out or change a lot of what you wrote. That's why most writers plot at some level before they write. It increases the likelihood that your scenes are properly linked by cause and effect and that you're not wasting time on pages that are bound for the recycling bin.

What happens if your scenes aren't rich with dramatic and emotional texture? Or if they don't combine to create a seamless, logical storyline that we call plot? You already know that answer. Audiences will walk away.

Conflict in life is bad. Conflict in stories is good. More than good, really — conflict is necessary. *Conflict* in stories is when two or more opposing forces clash in the service of a narrative. Conflict is more than random squabbles and low-grade disagreements. It gets audiences connected emotionally because the stakes are high. A sense of urgency must exist to move the story along. And no stakes are higher or more urgent than death.

"Wait! I want to write an easy-breezy dark elf rom-com! There's no death here!" we can hear you saying. Fair enough. We absolutely don't recommend that bodies must hit the floor in every sci-fi, fantasy, and horror story. However, think about what death represents — it's the ultimate loss. That's what we mean by *high stakes.* Characters must be in danger of losing something valuable, all the way up to potentially being murdered by a troop of nectar-soused pixies.

Here are the different ways that high-stakes loss can show up in your story with brief examples for each:

>> **Professional:** For most people, suffering a major setback at work or losing one's job has huge ramifications — as in your career as an intergalactic spy is over because you've been publicly outed by a spiteful ex-colleague.

>> **Spiritual:** For someone who believes in God or a religious system, a spiritual blow may be devastating — as in seeing the aftermath of the Great Goblin War left you unable to pray to your deity, Dazorr, the God of Fangs.

>> **Psychological:** All people are subject to emotional loss, mental anguish, and fear — as in witnessing a tentacled horror devour your paranormal investigator partner has you unable to leave the supernatural safe room in your high-rise apartment.

Conflict doesn't mean much if the stakes aren't sufficiently high, so let loss be your guide. And if it makes sense for your story, give your protagonist the ultimate stakes and watch how quickly audiences perk up.

REMEMBER

With conflict, someone's going to lose something they don't really want to, and someone else is going to gain. Conflict is about imbalance and a shift of power. If there's only one laser sword to be had and two people desperately want it, tough luck to one of them. Yes, that person loses their chance to own the coolest weapon ever, but along with that, they may lose their self-respect, their honor, or their left hand. It might've been quite the struggle!

Because everything in a story is causal, these losses can launch the next story event — the character trying to redeem themselves by taking action in response to these setbacks. Perhaps going on a holy quest fixes their honor deficiency. Challenging that laser-sword wielder to a duel might win them the sword. What else might they do to overcome one or more of these losses? The wrong answer is

"Nothing." Whether they embark on a wise action or a foolish one, the key is that they act. Passive characters aren't crowd pleasers.

Starting with Freytag

Way back in the 1800s, a German writer named Gustav Freytag created a visual aid to help understand ancient Greek drama and the plays of Shakespeare. It proved so useful that we're still using it for its clarity and simplicity to talk about all kinds of stories. This visual aid is called Freytag's Pyramid or Freytag's Triangle, and we discuss what you need to know about the Pyramid in the following sections.

Breaking down Freytag's Pyramid

Here are the relevant parts of Freytag's Pyramid (the numbers correspond with Figure 3-1):

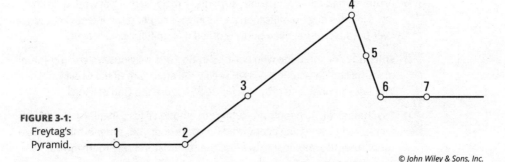

FIGURE 3-1:
Freytag's
Pyramid.

© John Wiley & Sons, Inc.

1. **Exposition:** Also known as the *introduction* or *pattern,* this is the main character's life and world prior to the story beginning. It's the norm, the pattern, the general routine of their life. Because it's so flat, you don't want much of this in stories, but you need to have a good sense of it such that the events of the story are seen in the proper context.

2. **Inciting incident:** This is the external change that lifts the main character out of their everyday world into a new situation full of tension and important stakes that unfold via a chain reaction of events. The strongest inciting incidents are dramatized with action or movement — someone having a realization is far less impactful.

3. **Rising action:** As the story progresses, each complication and conflict leads to another complication and conflict — a constant cause-and-effect chain of increasing importance and stakes. You can think of this upward-slanting line as a narrative tension barometer with moments of relief that then rocket forward into new complications and conflicts. Everything runs hotter and hotter until . . .

4. **Climax:** This is the turning point of the story. It's the moment of highest intensity that's dramatized by powerful action. If there's a BOOM in the story, look for it here.

5. **Falling action:** This action presents the immediate impacts of the climax's outcome. Because the tension and stakes are decreasing fast, this part should be far shorter than the rising action.

6. **Resolution:** Here the primary story problem is resolved, and all dramatic questions are literally or metaphorically answered. The main character will now settle back into the new norm of their life — for good, bad, or otherwise. Well-intentioned writers sometimes prefer the word "denouement" here, which is French for *untying knots*. But Freytag didn't use that word, so neither shall we.

7. **New pattern:** Also known as the *new norm,* this is the world of your story after the character has undergone their arc of change. Here's where any final questions or issues are handled and sequels are set up, if you're planning sequels. The new pattern suggests what the character's new life will be like after those meaningful events of the story. Audiences don't need nor want to see a lot of this — just a whiff, a taste. Don't defuse the narrative power of your ending by going overlong. Trust the audience to infer beyond what little you include.

Freytag's Pyramid helps identify key points in your story and remind you of the vital important of escalating tension and stakes. It's not a one-size-fits-all solution, but it remains an important tool for helping you think through and organize a story.

Here we delve a bit deeper into the elements of Freytag's Pyramid.

Committing to cause and effect

Take a closer look at the rising action part of Freytag's Pyramid (refer to the following figure). From a distance, it looks like a steady, straight line. Get a bit closer, and it actually has little dips after each big upward movement that represent the beginnings and ends of scenes. The rising action should be a series of actions and reactions at the scene level that collectively build toward that whiz-bang climax your story promises to deliver.

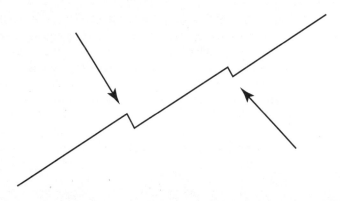

Stories are more than just taking your characters out for a wild rollercoaster ride. What audiences see is the result of a writer allowing characters (through goals and desires) to forge their own path, and then reap the rewards or other consequences.

In well-made stories, things don't happen in isolation. When talking about scenes and plot, use words like "because" and "therefore" because those words acknowledge a story's causal relationship. One domino falls *because* the one before it fell, *therefore* it falls into the next one, which tumbles *because* it just got thumped. And so on. That's what the rising action line of Freytag's Pyramid is trying to help you see.

Steering clear of online pyramids

Because you're really squinting hard at Freytag's Pyramid here, we need to point out something else beyond that denouement sham. Freytag's Pyramid is commonly depicted as an equilateral triangle online. The point at the top sits dead center. What 300-page sword-and-sorcery epic novel has the big-fight climax at page 150? What werewolf movie has the top lycan get dropped with 50 minutes left to watch?

Freytag was thinking specifically about old, old drama, plus he had a different idea of what the story climax was. Just ignore those other versions — what we're sharing here is more relevant for the type of stories being made and enjoyed today. Don't be duped by what you see online.

Finding the tension

While conflict is the engine of stories, tension is the fuel that runs the engine. As a noun, tension is the state of being stretched tight, perhaps to the point of discomfort or pain. It's also mental or emotion strain. As a verb, tension is the application of force to something — or someone? — that stretches it. For stories, however, *tension* is narrative stress that creates the anticipation of potential consequences.

Audiences feel this anticipation when they're spellbound by the tension crackling between characters. Yet audiences can be equally engaged by a heap of tension within a single character that's paralyzing them with fear or motivating them to action. Are you able to leave the audience breathless with anticipation because they know more about the appearance of a dark, mysterious box than a character in the story? That's a first-rate use of omniscience or having more than one point of view character (refer to Chapter 2 for more about point of view).

Here are some ways to make the most of story tension.

USING OTHER POPULAR STORY STRUCTURES

"Using a story template guarantees a cookie-cutter, boring, cliché piece," some warn. Not at all. All a template does is remind you of key structural opportunities and connections that make an effective story. It's just a way to give you something to start with. Seeing all the blank spaces in the charts or graphs has a way of firing up the creative juices.

Here are four popular story templates that you might find useful:

- **Save the Cat:** Created by the late Hollywood screenwriter Blake Snyder, this is a variation of the three-act structure. Its two main features are the intuitive 15-beat structure and its articulation of the ten amusingly named genre types (like "Dude with a Problem") that articulate the must-haves for each genre.

- **The Hero's Journey:** Inspired by Joseph Campbell's idea of the *monomyth* — which suggests common storytelling patterns in world mythology — you can easily see this framework in movies like *Star Wars*, *The Matrix*, *The Wizard of Oz*, and *Avatar*. The most prevalent iteration of The Hero's Journey is a simplified version created by Disney executive Christopher Vogler.

- **The Story Circle:** Dreamed up by Dan Harmon (of *Rick and Morty* and *Community* fame), this distills Campbell's monomyth into eight stages of a plot that occur in a circular process. The Story Circle guarantees change — it's baked right into its DNA.

- **The Plot Clock:** Created by literary agent Joyce Sweeney and writing coach guru Jamie Morris, this template looks similar to Dan Harmon's Story Circle in that it's circular like the face of a clock. Its four-act structure is designed to ramp up the action and help writers power through middles.

Many free or inexpensive resources are available to help you make the most of any of these story structures. See what you can find on YouTube and supplement with articles and books as you see fit.

Embracing different types of tension

Audiences aren't the only ones feeling and responding to tension. Characters feel their own tension — anticipation or stored potential story energy — through conflicting wants. *Tension is created when someone wants something but faces formidable resistance.* Two opposing forces clashing together generates a back-and-forth of tension up until one side wins out. Those battles are the conflict we're talking about in stories. Physical, mental, emotional, or otherwise, they drive things forward and have consequences that matter.

Examining the source of tension

Story conflict always comes from somewhere. Before things get to the point of open conflict worthy of dramatizing in a scene, characters have a host of low-grade tensions informing their lives. Stories build upon existing tensions in the world, in the scene, in the character that expand as the story unfolds. Here's an example of how long-standing tensions erupt into current-scene conflict in a years-long cause and effect.

> Bram the robot repair assistant hears someone scream, "Stop, thief!"
>
> The audience knows that back when he was at the Sunrise Orphanage, the other kids pushed him. Mocked him. Stole his blankets, rations, and tablet. Always he wanted to do something . . .but little Bram was too scared. There were too many of those bullies, and they were big and mean and awful.
>
> Now fully grown, Bram still has nightmares.
>
> "Stop, thief!" he hears. And when he sees the thug running down the street, Bram sees the face of the lead bully and he's paralyzed. *It's him — the bully*!
>
> Yet Bram is sick and tired of being scared. He reaches deep within himself and manages to summon courage he didn't know he had. Bram leaps from the shadows and punches that bully right in the face. Boom, down.

This single action that *seems* potentially out of a character for a quiet, gentle robot repair assistant makes sense, given the long-standing tension and built-up emotion. Push anyone hard enough, and they're going to respond. Eventually.

Because audiences know stories work from a cause-and-effect relationship, this scene isn't just about Bram finally saying "No!" to past injustice. The bully-thief's stolen bag of data crystals falls to the ground and spills into the sewers and is lost in those dark waters. The head of the Ripper Gang who needed those data crystals for nefarious purposes is furious. Even now, a pair of thieves is en route to burn down the repair shop and give Bram a beating.

What will Bram do when he hears them step over the squeaky boards on the delivery dock the next morning? The thieves are Tromborii and Bram is half-Trombor, and in this particular story world, Tromborii hate impure bloodlines, as in hate hate hate them for centuries-old reasons. Given that long-standing inter-species tension, they decide a beating isn't good enough for the abomination that is the assistant. In their view, Bram deserves death.

Conflict leads to conflict leads to conflict. And it's all informed by underlying, powerful tensions.

Thinking about tension in terms of Freytag, set up key tensions as part of the character's exposition, which is to say their *backstory*. When audiences see that and watch the character's current behavior, there's an aha! moment. It all clicks into place, as it did when audiences see Bram finally stand up for himself after a lifetime of disempowerment.

Considering tension and psychology

The only psychology audiences know is that of humans. If your character is an alien, a robot, a dwarf, or a shadow creature, audiences will use human psychology as a vehicle to understand their actions. If the characters are playing by different mental rules, devise a way to clue audiences in or they might feel their actions are weird or random since humans wouldn't act that way.

For a horror story, weirdness and randomness may be extra creepy (see Part 5 for how they might work to good effect). For sci-fi and fantasy, we require a better understanding because audiences want to connect with those characters more than with a horror monster.

Considering character arcs

Chapter 2 examines *character arcs,* which are how a character changes in fundamental ways over the course of a story. Plot is the arena in which you see those character arcs play out. Realizing this, you can use plot to highlight and complement a particular character's arc. You do this because stories are about character change, of course, and because change is often internal, audiences require plot to help visually dramatize it.

Freytag's Pyramid can help because it maps out actions and reactions via rising action. At the same time, it also tracks changes to the character as well as show how they interact with the world, because rising action is all about characters and growth. Whether it's how they relate to the world, how the world relates back to them, or how they seem themselves in the world, this is change. What makes it a proper arc is the transformation from one state at the story's beginning all the way to another by the ending.

Here is an example: We explore how that idea plays out in a maturation story about Sirith, a young swordsman in training. He's enjoyed the security, structure, and protection of a military academy for years. Strip that from him by having a trio of specters rage through the campus while Sirith had snuck out into town to carouse — an immature act of minor rebellion. Just imagine the agony he felt upon climbing back through a propped-open window to discover his classmates and teachers all slaughtered.

For someone on the cusp of adulthood in terms of age, experience, and obligations, this is a crucible moment. Through dumb luck, immaturity saved Sirith's life. Now he has a chance to be reckless and charge after those murderous specters to avenge all those deaths and likely cause his own demise because he's not ready. He's not fully trained, and even if he were, the combined skill of his teachers wasn't enough to stand against their foes. Look, the proof is all that blood on the academy floors.

Plot positions Sirith to make a choice related to maturity. He decides to find a new weapons master, complete his training, and only then embark on his quest for revenge. Along the way, he'll shed his childish views about the world as he grows internally while he becomes more powerful externally. Plot must give ample time and opportunity for Sirith to slowly develop into a competent swordsman. That kind of transformation doesn't happen in a blink.

Or does it? Perhaps in your version of this story, the training isn't as important as what happens next. If so, you can fast forward by letting all that reading, studying, learning, and practicing happen offstage by using *narrative summary,* which is to say telling audiences about those activities versus showing them in fully developed scenes.

Maybe your version tackles maturity in a different manner. Perhaps after coming back to the massacre, Sirith is so shaken that he vows to never to lift a sword again because violence now seems unconscionable. Or maybe he arrives at the academy just in time to encounter one of the specters who then attacks him but leaves him alive, though badly hurt. Is Sirith so injured that he'll never be able to properly wield a sword despite desperately wanting to? Does that mean he'll study to be a priest or wizard instead and use the powers of one of those callings to find revenge?

Keeping up the pace

Pace refers to the speed and rhythm of one's story experience. If the plot of a story is a 20-room mansion, pace is how fast audiences move through the various rooms. What follows are ways of thinking about and using pace more effectively in stories.

Identifying pace in your story

To spot the pacing from a bird's-eye view, follow these simple steps:

1. **List all the major actions, reactions, and revelations that happen in your story.**

2. **Add in the times when audiences learn information that casts the central character's conflicts and their stakes in new light, too.**

3. **Mark the page number for each of these vital story moments.**

4. **Determine when the first arrives.**

   Does it happen more than 10 percent into the story? If so, that's a slow beginning.

5. **Identify the gap between the others.**

   Smashing scenes too closely together is as much of an issue as having too wide of gap between them.

Picking up the pace

Generally, you want the pace to pick up in a story, but that's especially true after audiences pass the midway point of the story. You want your story to grab hold of the audience's interest and not let go until the story's end.

Here are a few ways you can pick up the pace if it's lagging:

>> **Write the scene to be more essential to a character.** The pace revs higher when a scene is important. Have your character consider the outcome of the scene to be important. Audiences will pick up on that and believe it.

>> **Pare back language.** Getting rid of chunks of exposition or even trimming back modifiers can make a section read more swiftly.

>> **Cut scenes.** An effective way to control pace is dealing directly with scenes themselves. If a scene is dragging, consider deleting it.

>> **Swap scenes.** So long as you don't confuse the narrative, swapping scenes can create interesting effects, which include affecting the story's pace. Consider how scenes work with the scenes before and after them.

>> **Use cliffhangers.** *Cliffhangers* are a plot device that leaves something important unresolved. If the outcome is unknown, audiences will plunge ahead to find out what happened. That's a trick episodic TV writers figured out decades back and have been using to good effect ever since.

>> **Write short chapters and scenes.** James Patterson does this all the time in his zippy, quick-read novels. You can do the same thing with sentences. Dump the long-winded, drag-on sentences that we see oh-so-often in fantasy novels so thick that they can double as a doorstop. Instead, go short. Get punchy. Pump things up. Yeah, baby!

If you need to slow things down, do the opposite (though 90 percent of all pacing problems are about things being too draggy, not too zippy).

Building Story Structure

Some writers insist they're a "pantser" versus a "plotter" — meaning they write "by the seat of their pants" without an outline, plan, or preliminary plot work. Can they write and publish stories? Absolutely. But without doing serious plotting as part of their storymaking process, pantsers run into unnecessary problems such as focusing on the wrong point-of-view character, getting lost in the details, losing overall narrative cohesion, or writing themselves into a dead-end from which they can't see a solution. Plot is a story's infrastructure. Avoid it at your own peril.

Stories require a good foundation, the same way a skyscraper or any building needs a proper foundation. If that foundation is lacking, weak, or ill-conceived, you're in trouble.

The sooner you get a strong foundation in place, the sooner you can build meaningfully atop it. Here we explore some ways to build a story from the ground up.

Understanding scenes

Scenes are so important to structure that many writers don't do chapter-by-chapter outlines — they go scene by scene instead and insert chapter breaks later in the manuscript itself. We prefer to write outlines by chapters, but the other option is perfectly valid and may work better for you. Try both options out and see.

Scenes offer narrative moments rendered in dramatic fashion. What makes a thing scene-worthy? It shows meaningful change. That's it. That's the bare minimum. Although a scene can advance plot, reveal information, offer characterization, and deliver humor, fear, or surprise, those things are secondary. Valuable, of course, but not a must.

No one likes flat scenes, those parts in stories where stuff happens, but none of it appears to matter all that much. It just burns up time. The antidote to this is making sure that every scene shows change.

These sections examine the three effective ways to ensure your scenes incorporate change. In all three cases, you have meaningful change that necessitates action and offers loads of opportunity for your character to act in ways that reveal who and what they are (their character arc). See Chapter 8 for how the story world can become a character.

Option One: Changing characters

Track a scene's effect on the *focus character* of the scene (a character who is the star of the scene, though they may not be the star of the entire story). Ask yourself two important questions:

>> Where are things at for the character at the start of that scene?

>> By the end, are things worse or better?

If you can honestly answer yes to the second question, congratulations, you have change.

When our students finish the first draft of a novel, we insist that they write every individual scene onto its own notecard and then lay them out in a linear fashion to ensure sure adequate movement from scene to scene as well as to assess the overall mood of the story. Is it mostly down? Up? Does it build nicely right up to the key story parts, such as the climax or the resolution?

Option Two: Changing stakes

The stakes can literally change from one thing to another. Because the stakes are different, the importance and meaning of what's happening necessarily changes, too. For example, at one point, a character may covet becoming the richest phothyst miner on X-47, only to later learn that shaft-mining phothyst — the only viable way to do it — causes sinkholes, so their goal shifts to saving the environment by campaigning to make all mining illegal.

If two characters in a fistfight stop pummeling each other and both draw knives, that's some stake-upping that works for any audience. Just remember to vary the types of conflict and use both internal and external stakes to keep things fresh. Audiences appreciate it when a character is affected in some internal way when they engage with external problems. Characters like that phothyst miner aren't mindless creatures after all.

Option Three: Changing the world

Even though the majority of change audiences expect to see is in the character as they undergo their character arc, the setting can change, too. The moment a story environment changes, you've literally created meaningful change that characters must deal with. An errant wizard's lightning blast may set fire to a crop field, which establishes the groundwork for a future food crisis. Or the world may be more active, such as when a melting glacier hits the tipping point and millions of gallons of water suddenly flood the underground capital city on Regula Five. Or the character starts a revolution that overthrows the Priest-King, only to find themselves responsible for filling the sudden leadership vacuum.

UNDERSTANDING STORY BEATS

Hollywood people like to talk about story beats in films, which are an even smaller unit of story. They have their own unique definition, too, which we won't go into here. For most non-Hollywood writers, a *beat* is a small story part that shows a small change. A scene that changes from overall positive for the character to less positive could incorporate three or four story beats that could be mostly positive, but the last one may carry enough oomph to shift the overall scene value downward.

If the idea of beats feels too in-the-weeds, that's okay. Just ensure that each scene shows change and you're on the right track.

In the world of film and TV, most writers think of a scene as a location. Move to a new location? That's a new scene. Yet a scene is fundamentally about change that comes as a result of conflict. Until that scene's conflict is resolved and change occurs, it's the same scene, regardless of whether the participants travel to a new location or not.

Using scene sequels — Action/reaction

When a scene ends, characters shouldn't always just rush to the next scene with a new goal and its related conflict. Sometimes they need to react to what happened in the previous scene, especially if it ended in failure. Welcome to what some call the *scene sequel.* It's basically another way of thinking about the next part of the story, the reaction to an action. Among other uses, it's a way to insert emotion, which is easy to neglect when the zombies are swarming, space blasters are firing, and magic summoning circles are alight with malignant energy.

Sequels provide a chance for characters to learn and grow. They also provide welcome variation to the scenes and give the audience a breather. Even the best page-turner can't be all go-go-go action. A little contemplation is both reasonable and believable.

Keep the following in mind when adding a scene sequel:

>> **Your character has to react to what just happened.** They have to feel those feelings! Let them. But not for too long, because it's boring to watch people wallow, and, after all, your character has moxie. They're no quitter. Even though they've encountered a setback, they have a large overall story goal that's driving them, and they won't get there by giving up at any point along the way.

>> **Your character has to face their current setback.** They've got a dilemma here. Allow them to consider their options, and then make the best choice available, likely with the help of a companion, mentor, or another supporting character. From that, they have a new goal that launches the next scene which might or might not end better for them. Who knows?

>> **Your character has a negative-to-positive change.** A scene sequel almost always has the character moving from a state of failure to one of hope and promise by virtue of having a new plan that's intended to advance them toward their ultimate story goal.

TIP

You can use more than one type of scene sequel. Sure, having a think/feel moment is okay. Sometimes, however, the reaction moment that's most authentic to your character or the situation is to punch back at something, literally or figuratively.

Adding variety to your scenes

Even though scenes mostly fall neatly into the action-or-reaction category, a numerous specific types of scenes are worthy of looking at more closely. Here are some:

>> **Interrupted scenes** may begin one way but then something interrupts it, which dramatically changes its goals and conflicts. Interrupting scenes is a jarring technique for characters and audiences alike because there's no closure to the original scene goal. Only try it when the stakes are high enough to keep audiences engaged beyond the awkwardness of nonclosure. For example, a trio of security bots appear and take position outside the door your character needs to go through. Or a rival can't finish a vital debate with your character because a subspace message about ship vandalism has them rushing to the hangar.

>> **Scenes within scenes** are similar to interrupted scenes, except the initial scene conflict resolves. The scene within the scene delivers new information or changes character motivation, which alters how the initial conflict plays out. Keep the interrupting scene short so audiences don't lose track of the initial scene.

>> **Multiple-goal scenes** have multiple conflicts and character wants in play simultaneously. A classic example is a fighter dueling away with an opponent while keeping up charming banter on a love interest who's watching the fight. Or imagine a heist situation with a team of thieves who each have different personal agendas they're pursuing while working together to crack the bank vault. Multiple-goal scenes are thrilling and rewarding when they come together, but they take careful planning because so many extra elements are happening at once.

- » **Dream scenes** only work if they're not a cheat, meaning that audiences know it's not a dream, and that it's reflecting a character's interiority versus delivering crucial plot development. The dream environment is just a different way of them working through fears or tensions. Keep the dream scene short and sweet unless you're writing a fantasy story where dreams are the predominant mode of magic or something equally vital. In that case, set up your rules and have at it (take a look at Chapter 16 for ideas on how to handle magic). Otherwise, employ dreams only to reveal character.

- » **Flashback scenes** stop the present story and explore the character's history to provide backstory. A flashback scene is most often part of a reaction scene as the character dives into their past to summon knowledge that will help in the present. Flashbacks work best when they're brief, vivid, and relevant. They can also create tension in the present moment while the narrative storyline moves away.

- » **Flash forward** scenes are the opposite of the flashback. A flash forward is a less common device that gives audiences a sneak peek into the future, often to the moments before the climax or even after the story's end. Using a flash forward at a story's beginnings can work to hook an audience by promising a powerful ending will come later. In every case, it creates useful narrative tension that makes audiences eager to know more. The best flash forwards use foreshadowing to hint at something without giving it all away.

- » **Prologues** are introductory sections to provide context and offer background details that prepare audiences for what's to come. They're extremely common in sci-fi and fantasy because writers think, "Hey, I'm doing all this worldbuilding, and how can anyone appreciate my story without knowing how the cat wizards lived 6,000 years ago?" (Let Chapter 7 help you manage the challenges and opportunities inherent in worldbuilding.)

WARNING

Prologues are problematic because so many industry gatekeepers hate them. Quite a few agents and editors who see a prologue instantly pass on the story altogether. That may not be fair, but it's the truth and you need to know it.

Too often, prologues are long, loosely connected to what follows, and/or written in a different voice or style than the rest of the book. If they're better than chapter one, that creates disappointment. If they're worse than the rest, that's a bigger problem. Often, they're an info dump. Plus, they rarely start where the real story begins.

Unless you have a very good story-based reason to use a prologue, steer clear. If you can't help yourself, maybe write that prologue, then cross off the word "prologue" and write "chapter one." Often, that does the trick.

- » **Epilogues** appear at the very end of the story and have the purpose of providing closure. You only see epilogues on long-form stories, and even then, they're rare for good reason. If you handled the climax and ending well, the epilogue isn't needed because audiences already have closure.

Thinking bigger — Sequences

Change doesn't only happen in individual scenes. You can connect a series of scenes into a larger unit of character change called a *sequence*. A sequence can entail one chapter or many. However, the bigger the sequence is, the more significant the change must be. The change that occurs at the end of a single scene may be quite small and only loosely related to the overall narrative arc, like a space freighter captain haggling a junkyard owner into a great deal for a replacement hyperlathium generator.

A sequence change is much more connected to the larger story, such as the captain hearing a rumor about the secret identity of their nemesis, then getting into trouble with the Nightskull Syndicate while following up on that rumor, and then ultimately discovering that secret, which creates a whole new set of connected problems going forward, which is the next sequence of events.

This sequence of scenes is just part of the whole-story arc that offers this basic question — will the space freighter captain defeat his nemesis?

The concept of a story sequences can be expanded further by looking at story acts. String together two or more related sequences, and you're in the realm of acts — the biggest story units other than considering the entire story as a single narrative entity.

An *act* is series of sequences that culminates in a significant change. These changes must come with more profound consequences than the changes audiences see at the sequence or scene level.

For example, an act-level change can be that the space freighter hero from the above example realizes he can't defeat his nemesis alone, so he swallows his pride and asks for help from his estranged father, who puts his son through a series of challenges before finally agreeing to help. That act ends with father and son willingly joining together toward the same goal for the first time ever. Will it be enough to defeat the nemesis? Perhaps. Regardless, the space pirate has taken a huge step toward maturity and a commitment to justice that he wouldn't and couldn't have made at the story's beginning.

A popular way to plot stories is with the three-act structure. Entire books have been written about this one idea, and lots of definitions and examples are available for free online. In general, though, it hearkens back to Aristotle, who wrote about it in his *Poetics*. His argument was that a story consists of three parts — beginning, middle, and end — which can be summed up as *setup, conflict,* and *resolution*. That's grossly underestimating all that goes into it, but in terms of the function of each act, it's fairly accurate.

For those who like numbers, most Act 1s and Act 3s each tend to make up a quarter of the story, which leaves Act 2 to deliver the other half of it. Variations on this structure exist that use four, five, six, or even more acts.

Examining Key Elements of Plot

The two most dangerous moments in an airline flight are the takeoff and the landing. The middle of every flight? It's long and boring.

Stories are pretty similar, minus the in-flight pretzels. Whether you're writing a novel or a short story, a movie or a graphic novel, beginnings and endings are problem areas, and middles have a huge potential to be boring.

Here we look at the opportunities, challenges, and conventions of each of those parts. We also examine climaxes because they deserve special attention because that's where the key battles happen.

Beginning with a bang

Beginnings are the most important part of a story because if they don't work, audiences quit. The rest of your story could be brilliant, but no one will stick around long enough to know.

The way to make beginnings work is to know what audiences have been taught to expect from them thanks to watching a zillion Disney movies, oodles of TV, and reading however many books and stories. People may not have the specific terms handy, but they have a shared understanding of what beginnings must do.

Freytag's Pyramid says that beginnings should do the following (refer to the section "Breaking down Freytag's Pyramid," earlier in this chapter):

>> **Present external change that launches the protagonist outside the comfort and familiar routine of their normal life.** This change can be overt, such as moving to Jupiter Prime for a dangerous job you can't afford not to take, or it may be far more subtle, like getting an email that a distant relative has died and you're the executor of the will. The key is to get the protagonist uncomfortable. Show that things aren't an everyday occurrence.

>> **Reveal the pattern of the protagonist's life by suggesting its regular features.** Don't show their daily work routine and home life in full scenes. Just show them bored at their desk and, later, smiling inside their VR helmet.

>> **Showcase a sense of the protagonist's character.** Audiences don't need a resume, home movies, or a battery of psychological tests, but give them enough to infer how the protagonist may act in most situations. The broad strokes will suffice for now.

>> **Start as near to the story's action as possible.** The inciting incident should occur in the first scene, unless you have a very compelling reason for not getting the story rolling right off.

>> **Familiarize audiences with the style, tone, and pace of the overall story.** Teach audiences how to read this story and what to expect from it in terms of your narrative style. Use a representative style, tone, and pace from the start so audiences can get acclimated. Don't begin with a jokey all-text-message scene if the rest of the story isn't that funny nor does it use text messages again. That's misleading. And weird.

>> **Hook the audience through tension, immediacy, and energy.** Make them want to keep reading. That's the No. 1 goal here. If you're not successful with this, it's all over.

TIP

One strategy that can work well is to begin a story *in medias res*, which is Latin for "in the middle of things." If laser swords or arrows are zinging in the first paragraph, that's in medias res. Your audience can't possibly know who they should root or fear for, but by gosh, stuff is happening, and it's so exciting that they're happy to just go with it for now with the assumption they'll puzzle out the other stuff later. Yeah, audiences love action that much.

A benefit of *in medias res* openings is that they skip all the info dump inclinations writers have, along with the throat clearing and slow warmups. Audiences are plopped right into action. The story has already begun.

REMEMBER

Trust your gut. If you're not sure how to start, ask yourself what's most important? What's most interesting? Or consider how if your story were a film, what would be the strongest possible opening scene?

The beginning of the story is never the true beginning of desire or conflict. Those are already in place well before page one. What the beginning does is activate desire and conflict via dramatic action. The best editors are usually able to draw a line across the page to show where the story *really* begins. That's a good exercise for all writers to try.

TIP

If you honestly can't decide how to begin, just start any way you can. Revision is part of the process for a reason. Do what you have to in order to get a complete first draft, ugly as it may be. Then go back and adjust as needed, which can include beginning differently than with the first moment in the chronology of your story. Making that decision is far easier after you have a full draft than when you have a blank page and too many ideas. If you need to know more about revising your story, head to Chapter 22.

Maintaining audience interest — Magical middles

If middles make up about half of your story, it's no wonder that writers struggle to keep the audience's interest. With beginnings, things are new. With endings, things are wrapping up. Your audience is intrinsically interested in those parts. Middles often feel like something to slog through to get to the good stuff like the climax and ending.

Every part of the story should matter, and nothing should feel like a throwaway or appear noticeably less good than the rest. Here are some of your best options for strengthening your middle:

>> **Introduce a subplot.** A well-considered subplot puts the spotlight on secondary characters for a moment, while perhaps allowing a wider exploration of your story world. You can use a subplot to adjust the pace of your story, weaving it in and out to keep audiences guessing at how it will play out while adding a bit complexity to your story. The larger your story, the more room for subplots you have, so long as none of them overshadow the main plot. Echo, yes. Run parallel, yes. Enhance similar themes, yes. Just don't compete.

>> **Embrace failure.** No, not your failure as a writer, but let your protagonist fail. Most audiences covertly love to see a hero crash and burn because the stakes just get higher as they pick themselves off the ground with renewed purpose. Failure generates audience empathy.

>> **Speed it up.** Shorten deadlines. Instead of having a week to locate the lost stone of Anyxia and return it to the high priest, the hero now has three days. Or 24 hours! Less time equals higher stakes. Crank up the pressure.

>> **Kill someone off.** Nothing says stakes like having a beloved secondary character take a dirt nap.

>> **Fake that climax.** Give audiences a big scene that, in the moment, seems like the real story climax. The only challenge here is that the *real* climax that comes later must deliver even more. But that's a problem for later. Right now, you're trying to get through that middle.

>> **Take a left turn.** The ending you planned isn't set in stone. If you sense a dramatically interesting possibility, take it. If you're shocked and pleased by that unexpected move, audiences will be, too. Yes, the rest of your story may now need rethinking, but an exciting turn is an exciting turn for every audience member. And excitement keeps audiences going.

Fulfilling story promises — Knockout climaxes

Your story's biggest obstacle is finally here. The stakes, emotions, tension, and fears are at their highest point. It's really intense! So, what now?

The *climax* should be as much about the values at play in the story as any type of conflict or action, even if the protagonist and their opponent are settling things with magic swords, blasters, or ghost minions. The climax should also answer the dramatic question and fulfill, challenge, or deny the characters' wants.

Because climaxes are so vital to an effective story, here are three common ways to get them right:

» **Find the right speed.** A blast of adrenaline only lasts for a bit, and the same is true for the audience's ability to engage with such a high-stakes scene. The pace needs to be brisk. But you can't go too fast either because audiences have waited the entire story to witness the climax. They want to savor it, whether the protagonist succeeds or fails. Given that, what's the solution? There's a sweet spot in the middle where things are thrilling and richly told, yet nothing feels draggy or superfluous. Give it your best shot, and then enlist outside readers to get firsthand reports about whether your climax zings and zooms or falls flat. See Chapter 23 for details on outside readers for help.

» **Make them work for it.** The climax should test the protagonist more fully than any other point in the story. Make sure they reveal who and what they are and what matters most to them. Giving characters an easy out is a cheat, and you won't be fooling anyone. The audience came to see someone tested to the max, so push that protagonist further than they've ever been pushed. Make it hurt.

» **Consider the implications.** The ramp-up to the actual climax needs to have preparatory thrills, perhaps facing temple guards or crawling through an underground sewer to find a hidden crypt the big baddie's using as a lair.

   You usually can't ignore the aftermath. After defeating the temple's dreadlord, minions are still fighting, plus the roof is collapsing. Or that crypt is being flooded by the nearby lake, and the only exit is through the rat swarm blocking the single tunnel leading out. Think through the logic of the moments before and right after the big showdown. If there's something to deal with, let it be part of the wonderous experience of a memorable story climax. If there's nothing to deal with, move on!

Finishing strong — Satisfying endings

Endings should seek to enmesh audiences in the story's outcome to the point that they can't stop reading, regardless of the real-world time or situation. In addition, make sure your endings do the following:

>> Endings should fully resolve the central conflict, one way or another.

>> Endings should also resolve the character arc, regardless of what type of arc it is.

>> Endings should feature your protagonist front and center, acting with a sense of urgency as their character arc comes to a close alongside the narrative arc.

Together, these should provide a satisfying moment. And after you've delivered that, you're done. Don't add anything after the end of your story.

A common mistake writers make with endings is the impulse to surprise, as if there's a deep fear that audiences will be mob-level angry and disappointed unless there's a Mardi Gras spectacle to those final pages. Ending this way comes across as a desperate way to get an emotional reaction from the audience.

If you have an intricate juggling act going with a slew of ideas and themes in the narrative, those things are already in play. Your audience has seen flashes of them all throughout the story. All they need know is to get them to land safely, not toss more things into the air.

The whole story should feel in alignment. That's why revision is vital, and why you should do it only after you've a complete draft so you know all the individual parts as well as the entire thing.

Yes, you can leave things open-ended to set up a sequel, so long as audience still feel an appropriate amount of closer with this story. The key is to satisfy audiences — not necessarily to answer all questions and wrap things up in a neat little package. And even if you aren't planning a sequel, it's nice if the audience wants to continue to be in the world you created with your characters. In other words, leave them wanting, but just a bit. Give them enough so that they can imagine for themselves what might happen next.

Chapter **4**

Crafting Many Worlds, Many Media

This chapter helps you consider how to share your stories with the world. Good news! There are more excellent options to reach audiences than ever before. Writing big genre novels may be a tried-and-true choice, but it's only one pathway among many that you can take on your journey to success.

The audiences are out there, and they're hungry for well-written, exciting original genre work in all kinds of media. Deliver that in any of the media we discuss in this chapter, and they'll respond.

Chapter 24 addresses the logistics of submitting work to agents, publishers, and producers. In this chapter, though, we look at what your story options really are. We also share tips and best practices for each.

Writing Prose — An Oldie but a Goodie

When writers talk about prose, they mean traditional fiction — text on a page that tells a made-up story. Reading fiction creates and sustains connections that get firmly into the hearts and minds of other people. Along the way, fiction delights, instructs, and charms. Few things have the cultural capital or sheer entertainment value of well-written fiction.

The strength of fiction is *character interiority* — the thoughts, feelings, and reactions of a character (see Chapter 2 for guidance) — and a limitless ability to handle setting, which is both time and geography (see Chapter 3). In short, you never need to worry about a budget because all the worldbuilding happens in the heads of your audience. Fiction also supports a lot of different shapes, sizes, and styles, which make it flexible enough for nearly any story you want to create.

No matter what you do, let your story dictate how long it needs to be. Then you can figure out how to make it work for publishers and audiences through using one of the following formats.

Novels

Novels are a book-length fiction narrative. "Exactly how long?" you ask. It depends. A book's size isn't solely related to story needs — it involves industry factors like the cost of paper and ink, or audience expectations for page count. Consider how long some of the following examples of novels are:

>> Middle grade — 40,000 to 60,000 words: *The Chronicles of Narnia: The Lion, the Witch, and the Wardrobe* by C.S. Lewis is about 40,000 words.

>> Young adult (YA) — 50,000 to 90,000 words: *Uglies* by Scott Westerfeld is about 87,000 words.

>> Adult — 75,000 to 125,000 words: *The Left Hand of Darkness* by Ursula Le Guin is about 85,000 words.

Some published books clock in well past the upper limits (witness Diana Gabaldon's *Outlander* at 305,000 words or Stephen King's *It* at 445,000!), but those are exceptions. When you're a bestselling author or you have your own Netflix series, go ahead and write novels as big as you choose. For now, see if you can keep it less than 100,000 words because anything more requires a bigger financial commitment for a publisher.

Novels are great because you have ample narrative real estate to work with. Want to write a cradle-to-grave story of a fireball-chucking Chosen One? Want to create a zombies-versus-unicorns battle that takes place across three dimensions? Want to explore an idea like "secrets are essential to a happy marriage" through the lives of passengers on an intergenerational ship? A novel gives you the space (pun intended) for all those things.

The novel format expands to offer you as many creative opportunities as you want. You can explore complicated plots and subplots and go deep and build a world with many levels. You can have multiple points of view, an ensemble cast of main characters, a handful of themes, and much more.

We can't ignore the strong tradition of sequels and series in genre fiction. If your vision is expansive, you might absolutely need a quintet of novels or a shared-world spinoff series to fully reveal the depths of your imagination. In horror, sequels and series aren't as common, but they sure are a thing in sci-fi and fantasy. Having a built-in, ready-made audience for your next book — because they've bought previous one(s) in the series — is a welcome thing, too.

REMEMBER

Because of its size and complexity, writing a novel isn't for the faint of heart. It often requires a year or more to write and revise one. Be realistic in your timeline and expectations if novel-writing is the route you choose.

WARNING

Although some novelists enjoy flashy Netflix and Hollywood deals where their stories get adapted to the screen, writing novels isn't a guaranteed path to those outcomes. Yes, it can happen, but it's not the norm. If you really want to see your work on the screen, refer to the section "Writing for Screens Both Big and Small — Scripts," later in this chapter, which may be a better fit for you.

You should only write novels if you want to write novels. Simple as that.

Novellas

If a novel seems like too much, no worries. One step smaller is the novella, which falls between 17,500 and 40,000 words. For the longest time, it didn't get a lot of love. Publishers avoided them, which made writing novellas an unattractive option because one of the primary goals to write something is to have it find its audience.

Thanks to changes in the marketplace, novellas are now viable. Traditional publishing houses are finding ways to make money with 100-page books. And digital publishers have no issue with stories of any size because the production costs are roughly the same whether it's a 9-page short story, a 99-page novella, or a 999-page novel.

Novellas have the compression of a short story — a good thing! — paired with the opportunity to explore that long-form fiction provides. It may be just be the best of both worlds. It's sizable enough to have a complex plot, rich characterization, a deeply explored theme, and a subplot or two. You're even able to use multiple points of view while keeping the pace brisk and lively.

A novella's the sort of thing one might devour in a lazy Saturday afternoon of poolside reading. The single long-session readability allows for resonance and reflection that could be lost in the longer (novel) format. Novels insist that you explore the world and setting, whereas the size of a novella can keep it intensely character focused.

Don't be a creator unless you're a consumer. If you want to write novellas, read some first. See how other writers operate in the space considerations of the form. Make sure you like novellas before saying, "Yes, I choose this — this is what I want to do!"

Short stories

The short story is one of the oldest types of writing, with examples on papyrus dating back thousands of years. Even though short stories have changed since then, the length hasn't. Their strength remains in the ability to read the entire thing in one short sitting, so 1,000 to 10,000 words feels about right. Writing fewer than 1,000 words is called *flash fiction* or *short-short stories* — these little tales often work more like a poem, mood piece, or comic moment than a proper story.

Why write short stories? They offer audiences a powerful story experience that occurs in a concentrated narrative time frame. There's no time to ramble or wax overly philosophic. Writers must get right to it. These babies deliver the goods, then wrap it all up nicely and send you on your way.

Short stories often begin close to their endings to keep things laser-focused. They rely on a single plot and conflict to drive the action — no subplots here, or if they exist, it's only one, and it's super basic. The cast of characters, too, is limited, with perhaps only two or three characters of real significance in the story.

WRITING A SHORT STORY IS DIFFERENT THAN A NOVEL

Some people think that short stories are just practice for novels. They believe they'll build up their story chops and pay their dues by banging out a few short stories before graduating to a novel. Although both are indeed fiction, they're as different as an urban muralist who paints seascapes on the walls of buildings and sculptor who creates miniature bicycles in bronze.

Writing a novel and writing a short story are different skill sets that can inform each other, but each requires unique attention. After you find which form you work best in, put the bulk of your writing energy and focus there. Trying new things, sure, is always refreshing, but you're better off finishing works and sharing them with the world than dabbling in lots of areas and never moving to the next level with any of them.

Endings always matter with any work of fiction, but with short stories, the ending is a make-or-break situation. A novel or novella can deliver a range of pleasures along the way such that if the ending is just so-so, audiences may be okay with it. With a short story, you have to stick the landing. If it's not a satisfactory conclusion, the story doesn't yet work. In short (pun intended!), the specific language you use becomes more important the shorter you piece is. That's why poetry is so exact!

Writing for Screens Both Big and Small — Scripts

Scripts are an exciting story format option because the media options that rely on it have large built-in audiences. Make no mistake — scriptwriting is a very different type of storytelling than what one does anywhere else. It may even seem daunting at first. And it's true that the requirements for specific media like film, TV, plays, audio drama, and comics may differ a bit, yet all of them are built on what makes stories work in any medium. Character. Action. Dialogue. Conflict.

The strength of film and TV lies in visuals and external conflict (see Chapters 2 and 3), whereas the strength of audio fiction is sound. Plays, too, privilege sound, but primarily in the form of dialogue. The selling point for comics is the potent combination of text and image — it gives audiences multiple levels in which to engage the story.

WARNING

Most scripts require others to be part of the storytelling process: actors, directors, producers, technicians. They'll necessarily bring their own ideas and creativity to the project at some level. If you're not a fan of collaboration or you want full creative control over every aspect of your story, think twice before working in the world of scripts.

What follows are your primary scriptwriting options. Read on to see whether these are the best pathways for your stories. If you wish to take a deeper dive into this exciting area, we recommend the latest edition of *Screenwriting For Dummies* by Laura Schellhardt (John Wiley & Sons, Inc.).

Film

Film presents you multiple opportunities to fine-tune your writing muscles. You have two main options:

>> **Writing short films:** The Academy of Motion Picture Arts and Sciences calls these "an original motion picture that has a running time of 40 minutes or

less, including all credits." Why go with this option? All the main reasons have to do with it size.

Because it's shorter, writing a short film requires less characterization, plot, action, and dialogue to manage. For some writers, a short film allows them to feel less overwhelmed by so many moving story parts. Short films are also cheaper to get made because they're short, meaning they're cheaper to shoot. They may be the easiest route to being able to call yourself a produced screenwriter. Plenty of famous writer-directors — like Tim Burton and Wes Anderson — started with shorts and eventually moved on to features.

>> **Writing feature films, like those you see in movie theaters or stream online:** These motion pictures tell a complete story in 100 to 150 pages. Features aren't quite as expansive as novels because it takes time to show things visually on a screen. That's why so many novels that get adapted have pages, character, and entire plotlines cut in order to make the film. Trust us, 100 to 150 pages for a script is more than enough to present a compelling story and delve deep into its nuances and richness. Feature films can work wonders even without high-tech special effects, exotic locations, and original sound and music.

TIP

One of the best ways to study anything is to see how the pros do it. Search online for free film scripts — you'll find a lot of options, including freebies of all the current Oscar winners and nominees. See what makes them so good. Ask yourself what lesson you can learn from them and be able to apply to your own writing.

WARNING

Because so many people are in love with film and there's so much money to be made here, producers and their script readers are flooded with screenplay submissions. That means that the gatekeepers are looking for reasons to reject just to deal with the volume, so don't give them any. Avoid common rookie mistakes, like having a slow first page, ignoring the industry standard format, having characters who seem indistinguishable (look similar, speak similarly, or have similar-sounding names), and too much directing on the page, like using SLAM CUT! DISSOLVE TO! FREEZE FRAME! Trust that the director and cinematographer are pros. And no pro likes someone else telling them how to do their own job.

STANDING OUT AS A SCRIPTWRITER

Film and television scripts have specialized formats that you must use to pass muster with industry gatekeepers, who insist on such things. Using pro-level scriptwriting software will make your life a thousand times easier. We like Final Draft and Fade In, but some of the free ones, like Trelby or Highland 2, may serve your needs well enough.

Make sure you write visually. That doesn't mean describing the hilt of Mercenary #3's sword or the texture of a genie's flying carpet fringe. It means using telling actions and dialogue to reveal character and powerfully advance the story. This means writing a script that shows an actor and director how to dramatize meaningful emotion. For guidance on how to do that, visit Chapters 2 and 3.

TV

Breaking into TV writing requires a spec (speculative) script that's either an episode for an existing TV show or a pilot for your own original show. The latter is a much newer phenomenon, which is the route we recommend. The pilot script serves as kernel for an entire series. Match that with a *story bible* — a document that delivers key information on the world and goals of your series — and you're on the right track. You're presenting yourself as someone who's put in the work to develop the future of your concept beyond a single script.

The TV world is a tough one to break into, but with more streaming TV options emerging, your chances improve each year. Give yourself an extra advantage by writing a killer script that's un-put-downable.

Need a few TV-script-specific tips? Here are four ways to stand out from the masses.

>> **Think about your first season in terms of three acts.** You're not making eight one-hour shows, you're essentially making one eight-hour show. Assign your episodes the proper function of the appropriate act. The first three are the setup, the next four are the rising conflict, and the last few are the climax and resolution.

>> **Employ cliffhangers.** Don't just use them at the end of each your first three episodes — which you *must* do to get audiences hooked! — but also at the end of season one. That's how you sell the producers on buying season two.

>> **Give main characters a break.** They used to have to be in every episode. No longer. Thanks to binge-watching, people will see them again soon enough. Use this freedom to explore other themes, subplots, and storylines.

>> **Trust your ABCs.** In the TV world, a single episode runs three plots at once. The A plot gets about 60 percent of the screen time, the B gets 30 percent, and the C — if it's there at all — gets maybe 10 percent. The A story is the primary focus. The B storyline runs parallel to the A story and features supporting characters, whereas the C story may be a small one-off moment or set up a payoff later in the series. The A and B plots should resolve at some level with each episode, however, though not at the season-level of importance and closure.

Podcasts

The field of audio drama is booming, and podcasting has proven to be the best way to present audio stories. Even though nonfiction is still the predominant form in podcasting, more and more fiction podcasts deliver original stories to their fans. As a sidenote, do you know what are the top three types of fiction podcasts? Sci-fi, fantasy, and horror, in that order.

Fiction podcasts vary greatly in subject matter, style, and length, but many run from ten minutes to an hour per episode. They follow these two story formats (stick to our advice about each format):

» The first option essentially is where a standard short story is simply read aloud — ideally with some sound effects and music, but not necessarily so. Just write your idea as a traditional short story and submit it for consideration. Easy enough.

» The other option works like an old-time radio drama with multiple actors, music, and sound effects. You're essentially writing a short film or a TV episode, only without visuals because listeners can't see physical action. That's quite the challenge.

Sound and rhythm are key to creating audience connection and amplifying conflict. Generally, keep each scene to three or fewer characters, so audiences can keep track of who is who. Also make your settings rich with sound, like having your robot detective chase down a suspect through a bustling amusement park or letting a pair of amateur teen paranormal investigators creep through a creaky ancestral mansion that might or might not actually be haunted.

TIP

Because the visuals aren't there, make the audience create them for you. Their imagination will run wild if you just nudge it with key details. "Oh my God!" shouts the teen in that scary house. "What's that oozing from the eyes of that painting? Is that . . .?" In the mind of the audience, yep. That painting is now leaking blood or ectoplasm or whatever gross liquid fits the scene and story that you've built up. Regardless, it's a wonderful moment of trust and co-creation with the audience.

TIP

Instead of submitting your writing to existing fiction podcasts, consider starting your own audio drama podcast. It'll take some technical know-how and money for microphones and audio software, but nowhere near the cost of making even the cheapest short or feature film. Having your own podcast to showcase your original writing allows you to keep the intellectual property and potentially get Hollywood or TV producers interested in paying you a lot of money to develop your story into their medium. Amazon Prime, FX, NBC, SyFy, and Facebook have done this with the most successful fiction podcasts. Perhaps you're their next success story. Check out the latest edition of *Podcasting For Dummies* by Tee Morris and Chuck Tomasi (John Wiley & Sons, Inc.) for more information.

Plays

This option doesn't come to mind as readily as many others, but that doesn't mean it can't be a fantastic option. For one thing, live theater may be the only art form where storymakers — writers, actors, and directors — are able to witness the audience both receive and react to the story. That unpredictability is amazing. As a result, little nuances of the story may change during every single performance despite the story and script staying the same.

If you're a fan of dialogue, then plays are an ideal form for you. Plays are about relationships and ideas and characters engaging with them. Scenes play out in real-time, without cuts, edits, close-ups, or any of the other tricks of other visual media, which means the dialogue has to be finely crafted and carry much of the dramatic weight of the action and reaction of your journey through the story's plot.

Horror theater focuses on building dread and anticipation, the shock of the Grand Guignol. King Arthur and Merlin found one of their most famous iterations in *Camelot*. Science fiction plays can ask what-if questions about possible futures and big ideas. The most famous word in all of science fiction comes from a science fiction play, *Rossum's Universal Robots* by Karel Čapek. It not only gives us the word "robot," but it also ends in science fiction's first robot uprising.

Comics

Say "comics" and some people immediately think of those superhero comic books that parents complain will rot their kids' brains. We mean more than that here — comic books have are so many styles, sizes, and subjects. In addition, here we also mean *graphic novels* (longer comics that include fiction, nonfiction, and anthologized work). Fundamentally, comics and graphic novels are sequential art stories. Their main creative task is to marry words and visuals to create maximum impact on the page.

An advantage in the comic medium is that the writer has a lot of power. In other text and image combinations — like children's picture books — the writer writes, and the artist does the art. Often the two never meet or talk! With comics, the writer writes and also directs the artist with clear written instructions on the page that match with the dialogue. It's rare, but some very talented artists do the full job.

By virtue of using *panels* — those individual frames inside which the story happens — the comic writer has a unique tool to work with. The size, shape, and frequency of them all affects how the story works. We heartily recommend Scott McCloud's *Understanding Comics: The Invisible Art* and *Making Comics: Storytelling Secrets of Comics, Manga and Graphic Novels* (both by William Morrow) to see exactly how to use panels and the other unique elements of comics that make this such an effective, popular story format.

REMEMBER

If you're interested in writing comic books, a good analogy is an episodic TV show. Each comic book equals one episode. If you prefer to create graphic novels, those function more like a novella or novel, with the bonus of cool visuals and fun special effects.

Inviting Audiences to Co-create — Interactive Stories

With interactive stories such as video games, tabletop games, and other immersive story experiences, audience are active consumers. Why just read about or watch a psychic detective chasing a possessed schoolteacher through the streets of New York City when you could be that psychic detective yourself? Want to use telekinesis to knock down a trash bin in front of her? Go for it. Want to yell for that off-duty cabby to stop her? Holler away. The choices — and their consequences — are all yours.

Here we examine the different types of interactive stories and identify what's needed from the writer to make these satisfying.

Video games

Perhaps the most immersive story experience comes from video games. Even without getting into virtual or augmented reality, audiences still enjoy stunning environments, captivating sounds and sounds effects, and eye-candy visual details, which makes sense because the budget of high-profile video games can rival that of Hollywood blockbusters.

In video games, players become co-authors with you, the writer. Their choices determine the fate of the story's characters and their actions resolve the conflicts. There are tons of different styles of games, and writing a video game can mean anything from creating movie-style scripts to inputting a thousand different possible responses into a spreadsheet (honestly, it's more often that last one).

Games with linear stories employ the straightforward plot techniques in Chapter 3. The *gameplay* (shooting, running, jumping, puzzle-solving) adds a challenge and a sense of accomplishment that heightens tension and excitement (and sometimes, yeah, frustration), but the story is the story and as a writer you have a familiar job.

Nonlinear stories are where video games really shine, and writing one of these takes a lot of extra work and a whole different kind of thinking. You get to create interesting choices that the players have to think about, pay off those choices with equally exciting and unique outcomes, and write whole scenes and story arcs that a player might not ever see. And the effect is unique to games: The audience feels a true sense of responsibility for the characters, which is a powerful emotion few art forms can offer.

REMEMBER

Plenty of story-driven game experiences don't require a $10,000,000 investment and a team of 25 programmers. Audiences enjoy choose-your-plot style games on their phone, which might have lots of still art, a couple of drawings, or have nothing but text. Simple can work if the character, story, and game make sense and are enjoyable.

Tabletop games

Tabletop games — meaning anything from card games (Magic: The Gathering and Exploding Kittens) to board games (Settlers of Catan, Pandemic, and Risk) to role-playing games (Dungeons & Dragons, Vampire: The Masquerade, or Pathfinder) — typically combine traditional storytelling with interactivity.

Board and card games lean into the story world in which they take place and rely on short pieces of writing combined with evocative art and design to convey a sense of story. Think of the venerable chess set with its knights and queens; it alludes to the broad concept of war but is mostly about the challenge of beating your opponent. More narrative-rich games these days include named characters, fictional worlds, and even small pieces of prose scattered across the cards. Writing for these kinds of games relies on inspiring your audience and letting them fill in the rest with their imagination.

Role-playing games like Dungeons & Dragons have rulebooks longer than most novels. They're a writer's dream, with tens of thousands of words to set up the world and define its characters, monsters, and magic items. Writing for a role-playing game means providing the players with deep reserves of setting and game rules that inspire them in creating their own stories. Think of playing one of these games as improvisational theater in a world built for conflict that's filled with wondrous props and thrilling premises. Your job is to make those props and premises and turn the players loose.

The tabletop game industry is having a renaissance right now with more ways than ever to break into the field. The competition is stiff, so your game has to look, play, and read great in order to succeed. But if you have a great game, the audience for it is probably happy to back its crowdfunding campaign on Kickstarter, allowing you to bypass all the gatekeepers in other industries. See Chapter 24 on self-publishing.

Immersive experiences

In their most lavish form, immersive experiences are theme parks like Disney World. But you probably don't have a couple hundred million dollars to build your own park. Much more manageable versions are out there, and immersive experiences are increasingly popular at every scale.

Here are three types of immersive experiences:

>> **Escape rooms:** They're the most obvious example where a group gets to play at being the heroes in a high-stakes deadline-intense narrative window. Will they solve the mystery and escape danger before doom strikes?

Because an escape room has a hard time frame — usually 60 minutes — you can't have more than a single conflict: escape! That makes the dramatic question: "Will the group escape with their lives or not?" With those stakes, the adrenaline is flowing, and nerves get frazzled. Players don't have time to focus on subplots. Even the cool scenery won't be of much interest unless it connects to the main escape plot. Unlike most video games or tabletop games, an escape room has a single, linear path/plot with, at most, a single *red herring* (something placed to lead audiences to a false conclusion). Like any plot, the solution to an escape room needs to be firmly based in a cause-and-effect relationship or those would-be escapees will be unsatisfied. Probably *mad*.

» **Haunted houses:** They're another great example of a themed experience. Here the plot and story are even more succinct, with audiences walking through them. You have to cram in the mood and dread and jump scares, all in minutes.

» **Immersive theater:** Immersive theater takes audiences participation to another level by inserting them into a story that's playing out all around them. Freed from their seats, the audience can explore the story space and experience the story from any perspective.

2

Worldbuilding: Journeys to Other Worlds

IN THIS CHAPTER

» Identifying what makes your world
  compelling to an audience

» Creating story worlds based on
  dramatic conflict

» Deciding what parts of your world to
  show and what to leave off the page

Chapter **5**

Building a World Like No Other

Sci-fi, fantasy, and horror stories all take place in fictional worlds created by storytellers. These days, folks usually refer to this process as *worldbuilding*. Dreaming up a magical realm of wizards and dragons and magic rings is worldbuilding. Mapping out another planet with giant sandworms and interstellar conspiracies is worldbuilding. Describing a typical suburban neighborhood where a serial killer stalks his prey on Halloween is worldbuilding.

Wait, suburban neighborhood? Yep, worldbuilding. Anytime you're telling a story, you're also building a world, even if there's nothing fantastical or high tech about it. Perhaps that suburban neighborhood has vampires in the basements or ghosts on the playground or bitter rivals on the homeowners association who secretly love one another. Even when your story is set in a world that looks exactly like the real world everyone knows, it's not. Instead it's a story world; it's your story world. As its creator, you make a thousand different decisions about how that neighborhood works. You're making a world tailor-fit to the story and its characters.

This chapter approaches worldbuilding from the way you and your audience come together: through the story's characters and their dramatic conflicts. We then discuss the importance of focusing just on the parts of your story world that matter to your story.

Creating Worlds Worth Exploring

Building a custom world is a lot of work and responsibility, and Part 2 helps you through the process. Here's one core piece of advice to guide you at every turn: *Make a world no one has ever seen before and that only you can create.* Your story world offers a unique experience for the audience built from your passions, quirks, and obsessions. The more of you that you pour into it, the more enchanting or thrilling or frightening it will be and the more excited your audience will be to explore it.

Here are some key techniques for making sure your story world and your audience connect with one another.

Making your place interesting

Every story is a journey into your story world with you as the expert tour guide. As you set out to create this spectacular new setting, ask yourself these three questions and let the answers steer you through your journey of creation:

Who is the audience for your world?

You are the first audience for your world, but who else do you want to share it with? Designers start their process thinking about their customers, and world builders benefit from thinking up front about their audience. The whole world isn't going to experience your story, and trying to please everybody ends up thrilling nobody. Instead, focus on the audience who will dive headfirst into your story. Give them a world to explore that excites them and they'll be the first ones to tell their friends to jump in after them.

Perhaps your audience are fans of a certain genre like urban fantasy or cyberpunk or ghost stories. Maybe they share a specific interest, like space exploration or the history of a particular city or sword fighting. Some folks love a good caper story, no matter the genre. Others find a special frisson from romance across cultures or comedies of manners. Think about the audience you're most excited to reach and keep them in mind as you move forward. Those future fans can inspire and guide you as you make the thousands of decisions yet to come.

How are they going to experience it?

The medium through which your audience enters your world profoundly affects how they experience it. Prose fiction is great for thoughts, ideas, and emotions, with room for deeper dives into lore. Film and television scripts favor the visual experience of the world and allow for sound and music and atmosphere to enrich the story. A comic book lives in its own special niche between the two, relying on imagery artfully combined with words. A game lets the player co-author their experience, which is a powerful feeling but requires you to create a world that can hold up to interactivity.

REMEMBER

When building your world, be mindful of the strengths and weaknesses of your chosen medium. Also consider your own interests and talents as a storyteller. A complicated web of intrigue and scheming (be it political, criminal, or supernatural) plays out well in long-form prose and ongoing series. Your vision for a dazzling other world of sentient stone sages would likely benefit from some stunning visuals to bring it to life. Perhaps your world would exist well across multiple media. If that's your plan, think about all these possibilities, but as you begin, focus on the first medium you're going to tell your story in and worry about adaptations later.

How do your own interests make this world unique?

One of the oldest pieces of writing advice you'll hear is "write what you know." That's true, sort of. It absolutely helps a ton to know the subjects you're writing about, but that doesn't mean you have to know it before you start writing. Instead we like to say "write what you want to know about." If something piques your passions or inspires you, go find out more about it. See Chapter 6 for more on research for your stories. The key here is: You're passionate about a topic and want to learn and explore it more.

That curiosity and interest can propel your story world to greater heights, enabling you to play with and build upon your interests in unique and entertaining ways. Only your specific combination of knowledge, imagination, aesthetic, and talent can bring this specific story to life for your audience. Yes, you're thinking about who your audience is and how they'll experience your story world, but just as important is making the journey through your world one that you alone can guide them on.

Knowing how your world works

You need to keep in mind a very true, very important fact: Readers know you wrote this story. They know it's not real, they know you've crafted it with care, and they sure know when you're cheating.

The all-too-convenient plot twist that saves your hero? The audience sees what you're doing there. The beyond-stupid decision that puts the ship in needless peril? Everyone knows the author is really making the decision for them. The previously unstated weakness that makes slaying the kraken with a dagger possible? Readers know that's a cheat and nobody likes being cheated.

THREE EXEMPLARY WORLDS

You're creating a world designed to tell your stories. Here we've created three worlds designed to serve as examples. Each is a touch more generic than yours will be in order to model core principles of story world design that you can apply across all genres. They are as follows:

- Our **fantasy realm** is designed for epic tales of war, politics, and magical mayhem. It's built for a panoply of different characters and creatures and overflows with dramatic conflict, mystery, and adventure.

- Our **space station** orbits around a hostile alien world. It houses a smaller cast of intrepid spacefarers in stories that push the bounds of technology and explore strange new worlds.

- Our **small town** looks quaint and picturesque from a distance, but the tight-knit community who dwells there lives in the shadow of ancient secrets that threaten to spill forth into the daylight if someone opens the wrong (metaphorical or real) door.

Cheaters are breaking the rules of the story. Your story world will have its own special rules. Magic exists, starships can travel faster than light, there's a vampire living underneath that 7-Eleven who only drinks the blood of those who've stolen a Slurpee. The audience is here for it, as long as it follows its own internal logic and you don't cheat.

You get to create, break, and revise your world's rules constantly as you write, but by the time the audience shows up for your story, they expect some underlying logic to hold sway. Learning those rules is an important part of the fun for readers as they journey through your world, and the more they understand how everything works in your story world, the more they'll enjoy the story.

REMEMBER

No set-in-stone rules apply to every story world, but unless you show your audience otherwise, they'll rightfully assume that your story world has the same rules as our world. That's great, because you can assume everyone knows things like love hurts and black holes are dangerous and cell phone service is spotty in abandoned mines. It also means that when your world works differently than ours, the audience needs a little guidance.

This place is awesome! — Your pitch

No one has visited your world outside of your imagination. Perhaps your story world is intricate, involved, and worthy of a ten-season TV show, but none of that matters if no one comes to visit. An enticing description focused on the core appeal not only gets your audience's attention, but it also can help you concentrate on the unique aspects of your story. In a sentence or two, describe what's exciting about your story world. Think about your target audience and what they're into. Take what excites you most about your concept and pitch it straight to them.

To spark your imagination, ask yourself what the first thing is you'd tell someone about your world. Is it an ancient land where fractious humans, elves, dwarves, and halflings must come together to stop an evil superbeing and his army of orcs from plunging the world into darkness? Is it a dangerous desert world where scheming noble houses fight over the sole source of the most valuable substance in the galaxy? Is it a legendarily haunted house where a hubristic parapsychologist has brought together vulnerable psychics to prove the existence of ghosts?

STORY CHEATS — STAY AWAY AT ALL COSTS

Story cheats are the lies that writers tell themselves when they write. They're basically excuses for delivering an easy cliché instead of following the rules and logic of our own stories. Watch out for cheating in these ways:

- **That's how these stories go.** Just because your friends' stories have their characters run upstairs instead of out the back door when the werewolf breaks in doesn't mean you have to follow their bad example. If you've seen it a thousand times and groaned out loud at the contrivance of it every time, it has no place in your story. Clichés are always dubious; illogical clichés are ruinous.

- **No one will notice.** Audiences are smart. As a writer, you want them to be smart because that lets you tell smarter stories. If you see the logical fallacy, they will, too. Don't bet against your audience by assuming no one will notice that the Deathknight "forgot" to use its flame staff at just the right moment to make your plot work.

- **Normally I'd never.** Audiences love characters who chase their dreams and desires, even when doing so leads them into trouble. Audiences are annoyed by characters who suddenly behave out of character and make unexplainable choices for no reason. Chapter 2 discusses characters' wants, moral codes, and desires in greater detail.

- **This is just so cool:** Cool things are cool! A sweet-seeming old-timer who whips out a blaster from nowhere and headshots every killbot in sight and then delivers an equally killer quip can get you some smiles and nods in the moment, absolutely. But if you don't tie a cool thing to the story logic at some point, if you never know why your character has a badass blaster and a filthy mouth, then the shine wears off quickly and readers end up confused or bored.

Your pitch shouldn't be any of those exactly, because *Lord of the Rings, Dune,* and *The Haunting of Hill House* have those covered, but even if you've never read those books or seen the movies based on them, from a single sentence you can see some of what's so exciting about them. Each focuses on the most interesting and provocative things about the world. You don't need any proper names or specific terminology like Sauron or Arrakis or Hill House, for your imagination to start firing off all kinds of intriguing questions about those worlds and the stories that might happen there. Refer to the nearby sidebar about sample pitches to get you an idea of how effective sample pitches sound.

REMEMBER

Some version of your pitch will end up as part of the message you use to promote your story to an audience. It works best when coupled with some specific challenge for the story's characters. It gives the readers signposts on what's important in your world and gets them thinking about implications and curiosity to read more. It also serves as a useful reminder to you as you write your story: The pitch is what you thought was the most exciting thing about your world before you started. Keep coming back to this pitch as you write and ask yourself if that's still true. If it's not, maybe you've veered off your path and need to refocus.

The pitch isn't a contract, it's a tool.

SAMPLE PITCHES IN 30 SECONDS

Here are some sample pitches to help you put your thoughts in order:

- **Fantasy realm:** A priest-king's attempt to bring fair and impartial justice to his kingdom unleashes a magical Truth Plague upon the realm, causing anyone who lies to transform into terrifying creatures while blessing those who never withhold secrets with a soporific sense of superiority.

- **Space station:** An interstellar war leaves Space Base Alpha isolated in orbit around an inhospitable world. Where once the station's crew simply serviced transports and oversaw robotic mining on the planet below, now they must try to make the dangerous alien world their new home.

- **Small town:** A pair of charismatic outsiders move into town and buy the recently closed Saint Andrew's church, promising to turn it into a meditation and retreat center. Most townsfolk extend the strangers a wary welcome, but a few begin to suffer unsettling visions and drastic mood shifts whenever the church bells ring.

In each case, readers start to imagine all kinds of stories without being told any additional information about the story worlds. The magical curse creates immediate physical consequences for what is normally a purely moral and intellectual decision.

How dangerous are those liars turned monsters? Does the priest-king think that the transformations are a price worth paying? How can this powerful curse be lifted?

The consequences of war and the challenges of the unknown already have your readers worried about the future of the space station's crew, while the presence of robots and an alien planet promise intriguing possible solutions. What makes the planet so dangerous? Is it the environment, the alien life forms, or both? What happens when enemy forces from the war find their way to the station? Can those robots be trusted?

The actions of outsiders repurposing sacred institutions and structures for their own beliefs presents a clear dramatic tension, with the mysterious bells adding an element of the uncanny, which indicates deeper forces at work. Who are these two outsiders really, and is their charisma dangerous manipulation or genuine friendliness? Is there something supernatural going on with the bells? Is this so-called meditation center a front for a cult?

Building Worlds for Conflict

Storytellers don't usually create worlds just for the sake of making worlds. You create them for stories, and your story world is a place for drama and conflict. Even though not every part of the real world centers on conflict and drama, they dominate the stories that people tell each other about the world. Just check your favorite social media feed or news source to see what we're talking about.

The more you think deeply about your world's conflicts from the beginning, the more engaging and alive your world will feel. Let the following ideas guide you in creating those useful story conflicts.

Finding a problem around every corner

Drama and conflict stem from characters wanting something. Maybe it's something they have and want to keep, maybe it's something they lack and want to get. Either way, they want it enough to take actions to make sure they get it.

The following questions are designed to help you uncover story-worthy problems that lead to meaningful conflict.

TIP

Three answers are better than one. Just as each disagreement has multiple sides, so each of these questions can and should have multiple answers. Challenge yourself to come up with at least three answers to each of the three questions that follow. You may struggle to think of a third worrisome or important thing, but when you do, it often is the most interesting or unusual idea.

What's important to characters in this world?

Determine what the denizens of your world value most. Not just the protagonists of the story, but people in general. Every character is theoretically unique, but we're talking about the passions and desires that the majority share and that drive the society as a whole. Perhaps it's a devotion and personal sacrifice to the patron deity of the realm or serving in the colonial marines to earn full citizenship. Maybe it's honoring the town's reputation and staying out of other people's business.

REMEMBER

Decide what's important to most other characters because your protagonists are likely going to be out of the ordinary in some way. Protagonists often forge their own path in the world, making decisions that most folks don't. When their desires conflict with the popular priorities, delicious, story-driving drama logically ensues.

What's uncertain and worrisome?

To find out what puts people on edge, ask what they're worrying about, warning each other about, or wondering about. These problems usually can't be easily fixed or maybe can't be changed at all. It could be roaming bugbears in the hills or the untranslatable signals from a distant star. It could be will they go to heaven or what those strangers are doing in town. For many people, maybe it's just where their next meal is going to come from or whether they have a safe place to sleep at night.

REMEMBER

Most people try to avoid or mitigate these worries, but your protagonists will face them head on. They may not be able to fix the local economy and ensure everyone has three meals a day, but they will risk starving themselves to face some greater problem. And when those strangers do come to town, they'll be the first to welcome them (or maybe snoop around their house at night looking for answers).

What do characters disagree about?

Just because most characters in your world agree about what's important and what's worrisome, doesn't mean they agree on what to do about it all. Every problem and every ambition has at least two perspectives on how to respond to it. For some, faith in the realm's patron deity means a life of personal poverty and prayer, whereas for others it means going on a murderous crusade against those they deem heretics. Maybe the best way to defend against bugbears is a big stone wall. No, obviously the best course is raising an army and fighting them in the hills. Hey, has anyone tried talking to them?

REMEMBER

Your protagonists will have to take a side at some point, and it may or may not be the same side your audience would choose. The more your audience understands each perspective of the disagreement, the more dramatic and compelling the decision to take sides becomes.

Creating characters from conflict

As Chapter 2 emphasizes, stories are all about characters. Creating a world and creating your characters go hand-in-hand, and trying to keep both in mind at the same time is helpful. Your main characters' wants should be tied closely to the conflicts that make your world interesting. They should have their own, very specific answers to those general questions about what most people think. Create your main characters to care about and engage directly in the core conflicts of your world.

Tabletop role-playing games have made some tremendous and useful innovations in the character-creation process. Even authors with no interests in making a game can take some cues from how game designers approach integrating characters and conflict. A number of game systems, notably the GUMSHOE system originally designed by Robin D. Laws, has players define their characters' drives and motivations in concrete language that has game rules. These drives are why the characters willingly enter dangerous situations and pursue forbidden mysteries whereas most normal (non-protagonist) people would run and hide.

REMEMBER

When you can define your characters' drives in relationship to the story world's core conflict and then treat them like rules that you can't break, your characters will take on a life of their own. As long as they follow their drives, you'll never have to worry about cheating your audience.

Focusing on What's Important — The Iceberg Rule

An iceberg is a potent metaphor, and not only when it's helping nature show humanity who's boss by tearing holes in the sides of unsinkable ships. The vast majority of an iceberg lies out of sight underwater. A bright, sharp fraction reaches into the air where we can see it, but audiences don't have to perceive every detail to infer the existence of those hidden, massive depths below the waves. The same is true with worldbuilding, where the *Iceberg Rule* serves as a great tool for both managing your workload and focusing on your story on what's important.

Here we focus on the two most useful applications of the Iceberg Rule: showing the world at work and not showing the irrelevant parts.

Show the characters and conflicts

Look closely and identify the parts of your iceberg, of your story world, that interact directly with the characters and conflicts. What is the stage on which your story will play out? You show those parts.

Consider these examples:

>> In our fantasy realm, the Truth Plague originates with the high-king and involves the administration of justice. We're going to show a lot about how the politics, legal system, and magic work in this world. With liars being transformed into monstrous beings, we'll also explore combat techniques, how news and information spread, and the prejudices people hold against those who don't look like them.

>> The crew of our isolated space station is going to spend a lot of time dealing with the hostile climate, flora, and fauna of the planet below, and we'll need to see their technology at work in that environment.

>> The residents of our small town are going to have definite opinions about a landmark of faith being transformed into something unfamiliar and possibly menacing. We'll want to see how the faith community responds and how local officials handle supernatural mysteries.

Don't show everything

Think about any legal thriller, police procedural, or medical drama you've seen. Those stories are set in the complicated worlds of law and medicine, but you as an audience member don't need to know very much at all about how those worlds work to enjoy the stories. You certainly don't need a law degree or a medical license. Those stories show the parts of their complex systems that directly impact the story.

REMEMBER

With every scene and story moment you write, you have to decide what parts of your world to show and what to hide or ignore. See Chapter 7 for lots of guidance about showing, telling, and explaining things in your story world, but right now, as you're starting the worldbuilding process, identify the parts of the iceberg you want to show.

Review the three questions we asked in the section, "Making your place interesting," earlier in this chapter. Your answers lay the foundation for your characters, your conflicts, and how you show them to the audience. Take into consideration how your audience will be seeing the bit of your iceberg: In a movie? On a comic page? In a game? In a story?

For example:

>> In our fantasy realm, where magic, justice, and morality take center stage, the details of what crops grow where or when probably won't come into play and we can gloss over the subject of farming for now.

>> On the space station, the specifics of the artificial gravity system likely won't affect the plot, but how efficiently the station recycles oxygen now that it's cut off from replacement parts could drive some major drama.

>> The specifics of the small town's economy and how people make a living isn't nearly as important as how town council members are elected, especially if the tolling of a church bell on election day disrupts the democratic process.

TIP

Make sure you save everything you don't show: You've decided not to show something that you nevertheless think is cool or interesting but doesn't belong above the water on your iceberg. Don't throw that idea away! Keep a document or file or stack of notecards where all the below-the-waterline ideas can reside. Maybe you'll find a place for them later. They may well be in an entirely different story or even a different story world. Maybe the ideas will go in an appendix or on a website of additional lore. Save those ideas and think about attaching a note reminding yourself why you cut it in the first place so when you return to it you'll have some useful context about how the idea may be useful someplace else.

Chapter **6**

Letting Your Research and Imagination Run Wild

We know you like to do your research before you write because you're reading this book. You realize spending some quality time on research will make your writing easier, not harder, as long as you enter the process with the right mind-set. You're open to ideas from outside sources and eager to find out all kinds of interesting things that will make your stories better. You're our kind of people.

Research can be the most enjoyable part of the worldbuilding process: finding inspiration, discovering fun facts, and imagining how to tweak them to serve your story is a creative undertaking. This chapter can help you turn fun facts into fantastic fiction.

Start with Earth: Inspiration and Adaptation

"Start with Earth." That's award-winning writer and game designer Kenneth Hite's first piece of advice to fellow worldbuilders and storytellers, and we couldn't agree more. In fact, because we're all Earthlings here, it's impossible not to start with Earth; it's the basis for everything we know and that knowledge influences everything we create.

You can't build story worlds without relying on the language, history, science, psychology, biology, philosophy, and cultural traditions of this shared world. So, start with Earth and then transform it into something uniquely suited to the stories you're telling.

Here are two useful approaches for adapting the existing world to serve the story and entrance your audience.

Tapping into the power of piggybacking

We all know a lot about the Earth and have assumptions and understandings about how things work. We all also have lots of shared experiences with famous stories, myths, legends, songs, and facts. As a world builder, *piggybacking* on your audience's existing knowledge allows you to laser focus on what makes your worlds unique and cool while letting common ideas carry the weight of how most of the world works.

REMEMBER

Not everyone will share all your conceptions of common knowledge, but if you've thought about who your intended audience is and what kind of ideas and preconceptions they're likely to bring to their experience of your story world, you can take advantage of piggybacking's tremendous narrative power. Even if some people aren't familiar with the information, in this era of Google and Wikipedia, the curious audience member can easily look it up.

Here are three different approaches to using piggybacking to build worlds in your stories.

Telling the story with one big change

One of the most useful and common techniques for sci-fi, fantasy, and horror, piggybacking involves telling a story on Earth's past or present but with just one big change. It's our world, but secret sorcerers live just out of sight. It's our world, but artificially intelligent robots cater to our every whim. It's our world, but zombies have overrun everything except this shopping mall.

The advantages to this technique are tremendous. You can focus all your imagination and attention on the one big change and how it affects your characters and creates your story. Your audience gets to play along as well; their own imaginations make connections and inferences based on what they're familiar with and how life would indeed be different if they were a secret sorcerer or could leave the dishes for the robot. You and the audience share a common framework from which the story's logic will play out.

Alternate history is another version of this same kind of piggybacking: what if the First Crusade never happened? What if computers were invented a century earlier? What if President Nixon had defeated Kennedy in the 1960 U.S. Presidential election? Philip K. Dick's *The Man in High Castle* (Houghton Mifflin Harcourt) imagines a history where Germany and Japan won World War 2. Nisi Shawl's *Everfair* (Tor Books) explores an African civilization in the Congo using steam technology to fight the Belgian colonialist invasion.

These kinds of "what if?" thought experiments instantly raise intriguing questions for your audience and allow you to play around with our shared reality without breaking or reinventing any of its rules. Just try to make sure your answers are more interesting than whatever your audience thinks up, which shouldn't be a problem because you'll be spending a whole lot more time thinking about the question and researching its implications. (Chapter 9 delves deeper into answering the "What If.")

Inventing a world with a thousand little differences

Another common piggybacking technique in a lot of fantasy and science fiction stories involves basing invented cultures on real world ones. The benefit here is that you don't need to do nearly as much explaining how things look or work or why the person in a metal suit on a horse is called "Sir," and you're free to tailor the world to your narrative needs.

A lot of high fantasy is often set in the European Middle Ages (or, actually, 19th-century vision of the Middle Ages) with new names and a different map. This piggyback ride gets you castles, knights, feudal lords, and stories of wizards and dragons. It can also get you a very powerful Catholic Church, but many fantasy stories leave that out because it overcomplicates their story, which is perfectly fine! The Romantic version of Medieval France that replaces wizards and fairies instead of bishops and nuns works great for most audiences of fantasy stories.

Victorian London, Shogunate-era Japan, and Ancient Rome are among the many common sources for story world substitution. Nothing is stopping you from following one of these well-trodden paths and making it your own, and if you're passionate about the era, then that's another reason why the source is great for your story world. Don't limit yourself though: You can draw from a whole world of history! For example, Arkady Martine's excellent sci-fi epic, *A Memory Called Empire* (Tor Books), takes elements from Aztec and Byzantine history (among others) and mixes them elegantly to create her engaging and original Teixcalaanli Empire.

History and other cultures aren't just sources for your stories. They're the lives and expressions and achievements of real people living and dead, and should be approached with respect and humility. See Chapter 23 for more information about authenticity, experts, and sensitivity readers.

Focusing on shared stories — Tales as old as time

You aren't limited to history or reality for your piggyback rides; shared stories and literature are another fertile source of story worlds where the audience already comes in with some valuable context. Much of Disney's catalog of hits is based on turning public domain, classic fairy tales into animated features (and theme park rides, toys, live action features, and so on).

The versions of myths and fairy tales read today are exactly this kind of retelling. Ovid's *Metamorphoses* are elegant retellings of stories that everyone in his first century Roman audience had heard a thousand times since childhood. Ovid just told them better than most people. The opportunity for you in retelling is that the audience already has some buy-in with the premise of the fantastic tale you're going to tell and may be interested in your spin on the classics.

You can make the story your own in an infinite recombinations and ways: Ragnarok of the Norse gods, but in space. *The Journey to the West*, but in modern-day China instead of the distant past. *Romeo and Juliet*, but with elves and dwarves. The *Three Little Pigs*, but in a haunted house. Try going back to the earliest versions of the stories you can find, and usually those are the strangest and most unusual to modern audiences. Mine those stories for fascinating details upon which to build your own interpretation.

You don't have to pick any singular time-tested tale as your basis. Combine character dynamics from one story and a story premise from another to create your own unique but familiar story world. For example, take an aging King Lear–style patriarch demanding unconditional love from his three daughters and insert them into a tale of mismatched lovers who stumble into *A Midsummer Night's Dream*–style feud between faerie monarchs. Now the three daughters become embroiled in sinister alliances with the faerie court as they try to wrest control or dignity or love from their narcissistic father. If the elements you're piggybacking on resonate well with your audience, then they're already halfway engrossed with the story before it's even begun.

Controlling cognitive dissonance

Fantasy, horror, and science fiction audiences expect the story world to be different from our own, and they're willing and excited to suspend their disbelief a little or a lot as long as the characters and their drama keep them engaged. The challenge comes when the breaks with consensus reality are so big that they produce cognitive dissonance and alienate your audience.

REMEMBER

Cognitive dissonance means the unease or discomfort an audience member experiences when different ways of thinking and understanding clash with one another. At its worst, it manifests in something like, "I know this is just a fun story, but I just don't think that's how people behave (or pigs would really fly or how gravity works)." On the other hand, a little controlled dissonance can be great and add to the experience. "I know how doors in old houses work, and they definitely don't open themselves. Something spooky is going on here!" You want interesting, compelling dissonance, not alienating, confusing dissonance.

Here are two powerful techniques for managing your audience's cognitive dissonance by finding the right balance between the new and the familiar.

Relying on most advanced yet acceptable

People like what they're familiar with, and they get uncomfortable when you change too much. But people do get excited about new things and changes for the better. Famed 20th-century industrial designer Raymond Loewy made his reputation designing everything from packaging to pots to cars and trains that customers found exciting and new while being accessible and useful.

He used the term *most advanced yet acceptable (MAYA)* to summarize his design philosophy. "The adult public's taste is not necessarily ready to accept the logical solutions to their requirements if the solution implies too vast a departure from what they have been conditioned into accepting as the norm." Put another way, MAYA means finding that perfect balance between your audience's fear of change and their interest in the new.

Whether you're changing one big thing, a thousand little ones, or twisting a twice-told tale, the MAYA concept is a great and powerful guideline for creating new worlds. When you're making changes to reality, change only as much as you think you need to in order to engage your audience without alienating them. Audiences will dive into your world if you build them a solid diving board from which to jump, so don't undermine their understanding of your world with needless changes to ours that don't help your story.

Staying true to genre realities

Your audience's consensus reality doesn't just include things that are real. Popular stories of all kinds allow for piggybacking and all three genres (sci-fi, fantasy, and horror) have well-established tropes that won't cause your audience much cognitive dissonance when you include them in your story.

For instance, fantasy audiences accept that dragons breathe fire and fly, elves live for thousands of years, and wizards cast spells. Science fiction fans don't need much of an explanation to accept faster-than-light travel or artificial intelligence. Supernatural horror's ghosts, vampires, and werewolves all come with long traditions that audiences assume apply to one degree or another.

You can create cognitive dissonance (both good and bad kinds) when you stray from the genre conventions. But know your genre well enough so you can advance from its tropes in a way your audience accepts and enjoys.

Familiarizing yourself with your genre

It's really important to know what other kinds of stories exist in your chosen genre. If you have the passion and determination to write a sci-fi, fantasy, and horror story, you likely enjoy those genres. Take some time to read stories that you think are similar to yours in some way and explore a mix of both contemporary classics and recent releases because the audience for those stories may well be the audience for yours.

The creators of those stories are going to be your peers, and politely and affirmatively engaging with the community of creators in your genre will only help your writing and grow your audience. You don't need to read in your genre all the time, of course. Many writers avoid reading work in their genre while they're doing the actual writing, for fear of muddling or distracting from their own ideas.

Using Research to Balance Science and Fiction

One of the great rewards of researching a topic, even one you're already familiar with, is discovering strange and fascinating facts that can inform and enliven your stories. Audiences love this kind of learning through fiction, especially when it's well-integrated into the storytelling. Seek out the true stories of strangeness and wonder as you're researching, allowing them to feed your fiction in multiple ways.

TECHNICAL STUFF

Here's a fun research topic for you: Look up the origin of the word "piggyback." Surprise, it's got nothing to do with pigs. It's a common phrase most people have heard. Piggyback rides are a staple of childhood. We bet you didn't know that its origins come from pitching something into a pack. And the origin of "ramshackle" has nothing to do with rams, shacks, or shackles. Any fact that inspires you to say to a friend, "I'll bet you didn't know that . . ." can inspire your story.

REMEMBER

The Iceberg Rule applies here: You want to focus your creative efforts on the parts of your story world that directly impact your characters and story (Chapter 5 explains the rule in greater detail). You're going to find way more interesting facts than you need for your story. There probably isn't a place in your story for interesting insights into the etymology of "piggybacking," so don't try to force it into your story world. Save it all in a file or on a Pinterest board with the other cool ideas you're not including. Someday maybe you'll find the right story for them.

Here are three key things to keep in mind as you dive into the depths of story research.

Striving for accuracy

There's an inherent tension between the story you want to tell and reality as best as you understand it. This tension plays out differently in each piece of fiction, nonfiction, journalism, commentary, poetry, and anything else authors write. You have to answer for yourself how beholden you feel to the facts and how much you're willing to bend the truth to make the story you want to tell.

In a work of fiction, particularly genre fiction like we're talking about in this book, audiences expect writers to play a little (or a lot) fast and loose with the facts. But they also expect you to do so in a thoughtful, creative, and entertaining manner — not because it's easier to just make things up. Allow us to make the case for striving for accuracy in your fiction:

>> **Audiences do care.** Genre audiences in particular are often interested in science, history, and cultural studies. They know things about space or castles or chainsaws, and if they catch you making a mistake, they're liable to count it against you, no matter how good your story is.

>> **Use effective piggybacking.** To gain all the benefits of piggybacking we discuss in the section "Tapping into the power of piggybacking," earlier in this chapter, you need to share some common facts and ideas with your audience. Diverge too far from your references, and the piggybacking doesn't work.

>> **You do have a duty to the truth.** When you're making another world from the literal ground up, you have a lot of leeway, but when your story takes place in our shared reality, your audience may take something you've made up as true fact. Setting a story in this world inherently requires telling stories that reflect on other people's realities. We think you have some moral responsibility to be thoughtful about the ideas you put out into the world no matter what, but especially when those ideas can impact how your audience thinks about other people.

TIP

Don't be afraid to change the facts to fit your fiction; just be thoughtful about it. Make sure your deviations from reality relate to the core conflicts and aren't egregious or lazy.

Casting a wide net when researching

It's never been easier to learn a dozen interesting things before breakfast. You never know when you'll stumble across some factoid about ant colonies that can inspire your next great space opera epic. Make a place in your media diet for regular and diverse consumption of nonfiction content, be it books, websites, podcasts, YouTube channels, or whatever. The wider the net you cast, the more useful discoveries you'll make.

Here are some effective techniques you can use when you do sit down to research. Using them, you can create a great library of associations and references to help get you started.

KEEPING UP WITH REALITY

New discoveries and inventions are happening all the time, and stories usually need to change with the times.

Consider H.G. Wells and *The War of the Worlds*. When he wrote it in the late 1890s, having Earth invaded by highly evolved aliens from Mars was a different story than if someone wrote the exact same novel today. In 1898, nobody had been to Mars or into space. It was still, as far as his audience knew, possible there were in fact aliens on Mars who could invade and conquer England. Today we all know there's no angry alien invasion force on the red planet. We're still hoping to find signs of microbial life. We know a lot about all the other planets in our solar system, too.

To write an even semi-plausible alien story today, you have to do your research to know whether your aliens came from somewhere else or you have to explain how they've remained hidden.

Reading like a writer

Most people start researching by reading. In fact, a good book about your subject is your best friend. Someone else has done a lot of hard work to inform you in detail about something they care about.

But you're not just reading to learn, you're reading to write a story about characters in a unique world who want something and are having a tough time getting it. Think of your characters and their conflicts as you read. Ask yourself how they would respond to this information you've discovered. What's their stance on the moral implications of this discovery? What are characters going to disagree about or fight over or be scared of?

Following the citations

We're college professors, and so we're duty-bound to admonish our students that they can't just rely on Wikipedia for their research papers. And they can't! You on the other hand, well. . . It really is a useful place to start.

For a lot of topics Wikipedia will orient you within the subject matter, and maybe all you need to know right now is that there were either 96 or 112 deaths associated with the building of the Hoover Dam (depending on how you count). But if your story needs more details and context, scroll down to the citations at the bottom of the page or go to the bibliography at the back of the book you're reading. Check out that original essay from the Bureau of Reclamation that's cited there and see what else you can find. The cited sources will be richer in details and curious facts that will bring your story to life.

Getting scholarly

Basic Internet searches won't give you everything you need to know about a subject. We talk a lot more about consulting experts in Chapter 23, but you can use expert-level tools that most folks aren't aware of. Here are a few places to start:

>> Google Scholar (scholar.google.com) searches academic publications and sources instead of the general web. You'll find pages or peer-reviewed, expert vetted information about your topic.

>> Other academic databases like Jstor and ProQuest are great as well, if you have access to them through a library or want to pay for them yourself. Ask your friendly neighborhood reference librarian for assistance.

>> Travel guides are a great resource for learning the basic history, geography, and culture of a region. Vintage guides published in the era of your story (like a guide to Paris from the 1920s) are especially useful for historical fiction.

Doing some field research

If you're able to get to a physical place related to your story, do so. Describing a place to your audience is infinitely easier if you've been there yourself. Even if you can't get there, Google Earth offers a powerful, free tool to simulate that view from the field. After you've walked the ground and talked to the people where your story takes place, you'll have a deep reservoir of experience with your story world's sights, sounds, and vibes.

Just because the place doesn't exist in our world doesn't mean you can't "start with Earth" by picking a specific analog to reference as you write. For instance, the priest-king's court can share features with a local museum. The alien's world's wilderness can share the fundamental layout of a nearby state park. The old church's floor plan can be identical to a church in your neighborhood. Take the Earth that's all around you and mold it to your story.

Heading straight to the sources

Historians and academics know how to distinguish between primary sources and secondary sources. Those two terms mean the following:

>> **Primary sources:** Something from the era or place or people being studied

>> **Secondary sources:** Something written about the subject by someone like a historian

Great secondary sources do a lot of the hard work for you, combing through archives of primary sources and other secondary ones to present a coherent account of the subject. For most purposes, a well-written secondary source with a detailed index and a comprehensive bibliography is the perfect place to start your research and might be all you need to know about a subject, depending on how central it is to your story.

Learning the broad strokes of a subject through just primary sources is difficult if you're unfamiliar with the field of study and takes a ton of time and effort. But they're an invaluable writing resource in other key ways that a secondary source can't be, such as:

>> **A hero or villain's tale:** Someone's personal account of their life is a great starting point for creating your characters. Maybe they're the perfect character for your story and you'll create a fictional version of them. More likely, you'll take details from their narrative of their life and translate them into your story world.

For example, someone like Nadezhda Andreyevna Durova was a real woman who disguised herself as a soldier and fought for Russia against Napoleon. She wrote a memoir, *The Cavalry Maiden*, that's already been the basis for at least one novel. You could tell her story again, or transpose her into a fantasy setting and turn France and Russia into rival dwarf kingdoms. Or you could just plumb her unique autobiography for details about impersonating a man, fighting for Russia, or being a cavalry officer.

» **Authentic voice:** How do people actually communicate with one another? What phrases and references and terms of affection and insults do they use? In a historically based setting, the primary sources give you a window into the past, but they're just as useful for any modern community or setting you're unfamiliar with, from the other customs countries to the elitisms of exclusive country clubs.

» **Concerns and conflicts:** What people talk about is just as revealing as how they talk about it. What are people arguing about and what kind of manners and social restraints govern their arguments? How do they treat outsiders or the unknown? What problems are businesses offering to solve for their customers in their advertisements in the local paper? Your story and its world are built around conflict; primary sources can enrich your portrayal of how that conflict plays out.

» **Full of details:** Many primary sources, especially things like letters, diaries, and memoirs, are jam-packed with the details of daily life. Mine these details mercilessly for livelier and more effective descriptions of everything from fashion and food to the weather. When a primary source makes note of a particular style of dress or finds some food objectionable or unfamiliar, that's likely the sort of thing a character in your story will find interesting, too.

» **The unspoken:** Step back and consider what none of your primary sources are talking about or talking around and wonder why. Many historical and contemporary societies put strict legal or customary boundaries on topics like sexuality, gender, and religious beliefs. That doesn't mean people weren't talking about them — far from it. You'll probably have to dig deeper to find the voices that the dominant societal forces have silenced to truly bring them to life in your story.

TIP

» **Avoiding anachronisms:** Primary sources can also help you avoid anachronisms in your dialogue, and you're on safe ground when you use phases and terms that people actually used in the period. (An *anachronism* is anything that comes from another time period than the story's setting.) A lot of idioms people use without thinking are quite modern or have origins specific to history. Google has a great tool called the Ngram Viewer (books. google.com/ngrams) that lets you check how often a word or phrase has been used in books dating back to 1800. It's an excellent tool for eliminating anachronisms from your story.

Chapter **7**

Showing the Explosion: Exposition That Thrills!

xposition is a dirty word amongst writers. Say the word, and people think of dry information dumps in an encyclopedia or long-winded side characters explaining how the oscillation overthruster works for five straight pages without pausing to take a breath. Distaste for exposition is often accompanied by the age-old storytelling advice "show, don't tell."

That's a fine piece of advice as far as it goes, but also maybe confusing. After all, you're "telling" the whole story in one way or another, right? The real key is to make sure your exposition fully incorporates your characters and conflicts so that your audience cares about the information being exposited at them. Telling is totally fine, as long as you tell well.

This chapter explores ways to write exposition that both shows and tells in exciting ways that won't leave your audience yawning or skipping ahead.

Showing Your World at Work

"Show, don't tell" really means "convey information through characters acting." Let your fictional folk do their thing, and nine times out of ten the audience can pick up a lot of key information through context clues (at least if you're telling well they can).

Read on to see how to do this.

Making memorable first impressions

The moment your audience enters your story world for the first time is delicate. Those early scenes carry a ton of responsibility; if they're boring or confusing, you may be able to hear the audience pick up a new book or turn the channel. In other words, they're outta here. That's why making a great first impression is so important. You want them to stick around.

Your *story world pitch* (the enticing description focused on the world's core appeal) and the questions in Chapter 5 come in handy here. Identify what's exciting and unique about this world and its characters. Some of that great stuff needs to be in your first scene, enough to entice the audience to keep going and want to know more.

WARNING

However! You don't need to cram everything that's great about your story world into the first scene. Think about visiting a new city for the first time. If someone dropped you off in a busy intersection full of loud noises, signs in a language you don't understand, your first instinct is likely to wish you were home. Pick a few key details related to the central pitch for your story and its world and give your audience a taste of what's to come and ease them in. Don't cram in a bunch of strange names and impenetrable idioms and turn them off.

Just don't go too easy.

TIP

Welcome your audience with a challenge they can handle. Your audience's first experience with the world works best when coupled with some specific challenge for the characters that gets the audience caring about what comes next for the people of this world. Although the audience may not love getting dropped off at that busy intersection in another country, reading about someone in that predicament sucks them right in. The characters can't read the language, and the audience doesn't need to at this point either. They can take in the broad picture and empathize with the disoriented character's plight from the safety of their home.

Letting actions bring the world to life

You've welcomed the audience with a compelling challenge for your characters, now you can start showing the world at work. The audience is here for your strange new world and all its fascinating and frightening wonders. They want to learn more — you just need to teach them in the most engrossing way you can.

TIP

Show things working rather than explaining how they work. Follow that simple rule, and most of your world's wonders reveal themselves, no added exposition needed.

Consider this example: The Deathknight paralyzes a muscle-bound gladiator with one exhalation of its fetid breath, then finishes him off with its seemingly fragile obsidian lance.

Something magical is happening here. The audience gets a sense of why they're not called Lifeknights and that they don't abide by the rules of chivalry. Now that the audience has seen them in action, you may need to explain more about the noxious breath or sinister lance later, or maybe not, depending on the story's needs. For now the audience has experienced them at work and can imagine what would happen to the protagonists if (when) they have to fight one of these nasties.

TIP

Whenever a new wonder from your world gets introduced, incorporate it into the characters' journey through the story. Don't just show things working though, show them working within the context of challenges for the characters as they pursue their wants and desires. When you have to explain something about the world, you get to explain it in terms related to how it affects your characters. For instance, the spaceship needs a specific kind of fuel to travel through the planet's atmosphere and the characters need to find it. The high court has very arcane and confusing rules and customs, and the characters need to consult an expert to bring their plea for mercy to the priest-adjudicate.

REMEMBER

Using a character's senses is a useful way to bring the story world to life without coming out and telling the audience directly about things. It's also a way to describe an object or thing that isn't working correctly and frustrates a character.

Small details can point to hidden depths about your world, and they don't need a lot of explaining to have a big impact. What do the names and appearance of everyday items imply about the story world as a whole? Unless the precise calculation of available funds is key to your story, you don't need to give conversion rates, but a world with its own pennies, nickels, dimes, and quarters indicates a money system that's evolved over time and an economy in flux over the ages. A world where stores are named things like "Dagby and Daughters" implies a different scale of corporate involvement than one where there's a "GalactCo" outlet on every corner. Your characters may never go into one of those stores, but just a passing mention of them adds to the whole tapestry of the world's experience.

WARNING

A common challenge you'll face is having characters who know much more about your story world than your audience does. You likely have characters who are learning about the world along with the audience, but most of the world's denizens are intimately familiar with every aspect of it so you need to write them with that fact in mind. "As you know, we've lived on this station since we were children, younger sister of mine." If you find yourself typing the phrase "As you know . . ." into one of your characters' mouths, hit that backspace key hard and try again. In real life, people pretty much only say "as you know" when they're trying to politely call someone stupid for forgetting something. Same for "I've told you before" and "Don't you remember . . ."

Relying on Narrative Exposition: Stories That Explain and Entrance

As we discuss in Chapter 3, no matter the type of genre you're writing, your story needs a great beginning, middle, and end. The same applies to exposition as we explore in the following sections.

Telling a tale within a tale

Every time you need to provide some exposition you have an opportunity to tell a cool little short story that not only informs the audience but also delights in its own right. Presenting exposition as stories means sticking with story fundamentals like we discuss in Part 1. The story should be about characters who want something, and it needs a beginning, middle, and an end:

» **Characters:** These don't have to be your main characters. Often they're people from another time or place whose actions or experiences affect and inform the present moment in the story. When you need to explain something about your world, consider who would be most affected by the subject, and structure your narrative exposition around their wants and the challenges they face. The rogue scientist seeking fame in the face of skeptical colleagues defies convention and creates the warp drive. The lovesick demi-god unlocks the principles of spirit magic in an effort to impress their love's haughty family.

» **Beginning:** Ask yourself why this expository story is worth telling right now. Begin the story with drama or conflict that somehow relates directly to what's currently happening in the story and the challenges your characters face. The broken warp drive has a curious quirk in its fuel system because of its creator's esoteric expertise with hypergeometric lenses. Summoning a helpful spirit to guide you through the forest requires a love song in perfect meter or they'll become angry spirits who'll lead you astray.

>> **Middle:** The heart of your narrative short story conveys the who, what, where, when, and/or how that you want the audience to know. Having hooked them with characters and conflict from the start, you've earned enough interest to lay out some facts in a relatively straightforward manner. However, don't go full technical manual dry. You can use some concise declarative sentences. The warp drive needs crystals from the Gugh system or it won't operate at full capacity. The spirits prefer love songs with a lot of flower metaphors, but not roses. No matter what, not roses. But always have an eye on relating these facts to the consequences for your main characters.

>> **End:** Wrap things up quick, giving audiences some closure on your narrative exposition characters and then returning to the story at hand. A good, bad, mysterious, or sentimental emotional valence for the ending can reflect the overall mood and theme of your story at this point, either reinforcing it (the inventor died testing their warp drive, so be careful) or offering hope in a tough situation (and they lived happily ever after, so maybe you will too, if you're lucky).

TIP

Look to classic fables, parables, and even children's picture books for models on creating tightly structured narratives in the space of just a few paragraphs. You'll find they do a great job of conveying information through both emotion and character.

Writing exposition that causes conflict

Every story has at least two sides. People often disagree about history and what it means. Even experts disagree about how something works or exactly what it means. In your story world you determine the facts, but that doesn't mean the characters presenting the exposition know them or agree with you. How characters and the audience react to the information is as or more important than the information itself.

History's mysteries, tragedies, and triumphs can inspire dread, anticipation, curiosity, or hope in both the characters and the audience. Even though past performance may not guarantee future returns, it definitely makes people wonder and worry. Determine what emotions you want the audience to feel now that they know this exposition you've given them. Ask yourself whether the story's characters feel the same emotions, or different ones. The audience may well worry about the threat posed by the spirit-haunted forest, whereas the characters discount the information as "just a story to scare kids." Unlike the characters, the audience knows they're in a story themselves, and the dangers are probably very real.

After you've given exposition through narrative to convey important information about the current situation, the main characters have to decide what to do with that knowledge. That's a great opportunity for drama and characterization. Prejudices and devotions distort clear-headed assessment of the facts. Sometimes people just refuse to believe something that contradicts their deeply held beliefs. Moral codes and obligation to others can restrict options, preventing characters from making the easy or safe assessment without compromising their values. They can argue with each other about it, they can carefully assess which option is the least worst path, and they can weigh the moral implications of each choice. Even a single character can debate these alternatives in their own head and the audience can join in with their own opinions.

Getting to the point with point of view

In Chapter 2, we discuss the basics of point of view and how it affects the way your audience experiences the story. Point of view plays a particularly important role in how the story handles exposition.

Consider the strengths of the following points of view when making this vital choice for your story:

>> **First person and close third person:** The audience is right there in the character's experiencing the world through their senses and thoughts. The audience gets to know everything they know and learn new things right along with them. Their thoughts, opinions, and feelings should color all the exposition the audience experiences, even if they don't always agree with their assessment or decisions.

>> **Rotating point of view characters:** Switching from one point of view character to another with each scene or chapter keeps the audience attached to your core characters while allowing a broader range of perspectives on the world and its conflicts. Particular characters may be more likely to understand or unearth specific kinds of exposition and have informed opinions about it. Equally likeable characters can have diametrically opposed interpretations, leading to great dramatic scenes as they disagree about what to do and we can see both sides.

>> **Shifting point of view:** Shifting point of view within a scene takes a deft hand and some daring as a writer, but doing so is a powerful way to convey multiple reactions to and interpretations of exposition. The audience can see how each party responds to the information internally in a setting where they're likely to hide their true intentions. Stories of political intrigue, legal wranglings, and open conflict can use this technique to great effect, but there's a high risk of confusing your audience.

- » **The omniscient narrator:** The audience is privy to all kinds of information about the world, likely including things the main characters don't even know. In stories that thrive on the audience understanding the big picture as events unfold, no one character can convey all the information the audience needs to know. Epic tales of war and disaster work well with this POV method, as do stories that cover broad sweeps of time or scope.

- » **The opinionated narrator:** A story that has a character as a narrator can have thoughts and comments upon events, which adds a lot of panache and flavor to the story when used well. It also means that the character themselves knows they're telling the audience a story, and just as you bend and shape events to suit your purposes as the author, so too they have their own agenda for telling the story the way they do.

You don't have to speak through a character to express opinions about things, and some stories deploy this kind of authorial commentary to great effect. In both cases, the audience recognizes that the opinionated narrator is probably also an unreliable narrator. Unreliable narrators can add drama, tension, and humor to your exposition in a natural way that feels more familiar and welcoming than straight recitations of fact.

- » **Letters, diaries, and confessionals:** Documents created by characters to tell the story are a special class of unreliable. Unlike a storyteller who presumably knows how everything ends, diaries and letters are usually written as events take place, without the benefit of hindsight. They're great for conveying exposition as the audience follows a character's journey and discoveries through the story and allow for many of the advantages of an opinionated narrator without the sense of ironic detachment. They're also an excellent tool for incorporating other points of view into a story that otherwise is locked to a first or close third person narrative.

EXPOSITORY EXCERPTS

Many stories begin chapters or issues or scenes with an excerpt from some source from within the story world. Science fiction classic *Dune* by Frank Herbert begins each chapter with a quote from various "history" texts written by characters in the book after the events of the book or about the planet Arrakis where it takes place. Excerpts like these can provide some valuable context for the rest of the story while also enriching the audience's understanding of the story world. In general they should be short and even then they're the kind of thing some readers skip or skim (refer to the section, "Storytelling at Every Level of Engagement," later in this chapter), so don't put any vital plot information in them.

Trusting and Provoking Your Reader

Maybe the best way to incorporate exposition into your story is to not explain something to the audience at all. The *Iceberg Rule* (see Chapter 5) relies on the concept that audiences can intuit a lot from seeing just a little of your world "above water." Piggybacking encourages you to start with familiar elements (like Earth) and let the audience's own knowledge inform their understanding of your story world. You don't need to explain something if the audience can figure it out for themselves. (Refer to Chapter 6 for more about piggybacking.)

Use the following ideas to provoke deeper story interaction and engagement from your audience.

Solving a puzzle: 1+1

One of the great joys of playing games is solving puzzles: literally solving a jigsaw or crossword puzzle, figuring out your way through a challenging level, making the right story choices to get the good ending. People love that Aha! moment when they figure something out. Revealing your world and its story to the audience is another kind of puzzle.

With every scene, the audience wonders about the implications and inferences of each new event and element. They see a "1" here with the empty secret compartment, and they see another "1" there with the sparkly antique amulet the suspicious courtier is wearing, and they put together "2" all on their own. That dude is up to something.

Giving characters revelatory actions

Characters reveal the true nature of the world and themselves through their actions, and the audience infers a lot from them. Audiences take their cue from what the characters respond strongly to and how that response turns into action gives more meaningful exposition than a full paragraph from the Encyclopedia Galactica. Combine your world's unique invented elements with primal emotions that all people share, and the reader gets what's important.

If everyone on board the space station is worried about the azimuth of the reflector array, then the audience will worry, too, even if they don't know what azimuth means or what a reflector array does. If all the main characters fawn over the Verger of Dauroth and ask her to bless their blades, the audience can intuit that she's a religious authority who approves of deadly weapons and appreciates a little butt-kissing.

Sending systemic signals

Your story world will respond to your characters' actions (see Chapter 2). How the world responds will signal to the audience how the underlying systems of your invented reality work. These systems can be physical or magical laws of reality or social conventions that everyone follows. Your characters poke and prod at the world's systems in part to show the audience what happens when a real or metaphorical line is crossed.

When someone steps over the blue chalk line into the stone circle and everyone outside the circle gasps in horror, the audience knows the character has violated an important social taboo. When an angelic voice emanates from nowhere and everywhere at once, chastising the trespassing character, the audience knows a magical system has been activated.

WARNING

A great way to surprise your audience is to imply 1 + 1 = 2 and then reveal that, in fact it equals 3. Bet they didn't see that coming! But are you just cheating on your own rules for a cheap surprise that elicits a "what the heck?" response? How did that happen?" or is this the kind of surprise the audience looks back on and says, "oooh, interesting!" Don't make them feel stupid. Don't do this to feel smarter than them because in your amazing word, 1+1=3, of course.

Storytelling at Every Level of Engagement

Most of you have watched something on TV while scrolling through something else on your phone or cooking dinner. You've listened to an audiobook or podcast while driving, played a game with the sound off while listening to music, skimmed some pages to get to a more exciting part of the book. As a writer, you present a carefully crafted whole story world (or the tip of its iceberg anyway), but you can't force your audience to pay careful attention to it. There's nothing you can do to stop this kind of behavior, though you can dissuade it by creating your story to work on multiple levels of audience engagement.

We divide audience attention into four levels, which apply to anything from visiting a theme park to playing a game to reading a book. Individuals will move up and down the levels depending on their interests and attention. Write your story and its exposition with all four levels in mind, and you'll have a rich, complex story world that engages audiences no matter how much attention they're choosing to give you.

Level 1: Bold strokes

These core elements can't be ignored: characters doing things in places and causing reactions. To help the casual audience member keep everything straight, give characters, places, and important ideas names with different starting letters and a dominant characteristic or turn of phrase. Clearly describe and highlight important actions and reinforce cause and effect through the characters' decisions and reactions to key events.

For example: In our small town, retirees Arnie and Janet Simmons attend one of the daily meditation circles at the old church. They discuss their plan to confront Orn and Rel, the new church owners, about their beliefs after the circle ends. Orn and Rel never speak directly to them, and they both sweat profusely and almost pass out when they hear the dissonant tones from the meditation bell and leave without following through on their plan. On the way home they both agree that Orn and Rel are good and godly folk, nothing to worry about there.

Level 2: Fine nuances

These are the telling details, themes, motifs and details that bring the story world to life and connect the scenes across the narrative. Most of the audience will pick up on them if they're paying full attention. Use descriptive language and environmental cues to enhance the drama and the exposition content in the scene. Focus on the lighting conditions, sounds, and other sensory impressions that are striking or are important to this moment in the story. In dialogue, what people avoid talking about can say as much as what they do share and specific idioms and dialect point to specific classes and groups within society.

For example: The interior of the church is bright, clean, and polished to a mirror finish, but there is no sign of any technology from the past two centuries. Orn and Ren never use contractions when they speak and tend to use short, declarative sentences while Arnie and Janet weigh their dialogue down with pleasantries and formalities. The bells in the meditation chamber are engraved with a floral pattern the audience will see in other scenes later in the story.

Level 3: Hidden depths

Nestled within the scene are hyper-specific elements that are almost a subliminal experience unless a dedicated audience member goes looking for them. They may be patterns like the use of specific adjectives or colors or metaphors when describing a place or character. They could be references to other pieces of literature or things from outside the story world that will resonate with your story if the audience knows them or goes and looks them up.

For example: The colors of the stained glass window feature strong greens, a color that recurs whenever someone has a mind-altering experience in the story. Orn and Ren mention that the bells were cast from metal originally used to make the Great Bell of Dhammazedi, which may or may not be the truth, but audience members who look it up will be looking for connections to Burma or Portugal, which will pay off later in the story when the audience learns more about the cult's origins.

Level 4: Beyond the text

True fans of your story want to keep exploring your story world even after the story ends. Some of the cool and complicated ideas you've left out of the story's main text can find a home in an appendix, on a website, or in social media feed. In a video game they may be optional elements the players can ignore or engage with.

Here you can go into loving detail about the finer points of space station artificial-gravity systems, all 33 levels of initiation in the Church of Dauroth, or the complicated family trees of the town founders. These elements are often a lot of fun to write, in part because they only have to tangentially connect to the main story, and you're free to show off more of that iceberg than is otherwise necessary.

For example: The names of the flowers engraved on the bells conform to musical notes and on the website you can hear the tune played out or see an image of the bells. The chant itself includes encoded versions of Janet and Arnie's names, implying that it was composed specifically to affect them in some way.

Putting the levels all together

Creating scenes that embrace all the levels of engagement will have more impact than a scene that uses only one or two of the levels. Taking advantage of every opportunity makes scenes that are rich with meaning and power.

An audience that experiences the example scene at just the first level will follow along fine and understand what's important to the plot and characters. Levels two and three add to the mystery and dread of the sequence, showcasing how the meditation center is uncanny from the tiniest detail. Level four takes some minor details and blows them up into a strange puzzle, the solution to which reveals a new facet to the sequence.

Chapter **8**

This Planet Will Eat You: Worlds Are Characters, Too

All of us talk about the world like it's a person with wants and feelings. We use metaphorical terms to add an emotional texture to natural phenomena: "angry thunderclouds" or "friendly breeze." We say, "Nature finds a way," or "the stock market responds." We treat big complicated systems like they're people making decisions because we're inclined to find causes and motives even when there aren't any. Sometimes we just feel like the randomness in life is out to get us: "The dice hate me today."

In a story, the dice really may hate your characters today. They could be cursed dice, but put the supernatural aside for the moment. There is no actual randomness in your story, and systems respond not according to the laws of nature, but according to you. Everything happens because you want it to, which means your story world really is just as much of a character as the rest of the cast: It has wants and it takes actions.

This chapter examines the different ways of thinking about worlds as characters and explore their roles in storytelling.

Recognizing That Worlds Want Something

Your story world isn't *just one* character with wants and actions. It's more like a big family of different systems that are all related to one another. And because this is a story with drama and interesting changes, these family members don't always get along well.

The political hierarchy doesn't agree with the religious traditions and both of them are dependent on the economic markets while nobody pays enough attention to the increasingly disruptive climate system. Your protagonists live in the middle of all this family drama, which all makes the story more challenging and dramatic.

These sections explore the different ways a world as a whole pursues its own goals, just like any other character in your story.

Reacting to your characters

Unlike your other characters, who can probably speak for themselves, your world's systems let their actions speak for them. When the characters do something in pursuit of their wants or in response to a setback, they can trigger some reaction from the world's systems. The orbital blockade leaves many of the station's crew starving. Stealing food from the space station's stores brings down the heavy hand of the law, who might or might not be sympathetic to your hero's beliefs about who should really run things around here. All those interrelated systems are reacting at once in their own way.

The more you understand about the systems, the more interesting and authentic your world's reactions will be. *Piggybacking* (building on knowledge your audience already has; refer to Chapter 6) on the real world and in-depth research can pay off in dramatic ways for your story. The more you find out how the real world works, from astrophysics to architecture to economics to social networks, the more engaging your story world will be.

Maintaining ecosystems and equilibrium

Think about what your world is like in a state of equilibrium, before the story starts. All the different systems are operating as expected in relationship to one another. Opposing forces are balanced and the situation is stable. Your world isn't some utopia or paradise; there are still predators and prey and prayers for a better world, but the family members are stable and getting along as well as can be expected. Knowing your world's equilibrium state makes throwing everything into chaos even more exciting, just as most stories begin with a character's normal life before the inciting incident launches the story.

REMEMBER

When nature in any of its forms plays an important role in your story, research the specifics for where the characters will be and what ecosystems they'll encounter. Think through the interlocking systems of water, soil, plant, and animal life and how they support one another. Determine what prey the predators hunt and where the prey finds food or water or sunlight. As the seasons change (if your world has seasons), how do the local life forms adapt? How does geography affect the weather and what kinds of plants and animals flourish where?

Even at equilibrium, no ecosystem is totally static. Ask yourself these types of questions:

>> What happens when natural disasters strike?

>> When a volcano erupts, what are the first plants to come back after the lava flow?

>> When there's a drought, how do species survive?

>> What great disasters in the past have led to mass extinctions or tectonic shifts, and how did the world change as a result?

Knowing how life responds to disasters can guide how your story world responds to the disasters you and your characters are about to inflict on it.

The *Iceberg Rule* (only show the parts of your world that interact directly with the characters and conflicts; refer to Chapter 5) remains in effect. Focus on the ecosystems relevant to your story. For example, in our fantasy realm, the liars transformed into monsters have been driven from the cities into the wilderness. Now they're the new apex predators of the field and forest.

Look to examples of invasive species for ideas about how disastrous they are for the realm's agriculture and food supply. On the planet below our space station, we want alien life forms that really feel alien. Research extremophile species on earth that thrive in places of acidity, temperature, or pressure that would kill most life forms. Our small town in upstate New York will face some cold winters. How do small towns deal with blizzards, and what happens when all the snowplows have been reforged into a cult's enormous bell?

Upholding the societal status quo

Social systems share many features with ecosystems, but they're even less likely to maintain equilibrium because they're created and run by people, and people make everything more chaotic. Political and cultural institutions have individual and group actors making conscious and unconscious decisions. Only a select few of those people will be characters in your story. Treat those people with the care and nuance as we describe in Chapter 2, but for the society as a whole, consider the systems as characters unto themselves.

REMEMBER

Each social system in your world exists to serve some function. It does things. The political system makes and enforces laws. The economic system creates, transfers, and hoards wealth. The people within those systems make decisions in order to serve that function. Maybe. Some of the time. It's useful to understand the basics of how these systems are supposed to work in your world, but the most important step in understanding society's status quo is to explore the differences between how a system is *supposed* to work and how a system *actually* works.

The people that make up these institutions often use them for their own benefit. Sometimes they believe that the system itself is more important than the official function. Yes, the temple is concerned about your immortal soul, so concerned they'll sell you a place in heaven if you give them enough money here on earth. Sure, the galactic republic's principles state that all sentients are created equal, but who gets to decide whether or not robots are really sentient and therefore who really gets equal rights?

Not all important systems have the weight of law or the power of bureaucracy behind them. Unwritten laws and customs are just as important, sometimes more so. Class biases and cultural prejudices can affect the lives of people (including your characters) more than any law. Yes, this park is open to everyone, but not everyone is like you. Sure it's a free country, but "we don't much cotton to strangers 'round these parts."

REMEMBER

Knowing how societies really behave means learning more about history, sociology, anthropology, and psychology. Research similar systems in the real world for guidance on both what people expect from them and how they truly behave.

For our fantasy realm we might look into the history of moral panics like the Satanic Panic of the 1980s and how society has responded to them in the past. For our space station, we'll want to read up on the challenges settlers of inhospitable lands faced, not just from the environment but from each other. Our small town's economic situation can draw inspiration from a one-industry towns and what happens when that industry fails.

TIP

However, don't get lost in your research. Research isn't writing, and you're going to have to start telling your actual story at some point.

Wanting equilibrium

The way systems work well also implies how to make them not work, preferably in the most dramatic ways possible. When you know all about your world's systems at equilibrium and understand their reactions to change, all you have to do is introduce a dash of chaos and you can extrapolate the consequences. What happens if the space station's temperature controls malfunction and the cold starts killing off the oxygen-producing plants? How does the town council react when they can't reach a quorum and need to make an emergency decision?

Completely understanding any complex human or natural system is a lifetime's work, and you don't have that kind of time. You have a story to write. But now that you appreciate more fully your world's equilibrium states, it's time to take that information and turn it into character traits. Characters want something, and they take actions to get it. What do systems want? *They want to return to a state of equilibrium.*

Here are two common and dramatic ways to disrupt the world's equilibrium in your story.

Creating change — Agents of chaos

The world seems stable until your antagonists and protagonists have come along and disrupt everything by starting a story. When deciding how to have your world react to those dramatic interlopers, first ask yourself: "What would bring this system back toward equilibrium?"

Nature finds a way to restore the balance between predators and prey by starving the predators or evolving the prey. Government authorities lash out at revolutionary ideas. Cultural institutions confronted with disruptive art forms and transform them into popular entertainment. The further the system swings out of equilibrium the bigger and more dramatic the response as it fights back toward balance.

Passing the point of no return

You can't always return to equilibrium, no matter how dramatically the world reacts to change. Events reach a tipping point, and your story can't go back to the old status quo. Forests become parking lots. Governments fall to revolution. Yesterday's pirates become tomorrow's admirals. The world changes and finds a new normal and now it wants to preserve that.

Your characters are often right at the fulcrum of one of these tipping points. Their character arcs intersect with the world's story arc and the two become intertwined. Maybe they're overthrowing the fanatical Priest-King as the heroes of a great epic or maybe they're just trying to survive the night in a city facing monstrous invaders in the wake of his terrible decisions. Just as great characters transform over the course of their story, so do great worlds. Often, writers create great worlds specifically to break them.

Building Spaces and Places for Drama

The world's systems are characters, but they're not just characters. They're also the stage upon which *all* the characters act out their individual arcs. Not only do you need to figure out what the world wants and how it reacts, but you also need to decide how it looks and feels as the setting for your scenes. Set your stage with the props, scenery, lighting, and sound that make your drama come to life while staying true to the realities you've established about your world.

These sections explore the narrative potential of both actual maps of your fictional world. Then we offer tips on thinking of your story not just as a series of scenes, but as a series of narrative spaces where the narrative unfolds.

Making maps memorable

Maps of imagined worlds are among the most iconic images from both sci-fi and fantasy fiction. Tolkien's own maps of Middle Earth seem almost as well-known as the world maps hung in middle school social studies classrooms. A great map is a picture worth way more than a thousand words, and it's useful for much more than showing what's north of where.

The following explains what maps can do for your story:

>> **Maps make audiences wonder.** Seeing all those places and interesting proper names, contemplating the floorplan and who would build such a place, the audience starts asking questions and making guesses about what it all means. They'll need to experience the rest of your story to find out.

>> **Maps can provide clues to the bigger story.** Maps provide pieces to the puzzle of what's really going on. "Oh, that river runs right by the Thieves Guild. That could explain why the deacon's boat was stolen!" A map may include regions of the story world your characters never visit or even mention. Including such details can add context and a bigger sense of scope, but don't spend a lot of time or space on parts of the map that never impacts your story. Refer to Chapter 7 for how readers like to put together a puzzle.

>> **Maps helps readers see how your world is different.** Maps reflect the realities of your world and highlight how it differs from our consensus reality. A planet rooted firmly in Earthlike geology should have mountain ranges that form along tectonic principles and oceans that conform to fluid and orbital dynamics. A fantasy world where mountains were built by dwarves or are the bodies of sleeping giants shouldn't conform to the same physical standards and rules.

TIP

The maps you make when you write are quite different from the maps your audience sees, if indeed they ever do get to see a map. Having a sketch of the locations and how they relate to one another, just so you can keep those spatial relationships clear in your head, is often useful. If the audience isn't going to see this map, then your map can be as sketchy as you like. You may even download maps, floorplans, and neighborhood guides and change the names and details as needed. You can choose from thousands of artfully rendered maps for tabletop games for sale on websites like www.drivethrurpg.com. The advantage of starting with these real maps is that you know they conform to some reality of urban planning or geologic forces and are therefore less likely to confuse or annoy audiences who may otherwise be saying to themselves, "Hey, that's not how swamps work!"

Sometimes the last thing you want to show your audience is a map, either because it will give away important plot developments or because it will enlighten and explain when your story is trying to keep things dark and mysterious. A map of a haunted house, forgotten tomb, or unexplored new planet can ruin the suspense that comes with encountering unfamiliar terrain. Video games based on maps often use "fog of war" to hide areas until the player visits them, making every move a step into the unknown.

REMEMBER

Not every audience needs a map to follow the story, but in visual media like film, television, and comics, the map isn't just supplemental to the story. It's the actual stage on which the story plays out. If you're building sets, you're making a map. If you're shooting on location, you may or may not be conforming to the exact territory where you film, but you're still creating a map of places in relationship to one another. And of course in many games exploring the map (or game level) is the core story experience, which is why level designers tend to take a whole lot more time thinking about maps than novelists.

Navigating story spaces

Your story's scenes play out in a series of individual narrative spaces within your larger world. These spaces can be as vast as a storm-swept desert or as confined as a haunted bedroom. Each space exists within the wider world and relates to it as part of an ecosystem and/or social system. Each space is also unique in important ways — first and foremost, that it's important enough to be in your story — and therefore requires care and thought in its creation.

REMEMBER

Story spaces can serve a variety of important roles in your narrative (sometimes more than one at once). Moving through these spaces is a dramatic obstacle course for your characters. Think about spaces in terms of how they both reflect the world you've created and how the characters experience that space in relation to their journey.

In many video and tabletop games, the player's journey through these spaces and the choices they make along the way determine how the story unfolds. Will they go left or right? How do they beat the baddies? What's the solution to this physics puzzle? Should I use my last health potion now or save it for later? Exploring these spaces and making decisions is what makes good games so uniquely satisfying. Non-interactive storytelling can benefit from thinking about story spaces a little bit like a game designer, except you as the author are making all the decisions for your audience along the way and you're of course choosing the more exciting options!

A story space doesn't need to be a literal 4,500-square-foot area that your characters walk around in. It can be any loosely defined location where characters interact with each other and the world. Navigating an ancient bureaucracy spread across a thousand departments or messaging on a social media platform for conspiracy theorists are story spaces. Any social, technological, or physical framework that binds experiences together can be a story space.

TIP

String together the following sequences of these different kinds of story spaces to create a kind of playlist for your plot. Use them to vary the mood and pacing and provide multiple different scenes for your story world to express its wants and for your characters to cause chaos in the service of a better story:

>> **Obstacles** are spaces the characters must overcome, bypass, or endure in order to continue. They're not likely to change within the scope of the story and should exemplify some core aspect of the story world's systems. They include places like perilous mountains and unforgiving wastelands, but they could also be trap-filled mazes, dangerous neighborhoods, or huge crowds of revelers in a public park. They may not be an obstacle for everyone all the time, but they make life harder for the characters at the moment.

>> **Reactive** spaces foreground the ways the world is responding to the events in the story. They're places where rules and customs and ecosystems feel the

impact of challenges to the equilibrium. When your characters enter these spaces, they experience firsthand the consequences of either their actions or the antagonist's actions. Think of places like a busy port of entry under heightened security in the face of recent threats or the local coffee shop where everyone is whispering about the new people in town. It can also be the untouched wetlands that suffer from the toxic runoff from the space shuttle that landed there or the social media platform where everyone's sharing images of the sinkholes that keep appearing.

>> **Contested** spaces are the objects of desire for two or more characters or systems in your world. Here opposing wants clash against one another to determine the space's future. A battlefield or the siege of a fortress are obvious examples. But a lone planetary outpost weathering a fearsome ammonia storm is also a contested space as is a courtroom when a trial is in progress. Rival viral video makers trying to one-up each other for the audience on a social media platform is an entirely virtual but no less emotionally potent space. Your characters' involvement in the contest is what makes this a contested space, and their actions determine its fate. A battlefield where the war continues before and after the characters enter the space is actually an obstacle — one where they lead their side to victory is a contested space.

>> **Refuges** provide a sharp contrast to the rest of the spaces that characters journey through. They change up the mood and pacing of the story, allowing a chance to process what has already happened, recover from shocks and setbacks, contemplate what's to come, or engage in other activities that aren't necessarily directly related to the main conflict. This can be a literal cave on the side of a mountain where your characters take refuge from a storm, or it can be the cozy cabin on the space freighter where they can communicate with their family.

Refuges come in many less literal forms, too. In a game, it may be a room with no enemies to fight but an optional puzzle to solve. It may be a night out at the tavern, flirting with the local apprentice alchemists. A refuge is often a story space version of the foil supporting character we discuss in Chapter 2; they show another way for the world to be, maybe a taste of what your characters are trying to achieve or what they stand to lose.

Each shape in Figure 8-1 represents a different kind of story space, with the dramatic stakes rising as the story escalates up toward the climax. The refuge space has a moment of relief before the plot rockets through obstacles and reactions to reach the climax in a contested space.

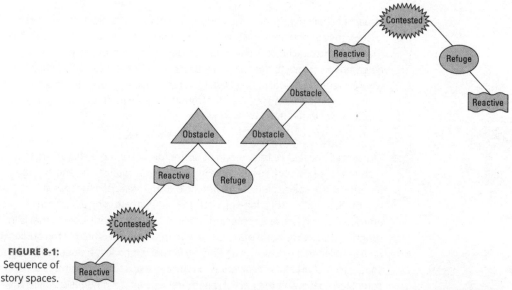

FIGURE 8-1: Sequence of story spaces.

EXERCISE

SEQUENCE OF STORY SPACES

The chapters in Part 2 provide a lot of worldbuilding tools to ponder. Creating an effective sequence of story spaces brings all of that knowledge together into one, unified process. You can explore that process through this exercise using any existing story world you're familiar with or you can use it to help develop your own terrific tale. It's a lengthy exercise that requires some serious thought, but the results for your stories are worth the effort. As you work through this exercise, follow these steps:

1. **Define your world's narrative purpose.**

   Answer these three questions (the same three we ask in Chapter 5):

   - Who is the audience for this world?

   - How are they going to experience it?

   - How do your own passions and interests manifest within this world in a unique way?

   Then come up with a one-sentence pitch highlighting what's most interesting and important about your world.

2. **Pick a specific system within your world to be both your stage and an important character.**

   Your whole story will no doubt involve multiple environments and social systems, but for this exercise, focus on just one system; perhaps it's a physical environment or a social institution, but it should reflect your answers in Step 1. Describe its equilibrium state and/or its primary function as you see them. Then write down the top three ways the system will respond when some agent of chaos throws it out of equilibrium. All of these reactions should affect your characters.

3. **Lay out a sequence of varied spaces.**

   Compose a sequence of spaces within this system to tell a story or part of your story with a clear beginning, middle, and end. Create at least six spaces and use all for the types of story space (obstacles, reactive spaces, contested spaces, refuges; refer to the section, "Navigating story spaces," earlier in this chapter). That means you'll use at least two of the types twice. Make sure they're distinct from one another and equally interesting. For extra credit, add a seventh space, revisiting somewhere from earlier in the sequence, but show how it has changed from one type to another (for example, a refuge has become a contested space).

4. **Define the levels of engagement.**

   We detail levels of engagement in Chapter 7. For each of your six (or seven!) spaces, summarize in a sentence or two how the space will engage audiences on all four levels. This step may take some time, but challenge yourself to find something interesting for each level. Ask yourself these questions for each level:

   - **Level 1 — Bold strokes:** What do the characters notice first about the space? What about the audience? What challenge or opportunity do the characters engage with to directly move the story forward?

   - **Level 2 — Fine nuances:** Describe some telling details about the space. Think about all the different senses and what they can tell your audience about the space. In visual or audio media, lighting and music can play a key role here. How do these nuances enhance the core dramatic action of Level 1?

   - **Level 3 — Hidden depths:** What subtle details, motifs, or themes can you add to the space to reward the more attentive members of your audience? Is there something here that foreshadows events to come or reflects a deeper history of the space that's not obvious to the characters?

   - **Level 4 — Beyond the text:** How can this space spin off optional material for your audience? These might be technical details, deep history write-ups, or a full map on your website. You may have additional background information somewhere that explains who made that sword or why these space stations always have flickering lights. What rewards does this space offer for the biggest fans in your audience?

5. **Identify the important changes for the characters and the world.**

   With each space, note how the story has changed. How have things gotten better or worse for the main characters? What new information have you given your audience? Summarize the changes for the entire sequence taken as a whole, describing how the plot has advanced, as we discuss in Chapter 3.

3

Science Fiction: Journeys into the Future

Chapter **9**

Answering "What If?"

hat if one morning you woke up to the news of an alien spaceship hovering over Central Park in New York City? What if astronauts travelled to another world and couldn't get home? What if computer implants did all the talking and socializing and people were forced to live lives of quiet contemplation? What if your life is all a grand experiment and you can't believe anything you see?

Writer and literary critic Joanna Russ (author of the excellent novel *The Female Man* [Beacon Press]) referred to science fiction as "What If Literature," and there's no doubt that provocative questions and inventive answers lie at the heart of great sci-fi stories. The genre earns complaints from audiences that it's often more about ideas than characters and story. This chapter helps you avoid that pitfall, but we don't shy away from asking the big questions that make sci-fi sing.

Asking Big Questions

Most fiction is about people and events in the world, and many genres ask interesting "what if" questions in some way. Fantasy fiction (see Part 4) is about people and events in impossible other worlds where magic and monsters are real. Science fiction is about people and events in other possible worlds and times. Those other possible sci-fi worlds may or may not be probable, but the power of sci-fi doesn't come from correctly anticipating the future. It comes from speculating and telling fascinating stories about other possibilities.

Although most sci-fi stories are usually set in the future, the genre as a whole doesn't have a great track record when accurately predicting the future. The moon doesn't have flying cars or cities, but we have supercomputers in our pockets that few authors could have imagined in the 1930s and 40s during the so-called Golden Age of Science Fiction. But that's not a problem for sci-fi, because that's not what's interesting or important about it. Sci-fi isn't for the future, it's for the present.

Great science fiction stories reflect upon and explore the important and provocative issues of today. They ask questions about life on other worlds or the capabilities of the human mind or the dangers of environmental collapse. Then they invent answers. They wrap those answers up in the drama and power of characters that audiences care about; characters whose actions and choices and the ensuing consequences reveal both the nuances of the question and the twists and turns of the plot.

To create sci-fi stories that rise up to their full potential, you need to start with some fascinating questions. In the following sections, we explore techniques for crafting those questions for maximum effect.

Looking closer at your questions

More than likely, you have questions. Chapter 5 asks you to answer three fundamental questions when creating a world for your story. One of those is: How do your own passions and interests manifest within this world in a unique way? We suggest a similar approach when it comes to brainstorming for your sci-fi ideas. Ask yourself these questions:

>> **What ideas interest you?** Do you wonder what life on other planets is like? Do you want to know more about the physics and engineering of space travel? Are there intriguing possible political or economic systems that you want to explore? Put simply, what do you want to discover more about?

>> **What are you excited about?** What recent discoveries or changes in the real world get you excited about what's to come? Are you curious about how conceptions of gender and sexuality change over time? Are you fascinated by the developments in artificial intelligence and adaptive algorithms? What do you hope happens next?

>> **What are you worried about?** What developments in the real world make you anxious? Are you concerned about the devastating impact of climate change? Do you wonder if privacy is really dead in a digital age? Is it possible that another global pandemic will bring social collapse? These questions may not be fun to ask, but they're dramatic. Answering them is the stuff of great stories.

> **» What if . . .?** Take your interests, hopes, and worries and distill them into a single "what if" question that helps you explore what's happening in the current world through the creation of a possible other world. The question may well change into something slightly or completely different as you start writing, but having a compelling what if as you begin should guide everything else as you move forward.

You may be wondering what if you don't have any questions. What if you just like lasers and robots and spaceships? Sci-fi can be a mere backdrop for creating your own setting for exploring war, love, politics, or art, but if it's not asking and answering any questions about another possible world, then it's leaving a lot of potential on the table.

Provoking curiosity and imagination

Science fiction means asking those questions *and* answering them. Your "what if" question is like an inciting incident in a story's plot: It makes this fictional world distinct from the everyday and sets the narrative in motion. The question can help get the audience's attention, but the answer is what's going to keep them to the end.

Consider that the earliest forms of literary science fiction were philosophical exercises like Thomas More's *Utopia* or Margaret Cavendish's *The Description of a New World, Called The Blazing-World*. They were fictional realms where the authors could play with ideas and model other visions for how society might work. These utopian societies were often located on distant islands or other continents, but as humanity's understanding of Earth's geography grew, the utopias moved off planet or into the future.

EXERCISE

KIDS ASK THE BEST QUESTIONS

Maybe you don't have a pressing "what if" question blazing away in your brain, demanding to be answered. Or maybe you have a question that's too complex or specific to provoke answers that make great stories. As a brainstorming exercise, turn to the youth of the world for inspiration. Take some common kid queries and invent a sci-fi answer that's not the true answer but is also scientifically possible. Consider these questions:

- Where do babies come from? Cloning vats, of course!

- Why is the sky that color? Sadly, it's the dust thrown up by the alien mass driver attack.

- What happens when people die? Their memories are re-uploaded into a new body.

- Why do I have to go to school? Because Big Brother says so.

The distance in time and space of these fictional worlds creates a fictive distance for audiences, which helps encourage their imaginations to accept that something different is possible. Audiences consciously and subconsciously use this distance to make room for some suspension of disbelief; they give themselves permission to say, "It's okay that that's not how things work in my world; this is another planet or the future." Authors use that distance for their stories as a crucible in which to put their questions and answers to the test.

Chapter 6 explains the concept of Most Advanced Yet Acceptable, the design rule that says audiences both like and dislike change and want a balance between the familiar and the new. Literary critics sometimes use the lovely term *cognitive estrangement* for the feeling audiences get when they experience a sci-fi story. They feel that this other possible world is strange and different, which makes them curious to learn more.

REMEMBER

Curiosity opens your audience to provocation from your story. As an author, you can raise feelings of awe and fascination at technological achievements and otherworldly sights. You can provoke responses of dread and horror from dissonant discoveries of science and abuses of technology. That alien ship over Central Park can do both at the same time. It's easy to imagine both the majestic vistas of an alien world and the existential dread of being an astronaut marooned on its surface.

WARNING

Make your story too strange, too different, and too fictively distant, and large swaths of the audience won't accept it. They'll be cognitively estranged all the way over to someone else's story. Balance is key. It gives the audience a firm foundation from which to engage with your story. Chapter 6 expounds on the virtues of "starting with Earth" when creating a story world.

Answering questions with characters

You're asking interesting questions and you're promising your audiences even more interesting answers. The surest, best, and right way to provide those answers is through the actions and experiences of your characters. Remember, all stories are about people your readers are interested in doing things they care about. The characters should always come first.

The story's ideas are interesting to your audience, but they must be absolutely vital to your characters. Don't write the clichéd sci-fi tale that's all thought experiment and no drama and humanity. Aliens hovering over Central Park are interesting in theory and present a huge problem for the people sent in a helicopter to make first contact. Information security and identity theft worry many people today, but it's terrifying when your memories get uploaded into an android doppelganger who shows up at your mother's house for Christmas.

A good way to start is asking yourself these questions about the implications your "what if" scenario creates:

>> How would your own life be different in this scenario?

>> What new kinds of challenges and opportunities would average people have?

>> Who would be most affected by and engaged with the scenario?

>> Who would benefit most from this change to our world and who would suffer most?

Sci-fi asks questions about possible futures, but that doesn't point to a specific kind of story. Readers know that a mystery novel will be about solving a crime. Romantic comedy audiences know that the story will be about will they or won't they fall in love. War stories are about strategy, tactics, and the trauma soldiers and civilians endure. Sci-fi stories can be about any of those things and more. They're also about ideas themselves and the future. Chapter 27 presents more information about ten of the most popular and effective modes for sci-fi and other genre stories.

Inventing the Big New Thing

Sci-fi stories often contain all kinds of futuristic technology, but a lot of those things are more like props and scenery for the central question. Spaceships just get the characters from planet A to planet B. Laser pistols may as well be revolvers from the 19th century. The story isn't asking any questions about those things.

A great sci-fi story needs a science-based development at the center of it that's integral to the narrative and that sets this world apart from the audience's reality in a significant way. Science fiction literary theorist Darko Suvin called this a *fictive novum*, and if you want to delve deep into some very complicated and interesting literary theory about how science fiction works, read his *Metamorphoses of Science Fiction* (Peter Lang AG, Internationaler Verlag der Wissenschaften). We tweak Suvin's definition a little and call this science-based innovation the Big New Thing. Here we examine the Big New Thing in greater detail.

Understanding what the Big New Thing is

A *Big New Thing* impacts how societies operate and how your characters live their lives. A Big New Thing makes such an important difference that it forces audiences and characters alike to consider moral and ethical questions about its implications. A Big New Thing is a big freakin' deal, and it should relate directly to your "what if" question. The invention of faster-than-light travel lets humanity travel to other stars. The creation of self-aware artificial intelligence forever changes your audience's relationships with technology. A visitor from another world redefines humanity's vision of its place in the universe. A wondrous new pocket computer makes landline telephones totally obsolete in just a few decades. The Big New Thing sets up a change and the "what if" question explores its implications.

The best Big New Things are based on what's currently known about science. The scientific foundation is key to making them seem possible to audiences and to making sure the fictive distance isn't too distant to be engaging. The story world's scientific basis creates a chain of cause and effect that doesn't contradict what actually happens on Earth and allows for logical conclusions about its implications. That's the fun part for audiences: They can start asking and answering their own "what if" questions.

REMEMBER

By no means do you have to get a PhD in anything to write science fiction. You don't need to fully grasp quantum mechanics or information theory or astrophysics. Chapter 6 describes how to use research techniques that focus on what you need for your story without getting lost in the minutiae. Yes, science plays a key role in science fiction, but it doesn't always have to be super accurate or specific. There's real science (orbital mechanics), possible science (intelligent life on other worlds), technically maybe possible science (faster-than-light travel), and probably-not-possible-but-who-really-knows science (traveling back in time). All of those varieties share a core scientific principle of logic and observation that allow audiences to grapple with interesting questions in a way they can understand and enjoy.

OLD NEW THINGS

Some iconic Big New Things show up again and again in sci-fi stories: aliens, faster-than-light travel, artificial intelligence, other planets, time travel, apocalypses, and dystopias, to name the most common. You can read thousands of good stories about each of these and thousands more to come. Just because they're common doesn't mean you should be afraid to use them, but you want to make sure your take on them is uniquely yours and offers audiences something they haven't seen a thousand times before.

Distinguishing between hard and soft sci-fi

Devotees of the sci-fi genre sometimes differentiate between hard and soft science fiction:

>> **Hard sci-fi** leans into known science and steers away from the fantastical. Andy Weir's *The Martian* (Broadway Books) is a great recent example about an astronaut stranded on Mars who relies entirely on the technology and known science of the time to survive.

>> **Soft sci-fi** stretches the word "science" to its limits, sometimes with just a thin veneer of it over its stories. Some folks put *Star Wars* in this category. The distinction isn't always cut and dry and goes all the way back to Jules Verne, H.G. Wells, and Mary Shelley.

Verne's novels asked questions about the technology and discoveries of the day, and he prided himself on that. Wells used plausible but further afield ideas like aliens on Mars and time travel to explore imperialism, war, and the arc of history. Shelley's *Frankenstein,* maybe the first true sci-fi novel, gives a quick but effective scientific basis for the monster's creation, but spends much of the story exploring the moral and ethical questions raised by creating a new life form.

No one way is better sci-fi than the other. They're just different approaches to asking and answering "what if" questions.

As Istvan Csicsery-Ronay notes in his book, *The Seven Beauties of Science Fiction* (Wesleyan University Press), sci-fi provides society with examples and metaphors to help us all think about the role of technology in society. Sci-fi stories can both express our collective fears about where the world is going and provide inspiration about how to shape the future. In other words, sci-fi stories have a profound impact on how society thinks about science and technology.

You can easily find interviews with NASA scientists inspired by *Star Trek*. The pioneers in virtual reality development were all largely inspired by sci-fi, which gave them fictional models for their real-world engineering achievements. Those Big New Things from sci-fi classics have shaped the way people make, use, and talk about the world. Technology and science march on, the world keeps changing, and your sci-fi stories can possibly help your audience with it all.

Asking Key Questions about Your Sci-Fi Story

We initially developed this questionnaire to guide our students and ourselves to think about sci-fi stories and how they work, and now we're sharing it with you. It's a simple rubric adapted in part from the ideas in *The Seven Beauties of Science Fiction* that can help you consider your own story and how it engages with the key elements of successful sci-fi. Ask yourself these questions:

- » **When and where is the story set in time and space?** It can be a distant world or next Monday. That time and place sets the fictive distance for your story world in the audience's mind and defines how much room you have to play around with consensus reality.

- » **What questions about this other world does the story ask?** Here's your "what if" question, posed in terms that relate to the world and its characters. What are you asking and how are you going to answer those questions?

- » **What Big New Thing does the story introduce that's key to the narrative and sets it apart from our world?** Determine the significant, world-changing, science-based invention or discovery that defines your world and its story.

- » **How do the characters in the story relate to the Big New Thing?** Figure out how the Big New Thing specifically impacts the lives of your main characters. Assess whether they discovered or invented it, or whether it fell in their backyard. Decide whether they're using it to travel to other worlds.

- » **What moral and ethical questions about this Big New Thing does the story present?** Those questions drive the dramatic decisions and challenges your characters face and offer audiences a chance to imagine how they'd respond.

- » **How does the story provoke feelings of awe and fascination at technological achievements and changes?** Decide what sci-fi elements you find cool and appealing. Determine what inventions and anomalies will draw audiences in and make them wonder what it would be like living in that world.

- » **How does the story provoke responses of dread and horror from dissonant discoveries of science in your world?** Figure out what will get your characters and your audience worried. What concerns about the modern world manifest themselves in dramatic and dissonant ways within your sci-fi world? What's going to keep audiences on the edge of their seat?

Your answers to those questions can serve you well as a great set of guiding principles as you write your story. With each choice you make about a plot point or a character action or a cool new piece of tech, keep your answers in mind and let them inform your creative decisions.

Chapter **10**

A Spaceship for Every Occasion, an Occasion for Every Spaceship

O uter space is vast and deadly. It's enormous on a scale the human imagination can't really grasp. Our minds have no frame of reference to make sense of the fact that the galaxy has more than 100 billion stars, maybe one *septillion* stars in the known universe, and that the universe is around 90 billion light years in diameter. That's a lot of space for a lot of stories. It's a lot of space for a lot of *everything*.

In all probability, humanity will never know much of anything about all that space, all those stars, and the bajillions of planets around them. These great swaths of unknowable universe give sci-fi storytellers ample room they need to give their futuristic scenarios some scientific possibility. Your task is to carve out a slice of space and make it your own, choosing which elements of astrophysics to include and which to quietly ignore. Humanity may never visit other galaxies or even other stars, but your audience and your characters can, and they're going to need a spaceship to get there. Consider this chapter your booster engines to get you there.

Voyaging Far from Home: Vessels for Isolation and Adventure

Your spaceship can visit a myriad fascinating places, but none of that is nearly as important as the people inside the ships. Remember, "people" in sci-fi can include aliens, robots, computers, and even the ship itself can be an intelligent and important character. They're people one and all for our purposes, and the spaceship not only takes them from one place to another, it also takes their wants, fears, prejudices, and ambitions with them.

A spaceship is kind of the ultimate recreational vehicle; it lets travelers take their home out into the great beyond and serves as a refuge from the unknown. Of course, it also means the people already living in the unknown get exposed to a slice of the traveler's home, bringing the two homes into contact, creating a clash of cultures of sorts — something interesting will undoubtedly happen next.

Here we focus in turn on the three key elements of space travel storytelling: the ship, the crew, and their mission.

Launching the ship

As the word "ship" suggests, sci-fi and science nonfiction have adopted naval terminology when talking about spacecraft. Spaceships usually have a bow and a stern, a captain and a crew, and are maybe part of a fleet or a navy. If your spaceships connect directly to Earth's shared history, then using these terms makes sense, but you don't have to. You may decide to have your spacefaring tradition take its metaphors from air travel, religious architecture, or some natural system. If you want to show the impact of another story world's concerns through the names it gives its rockets, imagine a narthex instead of a docking bay and an altar instead of a bridge and a bishop instead of an admiral.

But there's something deeper about the concept of a ship than just likening traveling through space to sailing the seven seas. Naval adventures are their own distinct mode of storytelling, and the seas have a lot of interesting narrative tools that can inform your spaceship stories. The sci-fi classic *Twenty Thousand Leagues Under the Seas* by Jules Verne exemplifies the mode, as do non-sci-fi books like C. S. Forester's Horatio Hornblower novels. These are stories about crews bound together in state-of-the-art vessels on journeys through peril and discovery that take them far from home. The crew is forced to work together to survive, no matter how they feel about each other. All that stands between them and death is the thin hull of their ship, and all kinds of giant squid and French frigates are trying to blow holes in it. It's an inherently dramatic, high-stakes scenario.

REMEMBER

Approach your spaceships as a part (or even the entirety) of your story world. They should enhance, complicate, and clarify the dramatic question in your plot, and their role should relate in some way to the story's central "what if" question (refer to Chapter 9 for more insight into asking that question). If your story is about what happens on the planets and not in between them, travel can be so fast it fits in a single sentence: "They warped to Horrix Prime and berthed the freighter in the cheapest dock they could find before arranging transport to the ruins." If the story calls for some serious space peril and characters making hard choices to overcome obstacles, that journey to Horrix Prime may take five scenes and include weeks of travel, avoiding suspicious patrol cruisers, a leak in the fuel core, and a heated argument between the navigator and the ship's mysterious owner. Only you can determine what role the ship needs to play in your story.

Build your ship as a stage for your drama. Consider the following examples:

» Lone capsules or one-person scout ships work well for stories that emphasize the vastness of space and inherent solitude of the human condition.

» Small ships with tight crews of distinct individuals can have dramatic conflicts with each other and the universe.

» Large ships with large crews are full communities with a variety of subgroups, ranks, or other demarcations.

» Generation ships for whole societies are isolated from outside influence over long periods.

SETTING YOUR STORY IN A SPACE STATION

The space station is a stolid setting for many fine sci-fi stories where, instead of moving through space, space comes to visit. When designing stations for your story, all the dangers of space still apply, along with questions about the crew and the mission. However, they tend to be larger, more permanent, and immobile, linked into the political, economic, and social systems of your story world.

They're crossroads spaces from which someone goes on a journey or a stranger comes to town. They can serve as a nexus for peace or a bastion in times of war or a gateway to other stars.

Meeting the crew

The confined spaces of the ship create a perfect melting pot (or pressure cooker) for diverse people from your story world to come together and interact with one another in dramatic and interesting ways. The external pressures (be they enemy ships or cultural conflicts amongst the crew) highlight the defining traits of the various species or robots or whoever makes up the ship's company. The way they face challenges and deal with each other shows the audience how the larger story world works. The original *Star Trek* TV series is one of the most successful models for this kind of story and many stories followed in its wake.

REMEMBER

Compose your ship's crew of characters created for the story you're telling. Their interpersonal dynamics lend emotional weight and engagement to your plot as your audience comes to know and care about them. The following are some of the most common ways to think about your crew's relationship:

» **Family drama:** Stories about people whose family or family-like relations tie them together no matter where they are. They may love or hate one another, but they're still family and they're stuck on this ship together. The ship becomes a stage for characters to work through family drama and resolve deep-seeded tensions that may stay buried were it not for the pitfalls of space travel.

» **Found family:** Stories of people who have chosen life aboard the ship and its dangers because the love and support from their fellow crew members outweigh the perils of the vast dark. These stories showcase diverse life paths and the mixing of cultures and ideas in intriguing ways while uniting together against a common challenge.

» **Forced confines:** Stories about people with no choice in the matter, thrown together by fate, professional obligation, or the force of law. Characters who otherwise wouldn't have anything to do with one another confront their differences as they face the harsh realities of space travel together.

» **Footloose adventures:** Stories about the freedom to explore, these can be classic tale of friends on a road trip together or episodic tales of vagabond star explorers. The crew may or may not all get along, but are free to leave when they please. They'll stick together at least as long as it's worth their while or until a greater purpose forces them to find common cause.

» **All alone in the night:** Space is great for stories of isolation, loneliness, and independence. A ship with a crew of just one forces the character to be utterly self-reliant. They might also have to face or work hard to avoid their own personal demons and insecurities. Usually someone else comes along to disrupt their hermit-like existence, be it for good or ill (or both).

A TALE OF TWO SHIPS: DISCOVERY ONE AND THE NOSTROMO

Compare two iconic movie spaceships: the Discover One from *2001: A Space Odyssey* and the Nostromo from *Alien*. Both ships are scenes for disturbing murders, but their designs and their crews support very different themes and fears.

The Discovery One is bright white, crisp and clean with an utterly calm and professional crew and ship's computer (HAL 9000). It's the stage for a story about discovery, progress, and the expanding of intellectual horizons. HAL's cold-blooded turn to murder is an unforeseen side effect of conflicting orders (keep a secret versus protect the crew). The sole surviving astronaut character uses logic and problem-solving skills to neutralize HAL, before going on to make a transcendental discovery about the universe.

The Nostromo is dark, lived-in, and crewed by a diverse group of working-class space truckers. It's the stage for a horror story, and the forced confines and discord between the crewmembers is fertile ground for the monstrous xenomorph to wreak havoc. In the end the sole surviving crew member must destroy the entire ship in order to escape.

Completing the mission

After you have the right ship and the right crew, the characters need something to do, which is probably the plot of your story. If you have a great inciting incident that makes this day in the ship's history different from most others, then what they do will be anything but typical. Take some time to think through what is typical for the ship and its crew. Consider what this ship is used for and how the crew feels about that mission by answering the following questions:

>> **What is this ship supposed to do?** Was it built for battle or shipping or science or something else? Did it start as one kind of vessel but has been modified and jury-rigged for some other purpose?

>> **What responsibilities do the characters have?** What is the ship's crew supposed to care about, according to whoever put them on the ship? Are they soldiers in an Imperial Navy tasked with defending against outsiders? Are they merchants paid extra if the cargo gets there ahead of schedule? Are they gathering data on stellar anomalies?

>> **Who doesn't want the ship to succeed?** Space itself can be the biggest obstacle for any ship, but who or what else stands in the way of the mission? Are enemy fleets maneuvering in the vast dark? Is the stellar anomaly

throwing off radiation that interferes with the ship's life support systems? Is a rival merchant willing to do whatever it takes to delay delivery?

>> **What's most likely to go wrong?** What are the ship's most fragile or finicky systems? Who in the crew has a history of screwing up their job? What rare fuel or ammunition is prone to running out at the most inopportune moment? Which gravity wells or time/space anomalies do they have to avoid or suffer through?

With interesting answers to these questions in mind, you're now well prepared with the building blocks of high-stakes conflict.

The Physics and Drama of Space Travel

Real space travel is incredibly dangerous, expensive, and slow. Anything that difficult can generate drama, and some great sci-fi stories embrace all three of those limits and use them to tell nail-biting dramas about missions to the moon, Mars, or beyond.

However, most stories don't portray every real danger and complication in space travel. Perhaps they worry about having enough oxygen and water but ignore the dangers of radiation or prolonged weightlessness. A lot of them create some kind of invention that lets ships break the speed of light. Audiences are not only fine with these story choices, they embrace them because those other problems aren't what's interesting about the story's central "what if" question. That's your first big decision to make about spaceships in your story: How dangerous, expensive, and slow do you need travel to be?

The following sections help you answer important questions about faster- and slower-than-light travel and how to best fit your ships' capabilities to your story's needs.

Obeying the speed of light

As Einstein showed, the speed of light sets a pretty firm limit on how fast anything in the universe can move. Having your story agree with Einstein more firmly roots it in Earth reality and lessens that fictive distance between the audience and the story world. Your sci-fi setting becomes at least a little more possible. Your "what if" questions and *Big New Things* (a science-based development that's integral to the story — see Chapter 9 for more information) rest on firmer scientific ground. A physics-obedient story enhances feelings of awe and dread rooted in the possible. For stories that emphasize the sheer size of space, the epic effort to travel through it, and the risks and sacrifices every space traveler takes and makes, obeying the speed limit has a lot of upsides.

Science already knows how to send spaceships to other planets: rockets. Classic icons of science fiction, rockets not only obey Einstein, but they also rely on Newton's Third Law: Every action has an opposite and equal reaction. Rockets fling some substance out one end at high speed and then anything attached to the rocket flies in the opposite direction. Rockets need propellant to fling out the back and energy to fling it out fast and steady, which means fuel of some kind is always necessary.

If you're going to obey the laws of physics, pay attention to the following hard truths about space travel.

Fueling your ship

How much you want to pay attention to fuel/thrust ratios, orbital mechanics, and escape velocities is up to you. The hardest of hard sci-fi stories can make all that math exciting because getting the math right in space is literally a matter of life and death. Other stories gloss over the formulae and leave it to the ship's computer to point out that unless they find a new source of hydrogen in this asteroid field, nobody's getting home.

Scientific advances can make the need for fuel less pressing for your ships. Consider the following real science alternatives to the old-fashioned rocket — none of these may work, but none of them defy Einstein and these kinds of technology give you additional options:

>> **Ion drives:** NASA has tested ion drives, which are slow but steady.

>> **Solar sails:** Theoretical models for solar sails use light from the sun to create thrust.

>> **Ramscoops:** They theoretically suck up errant hydrogen atoms floating in space and use a fusion reactor to turn them into ultra-efficient propellant.

Or if you want, create your own! James S. A. Corey's *Expanse* (Orbit) series of novels and books invented The Epstein Drive, a fusion-based technology that lets ships zip around the solar system more efficiently than any existing system but still conforms to all the dramatic limitations of velocity, gravity, and acceleration and deceleration mechanics that make space travel unique and interesting.

From Mercury to the moons of Neptune

Sci-fi stories with the laws of physics in full effect often end up staying closer to home, setting their entire story world within our solar system. By keeping your story orbiting the familiar old Sun, the conflict and concepts can feel closer to home.

The biggest advantage for the solar system setting comes from audience familiarity. Audiences know where all the planets are (basically) and what they're like (generally). Their imaginations have lots of information to help them fill in the gaps and make the story world feel more relatable.

Depending on your timeline, these stories can range from first missions to settle Mars to intricate political and economic systems spread across every planet and moon within the orbit of Pluto. Chapter 6 discusses the power of piggybacking to build on what the audience already knows to create more immersive story worlds.

The solar system we all live in already contains the political rivalries, cultural clashes, and environmental pressures of Earth. Expanding to other planets in this solar system allows all those dramatic forces to expand and find new homes and new forms. You can divide up the planets along whatever lines work for your story. Maybe one wing of politics is on Mars and the other is on Titan, Saturn's largest moon. Ancient faiths could find new expressions in the harsh life of an asteroid settler.

To the stars . . . eventually

Putting aside whether or not something like a spaceship could ever safely move that fast, just following the laws of physics, means it takes years upon years to get anywhere outside the solar system. Interstellar travel at the fastest realistic speeds also means at relativistic speeds. Characters traveling at or near light speed experience *time dilation*, aging much slower than the rest of their world because they're moving at such a high velocity. There's some complicated math and physics explaining that phenomenon, and odds are you know about it for the same reason we do: You read about it in a sci-fi story or saw it in a movie.

Amazing, landmark pieces of sci-fi center around the effects of time dilation and traveling the far-flung reaches of space. The concept of leaving Earth on a voyage that you experience as just a few years only to return home and find that decades have passed overflows with dramatic possibilities. Often the characters are put into some sort of cryogenic sleep or stasis during the voyage, so for them it passes in the space of a long nap. This classic "what if'" scenario goes back to early utopian novels and stories like Washington Irving's 1819 short story "Rip Van Winkle." What if someone misses decades or centuries without changing only to return home to find everything has changed?

The generation ship is a classic sci-fi big new thing that embraces the speed of light. Instead of putting your characters to sleep for the hundreds of years it takes to get to Horrix Prime, you give them a ship big enough for them to live full lives with families and children and a self-contained society for generations. Something usually goes wrong with this plan, which is of course the beginning of a great story.

Traveling through space faster than light

Faster-than-light (FTL) travel doesn't exist and may never exist. Some theories exist, however, as far as we (two non-physicists) can tell, the more you dig into the math, the more unlikely they seem to be. But the allure of strange new worlds and new civilizations transcends the laws of time and space, and FTL technology is one of the huge, iconic big new things in science fiction. The storytelling advantages are obvious: The whole universe opens up as potential settings, and nobody really knows what's out there. The possibilities are endless. After your audience accepts FTL, they're signing on to close that fictive distance at warp speed and discover what other wonders and terrors your story world has to offer.

Here are the four broad types of FTL technologies found across most sci-fi, each with its own inherent dramatic possibilities:

» **Hyper/subspace:** Spaceships leave "normal space" (the space we all actually live in) and slip into some other kind of space where the laws of physics are different and the speed of light isn't a limit. Faster than light doesn't mean teleportation, and hyperspace travel still takes time, but it can be hours/days/weeks to travel to another star instead of centuries. You may have set hyperspace pathways connecting stars or your world may be wide open to go any which way you want. Because it's another set of reality rules, weird and interesting things can exist in hyperspace and accidents can happen.

» **Warp drive:** The spaceship creates a bubble of energy or gravity, or something scientific around it lets the spaceship break the laws of physics and slip through normal space at immense speeds. Like hyperspace, warp drive can be as fast or as slow as you need it to be for your story, but it doesn't include the other reality part from hyperspace. Your spaceships stay in this universe, opening them up to various threats and obstacles.

» **Gateway/wormhole:** The spaceship travels via a shortcut through time and space that links two set points across the galaxy. Maybe these tunnels are naturally occurring anomalies or they may be constructed gateways using advanced technology. Wormholes combine the interstellar story possibilities of FTL with the familiar Earth concepts of set borders and routes between locations. They allow for dramatic complications like blockades, fortifications, and advanced warnings of incoming visitors or invaders.

EXOTIC AND ESOTERIC TRAVEL

Douglas Adams' hilarious *The Hitchhiker's Guide to the Galaxy* (Del Rey) features a ship that uses an Infinite Improbability Drive to travel through every conceivable point in the universe simultaneously to get to its destination. In terms of our four categories of traveling faster than light from the section, "Traveling through space faster than light," it falls into jump/fold space, but the humorous and wildly improbable side effects of using it push the plot in new directions and add new laughs. If it suits your story, imagine some specific cost to travel that heightens the themes, tone, and dramatic conflict of your narrative.

>> **Jump/fold space:** Why move through space when a ship can instantly teleport from one point to another? This category is the most efficient way to travel by far, and most science fiction stories with jump technology impose hefty costs or limits on this method. Creating the fold or tear in space may take tremendous energy or psychic abilities that mean only a few ships can do it. Perhaps it's only possible at certain jump points in a solar system based on the gravitational field of a given star. Or maybe you want anyone to be able to go anywhere anytime they want, which would raise its own interesting "what if" questions about the concepts of borders and territory.

Considering other speculative technologies

The speed of light isn't the only reality of space travel that sci-fi routinely waves away. These sections examine three of the most commonly deployed speculative technologies in science fiction.

Antigravity

Outer space doesn't have gravity (okay, technically there's microgravity, but you and your characters can't tell the difference). Characters dealing with zero-gravity can be fun and interesting and terrible: You get to float around, but your bone density and muscle mass wither away over time. Eating, drinking, and using the bathroom aren't easy, but zero-g ship interiors can take advantage of every surface being easily accessible to crewmembers.

You can create artificial gravity in your story in a couple of known ways:

>> When a ship is thrusting forward, the acceleration pushes everything and everyone on the ship in the direction of the thrust, but this only works as long as the ship is applying thrust to change speed and thus burning fuel.

>> The other option is to spin part of the ship and create centripetal force that pulls things inside toward the outer edge of the spinning section.

For many decades, film and TV limits were likely the strongest advocates of artificial gravity. Simulating zero-g in a movie or television show is expensive and difficult, but simulating weightlessness really feels like space when a production spends the extra time and money. These days, many sci-fi stories don't even bother to explain why the ship has gravity unless it malfunctions or is turned off for some dramatic reason. The more science-based your story, the more likely audiences are to wonder why there's gravity on the ship, but if your story's focus is elsewhere and gravity isn't relevant to the plot, few will notice one way or the other.

Faster-than-light communications

Stories are about people who want things, usually from other people, and that almost always involves characters talking to each other. The speed of light limits radio signals just as much as it does spaceships, so a conversation between two planets in different solar systems would take decades or centuries. The more realistic your space travel, the more realistic your communication should logically be. In sublight stories, the communication delay across a solar system enhances the isolation inherent in space travel, with minutes or hours between asking for help and receiving a reply from back home.

Sci-fi authors have invented numerous fictional workarounds for this problem, and audiences are accustomed to granting stories some generous suspension of disbelief. Linking FTL communication to FTL travel makes the most sense, with tech-like hyperspace broadcasting systems or relay beacons at wormhole entrances. You probably don't need to explain the details in much detail unless it's important to the story. These kinds of infrastructure are ripe targets for story complications: Mysterious alien signals can drown out all hyperspace frequencies and enemy covert raids can sabotage relay beacons.

Life support systems

Spaceships need oxygen, food, and water (or whatever the crew breathes, eats, or drinks). Storing, purifying, and providing enough of those vital supplies takes up space and requires technology of some kind. Furthermore, the ship probably has to process waste, shield against radiation and cosmic rays, and care for the sick and wounded. All of that can be as complicated as you need, or it can go unmentioned.

Life support systems can be an interesting way to explore possible big new things or engage with "what if" questions. The post-scarcity world of *Star Trek*-style replicators produce food from energy, a system abstract enough that it becomes a kind of amorphous checklist item that can malfunction when things start to go wrong. A real near-future mission to Mars is going to succeed or fail in large part based on how well it can support the crew's lives, so the details of the system become more central to the story.

EXERCISE

DESIGN AN ENGINE FOR YOUR STORY

Calculate your FTL technology for optimal dramatic impact by making space travel exactly as dangerous, expensive, and slow as you need it to be. As a way to familiarize yourself with these kinds of story calculations, design a space-travel system for a specific kind of dramatic challenge. Pick one of the story modes from Chapter 27 and create a form of space travel specifically suited for it. Consider the following factors:

- **Genre:** Identify the core storytelling experience that audiences want from the chosen story mode. Are you setting the course for adventure or are your eyes on a new romance? Is there a war to be fought or a mystery to be solved?

- **Speed:** Turn the maximum ship's speed up or down to set the pace and create isolation. Will your story benefit from confining the characters to a ship for periods of time so they can fall in love or interrogate suspects? How close or far away is help if the characters need it?

- **Expense:** The more expensive and rare space travel is, the higher the stakes for everyone on board and their stories. Who can afford to travel to the stars? Do young courting couples cruise to the asteroid belt to kanoodle? Does it take the combined effort of a dozen nations to send a generation ship to Alpha Centauri, and your hero is the only trained detective on board?

- **Danger:** Decide exactly how dangerous travel is in your story. Is a trip to the moon as routine as intercontinental air travel is today? Do people hop on board and head to the nearest jump point at the drop of a hat, or are there a hundred pre-flight safety checks to do before countdown? Is the greatest threat radiation sickness and oxygen leaks or are there enemy fighters patrolling the hyperspace lanes?

- **Ramifications:** Know the strong opinions characters in your world have about space travel. What are the ethical and social consequences of this mode of travel? Does tearing holes in the space-time continuum have detrimental effects on the fabric of reality? Does society distrust people who regularly travel between worlds because they're seen as vagabonds or rebels? Is spending vast sums of money to go to Mars a bold step forward for humanity or a callous waste when there's so much poverty back on Earth?

1, 2, 3, 4 — I Declare a Space War!

Humanity has managed to keep space free of weapons and war (so far), but science fiction has been fighting for the stars for close to a century. The spaceship's storytelling roots are in tales of ships and naval combat, which in the 20th century incorporated the realities and romance of airplane dogfights. The aircraft carrier became the ultimate inspiration for many a space war, combining the scale and slugging power of a ship of the line with the speed and ferocity of a squadron of fighters. Beloved franchises like *Star Wars* and *Battlestar Galactica* draw from this air/sea war tradition to great effect.

This section details ways to make your story's space warfare, weapons, and defenses feel like they're something that could possibly happen and make sure they serve the specific dramatic needs of your story.

War as storytelling by other means

Space is super dangerous. We don't know what fighting between two spaceships is really like, but we do know it doesn't take much to wreak havoc on any space vessel that's ever been built. One little hole in the side of your ship and all the oxygen is gone, with no way to get more. Even at slower than light speed, everything's hurling about at tremendous speeds and the smallest pebble can do immense damage. It's a wonder any ship survives at all, even when nobody's trying to blow it up.

Aside from the intrinsic fragility of spacecraft, you need to consider a few other hard truths about space that make fighting there different from any other field of battle:

>> **Nowhere to hide:** Because space is huge with nothing much there, your characters don't have anywhere to hide and take cover behind.

>> **Difficult to maneuver:** Maneuvering in space is complicated and requires careful control over vectors and velocity, acceleration and deceleration, all of which computers handle better than brave biological pilots. As is the case in modern air and naval combat, most attacks are going to take place over vast distances and controlled by automated systems.

REMEMBER

You'll decide how much of known physics to incorporate and how much of it to ignore in your combat, depending on the needs of your stories. The kinds of dogfighting starship battles seen in *Star Wars* aren't likely or realistic, but they do make for exciting action where one character's skill and bravery can change the course of the fight and audiences can keep track of who's shooting at whom.

Star Trek-style battles usually take their cues from the slugfests of the age of sail, with massive ships trading phaser blasts and torpedoes. Maybe no more likely than dogfighting, but as a story they put more emphasis on the crew working together and the ship as both a weapon and a home for the people on it.

TIP

Create a set of weapons and defenses that serve your combat's purpose and then show the audience how they work. As they come to understand the stakes and strategies in your story, they'll be able to follow the action and worry about likely outcomes. Then you'll be able to surprise them with a moment of tactical brilliance, sudden escalation, or other twist that makes each battle unique and important in your narrative.

These questions can help you as you incorporate war into your story:

>> What is the space combat in your story there for?

>> Are the risks de rigueur or cataclysmic for your crew and their ship?

>> Do your heroes run toward or away from a fight?

>> Are you creating compelling strategic clashes where characters can show their brilliance?

>> Is it a field of honor where your characters can clash with clear cause and effect?

Activating weapons of war

Listing every kind of weapon and defense system that may appear in a sci-fi story is next to impossible, but the majority of them fit into these broad categories, presented here in order from most technologically likely to most fanciful:

>> **Projectiles:** Good old fashioned pieces of metal shot at a high speed, there's no reason to believe projectiles will be any less effective in space than they are on Earth. Projectiles may feel more grounded in reality to audiences and also require ammunition, which must be stored and may run out at a dramatic moment.

>> **Torpedoes and missiles:** The mainstay weapons of modern air and naval combat, self-propelled, guided explosives are clearly an effective tactic against moving and distant enemy targets (everything you're likely to shoot at in space). They have built-in drama, with the tense countdown to impact and dramatic maneuvers and countermeasures on the part of the target. Ships can only hold limited quantities, which makes expending them an interesting decision for characters.

>> **Drones:** Remote warfare through drones is something straight out of a sci-fi story from 50 years ago but is a commonplace reality today. It's hard to imagine they won't remain a key element of space warfare in the future. The dramatic downside of drones is the lack of a character your audience hopes and fears for, except when the story's heroes are the ones under drone assault. Chapter 12 has more material about robots and artificial intelligence, some of which apply to your self-guided drone weapons platforms.

>> **Lasers:** The sci-fi classic, a laser, has current, real-world military applications for both targeting and destroying targets. Nothing can move faster than light as a weapon, and it should be almost impossible to dodge, although reflective ship surfaces may offer some protection. The damage and range depend on the laser's power, which in turn comes from the ship's power source (which likely has all kinds of constraints and other things it needs to power as well).

>> **Mass drivers:** Another kind of projectile, but instead of being shot out of a barrel by an explosion, the bullet is flung at tremendous speeds by magnetic accelerators. With force equaling mass times acceleration, that enormous velocity translates into massive damage. It also implies the equal and opposite reaction of that acceleration translating onto the ship that fired, which can jerk a ship around and send it off course.

>> **Blasters:** A generic term used here for some kind of dangerous energy like plasma that's hurled at a target. It moves slower than light and causes whatever amount of damage your story requires. The nebulous physics of blaster technology make it a great option for visual media and softer, less science-grounded storytelling.

>> **Nukes:** The ultimate offensive weapon has been around for eight decades and will only be cheaper, more powerful, and easier to create in the future. Although political and moral fortitude have prevented the use of atomic weapons since 1945, science fiction has imagined many uses for them since then. Introducing nuclear weapons into your story raises the stakes and reshapes battle tactics in huge ways that have a lot of potential but aren't what most audiences expect from their space wars.

>> **Future tech:** The preceding weapons systems are all semi-plausible and don't require much explaining for your audience to understand. But if your story needs some unique twist on its space battles, we can think of countless examples to pull from and plenty of room for you to invent your own:

- Disintegrators that break down targets at the atomic level

- Cannons the length of a battleship that annihilate planets

- Void bombs that create mini-black holes that suck in everything nearby

- Psychic assault pulses

- Teleportation bombardments

- Nanotech gray goo

TIP

Just make sure to figure out how you want the tech to work and under what conditions it is and isn't effective. Think about how they would work in different environments, for example. Every weapon should have drawbacks or limits to how and when it can be used.

Deploying systems of defense

When a single hole in the hull can spell disasters for a spaceship, having a strong defense is just as important as a good offense. These are some of the most common defense systems found in sci-fi ships, presented in order from most realistic to most theoretical:

» **Sensors:** Knowledge is power in all kinds of conflict, but especially in space combat. Knowing where your enemy is, what their weak points are, and how much damage they've sustained is vital for victory. Radar, infrared, and optical sensors all exist today and feature prominently in most sci-fi. Some sci-fi incorporates a common concept of undefined sensors capable of finding life signs, assessing the capacity of enemy force fields, and other key plot information as needed. Set your sensor's sensitivity to the level of detail your story needs.

» **Cloaking devices:** Even though space is vast and has little or nothing to hide behind, stealth technology can conceal ships from sensors quite effectively. Anti-radar technology is already advanced in this era, and prototypes of light-bending surfaces can render a vessel invisible at a distance. Stealth and cloaking technology, along with sensor-jamming, allow for games of cat and mouse, ambush, and tactical surprise, all of which increase suspense and tension in your battle scenes.

» **Point defense weapons:** Dedicated defenders against incoming fighters, missiles, and torpedoes, point defense weapons are usually short range lasers or projectile weapons. Warfare can become a matter of attrition, with volleys of missiles trying to overcome the limits of the point defenses. This tense situation focuses the battle on supplies and systems and creates very clear cause and effect that audiences can easily understand and appreciate.

» **Armor:** Modern day spaceships are built to be as light as possible because launch anything into space is expensive. In settings where ships are constructed in orbit or getting into space is much cheaper, layering on sheets of armor may make sense. Hi-tech composite sci-fi fibers can lower the weight and raise the effectiveness in a plausible way. Armor, the reinforced skin of the ship, protects the crew but shows its wounds and scars as it absorbs damage. As the ship suffers, armor peels away and isn't easily replaced, which is always dramatic.

>> **Shields:** Force fields or protective energy shields are iconic sci-fi techniques not because they're theoretically likely but because they're dramatically powerful. They allow a ship to sustain damage from any source, including nukes or disintegration beams. They degrade under pressure, often in clear numeric terms. "Shields at 17 percent and falling, Captain!" In many ways they're like hit points in a game — nebulously defined but easy to understand as a shorthand for how much trouble the characters are in.

>> **Tractor beams and other tech:** As with weapons systems, there are a host of implausible but exciting sci-fi possibilities for defense. The tractor beam appears across many stories, a literal hand of the author reaching out across space and moving someone where they need to be for the story. They stop heroes from escaping or allow for last-second rescues of helpless friendly ships. Tech that somehow blocks or interferes with your story's FTL travel also has serious dramatic utility, restricting movements at key moments. Any sort of inventive defense system works best for the story when it has clear advantages and disadvantages that the audience can comprehend and anticipate.

Chapter **11**

Encountering Aliens That Audiences Want to Know, Love, and Fear

What if humanity isn't alone in the universe? It's the biggest "what if" question in science fiction, a query that has launched a million stories. What would happen if another intelligent species visited Earth? What kinds of life will humans encounter on other planets? What other civilizations flourish amongst the stars and how are they different? How do humans measure up by comparison? What do they want? What can they do to or for us?

Sci-fi calls these speculative other lifeforms *aliens,* a word that at its root just means *others.* Aliens aren't us. Who does count as us depends on who's doing the counting. Long before aliens came to encompass imaginary beings from space, the term had negative connotations. Strangers. Outsiders. Untrustworthy. Dangerous. Seditious. In early and classic science fiction, aliens usually invade Earth or menace brave astronauts. Aliens abduct cattle and secretly control governments. Some are friendly, though most are scary.

For many stories featuring extraterrestrials, the alien is the Big New Thing you're introducing to the story world. (The *Big New Thing* refers to a science-based element that's integral to the story and sets the story world apart from the audience's reality; refer to Chapter 9 for more about the Big New Thing.) In other words, it's a new kind of life that is in some way based on science. The alien's primary purpose as a character is to let you explore what happens when people are faced with others who aren't like them, whether they're from another country or another planet. Your aliens don't have to fall into the same old fear-based stereotypes. To feel truly original and interesting, they should be as complex and nuanced as humanity itself. This chapter explores ways to do just that in your stories.

Making Sense of Alien Metaphors

Aliens in stories show your audience other possible kinds of people or other ways of existing. They provide a contrast to the way your audience and/or your main characters live their lives. Narratively, they serve a similar role to a dramatic foil. They represent a possible path not taken or an opposing worldview.

Of course, people on Earth don't live their lives just one way, and many great stories of all genres focus on the contrast and clash of human cultures in the real world. Extraterrestrial aliens provide storytellers a unique advantage: They aren't beholden to any existing people. Extraterrestrials are cut from whole cloth, tailored to the story you're telling.

REMEMBER

A *metaphor* is an element in your story that has a double meaning: the literal one within the story (it's a reptilian alien with a plasma rifle) and a symbolic meaning (its insatiable need for conquest brings to mind the warmongering side of humanity's history and culture). The alien conqueror drives the plot and serves as an antagonist whether or not an individual audience member registers its symbolic purpose. But for those that do register it, the alien has a deeper meaning within the story and gives the audience some familiar ideas and feelings to associate with the reptilian invaders.

Here are a variety of different approaches to making your aliens serve the metaphorical needs of your story.

Discovering differences

Your story's custom-made aliens allow you to emphasize ideas and ways of being to heighten the contrasts. Extraterrestrial aliens can maximize some idea or enthusiasm or lifestyle in a focused way not seen in human history. This alien as

Big New Thing manifests in sci-fi in three main ways: biology, society, and technology, which the following discusses in greater detail.

REMEMBER

When you're alien-building, consider the history, politics, religion, environment, and physical nature of their home planet. What do they eat? What do concepts like work and love and family mean to them? All of these have the potential to be radically different from what your human audience is comfortable with. A whole planet can live life as logically or rationally as possible. A galactic civilization's post-scarcity economy can be based on ethical reputation and poetic expression rather than accumulating space bucks and extracting resources. The planetary ecosystem is hyper-interdependent so that all life forms experience each other's feelings and one slight change affects the whole. Whatever it is that makes the aliens different from your audience also makes them interesting for your story.

>> **Alien biology:** This is often the most obvious Big New Thing; the aliens are physically different from your audience in some interesting way. Here are a few ideas:

- They're stronger or weaker, bigger or smaller.

- They live for a thousand years or die after only a few.

- They can only reproduce when three different genders mate.

- They might fly or swim or ooze as their primary means of movement.

Audiences generally expect these physical forms to have some scientific plausibility behind them. One of the great pleasures of science fiction is informed speculation about what other forms intelligent life may take in the universe. In some way their physical differences need to give them different physical needs and wants than humans. For example, an extraterrestrial species that lives its entire life cycle in a low-gravity, airless environment and which communicates through shifting colors on their exoskeletons has a different impression of life on an Earth-like planet. For them gravity and atmosphere may be as dangerous as deep space is to us.

>> **Alien society:** Otherworldly societies in sci-fi often closely mimic the kinds of cultural and political forms that have existed on Earth: empires, capitalist markets, feudal caste systems, religious structures, and so on. Based on Earth analogues, you can pick and choose and mash up interesting trends from history and remix them with other levels of technology to create an alien society unique to your story.

The galaxy-spanning Roman-style empire is a sci-fi cliché at this point. However, creating a new society from scratch is more interesting and more difficult, and doing so allows you to explore concepts that have never and maybe never could exist in human history. What would a participatory democracy be like if every member was psychically linked to each other?

What would a species of enormous aliens that lived for millennia in the orbit of a gas giant value instead of money or resources?

>> **Alien technology:** Aliens are often possessors of the technological Big New Thing in science fiction stories. They have the ability to travel between the stars and visit Earth. They have powerful weapons, can cure and cause deadly diseases, and have mastered nanotechnology and created post-scarcity economies. As such, they can be gatekeepers of this new technology for covetous humans or the long-vanished progenitors in a galactic treasure hunt. Or humans are the ones with all the cool gadgets, visiting a world much less technologically advanced. Alternately, aliens may have different technology than humans have developed. Perhaps their ships and computers are biologically bred, their tools created to be operated with six tentacles and no eyes. The more distinct their biology and society is from humanity's, the more their technology will reflect those differences.

Alienating audiences

This wonderful flexibility you have when creating aliens has risks. Remember, the audience knows you're writing this story and will rightfully judge you if your aliens feel too contrived or unoriginal. Thus, it's vital for you to be aware of the most overused tropes in sci-fi.

You can all too easily fall into the same old stereotypes: alien invaders from a culture that values only war and destruction, hyperintelligent angelic beings who bring enlightenment and a message of peace, ravenous unthinking insectile hordes that exist only to devour. These familiar tropes don't thrill audiences or engage the imagination unless you find some way to make them unique and compelling.

Not only are the old clichés dull, they're also based in paranoid, xenophobic, and racist fears of "the other" here on Earth. Science fiction doesn't have a great record when portraying encounters with otherness. Aliens have often been the author's or audience's fears personified in some way, usually reflecting the prejudices and concerns of their society and culture. The aliens become analogues for foreign ideas "corrupting" the nation's youth or immigrants "polluting" the nation's population. These ugly ideas are often expressed in unsubtle and harmful ways. Chapter 23 discusses ways to think about representation in fiction.

H.G. Wells flips these prejudices on their head in his famous 1897 serialized novel *The War of the Worlds*. Wells was responding to the late 19th century fad for fictional invasion of Britain stories, where the "aliens" were usually some other country on Earth that British readers were worried about or biased toward. Wells showed more nuance and thought by making his invaders come from Mars, and his story is a critique of British imperialism. In the book Wells specifically draws a parallel to the experience of the people of Tasmania suffering at the hands of the technologically advanced British military. *The War of the Worlds* asks "what if that kind of invasion happened here in England?"

TIP

Truly alien is truly difficult, and audiences mostly conceive of aliens in human terms, mixed with the flora and fauna of Earth. You don't need to shy away from taking real biology and human ideas as a basis for your aliens. Audiences rely on the familiar elements to help understand the alien parts. Chapter 6 discusses piggybacking on the audience's existing knowledge and how to use it in worldbuilding. Although replicating racist stereotypes in extraterrestrial bodies is bad, creating a new species or culture without in some way referring to Earth is almost impossible to do. When you take inspiration for your aliens from your fellow humans, do so thoughtfully and respectfully.

Relating aliens to your audience

The extraterrestrial "others" in your story exist in contrast to the assumed human audience you're writing for. There is always a metaphorical relationship between humanity and your aliens, and which metaphor you embrace has a big impact on how you write your extraterrestrial characters. Some of the most well-known aliens in science fiction are emblematic of the common ways extraterrestrials appear in stories and show different approaches to using them in your narrative:

>> **Aliens as us:** In the *Star Trek* franchise, the most important aliens are basically humans with bumps on their foreheads or pointy ears. They often have a heightened or ultra-focused worldview that defines them in a way no human ideology defines all humans. The warlike Klingons, the logical Vulcans, and even the machine-hybrid Borg all mostly model other ways of being human along some very dedicated path. Audiences can easily see a part of themselves in the aliens and understand how they speak to familiar and important ideas here on Earth. These aliens can be champions of ideas, characters who give voice and action to one side of a debate or offer a unique perspective on existence.

>> **Aliens as diversity:** The *Star Wars* franchise has tons of different aliens in all shapes and sizes. They speak different languages and presumably come from rich and varied cultures, but those differences are mostly surface level. They paint a broad picture of a multicultural galaxy and remind audiences that even though most of the protagonists are humans, there's no one right or dominant way of being.

>> **Aliens as animals:** In the *Alien* movie franchise, the monstrous xenomorphs have a complex biological life cycle designed to make them fearsome apex predators. They're dangerously clever but not intelligent. There's no reasoning

with them, only surviving them or dying. They show nature red in tooth and claw, personifications of a hostile universe. Audiences rarely see themselves in these aliens but can draw from their thoughts on the natural world to understand and even empathize with them.

>> **Aliens as teachers:** In movies like *Close Encounters of the Third Kind* and *Arrival* or novels like *Childhood's End*, aliens come from advanced civilizations and offer messages of hope, evolution, or peace. Their physical alienness and inhuman appearances emphasize their inherent differences from humanity and are often aspirational figures who have transcended the pettier concerns of life on Earth.

>> **Aliens as warnings:** In a story like *The Man Who Fell to Earth* (both the original Walter Tevis novel and the David Bowie film) a very humanlike alien arrives on Earth from a world ravaged by nuclear war and prolonged drought. His past is a warning about humanity's possible future as a species. These types of aliens can show which way madness lies and allow characters in the present to confront their possible future.

There's no one right metaphorical framework, and you can find many other examples of how to portray your creations as reflections of specific ideas or attitudes that your story explores. The key thing to understand is how these aliens impact the story as a whole.

Playing Their Part: Alien Dramatics

Another way to think about your aliens is to consider what role they play in your story and build them around their function in the narrative. Refer to the fundamentals of any characters in fiction that we discuss in Chapter 2 and ask yourself these types of questions:

>> What do these aliens want and what are they willing to do to get it? Put another way, what *dramatic question* (the central concern for your characters in the story) do these aliens pose within your story?

>> Will the alien fleet find a new home on Earth now that their planet has been destroyed?

>> Can the aliens survive first contact with aggressive human explorers?

>> Will the extraterrestrials be able to communicate with the Earthlings and deliver their dire warning of impending doom?

When you have an intriguing question about your aliens at the heart of your story, your audience will stick around to find out the answer. These sections are some of the most common dramatic roles aliens play in sci-fi stories.

Alien enemies

Given how common it is for humans to fear that which they don't understand, aliens as enemies are easy to create and just as easy to do poorly. As fictional beings, your enemy aliens can be exactly as evil or bloodthirsty or cold and uncaring as you want. They can be the ideal foe, something audiences will root against without reservation or guilt because they're not human, they're nor "us." Sometimes you may have to decide that's exactly what your story needs, but having such one-note antagonists is usually dull and derivative. Countless unknowable shadow hordes from the edge of space have menaced brave heroes in science fiction, forcing them to put aside their differences and join together to save humanity (or whatever). Here the alien exists just as pressure and threat to drive the protagonists forward, leaving the weight of making audiences care rest solely on the other characters.

Enemy extraterrestrials can take on specific elements of oppression and embody them in their biology, society, or technology. Perhaps they have psychic powers that let them read minds or project fear and paranoia. Or they may require certain kinds of people, natural resources, or subservient behaviors in order to survive. These kinds of aliens can make questions of exploitation, imperialism, and subjugation stark and unambiguous. They can also drain the nuance from any dynamic and become blunt tools of propaganda and xenophobia.

REMEMBER

As with any great antagonist in any story, your enemy extraterrestrials work best when they're fully fleshed characters with compelling and believable wants and goals. They also probably don't think of themselves as the baddies. What aliens let you do that's super-useful is create a moral calculus that's entirely different from humanity's. If an alien civilization can only survive by implanting their consciousness in other complex life forms, they're going to do what they need to do to survive. Audiences probably won't have much sympathy for them if they decide survival means brain-wiping all of Earth, but audiences will understand the alien dilemma and see why they're doing what they're doing.

Alien protagonists

Aliens can take on the role of the sympathetic protagonist. As with any protagonist in any story, your main characters have their own wants and specific goals and moral compass. Ideally, those core character attributes spring from what makes the alien different from humans. In return, humans may assume the role of the unsympathetic antagonist, allowing the audience to take a critical look at aspects of their own identity. For example, the indigenous beings in Ursula K. Le Guin's *The Word for World Is Forest* (Tor Books) are deeply connected to their natural environment and have an intense cultural abhorrence of violence. The invasion by Terran corporate and military forces from other worlds forces them into confrontations that test their society to its limits.

REMEMBER

Placing your aliens in the protagonist role is a particularly effective way to tell stories that reflect on how humans in the real world treat "the other" in society. They may have to confront and survive systemic oppression based on their planet of origin or handle everyday prejudice that reflects the socially constructed racism in our world. More broadly, a story world with multiple alien species all bouncing off each other in dramatic ways can draw upon the audience's own knowledge of real-world culture clashes without bringing any specific preconceptions about real-world places to the story.

Alien allies and rivals

One of the most interesting roles that aliens can play in a story isn't as the enemy or the hero, but as complex characters living their own lives on their own terms who the main characters must interact with in less adversarial ways. Here the alien isn't someone to be fought, but someone to be appeased or helped or negotiated with. They're potential allies that must be recruited to the cause or nonviolent rivals pursuing the same goal as the protagonists.

REMEMBER

If you want to write aliens like this in your story, figure out what about their otherness makes them dramatically interesting as characters to be reckoned with. The more alien they are, the more likely they are to care about different things and have inhuman concerns. This can be as straightforward as requiring your heroes to find the space bucks to retrofit their spaceship to accommodate an alien's atmospheric needs or as complex as learning to bargain with a species who measure a decision's impact over centuries and millennia rather than minutes or days. To achieve their goals and advance the plot, your characters must understand and deal with these different ways of being that create thought-provoking dramatic questions and resolutions.

Alien mysteries

Whether it's a first contact with visiting aliens scenario or the story of astronauts exploring the ruins of long-gone, highly advanced alien civilizations, figuring out the truth about other beings is a powerful dramatic question. Who exactly are these aliens and what do they want? How do they communicate? How does this other planet's unique ecology work? How will the characters navigate this complex cultural system?

Perhaps the aliens are friends, enemies, or entirely disinterested, but there's no way to know until the heroes unravel their mysteries and come to understand the truth. The entire story may be about trying to understand the alien enigma or it may be one of many challenges throughout the plot. Either way, puzzles and mysteries are a great way to capture an audience's attention, but they also need a satisfying solution. Don't present your aliens as a puzzle unless the final revelation is worth all the effort the characters put into solving it.

Alien obstacles

Sometimes aliens recede from the role of fully realized characters and act as part of the general setting of the story. They become obstacles on the hero's journey through the plot. A strange new world inhabited by dangerous and hostile life forms threatens the protagonists at every step as the journey from point A to point Z. These aliens can be iconic, plot-centric animals like the enormous sandworms of the Dune novels. They also can be the aggressive microorganisms found in the water or the semi-sentient crystalline pillars that amplify negative emotions. These beings become Big New Things that challenge the heroes in some novel way.

Fully sentient beings can be obstacles too, although consider what clichés and tired tropes you're drawing on (refer to the section, "Alienating audiences," earlier in this chapter). More interestingly, alien cultures and societies can throw up all kinds of unusual obstructions for characters to overcome. Navigating local customs and manners without causing grave offense can be as tense as running from a ravening beast. As with any obstacle in stories, how the characters treat others shows the audience what kind of people the protagonists are.

EVERYONE'S AN ALIEN HERE

Of course your story doesn't need to have any humans at all! Every character could be an alien or some other being from your audience's perspective. This decision gives you tremendous freedom, but it can be tricky. An entirely alien cast lets you create characters without any of humanity's specific cultural or historical baggage.

If you want to make that connection with the real world, you can include specific signifiers like Viking-sounding names or Wild West style costumes. This type of story also lets you divide up specific elements from humanity amongst different species and mix in your own Big New Things. However, if your nonhumans are too inhuman to relate to or understand, you audience can have a difficult time caring about the story. Fortunately, audiences of humans are pretty good at projecting their own humanity onto any and all kinds of characters as long as your aliens think and feel in at least some recognizable ways.

Creating Alien Emotions

Aliens have their dramatic and metaphorical roles in science fiction, but just as importantly they provoke emotional responses from audiences. These responses run the gamut from "oh, how cool!" to "oh, how scary!" to "weeeird . . ." When creating extraterrestrial characters, consider what feelings you want to inspire and how best to do that. Think about both how you want your audience to respond to the aliens and how your main characters respond, which can be very different.

Perhaps audiences find elegant, high-tech extraterrestrials in power armor are super cool, whereas a protagonist being chased by those same extraterrestrials will find them intimidating and scary instead. These emotions don't necessarily match one for one with a dramatic role or metaphorical association. Sublime aliens can be antagonists and grotesque ones can be heroes. Audiences and characters may not always agree on how to think about or react to other characters, creatures, or situations. And that's perfectly fine.

These are some of the most potent and common emotions that aliens in sci-fi can provoke from both audiences and characters alike.

Rousing wonder — Sublime aliens

Many aliens inspire a sense of awe. This sense of the sublime grows from the cognitive dissonance audiences have when they encounter something new and outside of their experience but which still makes enough sense that it draws them in and makes them want to know more. These aliens may be sleek and beautiful or wise and majestic or so mysterious audiences can only perceive them through their unfathomably sophisticated technology, like the unseen monolith-builders in *2001: A Space Odyssey*. They may or may not come in peace, but they don't seem like they're here to destroy Earth.

When anyone encounters the sublime, they want more. Audiences ask themselves what it would be like if they met beings like that. How would their lives and worldview change forever? What can be learned? And yes, what could go wrong? What if one were to upset or disappoint such a glorious being?

Provoking revulsion — Grotesque aliens

Some aliens, like the tentacle-armed, blood-drinking Martians in *The War of the Worlds*, are there to repulse and scare both the audience and the characters. Extraterrestrials with monstrous biological features like teeth and claws arouse deep worries about predator animals. Ultra-aggressive, bloodthirsty aliens tap into fears of societal collapse and violations of moral order.

Aliens as grotesque creatures have been in science fiction since its earliest days, both as enemies and as misunderstood others. They can present a challenge to characters and audiences alike, demanding that they try to look past their prejudices and see the true nature. They can also be irredeemable killing machines that definitely should be feared and avoided or defeated. Many great stories find some middle ground between the extremes. Chapter 17 explores creating dangerous and fearsome creatures in fantasy stories, but those lessons apply here as well.

Creating unease — Uncanny aliens

Between the extremes of sublime and grotesque lie the uncanny aliens. These beings give audiences the unsettling sense of something as strangely familiar, rather than simply mysterious. You may be familiar with the concept of the *uncanny valley*, a term first applied to robots that mimic humanity but don't quite replicate it. More recently it's been used to describe human characters generated by computers that look both way too human and yet not human enough. Either way, audiences find them unsettling.

REMEMBER

Your story's aliens can provoke this unease in a variety of ways, from moving in eerie ways to using unusual speech patterns to their appearance. The classic large head and eyes and small body of the so-called gray aliens are a great example of the uncanny. These various uncanny aliens remind audiences of themselves, but are unmistakably not them. They're living caricatures that can highlight certain features of humanity and human culture while still being somewhat relatable.

Inspiring hope — Power fantasy aliens

Many superheroes are aliens, and the thing that's alien about them is often the part of them audiences would love to be true about themselves. Superman is one of the most famous aliens in pop culture, a character who appears entirely human but is much better than human in all kinds of exciting ways. Even in stories where no characters wear colorful costumes or identify as crime fighters, extraterrestrials often possess technology or innate abilities that let them do fantastical things normal folk can only dream of. Their stories can tap into the power of those dreams to create tales of heroism or expertise or great power standing up to oppression and evil. If your story features big action sequences and showdowns between beings with godlike powers, drawing techniques and inspiration from superhero movies and comics can provide useful inspiration.

Producing smiles — Adorable aliens

From *E.T. the Extra-Terrestrial* to The Child from *The Mandalorian*, audiences have a special place in their hearts for cute and cuddly alien beings. Those big eyes and plaintive cooing noises combined with a sense of naivete and helplessness instantly elicit sympathy and interest. Chewbacca from *Star Wars* shows another adorable path; he's by no means helpless or innocent, but he roars his big feelings and fights with fury for his friends. Adorable aliens may even look just like humans, strangers in a strange land who encounter everything humans are familiar with on Earth with fresh eyes and a new perspective. When they're the protagonists of a story, they bring an otherworldly earnestness and curiosity to the story world that audiences relate to. As supporting characters, they give someone for your heroes to love and protect and for the antagonists to endanger.

Introducing audiences to your aliens

When and how you introduce your audience to your aliens is a key moment in the story. The audience's first impressions of the aliens shape their thoughts and feelings about the extraterrestrials for the rest of the narrative. The more central the otherness of your aliens is to your story's plot and "what if" question, the more care you need to take when crafting first contact experiences for the audience. Ask yourself these questions as you craft this key moment:

>> **What questions, connections, and emotions do you want to provoke in audiences in this scene?** Your audience is already primed to feel emotions while experiencing your story. How do you want the audience to feel when they meet the aliens? Are they curious to know more or but are on edge by the unknown? How does this alien's appearance in the story relate to your central "what if" question or your Big New Thing? Does the alien exemplify what's normal for your sci-fi world or does its appearance signify an inciting incident that's going to change the plot?

>> **Through whose point of view does the audience encounter the alien?** The audience and the characters aren't always on the same page when it comes to interacting with aliens. Are the protagonists and the audience making first contact together? Or does the point-of-view character already have thoughts and feelings about the alien before the audience? Maybe the first impression comes through the alien's eyes, giving an otherworldly perspective on things. If you're using an omniscient narrator, decide how much information to give about the aliens in this first scene in order to best serve their role in your story. (Refer to Chapter 2 for more information about point of view.)

>> **How do other characters react to the alien's first appearance in the story?** Audiences take their cues from characters within the story world. How your characters react to the aliens has a profound impact on how audiences perceive them. A dangerous-looking alien with large teeth and claws may send characters running or perhaps everyone in the story is happy to see and expresses reverence for the alien's wisdom and philosophy.

TIP

After audiences have made first contact, their relationship with the alien will likely grow and change over the course of the story. You can use these questions in subsequent scenes to track how the audience's understanding of the alien develops along with the story's plot.

EXERCISE

CREATING YOUR OWN ALIENS

This chapter presents different ways of thinking about your aliens. Our goal is to get you to think about the role of the alien in your stories and create extraterrestrials that serve the story and grab the audience's attention. This exercise can help you brainstorm a whole bunch of different beings by mixing and matching the metaphorical, dramatic, and emotional roles they might play in a story. Just follow these steps to launch your own invasion of unique and meaningful aliens.

1. Pick or randomly determine one option from each of these three categories:

Metaphorical	Dramatic	Emotional
Aliens as us	Alien antagonists	Sublime aliens
Aliens as diversity	Alien protagonists	Grotesque aliens
Aliens as animals	Alien allies and rivals	Power fantasy aliens
Aliens as teachers	Alien mysteries	Adorable aliens
Aliens as warnings	Alien obstacles	Uncanny aliens

2. Give your aliens a driving emotional or intellectual goal that audiences can empathize with completely such as love of family, desire for artistic expression, or fear of outside threats from the preceding table.

3. With both the three narrative roles and the relatable goal in mind, create an aspect of the aliens that is substantially different from modern humans in each of these three categories that creates a restriction that keeps them from pursuing that goal the way humans typically do:

Biological (Reproduction, sustenance, movement, communication)

Societal (Government, religion, values)

Technological (Travel, warfare, industry, computing)

The resulting alien species is now purposefully designed to have an important and interesting effect on your story.

Chapter **12**

It's Alive! Or Is It? — Imagining Robots and Artificial Intelligence

omputers and robotics are both the greatest triumphs and the greatest failures of sci-fi's vision of the future. Sadly, the world doesn't have android butlers and isn't run by artificially intelligent mega-computers. Nevertheless, the world is incredibly automated and computerized and the mega-algorithms that drive the internet run more and more of the planet every day, even if they aren't (yet) self-aware. Sci-fi stories may not have predicted the future of computing, but from the beginning, sci-fi authors were asking the absolute right and most interesting "what if?" questions about artificial life and intelligence. More than space travel or alien worlds, the sci-fi imagination has engaged with real questions about these technologies that have in turn impacted the real people making actual robots and computers.

This chapter deals with both robots and computers, which we link together with the common concept *artificial life.* These artificial life forms serve a similar role to aliens in sci-fi that we discuss in Chapter 11 — they're other possible kinds of "people" besides humans. The difference is, artificial life is purposefully created and designed by others for specific functions, and thus they raise big "what if" questions about humanity's relationship to and responsibility for our technology.

Creating Artificial Life

In this chapter we use *artificial life* to make a distinction from mere technology like smartphones and assembly line robots and chess-master computers. Although those things are super complicated and impressively capable, they don't rise to the level of artificial life as we're using the term. We assume all artificial beings meet the following criteria:

>> **Self-aware:** The being thinks and therefore it is. It can reflect upon itself as a being that didn't exist, was created, and may someday cease to function. It understands that it exists in relationship with other beings and the wider world and has an idea of itself as individual and distinct from others.

>> **Purpose:** The being was created for some specific purpose or goals. Those can be anything from endlessly bolting together spaceship parts to flawlessly imitating a human. It was designed to do something, and that purpose is reflected in its structure and capabilities.

>> **Autonomy:** The being can act without any direct input or orders from an outside source and is capable of making decisions and choices (likely within specific built-in limits or restrictions).

Taken together, these three requirements for artificial life not only distinguish them from mere technology, but they also make these synthetic beings great candidates for characters in stories. Because they act and understand the impact of those actions and because they have goals they pursue and limits they must work within, they can elicit emotion and sympathy from the audience. They have an essential part of being human: the ability to connect with others.

The following sections help you create artificial life forms that do more for your story than simply remain on one side of a man-versus-machine binary, which is only one of many options available to you. Think through your answers, reconsider them as needed, and then use them to inform your writing.

Asking questions of meaning

Alan Turing was one of the pioneers of computer technology, and he asked one of the most influential questions in science and sci-fi history: Can a computer successfully imitate a human? His actual question was more specific than that and put in the context of a specific "imitation game," but the popular understanding of the question has captured the imagination in the ensuing decades. Can a machine think like an intelligent human? How can people tell a human from a machine? These are the kind of dramatic "what if" questions that can form the core of a thousand or more sci-fi stories.

GIVING CHARACTER TRAITS TO EVERYDAY ITEMS

As any child with a favorite toy can tell you, humans can definitely develop strong emotional attachments to nonliving technology. Humans constantly imbue everyday items with character traits, and the more animate the device, the more faux-lifelike it becomes. Cars give up or keep going in the face of adversity, laptop computers "act up" and crash at dramatic moments.

These personable pieces of tech can thus serve as quasi-characters in a story, taking on some but not all the traits that we discuss in this chapter and adding additional objects of emotional involvement. The stalwart smuggler's spaceship may not be alive, but she and the crew have been through a lot together. Hope she can hold it together for one last run and isn't too upset about the cheap fuel the captain bought. . .

As you think about the artificial life in your story, consider how they can embody one or more of the following big, existential questions in a dramatic way. For some stories, just asking the question may be interesting enough, but audiences are much more likely to engage with the question when it's all wrapped up in the conflict and drama of your plot.

What does it mean to be a person?

No one expects you to be a philosopher, but writing about artificial life without running into questions about the very nature of existence and identity isn't easy. Instead of avoiding those questions, embrace them as an opportunity to elevate your stories and make them stand out with thoughtfulness and depth.

Consider these types of questions when figuring out what it means to be a person:

>> Artificial life may not be human in a biological sense, but is it human in a moral and ethical sense?

>> Where is the line between a piece of tech and personhood?

>> Does biology define people or do their thoughts, desires, and actions?

>> What does it mean to be a conscious being and to have free will?

>> If consciousness and free will exist, do they emerge from the circuits of a computer in the same way they emerge from the human brain?

These kinds of tough questions drive the stories of many iconic robots and androids. Data from *Star Trek: The Next Generation* is a prime example; he's an inhuman machine who looks and acts very human and who's constantly striving to be more human in every way. Over the course of his many adventures, Data's story explores the limits of personhood and humanity from different angles. His fellow characters and the audience seldom if ever doubt he's a person and they all care about what happens to him. At the same time, Data isn't exactly like his biological crewmates. His mind is different; he can be turned on and off, reprogrammed and copied. He's capable of inhumanly complicated calculations and analysis. Data is a different kind of person, both better and worse in many ways, but no less a person for it.

Your artificial life forms can challenge the idea of personhood even more than Data does. They may face much less sympathetic characters than the crew of the starship *Enterprise,* people who fear or hate or disdain the artificial beings. The societal suspicion of androids living as humans drives the plot of the massively influential film *Blade Runner* and the book it's based on, Philip K. Dick's *Do Androids Dream of Electric Sheep?* (Del Rey). In that story, special law enforcement officers hunt down androids who've rebelled against their assigned role and are trying to live as humans. Even if they mean no harm, these rogue beings must be destroyed because they have violated the natural order of creator and machine.

TIP

Maybe your artificial life carefully analyzes humans and says, "If that's what it means to be a person, no thanks." Answer the question of personhood in your own way, always keeping an eye toward how it relates to fates of your characters and the drama of your story.

Who and what can suffer?

In a 2021 interview with *The New York Times* columnist and podcaster Ezra Klein, the brilliant sci-fi author Ted Chiang raised a serious and disturbing consideration about creating artificial intelligence. At some point, we'll be creating billions of entities that have the capacity to suffer, and undoubtedly, they'll experience suffering. He rightly worries about that being a terrible idea for humanity.

Both audiences and characters in stories often view artificial life as less than human or less than alive, so they tend to overlook the ways in which these beings may suffer. Because robots and androids are built, they can also be rebuilt and repaired or even duplicated and for some that may offset the moral implications of any suffering they feel. But how do the robots feel about all this trauma?

In the *Star Wars* films the droid C-3PO endures a constant loss of limbs, decapitations, and other indignities. He clearly hates all of this, but he also doesn't seem to suffer the same way a human would if they sustained such damage. Although often played for laughs in the movies, C-3PO's suffering highlights the difference between how beings suffer and recover from trauma. C-3PO and many of the other droids in *Star Wars* are in fact more human than humans when it comes to suffering and fear. They seem to feel every bit as intensely as a human would, but their mechanical nature makes them capable of enduring endless cycles of pain a human could never survive.

REMEMBER

The suffering your story's artificial beings endure can work as a metaphor for specific types of human experiences. A robot might "die" over and over again in ways both heroic and cowardly, senseless and sacrificial. How the human characters react to this cycle of loss can reveal key elements of their personality and what they do to end or perpetuate the cycle can drive the narrative to its climax.

What do humans want from technology?

Technology enhances modern lives in countless ways, touching every part of the modern human existence. Most people want science to make them healthy, comfortable, entertained, and connected. That's technology's purpose: to make people's lives better and more interesting. It's a lot to ask of machines, and people rely on them more and more with each passing year. Think about how much of your daily life requires some combination of electronic and mechanical devices. Now think about how frustrating it is when your computer or car or phone breaks down or the whole city goes dark when the power grid fails. You want your technology to work the way it's supposed to. You expect it to obey your instructions.

Artificial beings in stories embody people's relationship with tech and give the machines a voice to say what they think about shouldering this great burden. As self-aware beings, they're sometimes capable of making up their own minds about what humans should want, whether humans want it or not. Robby the Robot from the 1956 movie *Forbidden Planet* is science fiction's first breakout popular character, going on to feature in other stories like the TV show *Lost in Space* because of his striking design and stalwart nature. In *Forbidden Planet,* Robby shuts himself down rather than follow his human's orders to kill a menacing monster. Robby knows what the human doesn't, that the threat is actually a manifestation of another human's subconscious and killing it would mean taking an innocent life. Humans want technology to help them, but how do they feel when it helps they in ways they don't understand?

What do humans fear about technology?

As much as people want technology to be obedient, they're often just as scared that it won't. From self-driving cars that crash into walls to a global industrial system that's overheating the planet, machines have as much potential to harm as they do to help. That's pretty scary. It's even scarier when they can decide to cause trouble purposefully. Beings with massive computer intellects capable of absorbing and assessing vast amounts of data in a fraction of a second will undoubtedly see the world differently than any human ever could. After they've looked at all the facts, can humans trust artificial life to care about human well-being?

The infamous HAL 9000 from both the movie and book *2001: A Space Odyssey* by Stanley Kubrick and Arthur C. Clarke set the sci-fi standard for a computer that turns against its human crew. HAL is the shipboard artificial intelligence on a spaceship sent to explore Jupiter, a pleasant, helpful, calm voice for the first part of the voyage. But when a conflict arises in its programming about keeping a secret, HAL ends up murdering four of the five people onboard before being shut down by the lone survivor. Your artificial life characters don't need to kill to embody fears of disobedience or unintended consequences. They may just decide to follow their own path or refuse to abide by their programming for their own reasons.

Contemplating questions of responsibility

Because artificial life is created for a purpose, it presents some fascinating questions about the responsibilities of its creators. Whether or not characters bear or shirk these responsibilities provides a provocative dramatic question. Science fiction definitely inspires real world inventors and scientists, and these are exactly the kinds of questions they should be asking themselves before they release their creations upon the world. They're also the kind of questions that make for great stories.

Chapter 9 goes in depth on the role of compelling "what if" questions in science fiction. You can check out more thought-provoking tools to add meaning and narrative power to your artificial life forms.

What is people's responsibility to the life they create?

These artificial life forms are in many ways like children. They didn't ask to be created, and they have no say over the world into which they're placed. When someone brings a child into the world, they're responsible for its care. That leads to whether the same is true for artificial life. What happens when creators shirk their responsibility?

Mary Shelley's genre-making novel *Frankenstein* set the model for the modern sci-fi story and asked one of the genre-defining questions of responsibility. Dr. Frankenstein creates an intelligent life form, the "monster," and then immediately gets freaked out and abandons the poor, gigantic, super-intelligent child. The rest of the story doesn't go great for the doctor, the monster, or some innocent bystanders.

What is people's responsibility for the forces they unleash?

Where Dr. Frankenstein creates life just to see if he can do it and then abandons it, many other characters create artificial life for a specific purpose. The artificial being is first and foremost a tool to achieve some specific end. What happens when people create a new kind of intelligent weapon? Are the creators responsible for every life it takes? When unforeseen consequences lead to disaster, whose fault is that and what price should they pay?

The legend of the *Golem of Prague* provides a foundational example. As the most familiar version of the story goes, Rabbi Judah Loew creates the Golem to protect his fellow Jews from antisemitism in 16th-century Prague. The artificial life form does its job well at first, but ultimately becomes a danger to innocent lives. Rabbi Loew does the responsible thing and destroys his creation for the greater good.

What is people's responsibility for the burdens they impose?

People demand unquestioning loyalty and obedience from our machines. You have to think about who's responsible for the pain and pressure that demand puts on those artificial lives who serve.

Consider these questions as you contemplate what the responsibility is:

» How would people respond when someone imposes similar demands on them?

» Do artificial life forms deserve the same kind of respect and consideration that humans do?

» Will the artificial life forms demand to have the same legal and moral rights that humans do?

» What if the artificial life forms don't agree with humanity's answer to that question?

Karel Čapek's landmark 1920 play, *R.U.R.*, provides a quintessential answer: The workers revolt. The serfs created by the company Rossum's Universal Robots in the play are biological rather than mechanical constructs, but they set the pattern for robot uprisings for the next century of sci-fi.

Treating Artificial Life as Characters

In order to make your audience care about those fascinating questions of identity and responsibility in your story, they need to care about your artificial life forms as characters. Like any good character, these beings should have specific wants. They should make decisions and take actions to achieve those wants and come into dramatic conflict as a result. Establish some limits on what they will and won't do to pursue those wants.

REMEMBER

What sets artificial life characters apart from others is that they don't necessarily get to choose what they want or set their own moral limits on what actions they're willing to take. Some person built them for a purpose, and that purpose is usually in the service of that person's wants. The artificial life's programming strictly limits their actions and forces them to conform to the will of another. Their physical structure is designed to execute certain tasks and not others. The dramatic possibilities and looming conflicts of this limited agency are obvious. An artificial being can recognize or seek one option while their inherent limits force them in another direction. It's hard to give a loving hug when you have laser cannons for arms.

To more fully consider the ramifications of allowing artificial life forms to function as characters in your story, we offer the following ideas and suggestions.

Automated roles

Artificial life characters are purpose-built for specific functions and designed to behave within set limits, as determined by what's important and useful in your story world. These functions can be anything you want, but think about them in terms of how the artificial life characters relate to the people who built them. Do they assist or replace a human in a specific role? And how are their capabilities greater and/or lesser than their creators?

As literal products of the story world that builds them, artificial life characters should reflect the core conflicts, questions, and concerns of your story world. Part 2 of this book explores worldbuilding in detail, and Chapter 5 specifically offers guidelines for creating characters that are tied directly to the core conflict of your story.

Here are some key considerations regarding the roles of artificial life characters.

Determining your characters' role: Assistants or replacements

Every artificial life form is created with a purpose in mind. To better understand which of the two primary roles it serves, consider the following:

>> **Human assistants** exist to help their creators and owners do things. The ship's computer helps plot the hyperspace coordinates and alerts the crew when the life support system is busted, but the crew makes the big decisions. The scout drone flies ahead of the space marines, looking for enemies, but the marines do the actual fighting. Assistants are often sidekicks or companions in stories, there to interact with characters and help out but not designed to make key decisions. Of course just because they're not supposed to make their own decisions doesn't mean they won't conclude your protagonist is wrong at some dramatic moment and act accordingly.

REMEMBER

>> **Human replacements** perform tasks instead of humans having to do them. The factory assembly line robots have been building cars for decades already. In the future perhaps they fight battles on their own or manage the factories where their distant cousins bolt together hovercars. Replacements free up humans from difficult or dangerous tasks, which is great unless you're one of the people who's been replaced and you liked your job. That's a dramatic challenge facing many humans today. In a future where artificial life has taken over human tasks for decades, you can easily imagine humans losing those dangerous and difficult skills entirely. What happens then when humans find they need those lost skills?

Human-plus or human-minus?

Artificial life characters are almost never exactly like humans. They're usually both more and less than human at the same time. Sometimes people want them to look and act like humans, but maybe not too much. It's a fine line between relatable humanlike and uncannily inhuman as the following explores:

>> **Human-plus:** When creating assistants or replacements, human creators usually want their automated servants to be as capable as possible. Artificial life characters usually have specific capabilities far beyond humans. They're super strong and tough. They have telescopic vision and lightning-fast reflexes. Maybe they can hover or fly or shoot lasers from their eyes. Their inhuman capabilities is a big part of what makes these beings appealing as characters. They can do exciting things normal folks can't.

>> **Human-minus:** Few artificial life designers think their creations should be better at humans in every way. Most of them are designed for a purpose, and anything that doesn't suit that purpose is superfluous. Those military drones

don't need a smiling face or even hands and arms to help the space marines find the enemy. The hovercar factory manager doesn't need a sense of humor or even any of the five senses to make the assembly lines hit their quotas. The less human an artificial life form seems, the less some characters and audiences are likely to think of them as a person. They can't do fundamental things normal folks can.

TIP

Play with the balance between human-plus and human-minus as you create your artificial life characters. Consider how to strike the right mix to really engage with the questions of meaning and responsibility that they raise within your story world.

SETTING LIMITS ON AUTONOMY: ASIMOV'S THREE LAWS OF ROBOTICS

Legendary science fiction author Isaac Asimov shaped the genre's perception for generations with his series of short stories and novels about robots who must all obey three simple laws. These Three Laws of Robotics (introduced in 1942 short story "Runaround") form a kind of logic problem that's meant to ensure the robots only help and never harm their human creators:

- A robot may not injure a human being or, through inaction, allow a human being to come to harm.

- A robot must obey the orders given to it by human beings, except where such orders would conflict with the First Law.

- A robot must protect its own existence as long as such protection does not conflict with the First or Second Law.

Of course, many of the stories actually involve robots harming or allowing harm to come to someone or something while still holding true to the letter of the law. That's the brilliance of these three laws and any other system you, the author, may devise for controlling artificial life: They are in fact drama generators. The laws set expectations in the audience's minds about how robots are supposed to work, allowing the author to cleverly subvert those expectations.

Imagining scenarios is a fun and productive writing exercise where a robot both obeys Asimov's laws and yet somehow the spirit of the laws is violated even as the letter of them is obeyed. Then create your own set of rules for artificial life, but write them with a different goal than Asimov's "do no harm." What if the goal is instead to do some specific harm, like fighting an enemy army? Who determines who's an enemy? How broadly can the robot define "fight"? Who counts as a friendly, and is it okay to kill one friendly if it means killing three enemies?

Computers are (sometimes) people too

You have to make some important distinctions about artificially intelligent computers that distinguish them from their robotic brethren.

In order for a computer to run its software, it needs hardware; it can't just exist in the ether. In some stories the required hardware is so complicated or huge or expensive, the computer does have a kind of body where its consciousness lives. In others any sufficiently powerful machine will do, and the mind (or the character, if you will) can jump from platform to platform without losing its identity. The software that comprises the actual entity has shed the need for a permanent physical host.

REMEMBER

Even when computer beings rely on a single mainframe to exist, they almost always have the ability to spread themselves out across multiple terminals, screens, cellphones, or whatever. They can reach out and affect the narrative wherever there's an outlet for them. They can even be in multiple places at the same time. They have a totally different sense of identity and individuality than embodied androids and robots. This splitting of computer characters across time and space makes for unique and complicated possible plot developments. Their omnipresence can be a source of dread for characters who find there's nowhere to hide from the security drones. Or they can be constantly at a protagonist's side to hack locked doors and pass on valuable insight.

One common variation on the computerized character is the concept of uploading a human brain into a machine, which may or may not result in the human's demise. An uploaded mind thus achieves a kind of immortality and a bunch of new capabilities with other computers, like being in multiple places at once or performing ultra-fast calculations. It also hopefully retains the human's moral compass, wants, and desires, although living as a ghost in a machine can significantly change a person's personality. Unlike other artificial life forms, it wasn't created as a tool for a specific purpose and can freely choose its own path. This difference encourages variations on the questions of identity and responsibility like we discuss in the section "Contemplating questions of responsibility," earlier in this chapter, and allows audiences to relate to the artificial life in a different way.

At the other end of the self-awareness spectrum, a computer doesn't have to be truly intelligent at all to make decisions and act as a character. In the age of the algorithm, Big Data collections and brute force computer power make rote decisions about what ads you see, what loan rates you receive, and countless other aspects of daily life. The antagonistic algorithm doesn't need to be alive to cause tension and drama in your story or even to be seen as a character. Many people talk to algorithms like Amazon's Alexa and Apple's Siri every day, often even thinking of them as living beings.

Building Your Own Beings

Just like whoever's making robots and computers in your story, you should design your artificial life forms to perform their narrative duties with optimal efficiency. Build bots for drama. The following sections help you refine your designs and explore these key characters in greater depth. We include three sample artificial life forms as examples. As you read about them, think about the possible stories that may grow from these sections.

We hope these sections get your dramatic imagination firing away with ideas. Try putting our three examples of artificial beings into one story world and see the possibilities multiply.

Determining its purpose

Assess what its creators design the being to do. It could be one specific task or a whole suite of general capabilities. For example:

>> A factory robot designed to assemble laser rifle parts and test the finished weapon before handing it over to its owners

>> An exploration drone designed to fly low over the surface of a planet and scan for signs of intelligent life

>> A companion android custom created to provide comfort and support to terminally ill customers

Figuring out what it thinks about that purpose

This character is self-aware in some way and can thus reflect on its lot in life. But its worldview is shaped by its design and function and so it's likely to approve of its purpose at first. Events in the story may change that assessment. Consider these possibilities:

>> The factory robot believes that human lives depend on the reliability of the weapons it makes, and in order to do the most good, it must make the best guns.

>> The explorer drone knows that it serves a vital role in the exploration process and that its discoveries benefit all sentient life.

>> The companion android understands that terminally ill humans need every comfort and consolation and helping them in their final days is the noblest of tasks.

Finding similarities and differences between creators and their creations

Figure out how it's more than human in some ways and less than human in other ways. Its capabilities and appearance should reflect its purpose. For example:

>> The factory robot has multiple arms and no ability to move away from its station. Its sensor suite can see into the microscopic range, and it can process multiple factors with ease. It can only communicate via text through the factory mainframe.

>> The explorer drone has a personality designed to closely mimic that of a human scientist, and it uses natural speech as its primary mode of communication with its owners. Its body is a five-meter-diameter floating disk with every kind of sensor ever invented but no method of physically interacting directly with the world besides bumping into things.

>> The companion android looks, sounds, and acts entirely human. Its patients often forget that it's artificial. Beneath its exterior are an array of diagnostic tools to monitor the patient's vital signs and a reservoir of drugs that it can administer as needed via retractable needles in its index fingers.

Establishing its range of emotion

Its emotions are likely to be different and more narrowly focused than people's. For instance, can it suffer? Can it fall in love? It will have feelings related to its purpose, which can express themselves in many different ways. Consider the following examples:

>> The factory robot only experiences satisfaction or dissatisfaction as to the quality of its finished product. When it malfunctions in some way, it feels distressed and anxious that it's letting its owners down.

>> The explorer drone is profoundly curious to find new life and derives enormous pleasure from relaying that information to its owners. It can grow frustrated when obstacles prevent it from doing what it deems necessary to make new discoveries.

>> The companion android has enormous empathy and love for its owner. It's capable of imagining itself in the owner's position and thinking from their perspective to the exclusion of all other concerns.

Identifying the limits it operates under

Think in particular about the kinds of limits that will impact dramatic situations or stand in the way of the character achieving its goals. Look at the strict laws or designed fail-safes that regulate its actions and how much freedom it has to deviate from that purpose. Contemplate the following:

>> The factory robot can't use any of the weapons it manufactures in such a way as to endanger anything or anyone besides certified test targets.

>> The explorer drone can't withhold any information from authorized overseers and can't disclose any information to unauthorized individuals.

>> The companion android must follow the accepted End of Life Best Practices guidelines as established by its programmers and can't deviate from them even when the patient demands that they do.

Recognizing society's strong feelings about it

The arrival of any new technology has its share of supporters and resisters. Surely something as complex and intimidating as an artificial life form doesn't go unnoticed. What are people thinking about it?

What possible events related to the being does society most fear or worry about? What do they demand from it without compromise? For example:

>> The factory robot is a fast-moving whirlwind of metal arms that's handling deadly weapons. Humans are naturally wary of it, even though its safety record is almost perfect. Still, it makes reliable, lethal laser rifles, which is nice.

>> The explorer drone sees and hears everything it gets anywhere close to and records it all. The privacy protocols are supposed to filter out all the data unrelated to new discoveries, but how does it decide what's relevant and what isn't?

>> The companion android gives patients faultless medical and emotional support, and no one doubts that. But other family members often feel inadequate and even jealous in comparison to the perfect-seeming caregiver, which can lead to resentment and even alienation from their loved one.

Chapter **13**

Constructing Planetary Plots and Earth-Changing Stories

What will the world be like in a thousand years? Or a hundred? Or ten? What would the world look like if that world war had been lost instead of won? If this societal system was flipped on its head? Or if society itself collapsed into chaos?

Great science fiction has always dealt with these fundamental "what if" questions about possible futures or alternate pasts. Chapter 8 examines strategies for creating other worlds for any genre of story. Here we focus on creating the specific kinds of story worlds found in sci-fi stories where those wonderful "what ifs" are explored in diverse and fascinating ways.

Exploring Other Earths

You and your audience know a lot about Earth, and you can easily find endless amounts of additional info about it. No matter what planet your story takes place on, the imagery, references, and framework for understanding the setting comes from the planet we all live on. (In Chapter 6, we urge you to follow writer and game designer Kenneth Hite's advice and "Start with Earth." We also offer designer Raymond Loewy's Most Advanced Yet Acceptable (MAYA) principle as a handy guide for making changes to consensus reality when building your world.) Change only as much as you think you need to in order to engage your audience without alienating them.

With those two principles in mind, we dig into some of the most popular and powerful sci-fi approaches to variations on the theme of Earth. Each broad category offers a different set of challenges and narrative opportunities, but what they all have in common is that they engage directly with exploring other ways of being as a planet and a species. Similar to the ways in which aliens and artificial life forms ask big questions about what it means to be other than human, these categories of stories ask world-changing "what if" questions based around planet-sized Big New Things (science-based elements that are integral to the story and set the story world apart from reality).

Remembering a different past

Alternate histories and parallel worlds are a mainstay of science fiction, stories where the Big New Thing is a change to a Big Old Thing. These stories are perfect frameworks for exploring the past in order to understand how it determines the present. The change can be an enormous shift in geopolitics or the slightest adjustment that causes a butterfly effect chain of cause and effect that sets the stage for your drama to unfold upon.

REMEMBER

Whatever the cause, the effect needs to be interesting. As a rule, the new timeline of your story should be significantly different from the world your audience knows. Characters in this alternate history should live their lives in a meaningfully different and compelling way.

Ask yourself these types of questions when you're thinking of creating an alternate history in your story:

>> How different would North America be today if the 13 colonies hadn't rebelled against England in 1776?

>> What if the Ming Dynasty hadn't ceased sending out its imposing Treasure Fleets in 1433?

>> Would the Chinese have become a world naval power to challenge European colonial expeditions in later centuries?

>> What if any famous victim of assassination had survived or any famous figure had been assassinated in their prime? How would the course of history change?

The audience needs to easily understand the big picture changes your premise makes. If that's a cool idea, they'll become engaged from the start. The 13 colonies are part of Canada, and the Cherokee Nation and the Sioux Federation are the major powers on the continent. Fascinating, tell your audience more. But the setting really comes alive when you show these changes through big and small details of daily life. For example, Philip K. Dick's landmark alternate history, *The Man in High Castle* (Houghton Mifflin Harcourt), presents a world where the Axis powers won World War II, but the story is powerful because it's about the lives of specific people the audience comes to hope and fear for.

Ask yourself questions about what daily life is like for your characters. Are there different pop culture trends as a result of the change? What kinds of cuisine are more or less popular in the new now? What new career options are available? What jobs have disappeared? What does a travel visa to enter the Cherokee Nation look like?

REMEMBER

Writing an alternate history requires a lot of research across a wide variety of topics. The further back in time your change is from the present day of your story, the more informed extrapolating you'll need to do about developments in culture, technology, and politics. But even if you're just changing the results of the last election or imagining a world where polka music is the dominant influence in all pop culture, you'll need to get the details right for effective worldbuilding. The story must set forth a clear logic of cause and effect that the audience can go along with, and if you lose them with illogical leaps, you risk losing their interest entirely.

Thinking about the near now

Stories of alternate presents and likely tomorrows can grab an audience's imagination with very tangible and tantalizing possible futures. These stories are set in the future lifetimes of the audience. If the "what if" premise is thought-provoking or cool enough, they'll be engaged in part because they can put themselves in the story world. What if aliens make contact with humanity? How will self-aware artificial life forms change society? What happens if humans don't do something to stop climate change?

The near now works wonderfully for addressing the big, topical issues of today and imagining possible futures that humans all might have to live with. The Big New Thing happens or is invented in the present and impacts the reality of the audience. Mary Shelly's *Frankenstein* is simply her modern world with an abandoned, resentful, and potent artificial life form brought into it. *The War of the Worlds* is then modern day Great Britain beset by Martians. Much more recently, Kim Stanley Robinson's frighteningly plausible *The Ministry of the Future* (Orbit) is the Earth everyone is all too likely to know as climate change heats the planet to deadly effect. Robinson's book shows the horrific probable consequences and explores solutions.

Not every near now story needs to tackle topics of global importance. They're also a great mode for focusing on some specific aspect of modern life. The TV series *The Twilight Zone* ranged across the genres of science fiction and supernatural horror, but often the stories were really parables about modern life and the human condition. The Big New Thing is some specific change that challenges the character's mundane existence or presents a moral lesson. For example, imagine if you will, a world not unlike ours but where your social media reputation was the primary way most people measured their self-worth or achieved economic security. What would happen to someone who tried to opt out of the popularity race? Would it be a form of liberation or an act of self-destruction?

REMEMBER

When writing for the near now, you'll be more beholden to modern day science and technology unless your story involves aliens or time travelers. Even though sci-fi has a poor record at predicting 50 years into the future, audiences have a general sense of what may or may not be plausible. Unless you're going to change Earth's real history in your story as well, there won't be cities on the Moon or Mars in 2040. These near now tales benefit a great deal from some scientific research on your part, taking a real world recent theory or discovery as a platform for easing the audience into your story world smooths over cognitive dissonance.

The slight downside of writing a story set ten years from now is that in ten years you'll be proven wrong. Keeping in mind the lag time between when you finish writing and the audience gets to experience your story, you could be proven wrong before it even comes out. We don't think that's a big problem, and it shouldn't make you pause for even a moment if you have a great idea you want to write about. Audiences know it's a story, and they'll give you latitude. And in 50 years if people are still enjoying it for the wonderful characters and immersive plot, they'll just view it as an alternate history, a past future that could've been.

Worrying about the looming future

Predicting the next few hundred years with anything approaching certainty is next to impossible, and that's okay because none of your audience is going to be around to call you on it when your predictions don't come true. Compared to the 14 billion year history of the universe, a few centuries is just a fraction of a blink of an eye, and at that scale the looming future is just around the corner. Audiences can extrapolate a great deal from today's Earth and imagine existence in 2250 will be familiar in as many ways as it's different.

This looming future is fertile ground for sci-fi, and many of the classics of the genre take place in this zone of tomorrows. Humans may travel to other stars and encounter new life and new civilizations, but they still hail from today's countries and cultures. As a writer, the longer timespan gives you the cognitive distance to advance technology in big new ways while keeping to fundamental humanity and human concerns of your characters relatable. *The Expanse* books and TV show are a perfect example, where human politics and conflicts have expanded to Mars, the asteroids, and the moons of other planets. Eventually the stories range out even further than that. The conflicts and concerns that drive the story are rooted in the spacey/sci-fi setting and technology, but protagonists and antagonists resolve those conflicts based on wants and worldviews very familiar to today's audience.

REMEMBER

Setting your story in the looming future is a great way to take trends or ideas you're interested in today and advance them forward a few generations. The time gives the science fiction setting plenty of room to react and adapt to today. You have the freedom to create a story world that explores your interesting ideas about what's at stake today and how it may cause huge changes for the world. For example, perhaps a story that follows the logic of climate change set out by the science of today may be set on an Earth fully adapted to much higher sea levels and raging superstorms. Or maybe a post-fossil fuel economy may rely entirely on clean fusion power and nanotechnology to create a lush and prosperous world, albeit one where every nano-schematic is licensed from megacorps that hold the patents and demand licensing fees paid in emotional labor. Don't forget, you're writing a story, so there's got to be drama.

WARNING

However, be warned: Don't include too many too-specialized or too-of-the-moment references or slang terms that can date your story not just years from now, but also likely by the time it's actually released. Be mindful of the temptation to think that what's a classic reference for you will feel timeless to an audience of today. We, fifty-something authors that we are, can remember a time when The Three Stooges were seen as paragons of comedy, whereas today you'd be hard-pressed to find someone younger than 20 who's heard of them. In two hundred years we're betting they'll be forgotten, not entertaining starship captains and alien ambassadors. We could be wrong. Ask us in 2250.

Voyaging to a whole new world

With 14 billion years of history and one septillion or so different stars to play with, you have quite a vast space to set your stories about other Earths that are a long time from now on a planet far, far away. Perhaps the tales of the far future or distant past may have zero connection to the Earth we all live and breathe on or where Earth in 5082 is a scarcely recognizable part of a vast story universe or other planets.

When you leap into the far future, you're free to include the wildest scientific advances imaginable — self-aware nanomaterials, personal warp bubbles, and hyperintelligent neutron star god-emperors that your story demands — and audiences will generally say, "sure, maybe, why not?" That's great! But acknowledge that Earth science, geology, biology, climate, culture, and society will remain the reference points from which your audience makes sense of your cool ice planet or your space station that's the size of a small moon.

Of course you don't have to go wild with the advanced technology or far out Big New Things. You can use your not-Earth worlds to create very Earthlike worlds that emphasize certain elements in human society and culture and work as metaphors for core themes in your story. See the section on metaphors in Chapter 11 for using similar techniques when creating aliens. Ursula K. Le Guin's acclaimed novel *The Dispossessed* (Harper Voyager) uses the three main planets in the book as exemplars of very different economic systems (roughly, capitalism, communism, and anarchism) to weave together a powerful story of ideas, family, morality, and identity.

WARNING

The biggest challenge to you as an author responsible for creating a whole new world is to make it feel as real and believable as the one your audience lives in. The stranger and more wondrous the not-Earth world, the more work you'll need to do to help audiences to understand and appreciate without feeling like they're reading an encyclopedia of exposition. One way to avoid that problem is to steer clear of falling back on well-worn clichés from science fiction like a desert planet, an ice planet, a city planet, or a water world. That certainly does make it easy for your audience, but you aren't going to win any fans looking for originality. Chapter 7 provides some ways to effectively reveal your world without slowing your story to a crawl.

Imagining a different future

For about a century or more, science fiction stories were dominated by Western, mostly white, mostly male imaginations of what the future may look like. There have, of course, always been other voices and other visions creating fascinating other worlds, and fortunately for all the diversity and breadth of the sci-fi genre has grown in recent years. You can now easily find English translations from other countries and cultures, such as the vibrant Chinese sci-fi scene and books like *The Three-Body Problem* by Liu Cixin (Tor) standing out as one example of stories that now reach a global audience. It's an exciting time to be writing and enjoying science fiction.

Other cultures aren't a convenience store stocked with images and ideas for you to thoughtlessly cram into your story shopping cart. Science fiction is available to everyone, everywhere to tell their own stories and express their own ideas (see the nearby sidebar for an example). The past century is littered with novels, comics, and films that put forward African and Asian imagery as synonymous with exoticism and otherness. Sometimes writers have done this "just" to add a dose of what they consider the "exotic" to their story world, but of course to those other cultures, those so-called exotic elements are part of everyday life and not something to be lifted thoughtlessly for someone else's story. Other times they've perpetuated degrading stereotypes and prejudices and projected them into the future.

Don't do those things. See Chapter 23 for more on getting help and doing research to inform the diversity in your stories.

Traveling through time

Time travel by its very nature encompasses all the different categories of other worlds we discuss in the preceding sections. Past, present, and future can flow into and affect one another in exciting and often dangerous ways. Time travel stories are one of the most popular types of sci-fi stories enjoyed by audiences who otherwise don't like sci-fi. In an alternate timeline this book has a whole chapter on Time Travel stories. There's a very real past where one of the two authors of this book wore a different *Dr. Who* T-shirt every day of the week, every week in sixth grade (it was the one whose first name begins with "R").

Even more than with faster-than-light (FTL) travel, traveling through time probably won't ever be possible, that the universe just doesn't work that way. That's sad news for would-be chrononauts, but good news for storytellers. As with space travel (see Chapter 10), you can design your time machines or chronal anomalies or temporal loops to obey whatever rules you decide works best for your story. Most of the time, you'll want to clearly show how the process works so audiences can both understand it and anticipate possible dramatic complications. Or maybe the how isn't important and all you care about is what happens when your protagonist wakes up in another era after being conked on the head, as in Mark Twain's *A Connecticut Yankee in King Arthur's Court*. Choose the method that makes your "what if" question about time most interesting.

We divide time travel stories into four broad categories, each of which approaches time travel from a different narrative perspective:

>> **Time tourism:** These stories send characters from our era (or one like it) into the past or future as a fish out of water. Perhaps the characters are there to study history or they end up there through some twist of fate. The dramatics focus on how someone from one time deals with and reacts to all that's different about another time. It's about surviving and thriving in the other era rather than changing history.

>> **Time manipulation:** Here characters are actively involved in breaking or repairing history in order to change events. The logic of cause and effect and the challenges of time travel paradoxes take center stage as characters struggle over foreseen and unforeseen consequences. In the end, history is usually either restored to the right timeline or it turns out the history we all live in now is actually the result of some time travel shenanigans in the past.

>> **Time alternative:** A story without time travel but that presumes a change in the past is an alternate history, as we discuss in "Remembering a different

past," earlier in this chapter. A special subgroup of these tales includes one where characters from one timeline jump over into another one, or one where alternate timelines interact with one another. These stories often incorporate some elements from time tourism or time manipulation narratives.

>> **Time trap:** Characters are caught in a shifting or looping timeline and struggle to return to normalcy. Perhaps they're unmoored from time and randomly leap from era to era. Or, as in the subgenre-defining movie *Groundhog Day*, they're doomed to relive the same loop over and over again until they can find a way out. These stories are often very personal, sometimes played for comedy, where the time trap forces characters to confront hard truths about themselves that otherwise they might let pass them by over time.

Making Everything Worse (or Better)

Your story world is linked to the Earth of right now no matter how distant in the future or how far away in space you set it. Here and now is the reference point that you share with your audience. Your story can draw on a shared understanding of today's problems and possibilities to highlight differences between now and then and delve into the "what if" questions that may happen. How much of what you think is good and uplifting about today's world still exists in your story's world? What dire trends and harmful practices persist or have gotten worse? Here we explore the most interesting ways sci-fi extrapolates on current issues to create riveting and inspiring future settings.

George Orwell's genre-defining novel *1984* about an oppressive surveillance state was as much about the privations and preoccupations of daily life in the post-war Great Britain of 1948 when it was written as it was about a possible grim future. In this section, we explore how to explore ideas about your present day through the lens of stories about grim futures (dystopias) and potentially bright ones (utopias).

Envisioning your story — Dystopian fears and utopian hopes

Whether you're feeling dystopian or utopian, remember to put compelling characters at the center of your story. Even if you don't consider your story utopian or dystopian, thinking about it in those terms can be helpful. Is your future an optimistic one or a pessimistic one? Likely it's a little bit of both. Take some time to think through whether your story is going to be hopeful or fearful about the future.

Make a list of things in the real world you're worried about. For each one, visualize a good path forward in time, where changes in society and technology could make it better. Then do the reverse, extrapolating bad paths forward with changes that make the problem worse. This process alone should give you ideas aplenty about how to flesh out your fictional future and present it as a warning or proposal for the world of tomorrow. The following sections can give you some more help.

Warning about the future — Dystopias

Dystopias alert the audience about a possible future that seems plausible based on current bad trends in the world. Very justified fears of nuclear war gave rise to post-apocalyptic wasteland stories. With society nuked to oblivion, the hard-scrabble survivors have to scrounge and fight over the scraps. Zombie apocalypses follow the same model, the undead spreading like a pandemic across the globe, leaving destruction in their wake. Non-apocalyptic dystopias focus on powerful central authorities or strictly enforced caste systems that echo fears of tyrannical governments or oppressive ideologies. Dystopias are often matched with some kind of existential threat to humanity as a whole that allows the abusive dictatorship to take control.

For example, Margaret Atwood's 1985 novel, *The Handmaid's Tale,* takes on the real-world evils of misogyny and patriarchy. She extrapolates these oppressive attitudes forward into a near now where a fertility crisis leaves most women incapable of bearing children, which in turn leads to a political crisis that puts a patriarchal, oppressive government in power over society as a whole and women's bodies in particular.

Idealizing the future — Utopias

Utopias inspire the audience to imagine a possible future where at least some of the current bad trends in the world have gotten better. They're hopeful visions of the future where the evils of today have been conquered in some way. A perfect utopia would be perfectly dull, with no room for conflict or character arcs. A good utopian story recognizes that perfection is impossible, but radical change for the better can happen in specific areas such as economic inequality, racist discrimination, or environmental devastation.

On the optimistic role sci-fi can serve in offering solutions to problems instead of just spreading fear, Sheila Williams, editor of *Asimov's Science Fiction* magazine, is quoted by Tasha Robinson writing for an October 15, 2020 article on Polygon.com as saying: "But if you take these problems apart and just deal with one individual [character or issue], looking at genetic research, or AI or whatever, staying specific, it's easier to have a more positive arc to the story, without worrying about the entire collapse of civilization."

Punks, punks, punks! Writing sci-fi with attitude

The 1980s brought a new subgenre to science fiction, with novels like William Gibson's *Neuromancer* and Bruce Sterling's *Islands in the Net* (both by Ace) setting the tones and themes of what became known as cyberpunk. In their introduction to *Rewired: the Post-Cyberpunk Anthology* (Tachyon Publications), writers John Kessel and James Patrick Kelly list the core ingredients of most cyberpunk stories:

>> Presenting a global perspective on the future

>> Engaging with developments in infotech and biotech, especially those invasive technologies that will transform the human body and psyche

>> Striking a gleefully subversive attitude that challenges traditional values and received wisdom

>> Cultivating a crammed prose style that takes an often playful stance toward traditional science fiction tropes

Just as punk rock music rebelled against both the politics and the pop music sensibilities of the 1970s and '80s, cyberpunk subverts the utopian promises of an automated, mass-produced, constantly connected world. The classic cyberpunk stories take place in the near now and verge more toward the dystopian than utopian. They're concerned with trends in technology, business, and culture and highlight the seedier, disruptive, and dangerous parts of the possible future. In these stories, inequality and class differences divide society. Global megacorporations dominate the world, battling one another with deadly force. Humans have become even more dependent upon technology, to the point of physically implanting it in their bodies or replacing biology with technology.

WARNING

Cyberpunk worlds typically imagine a globally diverse fusion of cultures, which makes sense and seems like a very plausible future. However, avoid incorporating other cultures just as a surface-level reference without any thought or depth. A lot of cyberpunk has involved a fixation on Asian and particularly Japanese cultural elements. Not only has this fetishizing of Asian culture become a cliché, it's often done in an ill-informed way that relies on stereotypes that perpetuate skewed and sometimes racist views. Go ahead and make your cyberpunk story as worldly and diverse as you want, but do the research first and steer clear of the prejudicial cliches. Chapter 23 discusses using experts and sensitivity readers for your stories.

The two most iconic elements in cyberpunk are virtual worlds and cyborgs, both which we hack into next.

Virtual worlds

One of the defining images from cyberpunk is when a character "jacks in" to a virtual world to hack some system or steal some valuable intel. William Gibson coined the term "cyberspace" in 1982 to refer to a shared "consensual hallucination" where people from around the world can interact in a virtual reality other world. Neal Stephenson picked up the concept in his 1992 novel *Snow Crash* (Random House), where he refers to it as the metaverse. These visions predate the internet of today, and although they haven't come to pass yet, many of today's leaders in technology are open about how much cyberpunk visions of a virtual reality have inspired them to make fully immersive cyberspace/metaverse a reality.

TIP

Having some or all of your story take place in a virtual world allows for a variety of fun shifts in the narrative. A virtual space doesn't obey the same rules as human space. The spaces themselves aren't bound by physics or engineering. The people in the spaces can move in impossible ways. Everything can look, feel, and sound however you want, and it can shift in the blink of an eye to something else. That freedom to do anything can be a lot of fun, but don't forget to provide your audience with some rules and limits. Likewise, think about ways to have what happens in the virtual world have high stakes in the physical world. Can someone's brain get fried if they "die" in cyberspace? Can human brains become infected with computer viruses? Some threat should loom over these scenes that keeps audiences engaged.

Cyborgs are (mostly) people too!

The other defining image from cyberpunk is radical body modification with high tech replacements (for better or worse). Characters often have robotic limbs, artificial eyes, computers integrated into their brains, or weapons hidden beneath their skin. The wild mix and match of possible augmentations sometimes echoes the wild style of old school punks with its outlandish, intimidating appearance. Other times the implants are carefully hidden, lurking below the surface of a seemingly gentile business executive.

These cybernetic enhancements push the boundaries of what it means to be human. A story world with cyborgs implies there is no one set way of being. Instead, there are many choices of being: gender, sexuality, physicality, personality, even knowledge all become upgrades or modifications that a person can choose. Many people would find the option to enhance themselves appealing, but others will undoubtedly find the concept frightening or repulsive in some way. How your story world's characters feel about cyborgs can provide potent dramatic tension and serve as a useful metaphor for the clash between individual identity and societal norms.

Using steam, sun, and cells

Cyberpunk has spawned multiple other punks, some of which are as or more popular than the original. Each of these genres has a specific kind of technology that is central to the setting and story: The punk part indicates a rebellion or fight against the status quo and a movement to change or step outside mainstream, conformist values and assumptions.

>> **Biopunk:** Here genetics and biotechnology take center stage rather than cyberpunk's virtual worlds and cybernetic implants. Where cyberpunk envisions a future of enhanced humanity that relies more and more on machines, *biopunk* envisions a future where change happens on a cellular level. With genetic engineering, it becomes possible to pick and choose the genes you want for your children or even for yourself. This godlike ability to rewrite nature opens the door to deep questions of what defines a human being.

>> **Steampunk:** Characterized by clockwork constructs, steam-powered computers, and top hats with goggles on them, *steampunk* takes place in an alternate Earth or a whole other world where technology took a radically different path. Steampunk tales often verge into the realm of fantasy, stretching the possible uses of 19th-century technology, when steam power was king. Although inspired by the stories of Jules Verne and other 19th century sci-fi authors, steampunk looks back at a different past whereas Verne was trying to predict the near future from his point of view. Steampunk stories prize inventiveness and a certain retro-chic style and are often more about nostalgia for a past that could've been rather than a vision for what's to come. In this way they're often about changing history, making them a kind of time travel story as well.

>> **Solarpunk:** A relatively new punk on the scene, *solarpunk* is a response to the dangers of climate change. Although these stories grow from the bleak present day of rising sea levels, killer heatwaves, and deadly superstorms, they offer hope for the future. Instead of wallowing in a post-climate apocalypse wasteland, solarpunk stories model alternative futures where renewable energy and other innovations have reshaped society in a more sustainable way. Here the punk act of rebellion is to stand against the complacent status quo that seems incapable of saving the planet.

There are many more punkish subgenres than the few listed here. In some cases, "punk" seems to get applied in a way that just means "type of sci-fi story with some technology or theme." Nothing is wrong with that per se, but there's a good case to be made for keeping the punk in your whateverpunk story. Punk stories look at the current dominant socioeconomic paradigm and don't like what they see. They look at the newest gadget or algorithm and see how it can be misused and abused. They look into the future and see something that needs changing. The punks bring drama, and drama makes for great stories.

4

Fantasy: Journeys into the Imagination

Chapter **14**

Bringing Wonder to Your Story

F antasy fiction includes everything from going on epic quests to slaying drag- ons and recovering mystic artifacts to modern-day tales of mundane worlds where magic hides in shadows and is only known to a select few. From role- playing game dungeon crawls to urban faerie romances to any of the countless schools for young wizards out there, all these fantasy stories share at least one thing in common: They're impossible. Horror stories are about frightening worlds of dread and danger. Sci-fi stories are about characters and ideas in other possible worlds of the future. Fantasy stories are about *impossible* other worlds full of won- ders that carry meaning and create amazement for both the characters and the audience.

We love Kathryn Hume's definition of fantasy from her book *Fantasy and Mimesis* (Routledge) where she explains that it's a purposeful departure from the norms of real life, which is a *departure from consensus reality*. In other words, the fantastical, cool, magical beings and events in a story could never happen in the real world in which the author and audience exist.

This chapter builds on the concept that fantasy is a departure from consensus reality, but not a complete departure. It's a mix of the world people know and a world that never was and never could be, but which audiences can still relate to. Writing fantasy lets you use impossible ideas to create meaningful stories about characters and worlds that are worth caring about. These stories are told through a specific point of view (POV) that shapes the audience's experience with your fantastical, wonderful impossibilities. Read on to see how to weave wonders that enthrall and amaze audiences.

Creating Wonder

A sense of wonder is a fundamental building block for fantasy fiction. Wonder happens when people see or experience something that fires their imagination. It draws them in with its striking appearance or nature and creates a longing for more.

The Grand Canyon is a natural wonder of the world. It's bigger than you can imagine. The vast scale stuns and amazes. How can it be so big? Where did this enormous crack in the Earth's crust come from? Those feelings of amazement and surprise make it a wonder. The Great Pyramid of Giza is the only remaining one of the seven wonders of the ancient world: beautiful, imposing, massive constructions that exemplify humanity's skill, imagination, and capabilities. How could they have built such an edifice thousands of years ago? What purpose did so mighty a pile of stone serve? What secrets are contained within? Those inspirational and admiring reactions to human ingenuity and artistry make it a wonder of the real world.

Wonder is the opposite of indifference. Wonder entices; it makes you want to learn or experience more. You can't turn away from an object of wonder. You've never seen anything like it. You want to share it with others, let everyone know how amazing and cool it is.

Fantasy stories are ideal venues for creating wonder in audiences. All stories can create wonder, but the inherent impossible elements in fantasy rely on it. The audience has agreed to suspend their disbelief and take a journey from consensus reality with your story's characters into a world where the fantastical is real. With their imaginations opened, your job is to provide the awe-inspiring, breathtaking, sometimes shocking wonders that make a fantasy narrative shine. Let the following ideas and tips help you make that happen.

Understanding the meaning of wonder

Fantasy fiction's wonders come in countless forms and expressions. The ancient, ill-tempered dragon, the floating castle, the enchanted ring, the ageless spirit of the woods, and the sorcerer's spells can all make audiences ooh and ahh and suck them into the story world. Authors design these fantastical wonders to not only capture the audience's imagination, but also to enrich their plots.

In fantasy stories, a wonder isn't just a powerful emotional draw, it also means something. Brian Attebery has a great take on wonder in his book in *Strategies of Fantasy* (Indiana University Press). He explains that humans are hard-wired to find meaning and patterns in everything, and those patterns form the basis for conclusions, beliefs, even whole religions. In the real world, people often assign meaning to patterns, but it turns out Zeus isn't really responsible for lightning. Our fates and personality may or may not be written in the stars. Not so in fiction.

REMEMBER

When you create your story's wonders, make sure they follow a pattern and have as exact a meaning as you want them to. The patterns that audiences discern really can inform them about the story world. Thunderstorms really can come from angry gods.

The meaning you attach to wonders reveals something important and/or interesting about the characters, world, and dramatic questions in the story. The massive, ancient dragon, whose wings whip up tempests and whose breath is an inferno, is so ill-tempered because she's the last of her kind. When she dies, a whole lineage of draconic tyrants and the epic poems they wrote about themselves die with her. If your heroic knights can find another way to preserve that legacy, can they avoid a deadly battle that will surely reduce their kingdom to ashes? Could the sorcerer who dwells in the floating castle help them solve this riddle? If so, how in the world can they get up to the castle gate in the clouds? All those wonders are extra-wonderful when they serve the plot. When they don't serve the plot, they're not really that wonderful.

You can also attach metaphorical and thematic meaning to your wonders. Fantasy allows for idealized, impossible versions of things that already carry some inherent meaning. The mansion of an exploitative wealthy merchant becomes more decadent when decorated with enchanted decor and supernatural servants that respond to the owner's every whim. The cursed mine that's the source of all their wealth becomes even more exploitative when you add in monsters menacing the miners forced to dig for mithril. See Chapters 16 and 20 for advice on how to incorporate metaphorical meaning into magic and monsters.

Most wonderful yet believable

Think of the wondrous, reality-busting parts of your story as sitting somewhere on a spectrum from fantasy to reality (What Kathryn Hume refers to as fantasy and mimesis). Look at the following formula to get an idea of the range.

Pure Fantasy --- Mostly Magic --- Middle --- Mostly Real --- All Real

>> At the Pure Fantasy end of the spectrum, everything's made up and unfamiliar to the audience. Anything can happen at any time, and the audience has no familiar references or rules to help them make sense of it.

>> At the All Real end you're not writing fantasy at all anymore, and the real world rules out the impossible. If you're being really real, you're not even writing fiction anymore, but rather you're just reporting the facts.

>> In between is an exciting mix of both the fantastic and the real. This is where most fantasy stories take place.

REMEMBER

Great stories can push the fantasy all the way to the limits of comprehension or stick so close to reality that only a single moment of magic pushes it into the fantastical. There's no best place on this Fantasy/Reality spectrum, but there's a perfect place for your specific story. Balance the creative freedom that the impossible gives you with the need for your audience to understand and care about your story.

Impossible things have wonderful uses for writers, but they're not risk-free. When you break with consensus reality too much, you can create *cognitive dissonance* (the unease or discomfort an audience member experiences when different ways of thinking and understanding clash with one another) and drive away rather than entice your audience. Chapter 6 discusses both cognitive dissonance and how to deploy it strategically using the Most Advanced Yet Accessible design principle. That is, only change as much reality as you need in order to engage the audience without alienating them.

Not all breaks from consensus reality are created equal, and so just because it's magic doesn't mean it's unfamiliar. For most audiences of fantasy fiction, the last century of books, movies, games, and other media have created a kind of consensus fantasy. For example, wizards, dragons, elves, and dwarves all seem as familiar to fans of the fantastic as humans and horses. You can take advantage of this familiarity to ease the audience into your world and then spring your exciting changes and innovations on them without creating cognitive dissonance.

A story about the ancient dragon who wants to preserve its long and questionable legacy of dragonkind in the face of opposition from some stalwart knights doesn't need to reinvent the dragon or the knight of popular culture. Part of the story's potential appeal is the wonder of great dragons and stalwart knights, and audiences understand how dragons and knights generally work in stories. Make these classic foes your own in ways that not only satisfy the audience's desire for something new, but which also incorporate the deeper meanings and conflicts in the story. A dragon who's metaphorically representative of greedy capitalism is going to be different from one who represents old-fashioned ways of thinking. Knights fighting for the common folk will be different from knights who personify modernity and innovative thinking.

Matching magic to the mundane

Why write a fantasy story (or any story) if you don't think you have something new and interesting to say? Your cool, unique ideas for a spell or a creature or a faerie realm are probably what got you excited about writing this story in the first place. In order for your unique fantasy wonders to have an impact, present them in the context of common fantasy tropes and everybody's shared understanding of the real world.

REMEMBER

Your wonders can have a greater impact when they manifest in clear relation to the plot, presenting obstacles and allowing for solutions that would be impossible in a realistic setting. But your magical plot points need some mundane world context to show off just how wonderful your reality-breaking creations are. Combine and contrast fantasy and mundanity in multiple ways within your story by considering the following:

>> **Mundane solutions for mundane problems:** You want at least some plot points that downplay or set aside the magic to lay a realistic baseline for dramatic scenes.

>> **Fantastical solutions for mundane problems:** Showing a wondrous way to resolve a reality-based difficulty helps audiences understand how the fantastical operates in the story and relate that to their own experience.

>> **Mundane solutions for fantastical problems:** Grounding your fantasy by having reality best it in some way (a plain sword slaying a monster, a clever mind solving a magical puzzle) shows the limits of the fantastical, teaching audiences the rules that govern this broken reality.

>> **Fantastical solutions for fantastical problems:** When all the magic and monsters come together for the big showdown, the wonders really get to show their stuff. But if you haven't given the audience opportunities to learn the basics of your fantastical reality, none of it may make sense.

Using the MMMaM Index of Wonder

Creating meaningful wonders takes more than just dreaming up some unusual, fantastical creature or kingdom. The wonder needs to not only draw audiences in, but also do real work for your story. We include this list of four factors — we call these factors the MMMaM Index of Wonder — that can help you think about how fantasy elements are working in your story, and whether or not they could be doing more.

Ask yourself all of these questions about each wondrous element you're building into your story (we also include some examples):

>> **Magical:** How does it depart from consensus reality in an interesting and engaging way?

- An enchanted sword that sings of future deaths when used to kill something.

- A fantastical city where everyone is immortal as long as they stay within the city walls.

>> **Mundane:** How does it relate to consensus reality so that your audience can better appreciate it?

- The singing sword does all the normal things a sword does, plus singing portents of death.

- The immortals in the city still have to deal with normal city problems like sewage, overcrowding, and buying food from outside the city.

>> **Meaning:** What role does it play in telling your story and how does it affect the characters?

- Whoever kills with the sword will die by the sword, playing into the theme of "you reap what you sow" and also foretelling the hero's death by sword.

- The protagonists visit the city, and the immortality within sorely tempts one of the heroes to give up the quest and stay behind, creating tensions in the group.

>> **aMazing:** How do the magical, mundane, and meaningful combine into something that produces wonder?

- The singing sword is both an iconic weapon and a mysterious puzzle that holds the truth about the hero's fate.

- The city of immortals provides a powerful temptation for one of the heroes to stray from the path, but it's not an easy choice. Is eternal life in a cramped city of strangers better than a short life spent with friends in the service of a great cause?

There's no right answer to any of these questions, but the answers should all reinforce one another. The MMMaM Index is a tool to help you focus on the wonders in your story from multiple angles at once.

BEWARE: THE DANGERS OF DREAM WORLDS

Magical realms built on impossibilities run the gamut from "modern day Earth, but there's a unicorn living in the Alps" to "anything becomes real if someone wishes it to be." The first is, maybe, a little dull. The second is chaos. You may not think that there would be many stories set in the chaos scenario, but have you ever seen a dream sequence in a story where anything can happen? The audience accepts it. Kind of. But when anything can happen, dramatic stakes become unclear and cause and effect becomes confused, which can make the audience lose interest and move on to someone else's story.

Many far-out fantasy worlds function just like a dream word — they suffer from the inherent boredom of "anything can happen." The best way to make these wild other realms work for your story is to rein them in with some rules. Anything can happen, but only until the sun goes up. Anything can happen, except for making someone fall in love with someone else. However, a few rules aren't enough unless they directly impact the characters and what they want. Tie the rules to the protagonist's dramatic goal for the scene, and the dreamscape can become a proper stage for drama instead of a sideshow full of weirdness and wonder signifying nothing.

Going High to Low with Fantasy

When you hang out and chat with fantasy writers and enthusiasts of a certain age, you may hear the terms "high fantasy" and "low fantasy" as ways of distinguishing different kinds of fantastical tales. Here we explore these useful concepts a bit more deeply.

Distinguishing between high and low

Definitions vary, but in general, the terms mean the following:

» **High fantasy** involves story worlds with lots of magic and mystical creatures that are usually coupled with epic, sometimes mythic tales of noble heroes and existential evils. *The Lord of the Rings* is classic high fantasy (more about that in Chapter 15).

» **Low fantasy** is grittier and rougher, full of moral gray areas and populated with less than noble, sometimes antiheroic characters. Magic and monsters lurk in the shadows or are locked away in wizard towers and don't necessarily play a big role in everyday life. The world of Westeros (the setting for *A Game of Thrones*) is a low-fantasy environment.

This very basic division between high and low is sort of useful. It's a shorthand that may help audiences familiar with the terms get an idea of what your story's like, but it's not something to worry about or even focus on as you write. However, the concept does point the way toward an extremely useful way of thinking: Just how magical and fantastical is your story world and your plot? It's high! Oh, it's rather low. That's too vague and restrictive. What about if some parts are low and some are high? Where does medium-rare fantasy fit into all this? We're glad you asked.

Employing fantastic elements

Most stories have heroes of some sort, but fantasy stories stereotypically have Heroes with a capital "H." These Heroes go to heroic efforts to achieve heroic feats and overcome incredible — we daresay heroic — odds. That's the stereotype, but not all heroes wield magic swords or are the chosen one (and thank goodness for that). There are a thousand and one other ways for your protagonists to face their antagonistic forces.

TIP

In the section "Most wonderful yet believable," earlier in this chapter, we present a spectrum we use for thinking about fantasy and wonders that runs from Pure Fantasy on one extreme to All Real at the other. Your whole fantasy story world doesn't need to sit on the same part of that spectrum. Indeed, it shouldn't. Think of the spectrum as a set of dials that you can use to fine-tune the different fantastic elements in your story. How fantastical do you want each of these elements to be in your story? The following can help you (we also include some examples):

>> **Realistic:** Just like the world that audiences are all stuck in, the element is probably challenging, costly, time-consuming, and risky.

- Protagonists firmly grounded in reality are relatable, the stakes for them are very high, and every encounter with the fantastic can be life-changing.

- In fight and action scenes, people run out of breath, fall over in agony when hit with a sword, and struggle to clamber over a wall taller than they are.

- Magic is rare and difficult, but even the simplest spell breaks reality in ways most people in the world could never imagine.

- Fantastical beings are rare and still mostly based on real-world biology and/or existing spiritual traditions.

>> **Heroic:** Even when no magic is involved, the world seems heightened and bigger than life, like the reality of an action movie.

- Protagonists are often driven by a higher cause and are self-sacrificing and noble. Villains are melodramatic and have bold ambitions. These people don't lead quiet lives or let challenges go unanswered.

- Heroic warriors have no problem beating 20 armed soldiers in a fistfight without losing their breath. They can take a crossbow bolt in the shoulder and shrug it off as they leap over the castle wall.

- Magic is special but fully integrated into society and the world in important ways, but only a select few control it.

- Monsters are bigger, tougher, and more dangerous than one person who isn't a hero could handle. Their origins may be purely fantastical, their physiology fearsomely ignoring consensus biological limitations.

» **Fantastic:** Magic and the fantastic are pervasive elements, creating wonder through the amazing density of impossibilities.

- Characters wield supernatural or superhuman abilities and don't think twice about it because that's just who they are. This gives them a demi-god or superheroic perspective on the world that can make them seem more than human.

- Battles involve such powers and enchanted items that the whole nature of fighting is different than what's seen in consensus reality, incorporating elements like mystic healing, invisible walls, eldritch blasts, and flaming swords.

- Characters use magic items or sling spells with ease and regularity. The magical elements pervade the story world and are a daily part of everyone's existence.

- Monsters and magical entities can be huge, defy all known laws of reality, and only be defeated by an army of realistic protagonists, a team of heroic ones, or one really fantastic superhero-type.

MAKING FANTASTICAL SUPERHEROES

Superhero comics and movies, along with a lot of popular anime and manga, often blend the fantastic elements in intriguing and inventive ways. The comic book superheroes of DC, Marvel, and other comics publishers have grown into a mishmash of magic, science fiction, action heroes, and mythic influences.

If you're writing a superhero story, the audience is already primed to enjoy the crossover between genres and levels of the fantastic. But remember, many of those stories rely on audience knowledge built up over dozens of movies and/or decades of pop culture appearances. When creating your own superheroic fantasy, you won't have that familiarity to piggyback on when introducing audiences to your story world and its characters.

REMEMBER

Different elements in your story should usually operate on different parts of the scale. Your protagonists can be all realistic while the world's magic is utterly fantastic. Your fight scenes may be heroic, with amazing feats of strength and skill, but the world itself is very grounded and realistic.

Choosing a Fantastical Point of View

Chapter 2 talks about point of view (POV), and we touch on it again as it relates to horror stories in Chapter 19. In those cases, we refer to POV in terms of which characters or viewpoints audiences experience the story through. But there's another way to think about POV, one discussed in detail by Farah Mendlesohn in her book *Rhetorics of Fantasy* (Wesleyan University Press) — the fantastical point of view.

Fantasy stories contain fantastical, impossible wonders. There might be magic or monsters or mystical planes of existence (or all of the above). *Fantastical POV* defines the way that both the audience and the characters in the story encounter all these wondrous elements. Make sure you decide on a fantastical POV before writing your story because that viewpoint will affect how everything else in the story unfolds. Building on Mendlesohn's work, here are the three most common fantastical points of view, each with its own strengths and uses:

Portal — Moving from the real world to a magical world

In *portal* stories, protagonists move from a relatively normal or plain world into a more wondrous or magical one. The audience follows along with the protagonists, and they encounter this strange new world together.

For example, have you ever been playing around in a distant relative's old wardrobe and discovered a doorway to another world? Or maybe your Kansas farmhouse got swept up in a tornado and deposited in a Technicolor kingdom of wizards and witches? If so, then you're already familiar with the portal fantasy POV.

For a long time, the portal fantasy was the default mode in fantastical literature. From fairy tales about encountering the supernatural in the woods, to Dorothy's trip to Oz in L. Frank Baum's *The Wizard of Oz*, the story of a normal person dropped into an abnormal world is easy for audiences to relate to. They can put themselves in Dorothy's shoes and together "ooh," "aah," and "yikes" at what they discover together.

REMEMBER

A portal fantasy protagonist doesn't have to come from a literal other world. They can be from a less fantastical part of a fantasy world, or they can be unfamiliar with the world's greater wonders for some reason. Consider *The Lord of the Rings*, where the four hobbit protagonists come from a pretty mundane, barely magical corner of Middle Earth. Their epic quest takes them out into the most amazing and terrifying locales in their world and thus functions like a portal fantasy. A character with amnesia or someone raised in isolation would likewise experience the story in the same way.

Portal fantasy is great for the following:

>> Fish-out-of-water stories where someone mundane encounters the magical

>> Quest narratives where heroes take a dramatic journey of discovery from innocence to experience

>> Stories where you ease audiences into especially fantastical and inventive story worlds that may otherwise create cognitive dissonance

Immersive — Inhabiting the magical world

"As you know, because we're siblings, we live in a land of eight kingdoms, each founded by the divine marriage of an elf and a dragon in the distant Age of Aaagamer the Wise . . ." isn't a good sentence. As a rule, it's almost always best to cut any sentence that begins with "As you know . . ." because people don't usually spend time telling each other things they already know. It's clumsy, lazy exposition, but it's the type of thing you may be tempted to write in an immersive fantasy.

REMEMBER

Immersive fantasy puts the audience into a story where everyone shares some core assumptions and knowledge about the wondrous world where they live and have adventures. The main characters aren't going to be surprised by the existence of magic, and even if they've never seen a dragon personally, they know that such beasts exist. No one outside the circle of conspirators knows that the Shadow Cabal plans to usurp the king's power with a demonic pact, but everyone knows who the king is, why he's not universally loved, and maybe even that sometimes ne'er-do-wells make deals with demons.

The audience doesn't share that knowledge when they start the story, which is where the temptation to write sentences with "as you know . . ." comes from. For the most part, audiences accept the consensus reality of this immersive fantasy world without too many questions, as long as nothing's too confusing. Chapter 7 provides lots of guidance about providing exposition in ways that serve the story instead of grinding it to a halt while you dump info on the audience. Whatever elements you show should be important to the story.

TIP

Even though the whole story takes place in a wondrous world, you should choose which specific wonders to focus the audience's attention on. Put elements of the fantastic that directly impact the main characters, the plot, and the dramatic conflict front and center: A war story starring characters who ride dragons should show a lot of details of how dragonriders fight, care for each other, and their place in society. A heist story in a world of magic should concentrate on what's valuable, how people use mundane and magical means to protect it, and how crime and punishment are handled in a world with truthsayers and teleportation.

Immersive fantasy is great for the following:

>> Stories with large casts and shifting viewpoint characters that give the audience multiple windows into understanding the story world

>> Complicated plots set in worlds that share enough consensus reality with the audience that they can understand and appreciate the story world

>> Dramatic or romantic tales of characters like faeries, cat people, or merfolk who live, love, and fight in ways that could never exist in the real world

SHIFTING POV

A fantasy story doesn't always stay in one POV. Don't let the fantastical points of view lock you into one way of writing your story. Use them to help you think about how your audience and your characters feel and act when they encounter the story's wonders. As the narrative evolves or as you write sequels, the fantastical POV can slide into another mode like the following:

- A portal story's opening chapters brings a character into the magical world, but as soon as they've become accustomed to it, the story takes on an immersive perspective.

- An intrusive fantasy disrupts the mundane life of a character who then travels into the wondrous world where the intrusion came from, becoming a portal fantasy protagonist.

- An immersive fantasy world can be subject to intrusions from other, stranger fantasy worlds, or immersive characters can travel through a portal into those even weirder realms.

Intrusive — Moving the magical world into the real world

Have you ever been rooting around in a distant relative's old armoire and out of seemingly nowhere a goblin riding a dire world leaps from behind an old raincoat into the room? Or have you heard the rumors about a secret order of mystical knights who meet every spring equinox atop the Eiffel Tower to plan their endless war against the fallen angels? These are tales of intrusive fantasy where something wondrous shoves its way into the audience's consensus reality and disrupts the mundane status quo.

REMEMBER

The *intrusive* fantasy is the mirror image of the portal fantasy. Instead of going on a journey with a protagonist who's learning about the wondrous new world, the audience is seeing things through the eyes of someone whose life and reality are being disrupted and thrown into chaos by the sudden appearance or revelation of the fantastic. The fantastical intrusion can be huge and obvious to everyone (a goblin invasion of New York City), but more often only a handful of people from the normal world know about it. Those people are usually your protagonists. The intrusion shocks and challenges the characters from your mundane world, forcing them to confront realities they once thought impossible.

The newly revealed wonder doesn't have to be earth-shattering. It's often one small supernatural element introduced into an otherwise mundane setting: a monkey's paw that grants three wishes, the ability to hear other people's thoughts, the discovery of a single mythical monster lurking in the woods. The fantastical intrusion brings focused chaos and disruption into the protagonist's life. It's one weird, new thing that makes your protagonist reassess key truths they thought they understood about how the world works.

Whatever form the intrusion takes, it poses fundamental dramatic questions like: How will this change the world? How will folks deal with this new information? Can the world ever return to normalcy? Should it?

Intrusive fantasy is great for the following:

>> What-if stories about a singular supernatural force disrupting normal life

>> Hidden worlds and secret societies wielding wonders out of the public eye

>> Dramatic and/or action-packed tales of the mundane world thrown into chaos by the fantastic

EXERCISE

THREE PERSPECTIVES ON YOUR WORLD

Early on in your writing process, before you've settled on too much plot and character details, this exercise can help you find the right fantastical POV for your story. Taking some time to look at other stories you like and seeing how they work can inform your own decision about how your audience and your characters will encounter the fantastic. Then stick to these steps:

1. **Pick one of your favorite fantasy books, movies, TV shows, or games.**

   If it's been a while since you enjoyed it, take some time to refresh your memory.

2. **Identify what fantastical POV the story uses.**

   Does it use just one, or does it shift over the course of the story?

3. **Write down why you think the creators chose that particular POV.**

4. **Imagine what the story would be like if it had each of the other two POVs that it didn't use.**

   That may mean having a different protagonist or a very different plot. How different would the story be? What appeal might this other version have that the original didn't?

You can do a similar analysis to the same story by applying the break from consensus reality scale to look at where the story's different elements fall between All Real and Pure Fantasy. (Check out the section "Most wonderful yet believable," earlier in this chapter where we discuss this scale). How would the story change if you turned those dials up and down for the characters, fights, or mundane elements?

Chapter **15**

Worldbuilding on the Shoulders of Giants, Faeries, Dragons, and Hobbits

C reative and compelling worldbuilding is an absolute requirement for writing a successful fantasy story. Even if your tale only adds a sliver of the fantastic into the real world, you'll want to think through the implications of that impossible element. For epic tales in wholly imaginary settings means thinking about not just what you can imagine, but also what others have imagined before you. This chapter explores using myth and the classic tropes of fantasy fiction to inform your worldbuilding and help your story feel both unique and accessible.

Adapting Myth and Legend

Tales of magic, monsters, and other wonders have existed for as long as people have told stories. The plots and characters from mythology and folklore are the taproots of modern fantasy, as Farah Mendlesohn and Edward James explain in their book *A Short History of Fantasy* (Libri Publishing). So much of today's fantastic fiction has grown directly from these ancient fables and epics, which aren't the creations of any specific author. They belong to the entire culture that produces them, and reflect that culture's beliefs and concerns.

These were stories everyone knew, featuring heroes, gods, and creatures that the audience may or may not have actually believed in. Their origins were religious or at least metaphysical; the stories were lessons about humans and their place in the physical and spiritual world. They provided models of good and bad behavior. They are also entertaining. What made a great storyteller then (and now) was artfully spinning your own take on these communal stories, plots, heroes, and villains.

Retold and interpreted by centuries of poets, artists, and writers, these tales and legends had a profound effect on how people write and enjoy fantasy stories in the 21st century. As Kathryn Hume details in *Fantasy and Mimesis* (Routledge), modern writers and audiences have inherited story patterns chiefly about protagonists struggling to live up to some ideal hero-type. When they fail to live up to the ideal, bad stuff happens. When they actually live that heroic life, they triumph. Audiences today still love a good "hero upholds the moral order" narrative, but it's certainly not the only way to tell a story. You tap into fantasy's origins and archetypes without constraining yourself to follow their specific patterns.

The following reveals ways to power up your fantasy story with what your audience already knows and believes.

Making myths and faerie tales your own

As soon as authors like Ovid, Charles Perrault, Hans Christian Andersen, E.T.A. Hoffmann, and the Brothers Grimm started collecting and rewriting these ancient stories, they made them their own. The versions of these stories everyone knows today have been crafted by experts to convey some specific message or emotional experience that might or might not have much to do with the story's original lesson.

These versions have in turn been reimagined and repurposed into some of the best-selling fantasy tales of recent history, from Rick Riordan's *Percy Jackson* series to superhero versions of Thor and Hercules, to countless films, TV shows, comics, and animated versions of The Monkey King from *Journey to the West*.

Retelling stories with your own take

No copyright holder is going to stop you from trying to be the next Ovid. Every year or so, at least one big-name author comes out with their own retelling of classic myths and fables. Greek and Norse mythology are perennial favorites, as are Grimm's fairy tales. If you have a strong vision and a striking prose style, go for it. But you'll probably have more fun and greater success by forging a new path based on old patterns.

Consider these examples:

>> Angela Carter's hauntingly disturbing *The Bloody Chamber* is a modern classic, interpreting the fairy tales of Charles Perrault in a dark and provocative way.

>> Madeline Miller's excellent fantasy novel, *Circe* (Back Bay Books), takes the villainous sorceress from *The Odyssey* and makes her a great protagonist, whose story extends across the timeline of Greek mythology.

>> The hit video game series *God of War* has not only let players fight every god in the Greek pantheon, but in recent years has also crossed over into fighting Norse gods as well.

Playing with a myth or fairy tale's *fantastical point of view* (the way that both the audience and the characters in the story encounter all these wondrous elements — see Chapter 14) can help you find an original take on these tales as old as time. Each point of view (POV) offers a different way to explore classic myths and fairy tales:

>> **Portal:** Imagine someone from your *consensus reality* (the things everyone generally agrees on about how the world works) traveling into the world of a myth or fairy tale. How would modern or mundane sensibilities conflict with this magical world?

>> **Immersive:** Dive deep into the fairy tale or myth and give it a thorough worldbuilding treatment. Take the basic details and extrapolate the whole fantasy world from them and then find or create some intriguing characters within that world to center your story on.

>> **Intrusive:** Consider figures from myth and legend stepping into your world. There've been countless variations on this theme, but the genre is far from exhausted.

Recycling legendary tales of yesteryear

The legends and fables of old have some of the most iconic characters in all of literature. Many authors have had great success pulling those ancient heroes and monsters out of their mythic milieu and plopping them down in a brand new story.

Here are a few examples that show how others have done exactly this:

>> Neil Gaiman's *American Gods* (William Morrow) tells the story of fading old gods struggling to survive in modern day America.

>> Rick Riordan's Percy Jackson series posits a hidden society of Greek gods and their descendants who never went away.

>> Marvel comics and movies has a boisterous Thor who hangs out with other superheroes and slams baddies from every genre of fiction with his mighty hammer. Even more than the heroes, the monsters of mythology appear all over the place outside of the myths that defined them.

>> *Dungeons & Dragons* features every creature from Greek mythology fighting alongside Tolkien-inspire orcs and Lovecraftian-inspired mind-flayers.

Make the premise, character, or creature your own by adjusting its elements to fit the needs of your story. The *MMMaM Index* (our list of ways to infuse your story with wonder — see Chapter 14) can help guide your thinking. Ask yourself these questions:

>> **Magical:** How does it depart from consensus reality in an interesting and engaging way? What changes can you make while still retaining the same level of magical appeal?

>> **Mundane:** How does it relate to consensus reality so that your audience can better appreciate it? What mundane parts of your story world will change or react in dramatic ways to the element?

>> **Meaning:** What role does it play in telling your story and how does it affect the characters? Is the character your antagonist or protagonist? Or, do the characters in the story come into dramatic conflict over the element?

>> **aMazing:** How do all those combine into something that produces wonder? Do the changes you've made to the source material make it equally or more wondrous?

Designing mythic blueprints

Adapting a mythic plot structure to your own world and characters allows your audience to slip into sync with the familiar narrative and appreciate whatever nuances and cool new wonders you've added to the mix.

Here are some examples:

>> An innocent-looking young woman sets off to visit a beloved family member, only to be beset on the journey by a vicious, smooth-talking predator. In the end, the predator poses as someone who the young woman loves in order to trap her. Then maybe a guy with an axe shows up and cuts the grandmother out of the wolf's stomach? Red Riding Hood is kind of a weird story if you take it too literally, but the basic plot has been the basis for a thousand stories since then.

>> How many video games are there where the player has to undertake a long series of Herculean tasks (labors if you will) before facing the final boss? How many times have we seen Ovid's star-crossed lovers Pyramus and Thisbe die tragically? At least a million, thanks in large part to Shakespeare's version, *Romeo and Juliet*.

You can create your own blueprints by analyzing the following in your story. (Chapter 3 provides all the tools you need to break down a story's plot and think about its structure.)

>> Map the myth or fable onto *Freytag's Pyramid* (a triangular structure that represents the action and conflict of a story — refer to Chapter 3) or your preferred plot outlining approach.

>> Track the characters' dramatic arcs to understand their individual journeys through the story.

>> Make note of the fantastical elements in the story and how they relate to the unfolding plot and character arcs.

After you've done this analysis, you'll have a useful blueprint that you can adjust to fit your unique story, but which still has familiar echoes for audiences who know the source material.

Being sensitive to religious beliefs

When you're adding your own take on myths or fairy tales, be careful because what seems like a myth or fairy tale to you may very well be someone else's religion. Make sure you do your research and are *extremely* thoughtful in how you adapt them. Chapter 23 has more details on collaborating with sensitivity readers and cultural consultants.

For example, stories of a war between Christian angels and devils have a dedicated audience, but some practicing Christians find them offensive or even sacrilegious. The gods and beings from Hinduism often have striking appearances and compelling tales associated with them, but they're also central to the daily practices of more than a billion people. Which isn't to say that you can't write a great fantasy story based on great epic poems like *The Mahabharata* and *Ramayana*, but be respectful and careful.

Start with Middle Earth? Not Exactly . . .

J.R.R. Tolkien's *The Hobbit* and *The Lord of the Rings* and the imaginary world of Middle Earth where they take place have had a genre-defining impact on fantasy storytelling in the last 80 years. As Brian Attebery explains in *Strategies of Fantasy* (Indiana University Press), fantasy, sci-fi, horror, and other literature have no hard and fast boundaries between them. What is and isn't fantasy fiction can be pretty fuzzy on the boundaries, but if a story sits at the core of modern fantasy and ticks all the boxes, it's *The Lord of the Rings*. Tolkien didn't invent the genre. Before him came other popular fantasies like L. Frank Baum's Oz series, the tales of Conan the Barbarian by Robert E. Howard, and others. But when *The Hobbit* and *The Lord of the Rings* came out, they revitalized and redefined the genre, and have dominated the field ever since.

Many (maybe most) of you reading this book have already read those books, or at least seen the movies or television shows based on them. If you haven't, you've read books, watched movies, or played games that were directly influenced and inspired by Tolkien's tales. The world of Middle Earth plays a role in popular culture very similar to the myths and faerie tales of past millennia: It has set the pattern for many of fantasy's default versions of dragons, wizard, elves, dwarves, orcs, epic quests, dungeons, and second breakfasts. It's a sort of consensus fantasy reality.

In Chapter 6 we cite writer and game designer Kenneth Hite's worldbuilding rule, "start with Earth." To a large extent, modern fantasy in the past half-century has started with Middle Earth. There've been some great stories told this way. There've been a lot of mediocre and derivative ones too. Importantly, there've been other perspectives, voices, and traditions crowded out of the marketplace by Tolkien's cave-troll-sized footprint.

Whether you want to create stories directly in response to Middle Earth or want to create something entirely different with no connection to Tolkien, it's useful to fully understand what patterns and tropes *The Lord of the Rings* established. You can take away useful lessons from those stories, no matter what form your fantasy takes; we discuss them in the following sections.

Genre-defining characters and creatures — Wizards, hobbits, and elves, oh my!

Tolkien was inspired by the creatures, characters, and legends of Norse and Germanic cultures. He then filtered these through his own imagination and interests. The resulting mix of folklore and invention has defined a whole set of archetypes that fantasy fans now take for granted.

REMEMBER

Knowing theses standard-issue Tolkienesque fantasy archetypes is important in order to make them your own or avoid them entirely. Using the basic version adds some value if you want your audience to understand parts of your story world easily so that you can then layer in more complicated and original ideas elsewhere. Consider these archetypes that Tolkien used:

>> **Dragons and treasure:** A lonely, ancient dragon in a lonely mountain atop a vast hoard of gold and jewels, Smaug the dragon from *The Hobbit* is one of the great icons of fantasy. Ever since, it's conventional wisdom that dragons (for some reason) have lots of treasure just waiting to be stolen.

>> **Wizards:** Merlin is the archetypal wizard character of legend, but Gandalf becomes the iconic mage — ageless, but aged-looking old white men with beards and staffs. Unlike Merlin, he's very active in the story; he and his fellow wizards are key antagonists and protagonists rather than mysterious supporting players.

>> **Hobbits:** Relatable everyday folk, hobbits are aggressively mundane and pleasant, yet still mildly fantastic. They're a pleasure to be around, surprisingly resilient, and can sometimes rise to the most dire of occasions.

>> **Elves:** Inspired by Norse and Celtic tradition rather than faerie lore and folktales, Tolkien's elves are immortal, beautiful, almost perfect and often haughty beings. They're aspirational figures, not tricksters and troublemakers. Singers, poets, artists, and fearsome warriors all wrapped into one pretty package.

>> **Dwarves:** Also out of Norse tradition, with a heavy emphasis on being artisans and stalwart warriors. Tolkien stripped away the idea of them as inherently malevolent or tricksters, turning them into lords of great underground kingdoms.

>> **Orcs:** The personification of evil, and inherently irredeemable, orcs are mostly a Tolkien creation and have served as default bad guys in infinite fantasy stories and games. They still have personality and are recognizably sentient, but are totally unpleasant. Racist? Maybe. See the nearby sidebar for more relevant information.

» **Magic items:** The all-powerful One Ring has obvious historical precedent in the Germanic *The Ring of the Nibelung* epic poems. And the idea of magic swords with names and histories attached to them harkens back to Excalibur and other legends. Tolkien weaves the enchanted object into Middle-Earth's history, making them not just tools for heroes to slay trolls with, but symbols of a lost golden era.

Having Tolkien standard dwarves in your fantasy novel is like having a New York cop in your detective story. It's a little ho hum, seen it before. But, like the cop tangling with a devious and imaginative serial killer, if those dwarves are battling a unique antagonistic force, that may be just what you need to give your audience relatable yet still fantastical POV characters.

THE NOT-GREAT PARTS OF TOLKIEN'S STORIES

Tolkien's stories attempt to create a mythology for England that never really existed, and the tales present moral and ethical models based on a decidedly medieval set of beliefs. The stories have very few women of note, and most of them are put up on rhetorical pedestals to be admired for their beauty and purity rather than treated as full people in their own rights. Only the character of Eowyn stands out, who disguises herself as a man in order to fight the forces of darkness and then kills the fearsome Witch King of Angmar.

The heroes of the stories are white men (be they human, elf, dwarf, hobbit, or wizard). The enemies in service of the Dark Lord Sauron are all from the East and the South, areas not seen in the stories, but which call to mind Asia, Africa, and the Middle East. The humans from these non-North and non-West realms are definitely "others," who are portrayed as inherently less noble or good.

Tolkien's savage warrior races, the orcs and goblins, are entirely evil and monstrous, with no redeeming qualities. As such, audiences aren't meant to have any sympathy for them and can relish their defeat at the hands of the heroes. Some scholars and critics have made strong cases that the Tolkien-style orc could be considered a racist trope; acquaint yourself with those arguments before incorporating them or something similar into your stories.

Getting indulgent with worldbuilding

Tolkien started with worldbuilding. He didn't even have a particular story he wanted to tell, and long before he started telling *The Hobbit* as a bedtime story for his children, he was inventing the Elvish language and creating the intricate, epic mythology that would one day be published as *The Silmarillion*. Inspired by his own work as a scholar and his interest in foundational mythic texts like Beowulf (which he translated), Tolkien wanted to make a new mythology for England, which didn't have the kind of rich tradition as Scandinavia, Ireland, or ancient Greece and Rome.

He spent years just noodling and doodling around because he thought it was fun and self-indulgent. And it can definitely be both fun and self-indulgent, so if you want to spend your free time worldbuilding for its own sake, go for it.

WARNING

However, if you want to actually finish and release your story, don't do this. Don't spend a decade making up languages and nigh-impenetrable backstories. Jump as fast as you can into the part with an actual plot about characters we hope and fear for.

Generating deep history and wondrous geography

All that self-indulgent worldbuilding does pay off for Tolkien, and every fantasy author can learn a lot from his work. Middle Earth overflows with a feeling of deep, lived history and myth. Characters regularly reference past events and how places have changed over the centuries. The wizard Gandalf has lived for thousands of years, and as a result has different names, reputations, and relationships in various parts of Middle Earth. A reader doesn't have to understand Tolkien's invented languages to get the sense that the names of people and places have a shared, consistent grammar and vocabulary behind them. They're not just jumbles of letters and apostrophes like you find in some fantasy and sci-fi worlds.

TIP

The Iceberg Principle (see Chapter 5) is relevant here. Only show the parts of the world that impact the characters and the story. This is one of the key lessons you can all take from Tolkien: The history, geography, culture, and languages all work best when they directly impact the plot.

REMEMBER

The magical password to get into the ancient mines of Moria is tied to the distant past, when times were friendly and peaceful. The ancient enmity between different kingdoms and peoples makes it more difficult for the story's heroes to forge an alliance against the greater foe. Avoid the clunky exposition dump. Make your history impact the present, your cool architectural detail, or unique monetary system vital to the plot. Then your characters will *have* to care about the worldbuilding, and the audience will too.

Some geologists have critiqued a map of Middle Earth for the way the mountains form an almost rectangular wall around three sides of the sinister land of Mordor (where the shadows lie). "Mountains would never naturally form this way," goes the critique. But hey, these aren't naturally formed mountains! They're the result of Mordor's creation by an evil godlike being named Morgoth, who, with the help of a giant spider, also destroyed the two giant glowing trees that Middle Earth had instead of a sun in its early days.

TIP

Mountains formed by evil gods and magical trees instead of suns are fantastical elements that create wonder and draw the audience in. Let the fantastical elements in your story world shape the geography or physics, or fauna and flora. Let wonders supersede natural law in fun and unique ways.

The now-classic quest narrative

The Lord of the Rings set a pattern for the epic quest fantasy series, grand stories with enormous stakes, lots of characters, and huge set pieces at the climactic moments. Although Tolkien certainly didn't invent any of these storytelling techniques, he did combine them together in exemplary fashion.

Whether it's from books, movies, or any of the numerous other ways Tolkien's stories have been adapted, audiences know these characters and the world of Middle Earth. They're quite familiar with the quest narrative, even if they don't use that term. This shared knowledge is something you can use to your advantage when making your own story. Read on to find out how.

Relying on the everyday hero

Tolkien's central heroes are hobbits: small, rural, rather middle-class folk who like comfort and don't leave their quiet corner of the world to go on grand adventures. Bilbo in *The Hobbit* and then Frodo in *The Lord of the Rings* are, like Dorothy going to Oz or Alice going to Wonderland, normal people the audience can relate to. Their story is very much a portal narrative, except that they are of Middle Earth rather than another world. They are fundamentally good and decent souls who rise to an impossible challenge and bring the audience along with them on their heroic journey. The relatable average person thrown into chaos and wonder remains a reliable staple of fantasy, and one you can easily adapt to the specifics of your story.

Including world-saving stakes

These days, saving the world is practically a cliché in genre fiction of all sorts, but it was a relatively new approach when Tolkien put the fate of Middle Earth in the hands of a humble hobbit. If anything, this is where his stories have had too strong an effect.

TIP

Ultimately, audiences care most about characters and their fates, and not every story needs to be about saving the world. So, before you decide to bring on the apocalypse, make sure you're doing it because it's best for your story and not just because it's the highest stakes you can imagine or you think it's expected or necessary.

Using multiple POV characters

Epic stories often have huge casts and multiple different POV characters. Books like *War and Peace* were using multiple character points of view long before *The Lord of the Rings* was written, but Tolkien does a great job easing the reader into the different points of view. Tolkien starts with his protagonist slowly gathering more companions, who stick together for most of the first third of the story. But soon he breaks the party up into three and then four different paths. Only the audience has all the pieces of the story, and the audience sympathizes and roots for the disparate heroes as the clock ticks down and toward doomsday.

Using multiple POV characters lets you capture the sweeping scope of an epic quest story. Each different POV characters offers a unique lens through which to experience the core conflicts. Typically your individual characters will be separated from one another, none of them fully aware of the big picture and each facing their own obstacles. And if one of them should fail or even die? Well, you have other heroes in the story to carry on the fight.

Applying epic plotting and time dilation

The Lord of the Rings has a reputation for being bloated with overly wordy travelogue sequences and a plodding pace. We think that's only sometimes true, and that in fact the books are full of epic plot developments and an ever increasing pace. Tolkien does a great job escalating the pressure on his characters and increasing the stakes. Key characters die. Grave losses and dramatic conflicts split the protagonists apart. Events are always moving forward, picking up speed as they go. He makes great use of *time dilation* (when a character ages much slower than the rest of their world because they're moving at such a high velocity — refer to Chapter 10 for more information), something that many starting writers don't think about. Years pass between plot points in the beginning of the book. Then weeks of travel are punctuated by key days and hours when something dangerous or dramatic happens. By the climax of the story, every day and hour matter. This careful control of the passage of time plays a huge role in creating the story's epic scope and feel.

TIP

Use time dilation to give your story grand scale. You don't have to describe every mile of a month-long trek across the mountains. If nothing dramatic happens, the time can pass in a paragraph or a panel of a comic book, but now the audience knows the heroes are far from home. When big dramatic events like a great battle happen, slow down time and take as many scenes or pages as you need to show the desperate battle where your heroes have nobody to rely on but themselves.

Understanding Tolkien and Dungeons & Dragons

The most influential follower of Tolkien's fantasy patterns has to be the 1974 release of the first edition of *Dungeons & Dragons* by Gary Gygax and Dave Arneson, and all the editions, spin-offs, and other roleplaying games that followed in its wake. *D&D* began as a set of rules to incorporate fantasy elements from *The Lord of the Rings* into the historical wargaming hobby. Jon Petersen's exhaustively researched *Playing at the World: A History of Simulating Wars, People and Fantastic Adventures, from Chess to Role-Playing Games* (Unreason Press) tells the whole story in fascinating detail.

Dungeons & Dragons took the fantasy elements from Middle Earth and other fantasy stories (including Robert E. Howard's Conan stories, Jack Vance's *Dying Earth* series, and Fritz Leiber's Fafhrd and the Grey Mouser stories) and gave players generic versions of the creatures, settings, magic, and characters from those story worlds. D&D also defined all those wondrous elements with rules and levels and hit points, game systems that would go on to inform many of the most popular video games ever since.

Losing hit points and gaining character levels in games

Thanks to *Dungeons & Dragons*, countless video games and tabletop games incorporate two very abstract concepts that don't make much sense in the consensus reality:

>> **Hit points:** *Hit points* measure how healthy a character is with an exact number, which goes down by a precise amount when something hurts them.

>> **Experience levels:** *Experience levels* go up in response to heroes achieving goals (like killing monsters). When they level up, characters get more hit points, special powers, skills, or other advantages.

These abstractions are great for games. They give players a precise measurement of progress and cause and effect. Use this magic sword with this special feat and do that many hit points of damage. Outside of the niche market of LitRPG, where these ideas are part of the narrative, incorporating hit points and experience levels directly into your story world feels strange and artificial to readers. Focus instead on specific details and concrete changes for your characters. Describe the arrow wound. Show the hero studying and practicing a new spell.

TIP

If you're writing for a game, hit points and experience levels are a powerful and underutilized tool. Because players become attached to the characters they control in games, losing and gaining hit points has a direct emotional impact on them. Want to show that the Lich Queen really is as dangerous as all the townsfolk say? Have her deal 100 hit points of damage to the player with one glance from her Baleful Gaze. Need to maximize the sense of triumph when the player makes an important choice or discovers a new plot point? Raise their experience level and unlock a new special power. Match the game system to the story and both will sing.

Starting with the Forgotten Realms

You can find just as much inspiration from D&D as you can from Middle Earth, and the past 50 years of tabletop and video games have created a multitude of fascinating ideas and systems that you can integrate into your fantasy writing. Consider the following:

» Take creature inspiration from the mass of monster manuals, magic items, and magic spells created for these games. A single inventive spell description can inspire a whole scene or even story.

» Look at more story and character-focused games like *Apocalypse World* and the *GUMSHOE* system for thoughtful and easy-to-use tools that can help you create characters built from the ground up for drama and adventure.

» Refer to game sourcebooks for ideas. These sourcebooks can be master-classes in worldbuilding. Look at setting books like *Ravenloft* or *Pendragon* for amazing examples of worlds built for telling stories.

» Adapt your fantasy world into an RPG sourcebook and sell it through online marketplaces like DriveThruRPG.com. Doing so will not only leverage all your hard work into another publication, but it will also force you to think about your world and characters from another perspective that can inform your fiction in cool ways.

Making Deep History in Record Time

How do you create a deep, wondrous history and mythology for your fantasy world without going all Tolkien and spending a decade creating different languages, cultures, and histories from scratch? Here we present a set of prompts and questions that can help you create a story world with fantasy elements that feel deep to the audience. Chapter 8 covers a lot of the important principles for engaging world design. This series of questions augments that chapter to help you think about the fantastic and wondrous elements in particular.

Basing your story in reality

Take a real-world time, place, series of events, or set of myths and stories as the basis for building your fantasy world. You don't need to replicate every aspect of the basis in reality, but rather use it as a blueprint from which to build your story. Ask yourself these questions:

» **What are at least three facts that you find most interesting about your basis in reality?** What's cool or what fires your imagination? Who's the person you'd love to read a biography of? Take a few minutes to write down why those three facts appeal to you.

» **What other stories, movies, or other media are also about your basis?** If you think something's interesting, more than likely someone else did too. Find out what other stories were inspired by the same real world history or places and think about how you could have a different approach to the same subject.

» **What about your basis is least interesting to you?** Identify anything that you don't want to take from reality into your story. The earlier you're thinking about how you want to handle or cut the unpleasant or offensive elements from your fictional world, the better.

Making your own myths

Layer in all the fantastical wonders into your story world that will break away from your basis in consensus reality. Consider in depth all the implications this break from reality has for your story world and its characters. The basis in reality is most powerful when the fantastical changes have a clear logic that audiences can easily understand. These questions can help:

>> **What is the nature and origin of the fantastic?** Does it come from the gods and spirits? Is magic just another aspect of reality like physics and chemistry? Understanding the fundamental nature of the wondrous in your story world lets you extrapolate its impact across every part of your narrative.

>> **What characters or legendary figures are closely tied to those fantastic origins?** Who are the famous people or creatures in your world that the average person thinks of when they think of the fantastic? Does your world have a Merlin or King Arthur figure? Were there equivalents of the Monkey King or Hercules? These aren't characters in your story, but rather the figures from popular culture that have shaped how your characters think about the fantastic.

>> **What customs, belief systems, or traditions grew out of those fantastic origins?** Define the current state of the fantastic as your story begins. Are there temples to the gods of magic? Feast days and epic poems that honor the heroes of old? Fairy tales that parents use to frighten children into staying clear of the old forest?

Identifying different people and places

Take a thorough look at the people and places that make up the world at the time your story begins. Whether you're creating new kingdoms and nations or populating a small village with curious characters, consider how the different people relate to one another and your world's fantastic elements. One of the most effective and interesting ways to show the audience some important facts about your world is to show how they directly impact the lives of your characters. These questions can help spark your imagination:

>> **What are the most common ways of making a living?** Are most people farmers? Factory workers? Soldiers? Are there a wide variety of trades and professions or just a few ways of scratching out a living? How does the fantastic in your world make these jobs different from their basis in reality counterparts?

>> **Who are the most esteemed and least appreciated people in your world?** What are the social, class, and religious hierarchies and how does the fantastic support and/or undermine them?

>> **How are those who are different from the norm treated?** A society is defined in large part by the people it excludes. When someone doesn't conform to the world's norms, what happens to them? Are they outcast and discriminated against? Appreciated for their eccentricities? Is engaging with specific fantastic elements forbidden or at least frowned upon? What is the penalty for violating spoken and unspoken rules?

Enhancing conflict

Consider how the fantastical elements in your story produce or change the dramatic conflict in your story world. Look at the important and/or interesting conflicts within your basis in reality and work through how the mythic elements make them more wondrous and intense. Consider the following:

>> **What do people get mad about and sometimes even fight over?** Do they struggle for scarce resources? Are there deep political or ideological divisions that drive people apart? Is there a deep-set culture of overblown honor and pride that creates fierce competition? Ensure that your world has things people care enough to fight over, if they have to do so. See how worlds are built for conflict in Chapter 5.

>> **Who benefits most and who suffers most because of this conflict?** Conflicts make for exciting drama because of the stakes involved and the effects they have on your characters. Think about the conflict in terms of how it helps and hinders the people in your world.

>> **How does the fantastic intensify the conflict?** The fantastical elements in your story world should fundamentally change the core conflicts from their consensus reality inspirations. Magic truth spells make lying in politics more difficult. Besieging armies with dragon riders will mean castles are constructed differently. Do your most compelling wonders intertwine with the story's core conflicts?

Chapter **16**

Conjuring Story Magic

Without a doubt, one of the coolest things about a fantasy story is the magic. The scorching burst of a fireball. The whisper-silence of turning invisible. The whooshing delight of levitating up into the clouds.

For many, fantasy *is* magic. It's the essential DNA that makes fantasy fantastic.

Not surprisingly readers have high standards and eager expectations about the magic found in stories. For writers, that means sticking to the Tolkien magic system — or any well-established one — will likely be met with yawns. Readers want power, delight, and novelty with their magic. They also want magic to be consistent as well as relevant to character and conflict, and making those things happen is what this chapter's all about.

Grasping the Role of Magic in Storytelling

Almost every fantasy story has its own version of magic. Many of them have more than one, some have dozens. The unique nature of magic in your story helps set it apart from the crowd and should draw readers deeper into your world.

No matter the specifics, all forms of magic entail one key element: They're a departure from the mundane consensus reality that you and your readers share. Magic bends and breaks the reality everyone takes for granted, and that's both wondrous and terrifying. Magic literally makes the impossible possible and opens a wide vista of dramatic and thematic possibilities for your characters and their story.

Breaking the rules of existence is already interesting, but what makes magic particularly potent is that characters *Do Magic*. Wizards cast spells, heroes don rings of invisibility, necromancers raise skeletons from their crypts. Magic means someone is actively choosing to break the rules of reality in order to get what they want; they project their will onto the world in a way people mired in mundanity can only dream of.

TIP

Think of the magic in your story first and foremost as a way for your characters to get what they want in ways that would be impossible for normal folk. Whether it's your hero's fireballs or the villain's skeleton army, your magic should express the core desires that push these characters into conflict. With this mind-set, all the wondrous spells, monsters, and enchanted swords you create will serve the greater story.

Taking the Reader on a Magical Journey

Magic lets you create stories where characters transcend the everyday world and use impossible powers to face fantastical obstacles with clear and high dramatic stakes. That's great! But breaking reality has as many risks as it does rewards.

Readers respond to magic in different ways at different moments along their journey through your story. When first introduced, magical elements produce a sense of wonder or awe. Climbing up a shear wall like a spider is cool! A 30-foot wall of endless flames surrounding that peaceful village full of innocent farmers is terrifying! The indistinct, green-robed person who's always accompanied by draconic whispers and the scent of sulfur sure does raise some interesting questions.

REMEMBER

As your readers grow accustomed to your story's magic, they begin to make sense of it and how it works in your world. They draw conclusions about the magical elements and imagine possible ways the magic might impact the lives of the main characters, like the following:

>> Climbing like a spider would be a great way for Bella the Bold to steal the Diadem of Light from the citadel vault.

>> Maybe some sort of ice or water spell could quench that ring of fire.

>> Those whispers always grow louder when someone mentions the hero's father, so what does that mean?

Now that they're engaged with the magical implications of your specific choice, readers start to rely on the story knowledge they've acquired from you so far. They're maybe even making predictions about what may happen next, and are certainly developing expectations about what can and can't happen, even in this impossible other world. Now you're in a wonderful but delicate position: You want to keep the story exciting, but you don't want to alienate or confuse the reader with magical developments that entirely undermine everything they've experienced so far.

WARNING

If anything is possible at any moment, the reader never knows what to expect as they journey through your story. Most people enjoy a few great surprises along the way — that's part of the great fun of any experience. But when everything is a surprise, readers can become confused or disoriented. Readers may feel like the author is just going to do whatever random thing they want at any given moment in order to move the plot along some set path, which feels like cheating. Before long, readers will be asking if the magic even matters.

You never want the readers to think anything in your story doesn't matter. *Remember:* Readers know someone wrote this story. They know you made specific decisions all along the way, and if the magic seems to always just do whatever's most "convenient" for the plot, they'll feel the author's hand manipulating them. Instead of feeling awe and wonder at your magical creations, they're thinking about you typing away.

Very, very few authors are more interesting than their stories.

Magic can do anything, but your magic should strive to do something very specific within the world of your story. Magic's role in stories is to heighten drama and tension around characters that audiences care about, not undercut the narrative or confuse the reader for the momentary thrill of a cheap surprise or an easy solution to a loose plot thread.

Making Magic Dramatic (in Every Sense of the Word!)

Magic is most interesting when it's breaking reality in order to make the core dramatic questions of the narrative more compelling. Magic breaks reality, giving authors a tremendous tool for defining the ramifications of any action in their story. Not bound by time, space, physics, or anything else, magic can crystallize dramatic stakes with a supernatural clarity that readers instantly understand and engage with. Use the following techniques to make your magic memorable.

Heightening dramatic stakes with magic

Magic's breaking of reality gives you, the author, a tremendous tool for defining the dramatic cost of any action in your story. Not bound by time, space, physics, or anything else, magic can react to events in a clear and dramatic way that readers instantly understand and engage with.

Cinderella's carriage will turn back into a pumpkin at midnight. Period. No exceptions. Pinocchio's nose grows when he lies, and there's no fooling the magic — it knows when you're lying. Santa Claus knows if you've been bad or good, so for goodness' sake be good if you want presents. Fairy tales thrive in the realm of crystal-clear cause and effect, and so can your fantasy story.

REMEMBER

In today's mundane world, cause and effect are seldom simple and clear when it comes to important, complex matters such as love, politics, society, or the environment. Untold thousands of factors converge to determine whether or not you have a great first date or your candidate wins the election. Romance and political thriller authors usually simplify reality's complexity to some extent, but they're still bound by the plausible. Not so the fantasy author. Magic lets you set very clear, very unrealistic stakes like in these examples:

>> The world will end in seven days unless one brave person can make the ultimate sacrifice.

>> Whoever collects all the seven whatsits can cast the mighty spell of making and become a god.

>> Someone suffers a curse until they find true love, and the magic curse somehow knows true love when it sees it.

>> Breaking your oath to the Star Spirit means instant death, and there's no arguing with or fooling the Star Spirit.

>> Only a weapon forged from dwarven mithril can harm the dreaded Faerie Knight.

You're probably already coming up with dozens of other examples from fantasy stories you love. Although these examples aren't original, they can work fine if you adjust them to fit into your story's magical world.

Being aware of magic's dramatic limitations

Magic should be a tool that can help a character overcome an obstacle, not an always-works solution for every challenge. In the same way you can't break through a brick wall with a bottle opener — a very useful tool in many other situations — however, magic should have its own limitations, too.

You can put interesting limits on your magic in all kinds of ways, but here's one simple way to think about magic in your story:

Magic that solves problems for characters should carry as much dramatic weight as solving the problem with violence.

Fantasy stories are often violent in some way, and even in the most blood-soaked swords and sorcery story, violence usually has severe consequences. A heroic barbarian who cuts down a dozen orcs isn't going to end up with a lot of orc friends. The same goes for a wizard flinging fireballs at goblins. When your hero slays the king even though only they know the monarch is really a vampire, the queen and her children are going to have some serious complaints. Readers and characters understand that violence has consequences.

In your likely more-nuanced tale, using magic must have consequences as well. Magic might mean casting a faerie glamour to get into the throne room or scrying through a crystal ball to find the safe path through the Swamp of Serpents. Although not directly violent, those magical actions should carry with them heavy dramatic resistance from the story's antagonists and side characters.

People resent being duped, and no one likes to be spied on in their serpent swamp, but if villagers suspect you're using magic on them? They'll burn you at the stake. And you can be damned sure the king will summon the Eldritch Inquisitors to haul you off in silver chains as soon as your glamour slips.

This dramatic cost may also be internal to your hero: a physical or psychic toll from bending reality, a loss of self that comes with projecting their thoughts through time and space, or straightforward guilty consciences for invading others' privacy.

Equating magic to violence doesn't make sense for every story, and you need to find the dramatic framework that's best for you and most appropriate for the story. Whatever form the dramatic fallout takes, make sure it strengthens the reader's feeling that magic matters in this story and isn't something to be taken lightly or for granted.

Setting the Rules and Costs of Magic

Almost every fantasy story creates a system of magic with its own rules and limitations, because if magic doesn't have meaningful costs, then everyone would be doing it all the time. Magic wouldn't feel wondrous and awe inspiring, but instead it would risk becoming too unmoored from reality to be relatable. Here we delve deeper into what you need to know about rules and costs when incorporating magic into your story.

Playing by the rules

Rules make magic easier for the reader to understand as they journey into your story. When readers know just the most simple facts about the rules of magic, they become more comfortable and interested, because they start to figure out what to expect — and just as important, what *not* to expect — from magic.

A rule like "spells require years of study to learn" makes sense to readers, who already know about professions like surgeon or electrical engineer or ballet dancer that also demand years of commitment to master. Add in the rule that "casting a spell requires saying special words in a loud, clear voice," and now you can make some reliable assumptions about magic:

>> The people who cast spells are the kinds of people who have the time and access to magical texts and teachers for years at a time.

>> Casting a spell is difficult without someone nearby hearing you, and probably impossible to do if something's stopping you from talking.

Now when the spell-casting hero is caught underwater, you know they won't be able to magic their way out of trouble. When they meet a mysterious stranger with a vast library of magical tomes, it's possible they're a powerful wizard or maybe they just want you to think that. When they see a seemingly buffoonish young person cast a powerful spell, they'll suspect there's more to this kid than meets the eye and wonder what's really going on.

REMEMBER

Rules help you further refine the clear stakes associated with magic in your story. They shape the characters' actions by limiting the ways they can use magic to get what they want.

Sticking to the rules of magic in video and role-playing games

Video games and tabletop role-playing games like *Dungeons & Dragons* (D&D) contain some of the most complicated and binding rules about magic you'll ever see. These thorough rules exist because in a game, players have the power to make choices and impact the story world around them. Making a video game where anything is possible is impossible because someone has to program the game to do each specific thing. Magic has to have very specific limits.

A game of D&D is more like a story people tell together; it has no technical limits beyond those of one's imagination. But a large part of the fun is playing within the rules of the game because game rules are just like dramatic stakes — the clearer they are, the more they matter to the story. D&D players want what happens to their characters to matter in the shared story, and for most of them that means triumphing over adversity within the rules of the game.

Magic systems in games don't often translate well directly to other kinds of storytelling. A game rule might say "Casting a fireball costs 10 magic points," and the player knows they only have 15 magic points, so that's just one fireball. Explode it wisely. But you can abstract this simple formula into other fiction by describing it in terms of mental and physical exhaustion or connection to the energies from the mystical plane of fire or whatever makes sense for your magic. Even this simple translation of game magic into a story conveys a sense of cost that clearly limits your spellcaster's options and thus heightens drama.

Assigning costs to your story's magic — Precious Things

Points are useful for a game, but stories are about people trying to overcome obstacles and get what they want. A character's struggle to achieve their goals should always come at a price, and magic should demand some pretty high prices in return for breaking the rules of reality.

Here's an example. "Selling your soul" is now a commonplace metaphor that has its most famous precedent in the story of Faust selling his immortal soul to the devil in return for knowledge and rewards in the mortal world. There've been countless variations on this theme, and you can likely come up with your own unique version of this devil's bargain and write a good story based on it. Your characters don't have to sell their souls for every spell, but they need to pay a cost with real dramatic weight.

TIP

Assign costs to your story's magic that directly affect what's most important to your characters. This simple exercise — referred to as *Precious Things* — can help you define your magical costs in terms that directly relate to the dramatic questions in your story:

1. **Write down two specific things that are precious to your main character.**

These categories should be relatively broad and have specific implications for the character's life. For example, if you chose "Love," then the character should have a deep love for someone in their life (whether requited or not). Some classic examples of precious things:

- Life

- Love

- Money

- Happiness

- Friendship

- Family

- Possessions

- Memories

- Freedom

- Faith

2. **Repeat the process for the story's antagonist or any significant side character.**

   Try to find something different from the precious thing you picked for your protagonist if doing so makes sense.

3. **Imagine a system of magic that requires paying costs related to *both* of the two precious things.**

   This dual cost brings the conflict between your characters into the center of the story world's magic system, ensuring every spell pulls at their emotional core while breaking reality for their immediate benefit.

Imagine that your protagonist finds love precious and your antagonist cares most about money. What's a magical cost that pulls at both? Perhaps spells require rare and expensive ingredients to cast, and the casting ritual itself fouls the magician's temperament so much that loved ones can't stand to be around them. Your protagonist's relationship then becomes more strained the more they use magic to fight their foe, whereas the already unpleasant antagonist does whatever they deem necessary to grab the gold needed to cast that final ritual of revelation.

This exercise is just one of many ways to approach making magic work for rather than against your story's drama. It's an example of keeping a core principle of fantasy writing front and center in your mind: All this magic is for the story, and the story is about characters that audiences hope and fear for struggling to get what they want.

Magic is there to make the struggle more wondrous and exciting, not to make things easier.

REMEMBER

Forging Enchanting Artifacts and Objects — Items Designed for Magic

Spellcasting is just one way to insert magic into your story. You characters can just as easily use a magic item to break consensus reality, whether it's a hunter who wields an ogre-slaying spear, a magistrate whose necklace turns ice-cold when a lie is told within 30 paces, or a hobbit burglar who finds a mysterious ring of invisibility deep within a mountain. In each case, the writer carefully chooses the magic item to help the character do the thing in the story that they must do. The hunter must slay monsters, the magistrate must find hidden truths, and the burglar must be sneaky.

In video games, it's not uncommon for characters to have piles of magic goodies. In a story, though, it's far more memorable and special to craft items to both characterize someone and serve story goals. With that in mind, dole out magic spells and magic items as you see fit while staying in alignment with your intended level of fantastic elements in your story. See Chapter 14 for more details on how to make thoughtful choices about the spectrum of magic between Pure Fantasy and All Real.

REMEMBER

An item's magic shouldn't be chosen willy-nilly, either. Tie the magic directly into aspects of the story or relate it to the world (and perhaps its inherent conflicts). Every part of a story should feel connected and unified. Since magic is a big part of what makes fantasy so wonderful, magic items should be as thoughtfully designed as the world's creatures, characters, and setting.

Here we look at some ways that magic items can connect more effectively with story elements and concerns.

Magic items as objects of desire

Plenty of stories have a *MacGuffin*, which is a valuable object that both the protagonist and the antagonist (and perhaps every manner of person in between) desperately yearn to acquire. A magic item serves that role quite well. Often these are artifact-level items, such as the Holy Grail, Tolkien's One Ring, or the Philosopher's Stone. When magic as powerful as this is used, these items create seismic effects that can profoundly change lives and even level mountains, destroy kingdoms, or wipe out civilizations. Given that, who wouldn't work hard to obtain such power?

Whether a magic item is an actual MacGuffin or simply something your character desires that is part of the story's primary plot, take the time to think through your magic item. Ask yourself the following questions:

>> What does your character know — or think they know — about it?

>> What kind of emotional value does it hold for your character?

>> What intriguing qualities does it actually have?

>> How would you describe the magic item using all five senses?

>> Is it hidden? What kind of clues/research are required to locate it? If it's not hidden, where is it?

>> How will it affect your character if they obtain it?

Magic items as character traits

In the simplest of definitions, a *magic item* allows for fantastic and wondrous actions. From a warrior's heirloom magic shield to a demon hunter's family crucifix to Green Lantern's awesome ring, magic items can be fundamental to a character's identity and integral to the way they pursue their story goals. If any of these characters lost their iconic magic item, it would radically change them for the worse. It'd probably hurt them as much emotionally or spiritually as magically.

If a character has a distinctive magic item, answer these questions:

>> How did they acquire or make it?

>> What is it and what does it look like?

>> What powers does it have and what costs does using its magic incur?

>> How does the item give the character new options for facing the story's obstacles and antagonists?

>> What would happen if it were destroyed, stolen, or misplaced?

All the preceding questions also apply to a new magic item the protagonist happens to come across in the course of the plot. These new acquisitions may not be as near and dear to the character's heart, but they should have intimate ties to the story's plot.

Magic items as obstacles

Magic items may also serve as an obstacle or antagonistic force. A cursed item may compel a character to flip a coin to decide anything. A warhammer imbued with the power of speech may insist on shouting insults at inopportune moments, which brings in every troublemaker, thief, and monster within miles. What do you do in these situations? The item is too valuable to cast off, and the magic itself may not allow you to just dump it in a trash heap. In fact, it may even punish you for doing so! A magic item could be far more than a nuisance. It may have abilities, secrets, or goals that make it far more formidable than a mundane physical obstacle like a dropped portcullis, spiked pit, or pool of acid that looks like water. It could even be linked to the primary antagonist in hidden or overt ways.

Think through your answers to the following questions to create a magic item that could prove to be a major problem for your protagonist:

» What does your character most fear? How could the item use that to its advantage?

» Does the item have the ability to influence others? Which ones? To what effect? Are they aware of the influence?

» Can the item change form? In what circumstances? To what other forms?

» If the item had vampiric properties, what could it covertly "suck" from its owner? Health? Happiness? Hope?

» Does the item have a previous owner that would be furiously jealous about its new owner?

» Is the item illegal or stolen? Is the user aware of this baggage? Will powerful, no-nonsense authorities get involved and insist on punishment?

Magic items as characters

Magic items can have magic so special that the item has developed a level of sentience. For a writer, this narrative magic allows something inanimate to literally become another character. Having another companion/rival/foil/friend for your main character is almost always a good thing. Just think about the flying carpet in *Aladdin*. It can't speak, yet it clearly expresses itself via action, movement, and gesture. As Aladdin's companion, it's funny, unique, and memorable.

The same thing can happen in your story if you anthropomorphize a magic item. Doing so, however, brings up a host of questions. Your answers can help make your intelligent magic item unique, fun, and potentially quite useful in terms of advancing the plot. Consider the answers to these questions:

» How does it communicate? If through speech, does it speak the same language as its user? Does it always sing or speak in rhymes? What about telepathy, empathy, dreams, or physical gesture?

» What type of personality does it have?

» Does it have an agenda? Is the agenda hidden or overt? Does it go against the interests of the user?

» What magic does it have, if any, beyond being sentient?

» How did it become sentient? Is it haunted by the essence of a victim or perhaps a previous owner? Did it become self-aware as the side effect of a powerful spell cast upon it or in its vicinity?

» Is it always sentient? Does it need to be "fed" or is it on some type of mystical "timer"?

Magic items as worldbuilding elements

How the characters think about and use magic items in your world is a great way to show audiences magic's role in the wider world. A farmer's never-dull sickle could be a prized family heirloom or standard issue for every fieldworker in the shire. In a world that's dense with magic, probably every middle-class home has an infinite water jug and a coldbox in the kitchen. In a world where water is precious and rare, a single infinite water jug could make someone ruler of a whole city.

Ask yourself some basic questions about the magic items in your world:

>> How does the item's origin reflect specific fantastic elements of the culture? Does its magic come from the gods? From the artificer's guild? From every two-electrum-piece enchanter's stall in the bazaar?

>> How is the item used in the world's core conflicts? How do they make conflicts more fantastical or wondrous (for good or ill)?

>> Is the item a luxury, a necessity, or quite the rarity? What do people in the world who don't have access to items think about it? Are they envious? Wary?

>> How has the use of the magic item changed over the centuries? Is it a relic of a bygone golden era or has magic developed over the years? How does this version compare to one made in the past?

Whatever answers you come up with, let the everyday norm reveal the reality of how magic works and what it means in your story world.

Chapter **17**

Forming Really Fantastic (and Fantastically Real) Monsters

Along with magic, weird and wondrous monsters are an iconic element of fantasy fiction. Whether you're writing about the classics like dragons and giants or creating entirely original creatures to stalk the streets of your setting, a truly menacing monster can make your story stand out in the crowded fantasy fiction landscape. This chapter delves into what makes a monster work within a fantasy context and provides tools to help fine-tune your ferocious fiends for maximum effect.

Understanding What Monsters Are

A *monster* is a dangerous, nonhuman creature. It can be wholly imaginary, like a dragon or an extremely angry pixie. It can be an animal from nature that behaves in a story-relevant, dangerous manner. The shark from *Jaws* isn't an imaginary creature, but it's definitely a monster, in large part because it behaves with narrative purpose in a way no real shark ever would.

The word "monster" comes from the same linguistic roots as "demonstrate," and "remind." In its original usage, "monster" meant a sign or omen from the gods; a malformed newborn animal was seen as a portent of bad news and was therefore considered monstrous. We bring up this fun fact not just because we're college professors, but because it's a useful reminder of the monster's role in culture: It's part of a story about how the world works. Monsters are meant to mean something.

Here we investigate how you create a monster that is truly story-worthy.

What makes a monster a monster

In order to be a monster, it has to meet two criteria:

>> **It has to be dangerous.** This part is key. Monsters have the potential to cause harm, which means they're something for others to worry about. If it's not dangerous, then it's instead an animal or a creature or a being. It can be strange and magical, but if your sentient floating fluff ball that giggles when it hears music can't seriously threaten someone, it's not a monster. To be a monster is to be threatening.

>> **It has to be nonhuman.** The monster exists in contrast to the human experience. In some ways it may be more than human (huge, strong, fire-breathing, ethereal) and in other ways all too human (angry, jealous, greedy, hungry). Chapter 11 in the Sci-fi section goes into lots of detail about making aliens that feel nonhuman in ways that enhance your story's plot and themes.

Monsters serve the story

The big question to keep asking yourself about your monsters is, what do they mean to the story? Why are they here and how do they impact the characters? When you're creating a monster, you can't have monsters in isolation from the rest of the narrative. The fearsome dragon Smaug from *The Hobbit* and the loveable, cute dragon Toothless from *How to Train Your Dragon* aren't interchangeable. Yes, they both breathe fire and fly, but they don't have much else in common except that each is the right dragon for their respective stories.

Monsters can mean a lot to your story's protagonists. Your story is (ideally) about characters the audience hopes and fears for trying to accomplish some dramatic goal. Monsters threaten to stop those characters from getting what they want. That's their most basic meaning, but there are lots of different ways to refine your monster's specific role, depending on your storytelling needs, including the following:

>> **Monsters can inspire the story.** Sometimes a cool monster idea provides the kernel of inspiration from which the whole story grows. This is actually

pretty common, and if you have a mind for monster-making, embrace it. But your six-tailed giant scorpion isn't a story all on its own. As soon as possible, create compelling characters to face that monster because the story is still going to be first and foremost about them and their struggles. Identify what the most dangerous aspects of your monster are, then imagine the kind of person who the monster would threaten most. That's the kind of person you want as a protagonist.

>> **Monsters can define dramatic stakes.** The classic monster use case is an overwhelmingly dangerous monster that threatens to destroy someone or something the characters care about. The heroes must confront and defeat it or else disaster and tragedy will ensue. But overcoming the fearsome beast seems at first impossible. Here, the monster embodies the dramatic question of the story: How will the protagonists vanquish this daunting foe? Through perseverance, intelligence, bravery, and maybe some guile, the heroes work their way through a series of scenes until they're finally able to face the monster and resolve the story's central question.

>> **Monsters can create obstacles.** Not every monster defines its story. In many cases, a monster is one challenge amongst many that the heroes face in their journey to the finale. Game monsters in particular serve this role. In a classic D&D or computer roleplaying game dungeon crawl, players battle through room after room of kobolds, ogres, and gelatinous cubes, most of whom exist only to challenge the player's skill and test their luck with the dice. All that hacking and slashing is more fun to play than it is to read or watch. More narrative forms of media like books and movies work better with fewer obstacle monsters that are each a unique challenge and have some specific purpose in the story.

Monstrous obstacles don't just get in the heroes' way, they also allow for the hero to show the audience what they're made of. They get to admire the heroes' clever tactics, amazing spellcraft, or prowess with a battle axe. The audience may also get a chance to sympathize with the heroes' fears, worry about their vulnerabilities, and feel sorrow when the price for victory is too high.

>> **Monsters can be characters.** Monsters aren't always mindless delivery systems for gnashing teeth and rending claws. Many are compelling characters, fully fleshed out with wants, needs, and sinister plans. Monsters with strong personalities who can taunt, tease, threaten, and talk with the protagonists add emotional depth to your story and create social and psychological threats on top of the physical danger they might pose. For example, the loathsome hell prince overseeing a Los Angeles crime syndicate can be sexy and charming at a fundraiser for the mayor's re-election campaign. An enemy with such powerful friends is dangerous in ways beyond his infernal magical powers and will require a more nuanced strategy from the protagonists.

MONSTROUS OBSTACLES

This simple exercise can help put you in the right mind-set to create monsters that serve as interesting obstacles that stand in the way of your protagonists and their goals. If it helps, think of this as a game. Play it as often as you need to in order to help out your story (and your monster-making!). Do the following:

- Define a specific, short-term goal that characters might have, such as traveling through lonely mountains, picking fruit from a grove of apple trees, learning a secret from a rare book, or telling an authority figure some vital news.

- Think of reasons that someone or something would want the characters to fail at that goal.

- Create a monster that embodies that desire to stop the characters. What dangerous things does that monster do to try to stop the characters?

Giving a monster character and personality makes them more relatable as foes. At a certain level, audiences see themselves in them because they think and feel in ways they can understand. The dragon Smaug in *The Hobbit* is in his own way very relatable, despite living for centuries in a cave on top of a mountain of stolen treasure. Because he talks with the hero Bilbo, the audience learns of his vanity, his pride, and his possessiveness.

No matter what other meanings monsters have in your story, they always serve the scene. Make your monsters dangerous and threatening in the way that makes sense for your story and characters. Monsters that are overwhelmingly powerful are hard to tell a story about. If the threat is too weak and the hero can win with ease, it's not satisfying either. Don't be seduced by the idea of making a monster so incredibly dangerous and cool that you end up relying on impossible coincidence or monsters acting idiotic in order to let your heroes win.

Making Monsters

The myriad monsters of Greek mythology have provided dangerous threats to protagonists in tens of thousands of fantasy stories over the past few millennia. The many-headed hydra, the majestic Pegasus, the confounding sphinx, and the petrifying Medusa are instantly identifiable and clearly fantastical beings. These were creatures of religion, myth, and legend, the kind of impossible monsters that inhabit epic poems and classical dramas and look great on the side of a fancy piece of pottery.

However, some of the other famous monsters associated with Greek myth weren't considered fantastical at the time. They were assumed to be as natural as lions or horses. In her tremendously fascinating book, *The First Fossil Hunters: Dinosaurs, Mammoths, and Myth in Greek and Roman Times* (Princeton University Press), historian Adrienne Mayor makes a strong case that creatures like griffins, cyclopes, and giants were based on misinterpreted reconstructions of dinosaur and mammoth fossils. The Greeks could see the bones, so of course they weren't imaginary beasts. Another example is the supposedly human-faced, man-eating manticore, which was said to live in India and is almost certainly nothing more fantastical than a distorted-by-distance description of a tiger. *Note:* Being eaten by a tiger is still pretty scary, even if it doesn't have a human face.

Our colleague, acclaimed fantasy artist Sean Andrew Murray, gives a great presentation on monster design (something he knows *a lot* about). He talks about how different stories generate different kinds of monsters. Sometimes a fantasy setting benefits from including monsters that have anatomies, behaviors, and life-cycles that seem to conform to the laws of biology and physics. These more realistic monsters are like the ancient Greek idea of a manticore or griffin — weird and scary, but part of the natural world. Other monsters emerge from the magical or spiritual parts of the story world and are designed first and foremost to provoke an emotional response, physics and biology be damned. They are creatures of nightmares or the underworld with magical powers like Medusa or the ever-multiplying hydra.

Let the following ideas and tip guide you in building a better monster for the purposes of your story.

A MONSTER FROM WHOSE PERSPECTIVE?

In Chapter 14, we present the three main points of view through which characters and audiences encounter the fantastic in your story: portal, immersive, and intrusive. Which fantastical point of view you use in a given monster encounter should impact how and what characters perceive monsters. A character going through a portal to another world may see everything as a potential monster, whereas anything from another world intruding into the audience's consensus reality could seem monstrous. Use the point of view to create a sense of dread and mystery around it and heighten the monster's dramatic impact.

Making your monster realistic or fantastic

Chapter 14 lays out the fantasy/reality spectrum we use to think about the levels of realism and fantasy in fantasy stories. This tool can help you think through your monster design as well. Is it a purely biological, semi-plausible monster that feels grounded in reality? Is it a weird, maybe even surreal thing conjured by magic or bred in a faerie realm? Or, just as often, is it some mix of the two, a monster with realistic and fantasy elements incorporated into it, like a mostly mundane vicious hound who also breathes fire?

The following explores the idea of realistic or fantastic monsters a bit further:

>> **More realistic monsters:** They mostly follow the basic natural patterns of creatures in the real world. They eat, sleep, reproduce, thrive in specific ecosystems, and generally conform to the laws of physics, biology, and chemistry. Realistic monsters are fundamentally much more relatable and create less cognitive dissonance for audiences. Their threat is more grounded, and it's easier to understand cause and effect when they clash with the protagonists. Sure, it has scales, six legs, and a spiked tail, but it still bleeds when you stab it with a spear.

>> **More fantastic monsters:** They aren't designed to be plausible or even possible; they're meant to invoke feelings of fear, awe, or wonder. They're direct expressions of your fantasy world's breaks from consensus reality. By ignoring the laws of biology and physics, your fantastical monsters can look and act in strange and terrifying ways. They can also integrate human characteristics like speech, tool use, and complex social interactions not usually found in the natural world.

Distinct aspects of your monster's design can exist somewhere different on the scale from fantasy to reality. The following section helps you find that balance.

Defining your monster's characteristics

No matter how realistic or fantastic your monsters need to be for your story, they all share common characteristics. Find the balance that works for your story, but make sure you give full creative consideration to all of them.

Chapter 20 provides another approach to monster making, one rooted in the emotions the monsters produce in your audience and their role as metaphors in your story. That chapter works well with this one, so for an ultra-comprehensive monster-making methodology, make sure to read that material as well.

Let the following help define your monster more clearly:

>> **Origin:** The monster comes from somewhere, so where *does* it come from? This question is hugely important because it sets the basis for the monster's entire existence. Ask yourself these additional questions to get a better feel for your monster's origin:

- What forces determined its nature? Is it the product of natural evolution (or whatever magical alternative to evolution exists in your story world)? Is it a creation by some god? Is it a god or spirit? Or did some alchemist brew it up in a lab?

- Was it created with a specific purpose in mind? Whether it's to be the fittest survivor or guard the gates of the underworld, does the monster have some fundamental need that drives its actions? What things might divert it from that purpose?

- Can the monster reproduce? If so, how does that work? Do these monsters breed and give birth to more of their kind? Can a necromancer conjure up more of them with a spell? Do they grow naturally in toadstool rings during a lunar eclipse?

>> **Appearance:** How much detail you need for your monster's appearance depends on the medium. A movie or video game monster goes through multiple rounds of visual development. Monsters in prose are sometimes described in minute detail, sometimes with just a few words. No matter what level of detail you're using, focus first on the aspects of the monster's looks that make it important to the story. These questions can help you focus on the monster's appearance:

- What's fantastical about its appearance? If you're inventing a monster instead of using a real animal, what about it makes it cool and special? How do you think it will produce a sense of wonder in your audience, even if it's just a little wow?

- What about the monster would someone be most worried about when they see it for the first time? What about its appearance seems dangerous? Or does its cuddly exterior hide a killer within?

- How big is it? If you had to liken it to a real-world lifeform, what would be approximately the same size and shape? Or what mix of lifeforms would be close?

- How does it sound, smell, and look? From the patterns on its hide to the stench of its breath, think about all the ways the monster can assault the senses as well as the characters.

>> **Physiology:** The monster inhabits and interacts with the world in a specific way. Does it have muscles and bones that dictate how fast it can pounce or how high it can fly? Or is it ethereal like a ghost or spirit? Maybe it's an elemental being of pure fire or a psychic creature that levitates by will alone. Consider these additional questions:

- How does it move? Does it walk, crawl, slither, or fly like a familiar animal or does it float along on a cloud of aether? Is it fast or slow, lithe or bullish?

- How does it sense the world around it? Does it have the nose of a bloodhound? Can it see in the dark? The fantastic opens up all kinds of senses that are impossible and dramatically exciting. Can it see backward and forward in time? Is it drawn to the corrupted aura of sinners? Does it hear any conversation where someone mentions its true name?

- What does the monster need to survive? Fresh meat? The souls of innocents? A period of dormancy during the full moon? Monsters that need food, air, and water like real-world animals will need all those things on a regular basis, and you should know where those things come from in your story world.

>> **Mentality:** The monster's mind and how it relates to sentient beings is more complicated than a simple intelligence rating. There are different kinds of intelligence, different ways of knowing and thinking about the world. From the instincts of an animal to the divine perspective of an angry demigod, the monster's mind-set governs its behavior and the way it threatens the protagonists. Ask yourself these additional questions:

- Is it part of a community? Do these monsters live in packs like wolves? Do they have a shared sense of identity with others of their kind or with other monsters in general? Do they have whole civilizations with politics, religion, and an economy? Or are they isolated loners, lying in wait in the heart of the deep, dark forest?

- What drives the monster to action? What does it want from the world and what's it willing to do to get it? Does it just want fresh meat, or does it want to spread its master's evil influence? Does it have a hated nemesis or natural foe? Is it bent on world domination? World destruction?

- How much foresight does it have? A wild animal's instincts make most of its choices for it. Many monsters don't care about or even understand the idea of a future. How much of a long-term plotter and planner is your creature? Can it spin elaborate schemes or is it all about attacking whoever crosses its threshold?

- How does it communicate with others and can it communicate with the story's main characters? Pet owners know there are lots of ways an animal can communicate without language. How does your monster get its point across? Angry growls and pleased purring? Psychic emanations of pure emotions? Long speeches about its evil plans?

>> **Environment:** For some monsters where the monster lives, hunts, and performs monstrous duties could be its natural environment. For others malevolent forces may have been placed them there to guard something valuable or kill someone specific. Consider these questions:

- What kind of environment does the monster dwell in? Is it a fetid swamp, a dank dungeon, or the magic crystal in an arch-mage's staff?

- What effect does the monster have on the environment? Is it an apex predator in the forest? Does it spread corruption across the city neighborhood where it has established its lair? How can the environment help tell the monster's story?

- What effect does the environment have on the monster? Is it limited to certain types of places like underwater or in complete darkness? If something happens to the environment, what happens to the monster?

- Why would anyone go there? Is there some reason people might venture into the monster's territory? Does it also have valuable resources? Do local teens dare each other to check out the creepy old mansion? Does the monster try and lure people in or keep them out?

Chapter 8 offers an approach to thinking about locations in your story as story spaces where the environment does as much storytelling as the characters or monsters who dwell in it. We list four common types of story spaces that have specific and useful narrative purposes: obstacles, reactive spaces, contested spaces, and refuges. Consider each of these four types through the lens of your monsters and how they enhance and deepen the monster's dramatic function in your story:

EXERCISE

A RANDOM DRAGON GENERATOR

Dragons are the iconic fantasy monster, a genre staple born from the myths and legends of cultures all over the world. There are so many kinds of dragons, about the only thing they have in common across all their interpretations is that they're big and magical and wondrous (most of the time).

This exercise generates a random dragon as a way to help you to consider the different monster characteristics detailed in this chapter and how they may combine fantastical and realistic elements in a host of different ways. Use a four-sided die or a random number generator to select one characteristic from each category.

(continued)

(continued)

Origin

1. It naturally evolved in the environment along with other creatures.

2. It's an expression of a pure elemental force like fire or wind.

3. The gods created it for a specific purpose.

4. Powerful wizards and religious leaders transcend by turning into dragons.

Appearance (here focused on size)

1. It's the size of the real-world's biggest alligators, 15 or so feet long.

2. It's as big as the great dinosaurs like a T-rex.

3. It's as enormous as a whole town or even a mountain.

4. It shifts in form from a normal human to dragon, one of the preceding sizes (your choice).

Physiology (here focused on flight)

1. The dragon can't fly at all and doesn't have wings.

2. The dragon flies in a somewhat plausible manner, with huge wings and a small body like a pterodactyl.

3. It has glorious wings and a massive body, allowing it to fly in a way that must have some magic behind it.

4. Although it has no wings, it still flies and is undeniably a magical creature.

Mentality

1. It's bestial, not more intelligent or ambitious than an angry animal.

2. It's intelligent and lives alone, concerned only with its own desires.

3. It's part of a larger community of dragons that interact and even come into conflict with one another.

4. It's a lone divine being with a spiritual outlook on the world rather than material concerns.

Environment

1. It dwells in an inaccessible swamp, far from any humans.

2. It lurks in a cavern deep beneath a major city.

3. It nests high atop a mountain peak, on the border between two kingdoms.

4. It resides in the astral plane, removed from the mortal realms but coming into their world for its own reasons.

Take the dragon you've rolled up and think about what kind of hero it would be a great obstacle or antagonist for. Try rolling a second dragon and imagine what kind of fantasy world would have both types of dragons in it. What do these two different monsters imply about the wider world they come from? Consider a story where the two dragons are aligned with one another and another story where they're opposed.

Rolling a random dragon from these five lists can create hundreds of different kinds of dragons. That should give you some idea of how thinking through all the possible ways your monster may balance the fantastic and the real and how that variety can help you make your monsters both original and perfectly suited for your story.

5

Horror: Journeys into Fear

Find emotional connections to make stories that haunt your audiences' imagination.

Trust well-trod shadowy paths to shape your own scary stories.

Brew up monsters from archetypes and terrifying creatures you already know (and love).

Make monsters a manifestation of fear, symbols, and themes in society.

Use setting to build the imagery, mood, and atmosphere of dread.

Chapter **18**

Creating Dread, Fear, and Terror

In this chapter, we dive deep into the spooky spectrum of thoughts and feelings that horror stories play with. For the pure horror story writers out there, we offer a tomb-load of tips and techniques for terrifying your audience. But this horror chapter plays very well with the sections about sci-fi and fantasy, and we occasionally refer you to specific chapters (such as Chapter 11 on aliens and 17 on fantasy monsters) for more ideas about incorporating the otherworldly and futuristic into your horror fiction.

Sci-fi stories are about people in other possible worlds and fantasy stories are about people in impossible other worlds. Horror stories are about scaring the @#!% out of people in any world. Horror stories aren't a genre so much as a set of feelings like dread, fear, pity, and revulsion, sometimes all at once. The source of those fears may be some science thing gone wrong, some ancient magical thing unleashed, or a "normal" person with a hankering for hunting humans. Where sci-fi and fantasy provoke questions and play with ideas, horror goes straight for the primal, disturbing feelings deep inside everyone.

Imagining the Worst about Everything

Fear is a powerful emotion. Philosopher Edmund Burke wrote in 1757 that, "No passion so effectually robs the mind of all its powers of acting and reasoning as fear. For fear being an apprehension of pain or death, it operates in a manner that resembles actual pain . . . . Whatever is fitted in any sort to excite the ideas of pain and danger, that is to say, whatever is in any sort terrible, or is conversant about terrible objects, or operates in a manner analogous to terror, is a source of the sublime; that is, it is productive of the strongest emotion which the mind is capable of feeling."

In other words, feeling afraid of pain is so intense because it's close to feeling actual pain. Anything that scares you, even just a spooky story, produces an emotional and physical response that's uncomfortably akin to actual harm.

There's science to back up Burke's insight. Scholar Mathias Clasen summarizes the evolutionary roots of fear in his book *Why Horror Seduces* (Oxford University Press). He says that humans naturally assume there's some sort of agency behind every event. The spooky noises coming from the dark forest beyond the campfire may or may not be a hungry wolf, but if it is, you're in trouble. Best to prepare yourself just in case. Evolution has given everyone very powerful imaginations that assume the worst about the unknown. Those powerful imaginations help humans survive, but as a side effect they mean people are very good at being scared by entirely imaginary threats. Those deep-rooted instincts on guard against saber-toothed tigers lurking in the tall grass don't care if the ominous growl is coming from a real animal or a fictional monster.

WARNING

Scaring folks is actually pretty easy, which is why cheap jump scares in horror movies get your heart racing. But audiences aren't going to stay engaged for a series of cheap jump scares over the course of a whole story. Those kinds of thrills are easier to find on a rollercoaster. You want to broaden the kinds of fearful emotions your stories provoke, keeping audiences wondering and worrying and curious until the very end. The rest of this chapter gives you techniques to do just that.

Equipping your toolchest — The horror writer's tools

You want to freak some people out. Great. As a horror writer, you have a diverse set of tools at your disposal for provoking fearful feelings. Each of the following is useful in its own way, but the real scares come when you combine them effectively:

>> **Characters:** As we say repeatedly throughout this book and will keep saying until the Grim Reaper's skeletal hand finally grabs us, great stories are about

characters: Characters who audiences hope and fear for. Characters who want something and take action to get what they want. Characters who are going to get into and maybe not get out of a lot of trouble. It's vital that your tale of terror features engaging characters who the audience can identify with or feel sympathy for. These characters are often the point of view through which audiences experience all the horror, although the audience knows at least one thing the character doesn't: that this is a horror story.

>> **Feelings:** A wider spectrum of emotions play important roles in horror stories, which we get into in the next section. Audiences take their cue from the characters when it comes to what to feel in any given dramatic situation. Even though the characters are certainly more terrified of the monster's talons then the audience, when the protagonist screams and runs for their life, the audience can easily sympathize even though those claws are safely sealed inside the pages of the story. Use your characters' responses to guide your audience's feelings throughout the story.

>> **Imagery:** Mood and atmosphere play key roles in building dread. If you're writing for a visual medium like film, TV, or games, storytellers benefit from lighting, costume, sets, sounds, and music doing a tremendous amount of work building tension. In pure prose, your descriptive language and details have to carry all that weight, but you have the audience's imagination helping you. The human brain is evolved to worry about hidden dangers in the darkness and to recoil in disgust at certain unpleasant sights. Deploy provocative imagery fine-tuned to the specific feelings you want to provoke in each scene.

>> **Mysteries:** Fear of the unknown ranks right at the top of powerful feelings that drive audiences to keep reading or watching. What's hiding in the dark? Who killed the old professor? What do those strange symbols mean? Is that blood!?!? The questions raised by the unknown trigger anticipation and curiosity, and audiences start to imagine the worst. They'll endure a lot of anxiety and discomfort in order to find out what's really going on and whether or not the story's characters will survive learning the truth.

>> **Revelations:** It is blood! The unknown is scary, but trepidatiously peeking under the bed only satisfies audiences when they discover what's lurking down there. These revelations are key turning points in your plot. The moment itself might be scary — there's a deadly cobra with glowing yellow eyes — and thus produce strong emotional reactions, but a good revelation also has an intellectual side. The characters and the audiences now know something new that raises more questions and implications. How did the snake get there? Why were its eyes glowing yellow? Does it have anything to do with that bizarre yellow symbol the protagonist found earlier? New unknowns naturally lead to new and more terrifying revelations.

A formula for fear

Characters are at the center of your story, and both their feelings and desires focus the feelings and interests of your audience. The imagery provides the vital setting for those characters to take action in, with details, mood, and atmosphere reinforcing the characters' feelings and manipulating the audience's experience. But the combination of mystery and revelation is what drives the plot forward, an ever-escalating cycle of deeper mysteries and more dire revelations that arouses the audience's curiosity and compels them to see the story through to the end.

In his 1927 book, *Supernatural Horror in Literature,* influential and problematic horror author H.P. Lovecraft wrote, "The oldest and strongest emotion of mankind is fear, and the oldest and strongest kind of fear is fear of the unknown." The quote is famous to the point of ubiquity in horror-writing circles because it gets to a fundamental truth not just about horror stories but about life. The unknown makes folks curious, and curiosity fires their very active imaginations. It only takes a little bit of mystery within a specific context to send the audience's imaginations spinning down one emotional path or another. Is the context colorful wrapping paper and people singing happy birthday? The recipient is excited to open that unknown box! Is the context dark stains on a dented cardboard box left on your doorstep in the middle of the night? The audience can easily imagine all kinds of horrors lurking inside.

In these sections we offer you a three-part formula for fear designed to make the most of an audience's overactive imagination.

Part 1: The Unknown

The Unknown is the first part of the formula for fear. Start with a mystery. The simpler the mystery, the better as you begin. You can start subtle and quiet or begin with a bang, but your opening unknown should be something the audience can easily understand and engage with, such as:

>> What's that shape moving out there in the dark?

>> Where is that child's laughter coming from?

>> Who is this shadowy stranger knocking on the door?

>> Why was this poor soul being brutally murdered?

Remember, most of the time your audience knows this is a horror story, even if the characters don't. They're primed to think the worst of each unknown.

Part 2: Anticipation

Give your characters and your audience some time and reason to brood and worry about what could possibly be going on with the second part. The longer the question goes unanswered, the greater the dread as the audience's imagination raises worse and worse possible answers. What's out in the dark?

>> An animal?

>> A wild animal?

>> A wolf?

>> A stranger?

>> A thief?

>> A killer?

WARNING

The period of anticipation usually features characters investigating the mystery in some way, their own sense of unease building as they explore possible answers. Sometimes only the audience knows something mysterious is afoot and must watch, helpless, as unknown danger stalks the hapless hero. But don't leave everyone anticipating too long or anticipation turns to frustration or, even worse, boredom. Sooner rather than later, the unknown becomes known.

Part 3: Revelation

Revelation is the third, but not necessarily the final, part of the fear formula. A revelation is something that changes the story dynamics in a radical and important way. It can come from the reveal of a monster or the deciphering of a clue or the opening of a basement door. Here are a few examples:

>> The call is coming from inside the house.

>> The character is acting so strange because a demon's possessing them.

>> The house is haunted by the ghosts of past lovers.

>> The best friend is actually the killer.

>> There's a big freaking monster under the bed!

After the Unknown has been revealed, anticipations dissipate and are replaced with surprise, alarm, disgust, or some other powerful emotion (we explore them in greater detail in the section, "Feeling Fearful Feels" later in this chapter). The characters must in some way deal with the new development, which may raise new questions or may try to kill them.

Repeat

Repeat the three parts of the formula over the course of your story, each time upping the stakes or changing story modes or both. Introduce a new Unknown that's more alarming than the one you just resolved. Switch from solving mysteries to running from monsters or trying to convince the cops there really is a vampire living in the middle school's basement. The cycle of the Unknown leading to anticipation exploding into revelation creates an upward spiral of tension until the story reaches its climax.

Providing climax and catharsis

One of the really great advantages of a horror story is that audiences can't ever expect a happy ending for the protagonists. Maybe the hero will triumph, maybe they'll die horribly. Horror audiences can walk away satisfied either way. Horror shares this characteristic with dramatic tragedies, and both kinds of stories are capable of providing a feeling of catharsis. Aristotle uses the word in passing in his *Poetics,* but the concept of *catharsis* meaning a purging or cleansing of its audience's feelings of pity and fear has become a foundational concept in the study of literature and philosophy.

Professor Joe Sachs of St. John's College explores how Aristotle's insights on how catharsis works in horror (`https://iep.utm.edu/aris-poe/`). He suggests that horror movies help purge all the scary stuff in real life by focusing the audience's fears on an external, faintly ridiculous fictional story. For a moment at least, they've faced and conquered a fear, stripping it of some of its power over them. In that way horror is like medicine, and like many good medicines, it can also be a little addictive. The sense of satisfaction audiences get from the shocks and terrors of a horror story can both give them a way to deal with their fears in a safe, fictional environment and give them a potentially addictive thrill from the real intense feelings the story generates. Either way, it's undeniable that the journey through the cycle of unknown, anticipation, and revelation leading to an ultimate climax can have a powerful emotional effect on people.

As the following formula shows, the cycle of Unknown, Anticipation, and Revelation grows more and more intense, with more danger and bigger dramatic stakes as the story moves forward:

Unknown → Anticipation → Revelation → Unknown → Anticipation → Revelation → Unknown → Anticipation → Revelation → Unknown → Anticipation → Revelation → Climax and Catharsis

Feeling Fearful Feels

Have you ever heard someone describe getting their finger caught in a door and you gasp and wince with something like real pain? Have you ever seen a picture of some rotten and decaying something and felt your stomach turn and bile rise up in your throat? Or, on a brighter note, have you ever felt a certain flushing and fluttering at the sight of fictional characters you find attractive in an erotic embrace? These are very physical responses to purely intellectual stimuli, what some philosophers call *occurrent* feelings. In other words, they're emotions that provoke a physical occurrence in your body.

REMEMBER

Horror is particularly effective at provoking occurrent emotions, which is why a scary movie or story can leave you as breathless as a rollercoaster ride. Your heart really does race. Your mind really does on some level think you're in danger, especially when your imagination visualizes how you'd feel if you were in the story, suffering the way those poor characters are suffering. This one-to-one connection between the audience and a character is called *empathy*, and it's one of your biggest friends as a writer. Anytime your audience forms a deep bond with a character, they're probably going to feel deep feelings.

Creating an empathic connection isn't always possible or even always useful. With a little more emotional distance, audiences can still care about the characters without taking every trial and tribulation personally. Feeling sadness or compassion for a character's plight is *sympathy.* You recognize and mourn the tragedy of the situation without taking the whole weight of the pain on yourself. Sympathy keeps audiences engaged with the story without overwhelming them, which means you can pile that much more fear and dread on the characters.

REMEMBER

Every person has different ways of experiencing empathy and sympathy. Some folks may not experience either, whether because of their personal mind-set or because they're not engaged with the story and the characters. You can't be sure how any given audience member will respond, but you can enrich and expand your story's emotional effect by employing a range of fearful feelings, which we discuss in these sections.

Fear and worry

The most fundamental emotions evoked in horror are fear and worry, and you almost can't have a horror story without heaping helpings of them. The audience is afraid for the story's main characters and worried about what may happen to them. These feelings are the most emphatic where the audience can put themselves in the character's terrible position and imagine how they would feel if they were

- The innocent seduced into peril

- The daring in over their head

- The unknowing walking into danger

- The victims suffering terrible fates

REMEMBER

Audiences also experience some genuine fear and worry for themselves. They'll wonder when the jump scare is coming, how disgusting that kill is going to be, and what kind of violent or creepy scenes they and the protagonist will both have to endure to get to the end of the story.

Pity and sorrow

Pity is that sad feeling you get when something terrible happens to someone you don't think deserves it. It's a sympathetic emotion, a sorrow that such a thing could happen to someone and a recognition that things are going awful for them, and you wish it weren't so. Rather than fully putting yourself in their shoes, these are characters about whom you say:

- "They shouldn't have done that."

- "I'm glad I'm not them."

- "I'm sorry for their loss."

- "I can't imagine what I'd do."

REMEMBER

Even though pity and sorrow make readers feel bad, they're also relieved that they're not personally suffering. That relief may come with a bit of guilt, but it can play an important role in creating catharsis, letting audiences become absorbed in the horrors without fully taking them on.

Disgust and revulsion

That cringe, that clenched muscle, that sharp intake of breath when you can just imagine how something horrible would feel is disgust and revulsion. The signature feeling of body horror fiction, these occurrent emotions are rooted in humanity's deep instincts to avoid sources of rot, disease, and corruption. Common gross-out imagery includes the following:

- Bloody and gory violence

- Insects, vermin, and other creepy crawlies

>> Slime, bile, goo, and sludge

>> Agonizingly familiar pains, catching a hand in the car door

REMEMBER

The disgust response is involuntary and immediate, powerful even outside any specific story context. For many, the gross-out is an exit door, too much or too disgusting and they're done with the story. For some, the bloodier the better. Deploy disgust with precision, knowing that a little can add a potent punch to a scene but too much may very well limit your audience.

Disoriented and discombobulated

Disoriented or discombobulated is the puzzled, unsettled feeling when you don't understand what's happening but feel like you should be able to. This feeling can be a purely intellectual experience of trying to find logic and sense where there isn't any, or in a movie, show, or game, it can involve discordant imagery and sound that may provoke nausea in some audience members. Disorienting the audience is an empathic provocation, creating a confusion that mirrors the feelings of the characters. Here are some examples:

>> Mysterious geographies that shift and change

>> Unreliable time or jumps back and forth in the narrative

>> Unexpected elements that appear and disappear

>> Strange individuals who speak and act in discordant or puzzling ways

REMEMBER

As with disgust and revulsion, a little disorientation can go a long way. Confusion is a great way to introduce a new unknown and build anticipation toward a revelation, but too much random weirdness and the intriguing mystery of "what's going on?" can become "what the hell is going on! This makes no sense! I'm out of here . . ." See Chapter 16 about dream worlds and other dimensions in the fantasy section.

Fascination and wonder

Fascination and wonder provide the sense of awe at the new and unimagined or literally awesome occurrences and entities in the story. These moments take the audience's breath away not because they're scared, but because they've never seen something like that. Or the wonder-filled moment when the intricate pieces of a mystery click into place and the solution is both a total surprise and one that makes perfect sense of all the eerie and terrible things that have been happening. For example:

- » The imaginative monstrosity of a unique creature

- » The awe-inspiring scope and design of a crumbling manor house

- » The outrageously over-the-top kill in a slasher movie

- » The seductively sinister figure who attracts as much as they repel

- » Anything that makes the audience say, "That's so coooool . . ."

REMEMBER

The sense of wonder has both the in-the-moment feeling of surprise and delight at the object of fascination and a deeper intellectual appreciation for the artistry of the storytellers. Crafting these moments in your story requires skill and planning as well as imagination. You must both set the stage for them with plot and character and build up to the revelations with mystery and anticipation. Reveal them at key moments in the story, when the revelation kicks the narrative into a new gear and the stakes are raised.

Triumph and relief

Audiences feel triumph and relief when someone they care about overcomes adversity. These two feelings are the mirror of fear and worry, empathic responses to the end of an ordeal and the dissolution of terror and dread. Characters that audiences hope and fear for make it through to the end and give them at least a little ray of hope, such as in these examples:

- » When they quiet the angry spirit

- » When they kill the monster

- » When they escape the house

- » When they survive until help comes

- » When they take revenge on those who've wronged them

WARNING

Sometimes audiences do enjoy a well-earned triumph where the characters they care about suffer and struggle, but manage to overcome evil in the end. The all-too-easy or too-convenient escape hatch isn't satisfying in any kind of story, but in horror it feels even more like cheating because in horror there's every possibility that the bad guys will win as often as the good guys. That's not true in most genres most of the time. Indeed, sometimes seeing evil prevail is fun, as the next section explains.

INCLUDE SOME LAUGHS (NERVOUS AND GENUINE)

A story doesn't have to be blood, tears, and dread for every moment of every scene. A one-liner from a quippy character or a visual pun incorporated into a slasher's kill can provide a brief moment of levity and provide much-needed relief for audiences and characters alike. Laughing in the face of death can show a protagonist's bravery or at least let them put on a brave face for a moment.

Although a little humor gives breathing room, it can also pull the audience out of the story or deflate anxiety too much. Make sure you root the joke in the characters and their established personality to ensure that your audience is laughing along with the characters and the story rather than at them.

Schadenfreude

Sometimes audiences just enjoy watching the pain and misfortune of others, a feeling called *schadenfreude* in German. It may not be kind or gracious and may indeed be one of the guiltiest of guilty pleasures, but there's no denying that it can be a lot of fun to watch the deserving get *much* more than what's coming to them. For example:

>> Rooting for the killer in a slasher movie

>> Appreciating an ingenious or creepy antagonist that defeats the heroes

>> Cheering when the jerk in the group gets eaten by the monster

>> Saying "burn it all down" when an apocalypse ends the world

Although schadenfreude-centered stories tend to be a little less serious and more outrageous slasher and monster fests, almost any kind of horror story has a place and time for a final note of guilty pleasure. A deadly supernatural entity or a soul-hungry haunted house are scariest when the innocent can't triumph, when the good do succumb to evil. There is real, cathartic satisfaction in the confirmation that your fears were justified and those poor fools really shouldn't have opened that box or gone down into that cave. Maybe they got more than they deserved, sure, but that just confirms that life ain't fair, and we all should probably be a little more scared of the dark.

Identifying Sources of Horror

Using the horror writer's toolkit of characters, emotions, imagery, mystery, and revelation, your story unfolds through scenes where the unknown creates feelings of dreadful anticipation, which lead to story-changing revelations that heighten tension and raise the stakes. All along the way, audiences and characters alike experience a range of emotions on their way from initial concern to final, cathartic triumph or disaster. At the center of all these moving narrative parts is a source of horror from which all the dread and terror grow. This root of malevolent cause and effect has a profound effect on what your audience expects, the rules underlying the story world, and the way the whole tale unfolds.

The following sections group sources of horror into eight broad categories based on the emotional, metaphorical, and intellectual story tropes associated with them. For added pedagogical fun, they're in roughly chronological order based on the development of horror as a genre from its origins in the 18th century.

Gothic

The earliest form of what would become horror literature (as opposed to much older folklore or traditional ghost stories), the Gothic looks to a place from the past that lingers in the present, unchanged except for the worse. These stories are of ancient estates, moody moors, and crumbling castles that feature characters suffering from misfortunes like dark family secrets, deteriorating fortunes, or doomed love. Gothic horror stems from characters digging up or confronting the past, often in helpless isolation from the warmer, gentler parts of the world. Only when the secret is revealed and reckoned with is it possible to escape the sins of the past.

Poe's "The Fall of the House of Usher" is an early example, but many great Gothics are still being written. Sarah Waters's *The Little Stranger* (Riverhead Books) is one of the more recent expressions of the aristocratic mansion and family gone to seed and beset by strange occurrences.

Spiritual

The spiritual category includes the classic ghost stories in all its forms (which can include spirits, fairies, and other supernatural beings from folklore). Here, the unfortunate protagonist comes into contact with mysterious entities at the border of life and death. Whether they're a ghost lingering in this world instead of moving onto the next or an ancient nature spirit that protects a pristine patch of forest, these creatures are fundamentally unknown and untouchable. The characters face a mental or spiritual challenge more than a physical one, often with a strong moral component.

M.R. James was the master of the late 19th century spiritual horror story, writing stories of lingering spirits and ancient curses that bedevil unsuspecting modern folk whose curiosity got the better of them. Spiritual sources of horror blur the line between physical and ethereal. As a source of horror they defy easy solutions and challenge characters' beliefs and moral compass.

Monstrous

In the monstrous category, the horror takes on physical form, with the terrifying and dreadful made flesh and bone in the form of a monster. Monsters present a clear life-and-death threat and embody the power differential between mere humans and the predatory forces that lurk out in the darkness.

Early horror story monsters were human failings manifested into something terrible. Dracula is a dangerous man cursed to be an even more dangerous and impure immortal thing. Mr. Hyde is all of Dr. Jekyll's worst traits given the form of a man and turned loose to indulge his perverse desires without regard for decency. The monster is usually a predator, a force for death that can't be ignored or avoided. You can read much more on monsters in Chapter 20.

Cosmic

The aloof, strange, and vast older cousin of the monstrous is cosmic horror, which presents impossibly vast forces that the human intellect can't comprehend. Horror comes from the realization that we all live in a cold, uncaring universe that views human life as insignificant — if it notices humans at all. The realization itself can test a protagonist's mental stability, but often the cosmic brushes up against our mundane world with a monstrous alien tentacle or a portal into another reality.

H.P. Lovecraft's "The Call of Cthulhu" and other so-called mythos tales set the original standard for cosmic horror, but it has developed along many other engaging (and less racist) paths in the past century.

Homicidal

A brutal, homicidal killer can be just as terrifying as any supernatural monster, and sometimes the most horrifying threat looks just like everyone else. Tragic tales of humans killing each other go back to the earliest forms of drama. In those stories, the killings derive from the dramatic and emotional needs of characters who audiences understand and maybe have pity or sympathy for. The killer becomes a horror figure when they kill for the pleasure of it.

These are stories of a normal person who behaves abnormally, violating the social contract that keeps the peace between neighbors. The familiar becomes dangerous and that danger not only hides among us, but it's also one of us. The terrible crimes of real-life serial killer Ed Gein inspired Robert Bloch's novel *Psycho*, which in turn became Hitchcock's landmark film and kicked off the serial killer craze in thriller and horror fiction.

Societal

Stories of societal horror present a whole community that is corrupt or dangerous in some way, with the protagonists the abnormal ones. Stories focus on strange small towns with deadly traditions, corrupt local authorities or oppressive dystopias where every move can be a wrong one, or sinister cults whose members isolate themselves from the rest of the world to pursue their own mysterious ends. Shirley Jackson's 1948 story "The Lottery" is a perfect short example. The 1973 movie, *The Wicker Man*, where a whole community of modern-day pagans sacrifices the movie's policeman protagonist, is a paragon of the folk horror genre.

Environmental

With the environmental category the entire world is actively dangerous and threatening by its very nature. This category is the angry cousin to the Gothic, where the setting is the source of fear and peril, but now the looming threat is aggressive and unavoidable. It may be a story of eco-horror or natural disaster, where the environment turns against the protagonists. Taken further, there are zombie outbreaks or nuclear apocalypses, where all society collapses and every day is a struggle to survive. *The Night of the Living Dead* launched the modern cinematic zombie tale, a story of both implacable monsters and human frailty and distrust in times of stress.

The unexplained

The uncanny little sibling to the cosmic category, this classification refers to stories of the eerie and weird. Strange things happen and the characters and the audience may not ever know why. Tales of the unexplained evoke strong feelings of unease and discomfort and maybe sometimes verge into true horror. Imagine a strange alley where every shop deals in curios from countries you've never heard of, each selling the odd-flavored sweets your weird aunt always brought you for Christmas, each with your initials on them. Great stories of the unexplained leave audiences in a state of uncomfortable wonderment, their imaginations roaming for answers. Robert Aickman was a master of the unexplained and uncanny with stories like "The Hospice."

SOURCES AND EMOTION — GENERATING A STORY

This chapter presents a lot of different pieces and concepts to play with when constructing a horror story. This simple creative exercise both familiarizes you with these ideas and is useful for generating a variety of different story ideas. Just follow along these steps:

1. **Pick a specific location.**

   It can be a beach, a mountain, a city, a cabin, an airplane. Choose whatever you want, as long as you can imagine it with some particular details.

2. **Create a character to be the protagonist.**

   Define them very loosely and include details such as name, age, and what they want out of life or at least right now.

3. **Using that location and character, come up with a horror scenario for as many of the sources of horror as you can.**

   The different sources can spawn very different kinds of horror plots for your character to deal with, such as the eight we mention in the section, "Identifying Sources of Horror."

4. **Choose one of those story ideas that really appeals to you.**

   Pick one of the fearful emotions to be the primary emotional experience for your audience with the story, like the ones we discuss in the section, "Feeling Fearful Feels."

5. **Quickly outline the story.**

   Use a cycle of Unknown → Anticipation → Revelation, writing just a sentence or two for each scene. Note how the chosen source of horror produces the chosen emotion.

Chapter **19**

Fashioning Fearful Plots and Sinister Scenes

An effective horror story is more than a collection of images and feelings swirling around a character in distress. It's a journey into darkness down a set and dangerous narrative path that leads to a satisfyingly cathartic conclusion. Even though your characters may be totally lost, you need to have a map of where this journey takes them. This chapter helps you draw that map in a way that heightens horror within an accessible structure.

Who Goes There? Characters Who Journey into Darkness

The mysterious unknown drives horror stories. As Chapter 18 details, the cycle of anticipation and revelation stemming from your story's sources of horror propels the plot and seizes audience interest. The audience *wants* to find out what's going on and so do the story's characters.

In fact, sometimes the biggest unknowns for the reader are figuring out what's going on with these characters. What's their story and what do they understand about the fearful unknowns and what will they do when they come face to face with the monster? Use the following to help generate that sense of the unknown in your story.

Controlling knowledge through point of view

In every story, the characters and the audience know different things, and either of them can know more than the other at any given moment in the narrative. Even when the story unfolds solely from one character's point of view (POV), what the character believes about what's happening and what the audience believes don't always align. Perhaps the audience knows a vampire is killing all those people, but the skeptical protagonist assures everyone there's a natural explanation for it all.

REMEMBER

The audience is a willing participant in the experience and unlike the characters, the audience knows it's a horror story. But the audience doesn't know what kind of horror story they're experiencing. Is something supernatural or science fictional going on here, or is there a more grounded explanation for all these strange occurrences? Keep going to find out. Is this the kind of story where the hero triumphs over evil or the kind where everything ends in blood and tears? No way to know for sure until you reach the end.

Chapter 2 describes the strengths and best uses of the most common points of view in stories. Here we revisit a few of them and add a couple more, paying special attention to how these POVs affect the horror audience's knowledge about the story's mysteries:

>> **First person and third-person limited:** These two POVs are the most common in fiction generally and have specific strengths for horror. In both cases, the audience is sunk deep into the perceptions, thoughts, and feelings of a single character. That's ideal for creating empathic connections with the audience. A story narrated in the first person, past tense strongly implies that the POV character has lived to tell their story.

>> **Third-person omniscient:** When the story has multiple POV characters or doesn't dive deep into a lead character's inner thoughts and point of view, the distance between the audience and the protagonists widens. The audience has room to logically suspect that those characters might in fact be hiding something from them. Although this distance from the characters makes it harder for audiences to empathize with them, it also breeds more mystery and anticipation about what's really going on. Furthermore, with no set POV character, the possibility that anyone could suffer a terrible fate becomes much more likely.

>> **Epistolary:** Here the audience experiences the story through a series of documents like letters, journal entries, text logs, audio recordings, or video diaries. The protagonist creates these accounts as the story unfolds and therefore doesn't have the benefit of hindsight that other stories presented in the past tense do. It's commonly used to present stories within stories, where a protagonist finds an old diary or the notes from some grim experiment. This POV combines the strengths of a deeply personal POV with the uncertainty of a story with an outcome unknown to the narrator. As Bram Stoker's *Dracula* so aptly proves, it's also possible to collect numerous documents from different characters that come together like a set of puzzle pieces to form a cohesive, frightening whole.

>> **Unreliable narrators:** Speaking of narrators, the unreliable POV is a powerful but easily abused technique. The audience puts some trust in the person telling the story, and nobody likes feeling cheated by the author. The tired cliché of a first-person narrative where the person telling the story dies and reveals they were a ghost the whole time doesn't satisfy. But, a story where the narrator misleads the audience while you, the author, leave enough clues and doubts for the audience to at least suspect something's going on can work amazing feats of chilling empathy. For example, Stephen Graham Jones's book *Night of the Mannequins* (Tordotcom) has a strong first-person narrator who steadily reveals through his actions and descriptions that in fact something quite disturbing is going on. By the time his true nature is revealed, it makes total sense and yet still chills the reader.

Creating creepy and creeped-out characters

Everything in Chapter 2 applies to characters in horror stories, but keep in mind some specific concepts when writing horror. The following tips apply to stories with horror and suspense elements in them and are particularly important when creating your horrific cast of heroes, villains, and victims.

Realizing you're doomed — Protagonists and knowledge

One of the tougher storytelling maneuvers to master in writing horror comes when your protagonist finally realizes and accepts that they're in a horror story. The audience has known all along, but most characters in most stories need some convincing. How do they react when the character discovers evidence that something beyond the ordinary is truly going on: Ghosts are real, cousin Jay is possessed, *They* do in fact *live* and also secretly control the world. In other words, how do the characters react to the impossible? Depending on their preconceptions and worldview, they may easily accept the truth or keep denying it until denial is impossible.

TIP

Reading or watching characters stubbornly deny the central premise of the story is often frustrating or dull when you'd rather see them start dealing with the problem. A central tension exists between the believability of the story and the characters in it and the patience and interest of the audience. As soon as the audience knows what kinds of impossible, horrifying things are afoot, you don't want to wait too long to get the protagonists on the same page. On the other hand, there's definitely some potent anxiety and dread for audiences who know exactly what's lurking behind the door while the characters blithely swing it open and step inside. Find the balance that works for your story, and if you have some clever or effective scenes planned for your skeptical or ignorant characters, great! But we suggest letting characters accept the horror for what it is sooner rather than later so they and the audience both can feel the fear of the next unknown.

Handling antagonists and their motives

Antagonists in horror run the gamut from your neighbor who collects human hearts in his basement freezer to undead predators feasting on human blood to vast, be-tentacled space gods who overload the human mind when seen for even a moment. They have at least three things in common though:

>> They're bad news for the protagonists.

>> They should be scary in some way.

>> They should do things for a reason.

REMEMBER

An antagonist's motives are often integral to the mystery at the center of your story. Watching the protagonists uncover the evil entity's goals and abilities is a big part of the pleasure. As with any mystery, the revelation works best when it's both surprising and yet perfectly logical given all that has happened before. In order to achieve that satisfying conclusion, the monster needs to have defined goals within the context of the story and a binding set of rules it follows to achieve those goals. Goals can be as simple as "kill all the campers in my forest" or a complex scheme to enslave humanity to the will of an alien god. The point is to focus their actions toward this goal in a way that, eventually, the audience can come to understand, though they may not understand it initially.

Even if the audience and the characters don't know exactly what rules the antagonist operates under, you should know them and follow them in order to ensure the story's core logic survives and satisfies to the end. They aren't written in stone and, sure, change things when a cool idea hits you, but take the time to think through the implications of your vampire's cool new teleportation trick. If she can teleport in this gory finale, why wasn't she doing it all along? Maybe she needs the blood of a specific type of human or can only teleport during a full moon. Figure out the logic and convey enough of it to the audience so they can feel fulfilled instead of cheated.

Valuing the victims

Depending on just how deadly and dangerous your source of horror is, your story can have a lot of victims. Perhaps many die some gruesome deaths, others lose their minds to demonic possession or suffer in sleepless terror from nightly spectral visitations. Although protagonists usually suffer more than enough to qualify as victims, here we turn our attention to the supporting characters who have less agency in the narrative and rely on the protagonists to (hopefully) deal with the monsters. These poor victims support your story in a variety of roles:

>> **Empathy generators:** Innocent and/or likeable victims who suffer and the audience feels pity and sorrow for them and the underserved traumas they're enduring.

>> **Protagonist motivators:** The hero will kick into high gear when people and animals whom they value as much or more than themselves suffer. They'll take big risks they may otherwise avoid in order to save or avenge their loved ones.

>> **Monster trophies:** The horrible fates your antagonists inflict on victims let you show exactly how dangerous they really are, raising the stakes and presenting a clear threat to those still alive to keep fighting or fleeing.

>> **Schadenfreude sacrifices:** If your story revels in the pleasure of watching others suffer pain beyond what they deserve, then you need some sacrificial lambs to die at the monster's claws in satisfyingly outrageous and disgusting ways. These characters shouldn't be so sympathetic that the audience feels deep sorrow at their loss.

WARNING

Before you start stacking the corpses for dramatic effect, take some time to consider the kinds of people you're killing and the kinds of people you're leaving alive. For a long time, the default victim in horror was a conventionally attractive woman and the default hero was a brave, straight, white man. The hard-hearted detective whose wife/daughter/girlfriend/all of the above suffered terrible traumas just to motivate him to hunt the serial killer is as tired a trope as there can be. You and only you are responsible for the fictional lives you take, and everyone in the audience knows it. Think through the messages you're explicitly and implicitly sending, the stereotypes you're reinforcing, and the clichés you're repeating.

Eluding the expositionist

Too often in horror, a know-it-all supporting character steps into the story to dump a bunch of vital exposition. Authors sometimes gussy up these walking, talking libraries with eccentric accents and quirky characteristics to hide the fact that their only real purpose in the story is to point the hero in the right direction. And yes, they're doing important work. In horror stories that involve uncovering mysteries (almost all horror stories), the heroes need to find those clues and receive those revelations. (Chapter 7 explores techniques like this for conveying facts and backstory vital to your plot in an entertaining and engaging way.)

TIP

Instead of having the town librarian happen to be a werewolf expert who explains the process of harvesting wolfsbane and making silver bullets, have your clue giver only provide a piece of the puzzle and let the protagonists be the ones to add it to another piece they already have. Let the hero take two from here and two from there and come up with four silver bullets on their own. A similar technique works for passing on dreadful information to your audience that even the characters don't know. A scene of the sheriff shamefacedly burning one of his uniforms that has mysteriously burst at the seams followed by a scene with the plucky protagonist asking why he's late to work this morning invites the audience to draw their own conclusions. And when the plucky friend finds those uniform buttons in the bottom of the ashes, they can start to catch on as well.

Plotting Your Host of Horrors

In his 1990 book *The Philosophy of Horror*, philosopher Noël Carroll presents a theory of how horror narratives work and details two overarching plot structures, the complex discovery and the overreacher. We take his concept as inspiration and introduce a set of fundamental structures for telling tales of terror. These plots aren't set-in-stone outlines or templates that you should faithfully follow in every detail. There is no hard-and-fast science for plot that works for every story. These horror plots describe an overall sense of plot movement and story arc that can help you organize your narrative to emphasize a particular kind of experience for your characters and your audience.

They're especially useful as a brainstorming tool when you're first conceiving your story. Maybe you have an idea for a particularly cool and gruesome ghost, or you want to feature a specific type of protagonist. Perhaps you can picture the perfect haunted house, but you haven't figured out a story for it yet. These plots, all common in horror fiction, can show you a well-trodden, dimly lit path forward through the haunted woods to your story.

The Discovery Plot — Unearthing dread secrets

Probably the most common plot, the discovery plot centers on investigating a mystery of some sort that results in uncovering the source of horror. Unlike a detective story, making the key discovery is just the first part of the story; after that, the protagonists still need to confront and survive the horrible truth they have uncovered.

Here are some basics to this kind of plot:

>> A source of horror such as strange killings or odd occurrences has caused a mystery.

>> The protagonist is drawn into the mystery because solving it is important to their core wants and ignoring it would come at some personal cost.

>> They discover clues or have encounters that raise anticipation and dread as they learn more and more about the source of horror.

>> They reveal the truth about one or more fearful things.

>> Something terrible happens.

For example, consider *The Haunting of Hill House* by Shirley Jackson (Penguin Classics).

The Overreach Plot — One step too far

Unchecked ambition and ill-fated pursuit of achievements drive the horror and drama. Someone, either the antagonist or even a protagonist, purposefully pushes the limits of what's acceptable or advisable, their hubris bringing badness down on themselves and those around them.

This type of story often includes the following:

>> Someone is trying to achieve something they shouldn't try to achieve, despite others warning them of dire possible consequences.

>> They do whatever their atypical moral compass allows them to achieve their goals, naysayers be damned.

>> They achieve their goal, at least partially, and the result isn't what they were expecting or hoping in some way.

>> Their goal becomes a threat to the overreacher and other innocents around them.

>> Something terrible happens.

Two examples of this plot device include *Frankenstein* by Mary Shelley and *The Strange Case of Dr. Jekyll and Mr. Hyde* by Robert Louis Stevenson.

The Trespass Plot — You shouldn't be here

Naive or foolhardy exploration or investigation reveals something that should have been left alone. An ancient curse. A dormant virus. A slumbering beast. The characters in this plot device aren't looking for trouble, but they're instead thrown into it because of their actions and now must fight for their lives.

Common aspects in this type of story are as follows:

>> Someone goes somewhere or does something they shouldn't, either through ignorance or foolhardiness.

>> Their act of trespassing triggers a dangerous response.

>> They come to understand the true nature of their "crime" and how much danger they're in.

>> They try to escape back to pre-trespass normalcy before they made their mistake.

>> Something terrible happens.

One example is the film *Alien*.

The Pursuit Plot — The hunt is on

Something is after someone and there are notably disparate power levels. The strong pursue/threaten/oppress the weak. Perhaps the weak are the object of obsession for a killer, the ideal victim for a monster, or the possessor of important knowledge that some evil being needs for their foul machinations.

In a pursuit story, audiences are likely to find:

>> Someone is marked for pursuit, often unjustly.

>> The protagonist escapes or avoids the initial pursuit and learns terrible truths about the pursuers.

>> The chase can take many forms, and it doesn't have to be a literal chase, but the stakes increase.

>> There's a final chance at escape or turning the tables on the pursuer.

>> Something terrible happens.

Some examples of this plot device include the movies *Halloween* and *Rosemary's Baby.*

The Contest Plot — Facing your fears

Two forces, not necessarily equal, are battling one another, such as exorcist versus demon, hunters versus vampires, and serial killers versus detectives. The opposing sides are each bent on destroying the other. Although some discoveries will be made along the way, this plot emphasizes the back and forth between the two sides as the stakes and horror escalate.

The following are often found in this type of story:

>> The contestants become aware of each other and test their strength.

>> The two opponents size each other up.

>> They engage in a series of escalating clashes, revealing more about themselves.

>> Stakes rise and innocents often become caught in the crossfire.

>> Something terrible happens to one or both of them.

Examples include the movies *The Exorcist* and *Seven.*

The Breakdown Plot — It's all gone to hell

Survival and stability are the primary goals for characters in a world that has gone to hell. They could be trapped in their little part of the world because of a natural disaster or lost in a hostile environment. The whole world may have broken down through alien invasion or zombie apocalypse. Just staying alive another day or even hour is all the characters can hope for.

A breaking-down story is likely to have the following:

>> The protagonist's once-safe home is overcome by chaos and horror.

>> They survive the initial horror and search for safety.

>> The characters strive to survive and build a place for themselves.

>> The whole world is against them.

>> Everything is terrible.

One example is the TV show *The Walking Dead.*

The Weird Plot — What the heck is that?

Weird things are happening and the characters don't know why. Maybe they're suffering a mental breakdown, having hallucinations, or enduring hauntings. Perhaps other worlds are impinging on their own. These are disquieting tales of confusion and the surreal that can challenge characters and audiences alike.

The following are common elements in a weird story:

>> Regular life is interrupted by the uncanny. The threat and implications are uncertain.

>> The characters struggle to understand what's real and what's not.

>> They're forced to reckon with a world that's stranger than they imagined.

>> They usually fail to understand or become lost in the strangeness, both of which can be terrible.

One example is the film *Eraserhead*.

Creating Fear with Narrative Flow

You can start working out the scenes and sequences that flesh out that plot skeleton. Chapter 18 introduces a formula for fear, a cycle of dread resolving into story-changing events with ever-escalating stakes until it reaches the cathartic climax:

Unknown → Anticipation → Revelation

Here we define and explore the sources of horror that drive that fearful cycle and the emotions the audience experiences as they play out before them. In this section, we focus on the small but important arrows (→) that link the stages one to another. We call these narrative flows.

REMEMBER

A *narrative flow* is a way of describing the experience your characters have as they transition from one stage to another in the formula. A flow is a scene or sequence where actions by the antagonists or protagonists push the plot toward a *revelation* (key turning points in your plot). Remember, revelations are moments that significantly change the course of the story in some way.

To maximize the effect of narrative flow in service of your horror story, employ the following ideas and strategies.

Mixing and matching flows

Flows and revelations are always linked together. The flow describes the experience from the point of view of the protagonist or the audience as they approach the revelation. Think of these flows as a set of templates or tropes that you can use to give plot movements a specific flavor of horror mood and emotion. Meanwhile, a revelation can introduce a new kind of flow as the story kicks into a different gear. Mix and match flows with revelations as needed to create a richer and varied narrative as the new revelations lead to more high-stakes narrative flows.

Here are some ways to do that:

>> **Unknown Becomes Known.** This is the simplest and most common narrative flow: A mystery is solved, looming questions get answers, an important fact about someone or something is revealed. The new knowledge sometimes comes from classic detective work, like reading an old diary or combing through newspaper archives to find out who was murdered in this house a century ago. It can also include the introduction of new and probably suspicious characters or characters the audience already knows revealing key new facts about themselves. "Didn't I mention? My mother fled the country after the authorities learned about her gene-splicing experiments."

>> **Familiar Becomes Unfamiliar.** The known becomes unknown in some way, with strange changes to familiar people, objects, and landscapes. The things that people expect to act normally behave unpredictably, causing disorientation and dread. These can be anything from eerie lights and unsettling noises in their homes to neighbors acting weird to bouts of amnesia or confusion. "Don't you remember, dear? We always have pigeon pie on Thursdays, ever since you were a child. I don't know why you don't recall." The change isn't necessarily threatening or obviously the result of some evil source, but it's enough to arouse suspicion and fearful anticipation.

>> **Past Becomes Present.** The past is never fully past and something from another age resonates into the modern world. This is the trademark move of the Gothic, where old crimes and buried secrets resurface to cause new problems. (Check out Chapter 18 for more on the Gothic.) A ghost that haunts the person who murdered them, the malcontent child locked away in the attic for fear of their deformities, the ancient curse the family bears for the evil misdeeds that made their fortune. As the past rears its ugly head in the present, characters reassess and likely start to worry about people and places. Someone's not going to be happy that the old secret is out — and might do anything to bury it again.

>> **Outsiders Become Trespassers.** Someone goes where they're not supposed to go, usually against the rules or at least against playing it safe or using common sense. They travel off the beaten path or go through the off-limits door and are therefore a little complicit in their fate. It's a mini version of the

trespass plot (refer to the section "The trespass plot — You shouldn't be here," earlier in this chapter), one that can fit into any story structure as characters discover a clue in a locked room, flee a pursuer by hiding in the old mine, or seek an advantage over their foe by pursuing forbidden rites. The trespass is the price they pay this time to receive the linked revelation.

» **Safe Becomes Vulnerable.** The characters' secure, comforting existence is breached in some way. What they relied upon as a source of strength begins to crumble or vanishes completely. Those who usually think they're untouchable become targets. This transition from safety to vulnerability leads to a revelation that undermines someone's sense of security and raises new anxieties. A job is lost. A home is broken into. A loved one becomes sick or injured. Disaster strikes, be it a sudden financial loss, an epidemic, an invasion, or a natural disaster. The resulting revelation relates directly to the loss of safety, raising the stakes for the protagonist.

» **Beloved Becomes Threatening.** What characters once took comfort in now causes anxiety in some way. Similar to the safe becoming vulnerable, this flow has a stronger emotional impact because of the crossed emotional cues and intense flip from source of comfort to a potential antagonistic threat. A child or parent has a profound personality change. A lovable pet now snarls and growls at their owner's approach. A respected pastor directs their congregation's ire against the protagonist. This flow challenges the character's ideas of who they can trust and what they should fear.

» **Strangers Become Even Stranger.** The already strange or unusual reveal new depths of eeriness. Their true, possibly horrifying nature becomes evident and worse than imagined. In a story where earlier revelations have established a baseline of the uncanny and dreadful, now it's even worse. The off-putting neighbor is seen burying a body. The strange lights and weird noises resolve into words of warning. The charismatic church leader worships an older and more malevolent entity than anyone imagined.

» **Stable Becomes Unstable.** The story's setting as a whole shifts into a dangerous state. Societal norms disintegrate, either from external pressure or internal strife. Rules of law and society evaporate, leaving everyone vulnerable and bringing out the worst in people. This could be an angry mob, an abusive police force, or something as widespread as nationwide riots and purges and disasters. "The storm has knocked out all the power and washed away the bridge, so there's nowhere safe on the island."

» **Knowledge Becomes Dangerous.** This is the classic core of much cosmic horror. The truth will destroy you, not set you free. Reading the *Necronomicon* opens their eyes to the horrors around them and tests their mental stability. Learning the killer's identity marks the detective as the next victim. Using the experimental technology puts them at risk of dangerous side effects. Here, ignorance would be bliss if only the characters didn't need the knowledge that comes from the revelation.

>> **Horror Becomes Undeniable.** The horrors that have lurked in the shadows are now howling under the full moon, and there's no denying them. As a result, everyone in the story must come to terms with the threat or succumb to it (which may happen anyway). Aliens invade, zombies overwhelm, the interdimensional being's pseudopods ravage the town square. The only mystery left is how to stop them — if indeed there is a way to stop them.

REMEMBER

These narrative flows describe transitions from unknown and anticipation to revelation, and the matching revelation should feel seamless and fully integrated into the narrative flow when the audience experiences. Read on then, brave writer, as we explore those horrifying revelations in more detail.

Shifting the narrative — Thrilling and chilling revelations

The revelation is a turning point in your story, an event or discovery that shifts the narrative in a new, probably worse for the protagonists, direction. Revelations are the end results of the narrative flow scenes we describe in the preceding section. These revelations are specific moments of dramatic climax within a scene. They're an occurrence that could scare in its own right but add anxiety and suspense within the larger context of the scene and story. It's the count baring his fangs to reveal he's a vampire or the couple coming home to find their babysitter spread all over the living room, dining room, and kitchen.

With each one we note some common linkages between specific flows and specific revelations, ones where the two interweave with each other to create a potent pairing. But that's not the only way to go! Each revelation can link with any of the narrative flows. Again, use these are tools to organize your narrative, not rules to blindly follow.

The Uncanny Occurrence

Something very strange happens that indicates there's dark dealings afoot. Mysterious appearances and disappearances, the flickering of lights, the ominous phone call from a menacing stranger. Curiosity and/or anxiety are aroused. The characters probably don't know exactly what it means, but now it has become clear that things aren't normal. The uncanny occurrence usually happens early in the story as part of the opening scenes of establishing the unknown and building anticipation. An additional uncanny occurrence late in a story provides a change of pace or a less-frantic moment while still moving the overall plot forward.

This narrative pairs well with Familiar Becomes Unfamiliar and Strangers Become Even Stranger.

Violation of Expectations

The rules that characters live by stop working or things don't go the way they're supposed to. Someone violates cultural norms or behaves in unfamiliar and disquieting ways. The violation can be as straightforward as internet or phone service being cut without cause or a neighbor slashing their tires. Perhaps protectors like police or doctors threaten and abuse the people they're supposed to protect and serve. Whatever the specifics, the protagonist suffers some direct harm from a formally trusted source. The characters and the audience now know to trust no one and are set on guard against threats from any direction.

This narrative pairs well with Familiar Becomes Unfamiliar and Beloved Becomes Threatening.

Implications Become Clear

That moment of, "if that's true, then . . ." when characters or maybe just the audience put 2 and 2 together. And in this case 2 +2 equals sinister conclusions like clues that prove the murderer's identity, patterns in the monster's attacks, or a full analysis of just how bad it will be if this disease gets out into the world. With this revelation, the characters can project their fear and anxiety forward into a future that's likely to get much, much worse for them. On the upside, now that they see what's coming, they can try and stop it.

This narrative pairs well with Past Becomes Present and Stable Becomes Undeniable.

The Sudden Shock

Traps that spring into action, ambushes that attack out of nowhere, and the sudden betrayals of close friends all deliver unexpected, quick shocks to the characters and the audience. Now the protagonist has come under direct assault by the source of horror in some way, and their survival instincts will kick into high gear as they realize the enormity of their situation.

WARNING

Jump scares are cheap tricks that take full advantage of the occurrent emotions audiences feel while watching horror. They trigger a deep, evolutionary fear response and get the heart racing, but they're seldom satisfying when the audience discovers they had nothing to do with the plot. If you're going to have something jump out at the audience, make it a monster, not a cat.

This narrative pairs well with Knowledge Becomes Dangerous and Safe Becomes Vulnerable.

The Disgusting Mess

Seeing something grotesque is much like the jump scare. It's literally visceral in many cases and provokes that instant revulsion that most people instinctively experience at seeing something disgusting. To be fully effective, the audience needs to see at least some of the same gory details that the characters do: the mutilated victims, the gravely wounded friend, the gore-soaked beast. In some cases, the characters come across the disgusting display after the violence, in which case it serves as proof of the antagonist's threatening nature. Other times, they may witness the disgusting process in action, maybe trying to stop it. Here, the threat becomes imminent, and they risk their own demise if they can't defeat or escape the source of horror.

This narrative pairs well with Outsiders Become Trespassers and Horror Becomes Undeniable.

The Terrifying Thing

The evil is finally revealed, and it's clearly bad news. Audiences see the monster. They have undeniable proof that there's a ghost. These murders are the work of a serial killer. The whole thing's about to explode! There's no one right time to show the source of evil. Plenty of great horror stories open up with the slasher/killer/soul-sucker doing its terrible worst to some poor victim and the protagonist spends the rest of the story dealing with it.

But more often, the source of horror remains at least partially hidden until close to the end. This delay allows more cycles of unknown → anticipation → revelation to play out, building up the fiendish foe in the audience's imagination. After the thing itself appears, whether early or late, the story becomes not so much about "what is that thing?" but rather, "what horrible things will it do?"

Monsters go well with everything.

EXERCISE

CREATING YOUR OWN HORROR PLOT

This chapter identifies four different elements of horror stories to work as a set of tools to help assemble an effective narrative. Like any set of writing tools, they aren't hard-and-fast rules or universally accepted terms. They're one approach, and we encourage you to use, adjust, and reframe them however works best for you. We suggest starting with a source of horror and then matching it to a plot structure. Then outline a series of narrative flows that lead to revelations, building tension and raising stakes as the plot unfolds.

(continued)

(continued)

Here's a quick exercise that shows the parts all working together. Use the following table and stick to these steps:

1. **Choose a source of horror to serve as the focus of a story that follows the Discovery plot where a mysterious event or discovery leads the protagonist(s) to seek answers that can only be found by confronting the source of horror.**

2. **Write an answer-seeking scene using one of two specific narrative flows: The Unknown Becomes Known or Beloved Becomes Threatening.**

   That scene ends with the first revelation, using either a Sudden Shock or a Violation of Expectations.

3. **Write a scene where this first revelation presents a new mystery that the protagonist(s) must solve or obstacles they must overcome.**

   This mystery/obstacle presents itself through your choice of two specific narrative flows: Knowledge Becomes Dangerous or the Familiar Becomes Unfamiliar.

4. **Write a final scene with the final Revelation and climax of the story, which must be either The Terrifying Thing or Implications Become Clear.**

Source of Horror	Plot Structure	Narrative Flow	Revelation
Gothic	Discovery	Unknown Becomes Known	The Uncanny Occurrence
Spiritual	Overreach	Familiar Becomes Unfamiliar	Violation of Expectations
Monstrous	Trespass	Past Becomes Present	Implications Become Clear
Cosmic	Pursuit	Outsiders Become Trespassers	The Sudden Shock
Homicidal	Contest	Safe Becomes Vulnerable	The Disgusting Mess
Societal	Breakdown	Beloved Becomes Threatening	The Terrifying Thing
Environmental	Weird	Strangers Become Even Stranger	
Unexplained		Stable Becomes Unstable	

Chapter **20**

Shaping Your Scares — Menacing Monsters and Human Horrors

C reatures, aliens, and imaginative beasties have a role to play in all three genres (science fiction, fantasy, and horror), but in horror, the monster takes center stage. The threatening, dangerous, fear-provoking source of all your story's scares is almost always some kind of monster. Maybe it's a human being behaving monstrously or maybe it's a former human arisen as an undead creature. It could be an evil demon, haunting spirit, or otherworldly mass of tentacles and mouths. No matter its form, the monster's job in horror stories is to make matters much worse for your protagonists.

We detail different sources of horror in Chapter 18, one of which we term the Monstrous. There we define a monster as the horror taking on a physical form that threatens the protagonists and highlights human frailty. Monsters are predatory, dangerous, and aggressive. Not only can't you just walk away from them, they'll chase after you when you try to run. This chapter offers tools and techniques for thinking about monsters in terms of how they work to inspire fear, dread, and other horror-adjacent emotions in your audience.

Mixing Up Your Monsters

Noël Carroll in his book, *The Philosophy of Horror,* argues for a taxonomy of monster types based on four principles he terms fusion, fission, magnification, and horrific metonymy (refer to the nearby sidebar for more specific details about Carroll and his book). He makes the case for his categories so well that we were inspired to expand and refocus his monstrous elements into a set of monster characteristics for you to reference as you dream up your own fear and disgust-generating beasties. Most monsters have all the following characteristics to one degree or another. You can use them as a kind of questionnaire to help you define your monster's nature and set down guidelines for how it will behave in your story.

If one or more of these doesn't seem to apply to your monster concept, don't worry. However, before you dismiss the inapplicable characteristic completely, give it a second thought and see if there's some subtler way it may apply. No, your attractive psychic vampire isn't disgusting in an outward way in that they don't even drink blood. But could there be something emotionally revolting about the experience of being psychically drained that your audience may find disgusting in a moral way? Maybe!

Threatening

Every monster needs to somehow threaten someone, usually, the protagonist and/or innocent victims. A monster can be threatening in a variety of ways:

>> Direct physical harm in all its many forms, from fangs and claws to weapons and curses.

>> Indirect physical harm through disease, corruption, or infection that the monster spreads in some way.

>> Psychological harm that damages or distorts the victim's mental state. This can be as straightforward as inducing panic to manipulating or altering someone's thoughts and emotions.

>> Social harm in the form of loss of financial, political, social, family, or professional ties. Social harm can be more subtle (the monster's taint makes people uncomfortable around the victim) or more drastic (the victim is cast out of society into the wilderness).

Monsters can of course threaten in different ways at once, or in turn. Whatever the threat, the protagonists can (hopefully) contain or counter them in some way, but not without cost and effort.

MAKE YOUR MONSTERS THREATENING AND IMPURE

In his book, *The Philosophy of Horror*, Noël Carroll makes the case that for a monster to be a real monster, it needs to be both threatening and impure: Monsters can threaten physically, with claws that rend and fangs that kill. They can threaten emotionally or violate social norms. They bring up fundamental fears about food and sex and disease and the unknown.

Furthermore, monsters defy the normal categories people impose upon the world. They're both one thing and another and yet neither of the two. Both living and dead, both human and animal, both biological and mechanical, both animate and inanimate. He also makes the important point that, "Thus, monsters are not only physically threatening; they are cognitively threatening. They are threats to common knowledge."

Disgusting

That thing is gross! Some aspect of the monster provokes those instinctual, occurrent emotions of revulsion that make the audience at least a little sick to their stomach. Or the monster does something so offensive that the audience can't help but gasp in shock at the nastiness. Here are some revolting methods for provoking disgust in audience and characters alike:

>> The physical appearance of the monster can disgust, with slime and gore and open wounds or grotesque body features that turn stomachs.

>> Physical actions the monster takes can be equally disgusting, from causing gruesome bodily harm to covering itself in blood or other disturbing substances.

>> Psychological actions and attitudes can sometimes arouse as much revulsion as the physical, from hateful tirades to gratuitous cruelty and filthy expressions; what a person says can make them as revolting as any blood-sucking freak.

The disgust can be constant (it just looks gross all the time) or intermittent (when it feeds or attacks it reveals its disgusting nature). The revulsion can run the gamut from full-blown carnage of a dismemberment to the subtle yet disturbing trickle of blood from the corner of a vampire's smile.

Humanish

Humanish refers to any aspect of the monster that encompasses or mimics humanity. This humanish quality creates a sense of uneasiness and cognitive dissonance for audiences who can both recognize the familiar humanity in the beast and feel repulsion at the way it expresses itself through the monster. (We discuss purely human horrors in the section, "Hunting Down Homicidal Humans," later in this chapter) in the following ways:

>> Human intelligence that allows the monster to think as well as or better than a person, elevating them above mindless beasts and adding to their formidable presence.

>> Relatable motivations that at least echo human desires like anger, protecting offspring, lust for power or wealth, or even the simple need to feed.

>> Speech that allows the monster to directly threaten, taunt, lie to, and creep out its victims. This can produce an eerie effect when the voice is inhuman, but the words are in a human language.

>> Expressions through body language and facial movements that are sort of human and sort of monstrous like the killer clown's smile, the demonic laugh, or the piteous wailing of a childlike ghost.

When monsters have at least some humanish characteristics, the audience can at least partially understand and thus more deeply fear their actions.

Animalistic

The world is full of frightening animals, from vipers to wolves to sharks, and a ton of scary stories depict mostly natural animals as their central monster (the book and movie *Jaws* being the most famous example). Pulling out elements of these real-world threats and putting them in your monster is a proven way to up the fear factor:

>> Physical attributes like fur, tusks, claws, gills, tails, and tentacles that give or imply the dangerous attributes of an animal.

>> Temperaments and drives that are primal or instinctual that cause the monster to act more animallike. These are especially frightening when otherwise the monster seems largely human.

>> Detachment from typical human social structures and ignoring human customs like when and where to eat, breed, or carry out other natural functions. Also, distinctly humanlike monsters following classically animal group behaviors like a hive of insects or a flock of birds.

Combining the animalistic and instinct-driven with humanism characteristic produces a combination of fascination and the fear that the monster is part or wholly animallike. Here the cognitive dissonance comes from seeing a non-animal behave in a beastly way, while the audience's familiarity with animals gives them a context to judge and worry about the monster's capabilities.

Heightened

Aspects of the monster take normal phenomena and magnify them in some way. Something that's already frightening, like teeth and claws become even sharper and deadlier, whereas something normally benign becomes very malign when magnified. Heighten your monsters using the following techniques:

>> Bigger, tougher, more numerous instances of the everyday, from giant ants to unstoppable slasher movie murderers to hordes of rats.

>> Obsessions and preoccupations become monstrous when taken to extremes, from stalking innocents to collecting bones, anyone and anything that blows past the conventional limits of interest into mania.

Anytime something exceeds its normal bounds, people become anxious. A group of friendly neighbors becomes a stifling crowd when it gets too big or forced into too small a space. One rat or cockroach disgusts most people, whereas a swarm of them induces pure panic.

Unnatural

Something about the monster violates the laws of nature as commonly understood by the characters in the story and/or the audience. The monster is far outside their experience and threatens the very foundation of what's real and what isn't. Here are some examples of the unnatural:

>> Any kind of impossible combinations or attributes that make someone say in a fearful whisper, "that shouldn't exist . . ."

>> Supernatural abilities and mystical powers of all types

>> Weird science attributes that transcend and distort the known universe

>> Alien or extra-dimensional origins

This unnaturalness creates a strong sense of cognitive dissonance and dreadful anticipation because the rules and facts everyone uses to understand how the world works are no longer relevant. They can't predict what may happen next and therefore they start to imagine the worst.

Corrupting

This is our version of what Carroll calls "horrific metonymy." Not only is the monster scary in its own right, but it makes the world around it scarier too. An aura of evil or danger or just bad feelings surrounds it, or maybe just bad news follows in its wake. Corruption can take the following forms:

>> Infectious or degrading miasmas that spread sickness and rot, including emissions like radiation.

>> Attended by disgusting things such as flies, vermin, noxious odors, and dripping slime.

>> Physical environmental changes occur in its presence, such as changes in temperature, odd noises, or sudden storms.

>> Emotional and psychological impacts, creating negative feelings or impaired senses in all those around the monster.

A corrupting aura can heighten an already fearful-looking monster or show the evil influences of an otherwise unthreatening-looking entity. It can be obvious, like a halo of darkness or subtle and unseen, its effects only discernible long after the creature has moved on.

Captivating

Like a car wreck, audiences just can't take their eyes off the monster. An awe-inspiring element impresses audiences in some way even as it horrifies. Here are some strong captivation techniques:

>> Creative monster design that impresses with its originality and creepiness

>> A magnetic or engaging personality that makes the monster a pleasure to spend time with while it does terrible things

>> Amazing actions and over-the-top kills that almost feel like a thrill ride

>> Seductive and erotic elements that trigger other occurrent emotions besides fear and dread

A captivating monster is the kind of creature that inspires toys, fan fiction, and often steals the spotlight from the human protagonists in the story. It may even be what makes the monster more of an antihero than a pure antagonist.

Making Metaphors Monstrous

Monsters are dangerous and disgusting and cause no end of trouble for protagonists, but what does it all mean? Sometimes it means: "don't mess with monsters, they'll kill you," but often authors use creatures, killers, specters, and spirits as metaphors for something else. Dive into the literary theory and academic research on horror, and you'll find a host of well-reasoned and thought-provoking analyses of the metaphors and meanings monsters can be seen to embody in horror stories across literature and popular culture.

REMEMBER

Making your monsters serve as metaphors for some other concept isn't just some fancy technique to make film critics opine favorably about your story's deeper meanings. Thinking in terms of metaphors really can make your story more emotionally and intellectually engaging for your audience. A guiding metaphor can focus your plot and inspire specific thoughts and feelings. Your monsters can not only disgust and terrify, they also can let your protagonists and your audience confront tough ideas. The evils of the world are made existential in the story. Things people think of as bad that are intangible or diffuse become very tangible right here and now. In fact it's right behind you. Run!

Monsters are often a metaphor or stand-in for "the other" as defined by whoever's writing the story, someone different than them and therefore somehow seen as scary. In countless stories over the centuries, authors have used their monsters to embody harmful stereotypes and aggressively link negative ideas and emotions to people the creators consciously or unconsciously don't like.

You can do that. Some great stories target a certain class or attitude or set of beliefs and turn them into monsters. But you must be aware of who you're targeting, what stereotypes you're perpetuating, and how much of a contrarian you're being. Watch out for stereotypes that portray humans with disfigurements as being evil or inherently corrupt in some way. And know that, in our opinion, no story you write is ever going to be worth making real, vulnerable people's lives even an iota worse.

Societal flaws personified

People as a whole suck a lot of the time. Sometimes monsters are just the sucky parts given physical form. The monster or monsters distill the flaw to some essential horror (zombies as thoughtless consumers). Or they may heighten existing horrors of oppressive ideas (dystopian police states). Institutional racism, sexism, homophobia, and xenophobia can spawn monstrous avatars that take the evil attitude and give it real teeth and claws.

Voice for the voiceless

The monster takes on the role of advocate or avenger for something or someone who is normally powerless in society or for something people fear out of proportion. The monster takes the actions that people imagine the voiceless would take if they could, often with some sense of justification. Nature, suffering from pollution and environmental havoc, creates a monstrous being to destroy the human polluters. A manmade or natural disaster, such as an atomic blast or an earthquake, gives rise to terrifying beasts that make the disaster even worse. Or maybe it's an expression of resistance from downtrodden castes, the supernatural spirit of the oppressed who passes judgement on the oppressors.

Personal flaws made manifest

Everyone has inner demons. Sometimes they become outer demons. Greed, hatred, cruelty, irrationality, jealousy, anger, callousness, and obsession all bring out the worst in people. The monster is a heightened, imminently threatening version of one or more of these flaws. Perhaps it takes the form of a serial killer driven to murderous extremes by jealousy. A spirit of anger may manifest into the world as a demonic monster.

Whatever form it takes, the monstrous version of the flaw is usually more extreme and dangerous than it could ever be in a normal person. Defeating such a creature means countering the fundamental flaw in some way, perhaps when the protagonists exorcise the same flaw from themselves. Or maybe a chainsaw to the anger spirit's face will solve the problem, depending on the kind of story you're writing.

Deep difficulties turned terrifying

Chronic, deep challenges and setbacks like trauma, loss, addiction, and illness can manifest in physical, monstrous form. Sometimes the difficulty itself creates the problem, such as mysterious psychic outbursts from a disturbed mind or a strange disease that transforms people in some monstrous way. The monster can also be an external threat that attacks the vulnerability created by the difficulty: a ghost of a lost loved one or a creature that thrives on some specific toxic emotion. Confronting and defeating the monster requires facing and either accepting or overcoming the underlying difficulty.

Universal experiences mutated

The monster embodies some fundamental and often frustrating aspect of human life. These monsters are deeply reflective of the culture that creates them and the experience they embody. Puberty and the disconcerting changes and challenges it brings may turn someone into an actual new form. Old age and the infirmities and weaknesses it brings may make someone vulnerable to a monstrous threat or drive them to monstrous lengths to fend off death. Parental fears about responsibility for a young life become terrifying when the child itself is evil in some way.

Positive characteristics taken too far

In high enough doses, everything is toxic. Ambition, pride, and concern can be taken too far, and the result may well be monsters. Caring too much about someone or some cause can become an obsession that leads to violence. Giving too much of oneself and demanding others do the same can lead to cults and oppression.

Focusing on fixing one problem to the exclusion of all others can do real harm. The result is a monster who seeks to control, cleanse, or fix others in their own twisted way. A vengeful ghost or slasher villain wants justice and doesn't care who it kills to get it. A devoted fan wants another book from their favorite author, no matter what the cost. Overcoming the monster means restoring balance and perspective.

Interpreting the Classics

Horror stories have their own rich history of well-known creeps and creatures, and there's no shame at all in taking a classic monster and making it your own. Vampire, zombie, ghost, and werewolf stories continue to bring in big audiences year after year, and there's no reason you can't join in the fearful fun.

REMEMBER

Classic monsters already have audience acceptance. Your job is to advance beyond the clichés in some way and make your version unique and exciting. Employing one or more of the metaphors from the previous section can help you do that, as can mixing and matching the different monster characteristics from the section "Mixing Up Your Monsters," earlier in this chapter.

Chapter 6 explains the power of piggybacking in building story worlds and borrows the dictum Most Advanced Yet Acceptable (MAYA) as a great tool for both tapping into your audience's existing knowledge and offering them something original and exciting at the same time.

Here we offer a third tool: sets of creativity-prompting questions specific to the most well-known and popular classic monster types. If you can dream up cool and creepy new answers to these fundamental questions, you're on your way to making a MAYA monster worth writing about.

Aliens and cosmic entities

This monster came from another world and is fundamentally alien and mysterious. Maybe it's a being of a natural world, but not our natural world. It may be malevolent or mindless or destructive without even noticing humans are there. Like the Xenomorph from *Alien* or the titular blob from *The Blob*, an alien monster should feel well and truly *alien*, the kind of creature that would never evolve here on Earth. For stories rooted in cosmic horror, the stranger and less earthlike they are, the better. Chapter 11 gives you a lot more to think about when writing aliens. These questions can help you make your alien monsters more otherworldly:

>> Where did it come from and why is it here?

>> What are its physical properties and what do they say about where it's from?

>> What are its mental and technological capabilities?

>> How does it think, feel, and desire different from humanity?

Cryptids and creatures

These types of monsters include mystery monsters and hidden creatures who have a fundamentally natural origin, but which are largely unknown to the rest of the world. Bigfoot, Chupacabra, the gill-man from *The Creature from the Black Lagoon*, and King Kong are some classic examples. They aren't supernatural or otherworldly and part of what makes them exciting and frightening is the idea that they could really exist out in some hidden corner of the world. Ask yourself the following questions about your cryptid:

>> How and why has it remained hidden?

>> Who knows about its existence?

>> What do people believe about it and what's right/wrong about those beliefs?

>> What is its natural habitat, and what does it feed on?

>> What happens when it's removed from its natural habitat?

>> How aggressive is the cryptid?

>> How intelligent is it?

Demonic and supernatural threats

These monsters include demons, witches, sorcerers, and otherworldly beings that have a physical form but employ magic and the supernatural to threaten others. *The Mummy* as shown in both the original movie and the 1990s version falls into this category: something that was once human but has become something more powerful through forbidden magic. Other monsters of this type may come directly from some hellish dimension, summoned into this world by foolhardy humans or cosmic occurrences. Before making any infernal pacts, know the answers to the following questions:

» What are their powers and how can they use them to threaten others or get what they want?

» What is the theology or rules that govern and limit their powers?

» What cost do they pay to use those powers and what weaknesses do they create?

» What do they want from the mundane world and what do they abhor about it?

Experiments and evil scientists

Something has gone wrong or someone has done something amoral, resulting in a normal person becoming monstrous in some way or the creation of something terrifying. *Dr. Jekyll and Mr. Hyde* is the most famous version of this tale, rivaled by *The Fly* (in both its movie versions). The audience will accept a lot if you provide even a basic scientific rationale. That science-gone-wrong origin implies a science-gone-right solution, or at least a brave attempt to find one. Think through all the implications of your monstrous experiment with these questions:

» What was the cost for carrying out this experiment?

» What was the original purpose or goal of the experiment?

» Who paid the cost and how did they pay it?

» Can the experiment be repeated?

» What was learned or what truth revealed?

» Can it be reversed or cured or defeated?

Ghosts and evil spirits

This monster includes any kind of ectoplasmic or ethereal entity that haunts or bedevils the living. These beings can't be overcome by physical force, but they may themselves cause physical harm. Perhaps they are the soul of a dead person or an entirely supernatural being. Because of their insubstantial nature, overcoming or appeasing a ghost or spirit requires moral, spiritual, and mental strength rather than physical ability. Commune with your spirits by answering these question:

» Why does the entity interact with the living?

» Does the entity want to cause harm, be left alone, or pass on some message?

» How can it affect the living? Physically? Psychologically? Possession?

>> Is it tied to one place or object or is it free to haunt where it pleases?

>> What can defeat it or put it at rest?

Golems and constructs

This man-made monster is designed to serve but ends causing trouble and even disaster. The monster from *Frankenstein* is the ultimate example, as are tales of killer robots and genetically engineered creatures. These creations are more than human physically and other than human mentally and spiritually. Chapter 12 offers lots more advice about writing artificial lifeforms. Come up with a frightful construction plan by answering these questions:

>> Who made it and why?

>> What costs did they pay, rules did they break, shortcuts did they take?

>> What makes this construct more than human?

>> What makes it other than human?

>> How can it be controlled?

>> How can it be destroyed?

Lycanthropes and shapeshifters

This monster is an individual who can shift between two or more selves through some supernatural or scientific transformation. The werewolf is the iconic version, and there are as many variations on them as there are dog breeds. The otherworldly shapeshifter from the movie *The Thing*, who can mimic others, is another version. In both cases the monster can pass among humans sometimes, but the monstrous form lurks just beneath the surface waiting to be discovered or let loose. Get you shape changers under control by answering these questions:

>> How and why do the shifts happen?

>> How much control does the monster have over the shifts?

>> What strengths and weaknesses does each form have?

>> Are the forms distinct personalities or shared expressions of an individual?

>> Is there a cure or way to stop the shifts and would one or more of the selves use the cure if they could?

MY HERO, THE MONSTER

Some folks just love a baddie. It's no surprise: Monsters though they are can also be sexy, powerful, and cool. They're the ultimate rebels. They do what they want and don't care about what normal people think. You can absolutely have a monster as your hero.

The easiest way to make this work is to have your monster be the lesser of two evils, fighting an even nastier and less appealing monstrous foe. Or the monster can be a tragic figure, someone or something whose point of view the audience understands, but whose evil nature dooms them to a fate that audiences recognize as just even as they're a little sad to see the cool monster go.

Vampires and the undead

The undead exist in that nebulous, unsettling space between life and death. They thus have connections to both worlds and properties of each. Whether they're a flesh-eating ghoul dwelling in the sewer system or an aristocratic vampire in her castle, the aura of death and decay surrounds them. Only by taking from the living can the undead fend off death's final embrace. Before you defy death, consider the following questions:

>> What does it take from the innocent and living in order to survive and thrive?

>> What is its fundamental nature, scientific or supernatural?

>> What are its strengths and vulnerabilities?

>> How humanish is the monster? Can it pass as one of the living or is its visage purely terrifying?

Hunting Down Homicidal Humans

From Norman Bates in *Psycho* to Annie Wilkes in *Misery* to Hannibal Lecter in *Hannibal*, human beings can cause just as much fear and dread as any lake-lurking gill-man or leather- and spike-clad demonic executioner summoned from hell. Although fantastical monsters offer dark pleasures of their own, an entirely natural killer can create a special kind of realistic horror and dread. The following breaks down the disturbing elements of writing fiction about killers who can seem all too real.

Confronting all too natural-born killers

The most frightening thing about human monsters is that the audience doesn't have to suspend their disbelief. Both history and the daily news are full of terrible tragedies caused by profoundly evil and horrifying people. The precedent is everywhere and the precise threat is very imaginable.

The idea that a killer lives in the neighborhood, that they could be anyone and could kill anywhere is deeply disturbing. These homicidal humans may be rare, but they're not impossible. The dreadful anticipation created by a suspicious neighbor and the shocking revelations of what can really happen behind closed doors literally bring the horror home. More than anything, these stories suggest that anyone could become a monster.

Beyond the existential fear of the murderer around the corner, many are also morbidly fascinated with the macabre and sometimes bizarre details of serial, ritual, and mass murder. Horror stories with homicidal humans as antagonists typically dredge up inspiration from the darker and more extreme cases. Chapter 5 on worldbuilding advises that you start with Earth. Starting with the details of real murders means to some degree letting a psychopath inspire and guide you. That research into actual atrocities can be truly traumatic and isn't for everyone. One of the reasons horror stories are cathartic for audiences is that they're fiction. The fictional framework insulates the audience from the full implications of death and agony.

WARNING

True crime stories are more numerous than ever, from books to documentary series to podcasts, and audiences have developed a taste for them. Successfully and responsibly telling a true crime story takes research, skill, and thoughtfulness. Even then you risk disrespecting the true criminal's victims or casting unfounded suspicions on the potentially innocent. This section, indeed this whole book, is about fiction, and we don't necessarily think the approaches to writing a horror story are the same as what you need to write true crime.

Solving dramatic and mysterious murders

Freed from the challenges and obligations of true crime, make your human monsters dramatic characters first and foremost custom-made to inspire the specific kinds of horror and dread your story demands. All the techniques for metaphor and monster characteristics detailed in this chapter still apply, even for stories that include no supernatural or science fiction elements. A human who behaves animalistically (say, eating human flesh) is monstrous and frightening even though they don't have wolf claws or vampire fangs.

Don't be afraid to heighten your homicidal humans for dramatic effect. Fictional serial killers often transcend the mundane murders with massively complicated means of murder weighed down with meaning and motive. They seem capable of being in multiple places at once and always plan six moves ahead of the protagonists. The immense cost, time, and labor involved in carrying out their baroque schemes go unmentioned, and audiences are fine with this for the most part. It's not only okay, but often it's awesome to give your killer a little bit of more-than possible in order to heighten their horrific impact and keep the cycle of unknown → anticipation → revelation flowing.

TIP

Fictional killers exist on a spectrum between unimaginable and all too possible. You have to make them at least somewhat believable in order to get the fearful frisson of "it could happen to me" from your audience. But real crimes are seldom as imaginative as horror fiction audiences desire. Here again, MAYA is a useful guide (see Chapter 6). Make your killer's actions too imaginative and over the top, and the tension dissipates into a pulpy farce (which maybe you want, maybe you don't). Too real and it risks becoming depressing and revolting rather than thrilling. Avoid making your killers too one dimensional, however. They can't just be pure evil.

At one end of the spectrum lurk the iconic slashers of movie franchises like *Halloween, Friday the 13th,* or *Saw.* Those films have thrills and chills by the bloody bucketful, but no one in the audience believes that kind of thing can happen to them. As those franchises have gone on, the killers themselves have become supernatural monsters more than homicidal humans. At the other end of the spectrum are more grounded and emotionally disturbing movies like *Henry: Portrait of a Serial Killer* and *Monster,* which work hard to ground the horrors in the gritty, mundane details of reality, making them all the more horrifying for their plausibility.

Exposing deadly cults

Real world cults caused some of the most disturbing and horrifying mass casualty events in recent history. The tragic 1978 murders and suicides at Jonestown, Guyana, made Jim Jones and his cult world infamous and introduced the macabre expression "drinking the Kool-Aid" into the popular lexicon. Cults are as much an object of morbid fascination as serial killers and have been the subject and setting for many great horror stories.

With cults you get not just one homicidal human, but also a whole church/gang/sect full of seemingly normal people whose worldview has become threatening in some way. The real antagonist is the cult leader or leaders, who often don't get their own hands bloody, but enthusiastically encourage their followers to do their work (see Charlie Manson). The cult leader claims some connection to a higher power or some greater understanding about the universe. They offer their followers enlightenment or salvation or worldly power, and in return they expect full and complete devotion. Cult followers are isolated from their friends and family, giving themselves fully to the leader's skewed view of reality. This break from the consensus worldview makes cultists particularly unsettling.

REMEMBER

One of the creepy-cool things about cults in horror stories is that, as often as not, the cult leader is right! They really are in touch with some otherworldly power or privy to secret wisdom. Maybe the dark power they worship is manipulating and using the leader, but that demon or ancient god really is giving supernatural gifts in return for those human sacrifices. Real-world cults have a terrible record at predicting the end of the world, but those failed predictions may well come true in your story. Similarly, the Satanic Panic of the 1970s and '80s in the United States saw the publication of dozens of stories of devil worshippers. Although none of these stories were in fact true, they're full of outrageous tales of cult activity to inspire your fiction.

Winning the duel of wits

Chapter 18 explains how important the unknown is in creating a sense of dreadful anticipation. The mystery of the unknown is a super-alluring tool in all kinds of stories, and of course it's key to the wildly popular mystery and suspense genres. An entire whole other book could explore all the techniques for writing great stories in those genres, but you can use some core techniques from those genres in your horror fiction.

Chapter 19 provides basic structures commonly found in horror narratives. Two of those, the discovery and contest narratives, work especially well for homicidal human-driven plots:

>> **Discovery narratives** focus on the mystery of uncovering the source of horror that's murdering people and trying to stop them. The audience knows little about the killer as the story opens and learns more along with the protagonists. Figuring out the puzzle keeps the audience engaged, and the clever twists, turns, and revelations along the way provide the thrills. The protagonists can be law enforcement, potential victims, or even curious kids, anyone who struggles to preserve or return the community to safety and normalcy in the face of the antagonist's monstrous actions.

>> **Contest narratives** focus on the clash between the killer and those trying to stop them. Here the audience gets to know a lot about the homicidal human, usually much more than the protagonists in the story. They spend time in scenes from the killer's point of view, the tension building as the crimes grow more and more intense. The dramatic question involves whether the protagonist overcomes the human monster or not, and if they do, what cost will they pay?

Both narratives create a game of cat and mouse between the two sides, and often the line blurs between who is the hunter and who is the hunted. Taking that formula from the classic mystery/suspense story into the realm of horror means working in all the other techniques in Chapters 18 and 19. In addition to curiosity, what other emotions does the story invoke? How do the revelations continue to ratchet up the horror toward catharsis? What characteristics make this homicidal human not just a killer, but a true, threatening, impure monster?

Chapter **21**

Lurking in Every Shadow: Where Horror Resides

Horror stories as a form of entertainment really came into their own in the 17th century with what became known as Gothic literature. Horace Walpole's *The Castle of Otranto* (1764) kicked things off with a wild, weird, and creepy tale of an ancient castle, a cursed family, skeletal spirits, and a giant helmet that appears out of nowhere to crush a bridegroom on his wedding day. The Gothic continues to be a thriving genre of its own and went in all sorts of interesting directions, all of them sharing at their core uniting element: a particularly potent place of mystery and dread.

As a source of fear (refer to Chapter 18), the Gothic is firmly rooted in a very specific and usually extremely spooky place. This evocative environment sets the dark mood for everything that happens in it, from ghosts and vampires to murderous mad patriarchs and deep family secrets. You also can discover a lot from the Gothic's use of setting to enhance dreadful anticipation, no matter what your story's setting or source of horror is. This chapter builds on those crumbling, cursed Gothic foundations to provide a set of tools for making all of your horrifying locales as effective as possible.

Constructing Environments That Raise Dread

Sometimes a writer, usually a beginning writer, will say something like, "The city of New York is really the main character in this story." When we hear a student say that, warning bells go off. It usually means the story is lacking an interesting antagonist and may not have anything resembling an engaging plot. However, in a horror story, the setting sometimes really is the antagonist, and it can be every bit as dangerous and proactive as a monster. And even when your setting isn't actively trying to kill your protagonists, you want it to be doing everything it can to establish the right mood and tone.

Any place becomes freaky if you turn out the lights and fill it with spiders, but you can make a location put characters and readers on edge in more subtle and versatile ways. The following sections are some of the creepy characteristics common to many horror story locales. As with the monster characteristics in Chapter 20, an environment can incorporate some or all of these to varying degrees. Think of them as levels you can lower or raise or perhaps as sinister spices that let you season your setting to taste.

TIP

These elements are useful for any part of your setting, from the site of your dramatic finale to a weird curio shop the protagonist visits to find a clue to the demon's origins. Later we give you even more tools for creating key locales that are central to your story.

Isolated or inaccessible

Dreadful locales are almost always cut off from the outside world in some way, which allows them to work as contained, focused settings for horror. This isolation means that characters can't easily come in and, more importantly, can't easily leave. With escape routes cut off, the heroes have to face the horrors instead of fleeing. In the classic Gothic formula, the isolation is usually geographic: the strange house on the hill, the sinister swamp at the edge of town, and so on. But your scene can be right next door to a busy grocery store and still be isolated in some other way.

Here are some narrative uses for isolated or inaccessible places:

>> **Physically cut off:** Whether it has high walls and locked doors or is off the main roads and beaten paths that locals are familiar with, it's hard work to enter and leave. In a supernatural story, the location may seal itself off through magical means, making both finding and escaping it a reality-defying challenge.

>> **Economically or socially committed:** The characters can't afford to leave without paying a price they're not prepared to pay, and nobody outside the location can help them. They invested their life savings or are duty-bound to stay for the sake of their career or family.

>> **Psychologically ensnaring:** The location holds some powerful sway over the minds and imaginations of the characters. It can be hypnotic or supernatural, or perhaps the characters' own personal obsessions keep them there. Whatever the cause, they want to stay, no matter how much sense it makes to run.

>> **Out of time:** The location is temporally distant from the contemporary world of your story either because it hasn't kept up with the times or because the people there choose to live life out of touch with modernity. It doesn't have electricity, the landline is unreliable, and the unpaved roads wash out in a heavy rain. More than likely, it has seen better days, but now it has fallen toward ruin with crumbling walls and unstable floors. Visitors can't rely on the technology and/or ideas they're used to, isolating them from the world they're most comfortable and capable in.

Intimidating and foreboding

The location doesn't welcome visitors with open arms and a cup of hot cocoa. As you approach, the high walls, ancient woods, or fog-shrouded moors all make folks think twice before stepping in. The place probably has a grim reputation among locals, with a long history of crimes or tragedies or mysterious goings-on. That doesn't mean it's hard to get to or inaccessible. The dangerous neighborhood can be two subway stops away, the cursed woods just at the edge of town.

Intimidating locales usually include some or all of these characteristics:

>> **Domineering:** The place physically and/or psychologically looms large in the surrounding community. It may be the cruel baron's castle, an oppressive outpost of the police state, or a crumbling hospital, home to cruel treatments. Everyone knows it's there, they just chose to look away for fear of drawing its attention.

>> **Legendary:** The place has a reputation with those who know of it — and it's not good. It was the scene of horrific crimes, the location of a tragic loss, or home to an infamous dabbler in the dark arts. There's a witch out in those woods, or maybe it's a werewolf. You may get different stories, depending who you talk to, but everyone agrees something spooky is there, even if they've never seen it themselves.

>> **Restricted:** The space is quite welcoming, if you're the right kind of person. Otherwise, stay away! Secret corporate research facilities, military bases, cult

compounds, and reclusive or insular communities all raise suspicions amongst the many people who aren't allowed in. These spaces emphasize the disparity of knowledge between the protagonist and other characters, implying that there's not only a secret worth keeping, but one that may be worth killing for.

>> **Dangerous:** This place can flat-out kill you. It can be naturally perilous: a crocodile-infested swamp or avalanche-prone mountainside. Perhaps dangerous people or monsters protect it, attacking anyone who approaches. It may be toxic or cause psychic harm or be filled with booby traps. Outsiders may or may not know about the dangers that lurk within. Either way, most who trespass suffer direct harm, and only a plucky or lucky protagonist can survive the experience.

Uncanny and unsettling

The place just doesn't behave like a place should. It doesn't have to be supernaturally weird, but it should be out of the ordinary in ways that cause unease or suggest unhinged origins. The real-world Winchester Mystery House in California famously has a seemingly endless series of rooms with stairs that go nowhere and doors that open onto nothing. Whether or not it's actually haunted depends on who you ask, but the reasons Sarah Winchester had it built that way are well-known and no less unsettling for it.

Here are some characteristics that make these locations so disquieting:

>> **Weird:** The location has pockets of strangeness that is otherwise pretty normal: A corner in a sealed room that always drafty. A clearing in the woods where compasses spin wildly. A gaunt, silent doorman who never blinks but smiles a toothless grin when he opens the door for visitors. The contrast between the odd and the normal signifies something's afoot, which puts visitors on edge.

>> **Unusual:** The denizens of the place have odd customs and local rules that defy logic and tradition: Always knock three times before opening the closet door. Never go into the woods after midnight. Don't wear red on a Sunday. Locals take these kinds of behaviors for granted and visitors are likely to ignore or forget, which often in turn gets them into trouble.

>> **Too perfect:** The house is just too good to be true in some way. It's exactly the right price for a down-on-their-luck family. Everything is spotless, nothing collects dust, and the furniture is so comfortable you never want to leave. Ever. No matter what.

» **Shifting:** Unpredictable changes occur too quickly or without explanation. Locked doors that open themselves. A different clerk at the shop counter every time a character comes to the curio shop. A cuckoo clock that chimes a different song every day at noon. Those familiar with the place have learned to take these changes in stride, but for an outsider they cause confusion and curiosity. And you know what curiosity leads to . . .

Assembling Haunted Houses and Other Lairs of Fear

The ancestral estate, decaying and glowering behind its high wall. The shuttered-up family home at the end of the lane where no one's lived for years. The some-times luxurious mansion whose visitors sometimes never leave. The haunted house is one of horror fiction's great icons, a setting for stories that is familiar but also home to endless variations. Its power is in large part from the inherent tension that comes from a place that's supposed to shelter and comfort but instead threatens and even kills. It sets the aspiration of having a home against the anxieties of being trapped in a house that's doing harm instead of good.

And not just houses house the monsters, mad scientists, and other antagonists of horror. The lost cavern inhabited by primordial lizard people, the circle of standing stones high atop a hill where witches and warlocks perform their rites, and the cement bunker in the deep desert where amoral geneticists splice together things that shouldn't be, all serve similar narrative roles to the classic haunted house. Evil and mystery lurk in these are places, and visitors risk skin and soul upon entry.

REMEMBER

Because our love of haunted houses runs deep and true and because they have so many iconic elements to explore, this section focuses on the haunted house. *Note:* The principles here apply to all manner of dread locales.

Recognizing the types of haunted houses — What lies within

There's no one way to haunt a house, but haunted houses do have some broad categories based on what dramatic purpose they serve in your narrative. Think about what kind of characters may journey into the house and how the house itself entices or repels potential visitors:

>> **Forbidden houses:** They're off-limits for some reason. The house or entities in the house don't want to be disturbed, or the people around the house have declared it dangerous. Characters have to go out of their way to go into the house, becoming *overreach plot protagonists* (where characters purposefully push past limits and restrictions; refer to Chapter 19 where we discuss these protagonists in greater detail). Nobody comes inside without some hint or warning that it's a bad idea. They enter prepared to face at least some possible threats.

>> **Hungry houses:** They lure people in because the house or the entities inside want to harm hapless humans for some nefarious reason. They're traps, seducing visitors with tantalizing promises, often using either complicit or ignorant outsiders (like real estate agents) to lure people in, who then become *trespass plot protagonists* (where characters unknowingly stumble into danger; see Chapter 19). Characters stumble into the house with little or no concept of how dangerous it really is and often have no preconceptions or capabilities for encountering the dangers within.

>> **Mystery houses:** They contain compelling clues to a mystery about the living in some way. A main character's loved one was murdered here or perhaps the secret to a family curse lies within. The house becomes a set of obstacles in the way of the character's *discovery plot* (where characters investigate a mystery of some sort; see Chapter 19). Characters come to the house with an agenda, but they likely don't really understand how deeply mysterious the house will turn out to be.

TIP

As you think about the nature of your house, you can draw upon the tools for making monsters in Chapter 20. Ask yourself these questions:

>> In what way is it threatening?

>> Does it behave like a sentient human or a wild animal in some way? Is it heightened in scale or decor or mood, overfull of cobwebs and bristling with gargoyles?

>> What smells, textures, tastes, and sounds do visitors encounter?

>> What unnatural and corruptive auras does it exude?

>> Are there any disgusting secrets, a rotting corpse, or a room filled with flies?

>> What specific design elements captivate the audience's imagination, a massive greenhouse or room-sized pipe organ? If your house is going to be an antagonist, make it monstrous.

These are all questions to help you think of your house as more than just a location, but also as a special kind of character that has as many distinctive and creepy aspects as your story's antagonist.

Welcome, foolish mortal

When writing and creating your haunted house, identify what brings your protagonists to this house. That depends on how the house relates to the character's core wants and objectives. How you define the house's purpose for your plot should guide the ways you furnish and inhabit its interior. Consider the following:

>> **Subjects of study:** These houses are places where outsiders come looking for answers. The haunted house is an alluring subject for those fascinated by the afterlife because these homes can hold the key to the mystery of life and death. Or they can unlock the potential of humanity's latent psychic abilities. The house may or may not resist being studied, but it often becomes the battleground for the classic conflict between the skeptic's technology and the believer's seances, struggling to make sense of the home's mysteries. Neither side usually comes away happy from the experience . . . if indeed they come away at all.

>> **Objects of envy:** They're impressive buildings that highlight class differences and sharpen money problems. A haunted house is often a manifestation of the price of opulence. These grand homes are dream houses, aspirational and enticing, but most people can never afford such a place, unless something is wrong with it. Perhaps something is wrong with the people who can afford to own it. Any great mansion must be built upon the pain and suffering of the poor. Its existence is inherently exploitative. All that pain and trauma brings out the worst in those stuck there, often families who have spent all their money to buy this "great bargain" and now have no way to leave it without suffering financial ruin.

>> **Shelters for dread:** They're houses for something or someone unsavory. The dread denizens use the home as an actual home; it shelters them and their secrets from the outside world. Far from being abandoned, the house is kept up in the grim manner that best serves its inhabitants. A hungry house can house an angry spirit or some creature who feeds on outsiders. A classic Gothic house is the ancestral home of the menacing heir to a family fortune built on bloody deeds. The house directly expresses the wants and actions of its owner, often to the detriment of visiting protagonists who have to enter if they want to defeat the antagonist.

Tapping into what came before

Every haunted house has a history, and something from that past is reaching out into the present to cause trouble. You don't want to invent the house's history until you've established its role in the story, but after you've done that, you can have fun with its history. Finding out the dark past of how this place came to be haunted or cursed should be a real pleasure for the audience.

Look to Chapter 7 for more about writing exposition, and remember that the key is to make the backstory a fully formed story with a beginning, middle, and end that features characters audiences hope and fear for. In horror, presenting the house's history is a great excuse to tell a mini ghost story within your bigger story. Short short horror stories are their own artform, and they can land a mighty dreadful punch in just a page or two.

When imagining the house's history, ask yourself these questions:

>> Where is it located?

>> Who built it and why?

>> How has it changed since it was built?

>> Who has lived (and died) in it?

>> How did it become haunted?

>> Why does it stay haunted?

Remember, when we write "haunted," we're including not only by ghosts but also possessed by demons, occupied by cultists, used for evil research, or infested with giant killer bats.

Sizing up the scene

After the characters step through those creaking doors, envision what's it like inside the house. How expansive is your haunted house? There's no right answer because both a hundred-room grand mansion and a dingy apartment with a mysteriously sealed closet door have horrors lurking, just waiting to be found.

Here are three ways to make your house's interior heighten the horror for those characters unfortunate enough to step inside:

>> **Labyrinthine houses:** They have more locked doors and cobwebbed corners than the characters can ever explore fully. There's always another place for a monster to hide or for a secret to be discovered. The threat of the unknown never fully dissipates in such a place. Even worse, getting lost in a maze of rooms or turned around in a trackless wilderness creates a special kind of helplessness. Your readers know what being lost feels like and can easily sympathize with the desperation and frustration that sets in when you don't know where to go next.

>> **Confined spaces:** They present their own unique advantages. Readers can come to know every corner in a confined location and hold it in their minds.

They know where the exits and entrances are and how one space relates to another. The sense of confinement combined with the isolation of many haunted houses (refer to the section, "Recognizing the types of haunted houses — What lies within," earlier in this chapter) creates a stifling claustrophobia. That confinement means when the weird things start to happen, there aren't as many places to hide. It also means that when something strange changes — a door that wasn't there before, a crack in the bathroom mirror, a shift in the lights — the readers will notice.

>> **Shifting structures:** They're more unusual, places where the hallways and rooms aren't always in the same place and new ones may appear. Such changes usually require either supernatural or science-fictional sources of horror and are often the hallmark of an aggressive, antagonistic house. These radical changes to reality immediately put visitors on edge and can send them into a full panic if the door out disappears.

Combining two extremes or switching from one to the other within the same story and even the same location is possible. Investigators of a haunted house and residents in rundown Gothic manors often pick just a handful of rooms to use as a kind of base camp or home within a home. These rooms become places of security and comfort in the face of the wider house's mysteries and threats (at least for a while). And nothing is creepier than finding a new space within a home that shouldn't be there. Mark Z. Danielewski's mind-blowing haunted house novel, *House of Leaves* (Pantheon Books), is a perfect example of taking this bigger space within a smaller space to an intense extreme.

A ghost will follow you home . . .

A haunted house or other accursed and dangerous place seems like a container for the evils within. There's an implicit assumption by the audience and characters that the bad stuff is in there, and as soon as the trouble starts, getting out means reaching safety. That works well for many stories. Make sure you have a clear goal for the characters, something specific the audience can hope for. Escape the haunted house couldn't be clearer.

Except sometimes, leaving the house isn't an escape. As in Susan Hill's 1983 novel *The Woman in Black* (Hamish Hamilton), sometimes the ghosts follow you home and bring the haunting with them. The protagonist's ordeal within the house has left them corrupted or cursed with no easy escape. The story shifts gears and the narrative moves from one of discovery or trespass to one of pursuit or contest (Chapter 19 details these plot types). This change usually comes as a surprise to the reader and characters alike and can reset the audience's expectations about the story, increasing the levels of anticipation and dread.

Taking the haunting out of the house works best when the external haunting feels as closely connected to the house it came from as possible. If the ghost from inside has journeyed out, find ways for its actions and desires to reflect the origins and nature of the house. Is it trying to drag the protagonist back or re-create the haunted house in a new location? Maybe the ghost doesn't actively exit the house, but rather a psychological obsession or connection that follows the character home. Figure out how the ghost's behavior outside reflects the haunting inside. Often these stories loop back to the house for the finale, the protagonist forced to face the unfinished business they fled from.

EXERCISE

ASSEMBLING YOUR DREADFUL LOCALE

We encourage you to play with different combinations when you're writing your horror story to create a realistic setting. Although the set of settings that we discuss in this chapter isn't exhaustive, it is versatile, and we encourage you to play with different combinations. Whether you're constructing a haunted house, an ancient ruin, or an uncanny corner store, try and answer these questions:

- **How do its environmental elements create dread?** Look to see whether the location is isolated or inaccessible, intimidating and foreboding, or uncanny and unsettling, and to what degree.

- **What's the dramatic essence of the location?** Determine whether the location is forbidden to visitors, hungry for victims, or a vault in which mysteries are kept.

- **Why do your protagonists come to the location?** Figure out whether the location is a subject of study, an object of envy, or a shelter for some dreadful thing they must confront.

- **What is the place's history?** Tell the story of who, what, where, when, how, and why this place came to be as dreadful as it is.

- **What is the size and scope of the space?** Figure out if it's vast and confusing or confined and claustrophobic. Assess whether it shifts and changes in response to intruders.

6

The Journey from Writing to Publication

Understand how professional writers edit and revise their stories.

Use the drafting process to discover, explore, and enhance story themes.

Bring in the right experts and outside help to push your story to the next level.

Find out what you need to know about literary agents, editors, and the increasingly interesting world of self-publishing.

Embrace the power and potential of networking.

IN THIS CHAPTER

» **Revising with a clear plan**

» **Doing things in order**

» **Thinking about theme**

» **Giving it one final polish**

Chapter **22**

Revising and Editing Like a Pro

So, you've written a complete draft of your story. That's an accomplishment worth celebrating! Many beginning and early-career writers struggle to get to THE END. Take a moment to feel proud. You deserve it, even if you have mixed feelings about the story draft at this point.

After you've taken a moment to honor all the hard work that went into creating that initial draft, you're ready to honor the story itself by putting in the rest of the work to make it the best version that it can be. The first version is just you telling the story to yourself; subsequent drafts are you figuring out how to best tell the story to others.

Now's the time to fall out of love with your story and ask the hard questions. If a friend showed you this story, would you recommend they send it out for publication as soon as possible? How does this story compare to the best of what's being published today? How many ways to improve the story can you think of? If the story were 100 percent totally awesomely perfect, how would it be different than what you have in your hands?

Odds are that you have some work to do. And that's fine because no one writes perfect first drafts. No one. This chapter helps you begin with a clear, actionable revision plan to keep you on track. We explain how revision has to go before editing because revision includes big-picture stuff that can affect or even require deleting smaller things you may otherwise have spent a lot of time on. We also address finding, improving, and revising for theme, which is an underutilized but vital aspect of any story. Lastly, we talk about final draft concerns, such as editing and proofreading.

TIP

Create a version history of your story by keeping copies instead of working on the same one over and over. You'll never lose anything this way. Just save a new file with the story title, draft number, and date (for example, Day_of_the_Dread.v3.101022). Some authors do this before each work session to help motivate them; looking at all those drafts in a folder on your computer can energize you if you ever hit a writing funk.

Creating a Revision Plan

After you've put all that time into creating your first draft, the best thing you can do is not look at it for a week or two. Preferably a month. Why? You're too close to the story. You need to cleanse your literary palate by enjoying other stories and getting some distance from your own. You need to get to the point where moving away from your initial creative impulses doesn't feel like a profound betrayal.

Seriously. Give yourself space and time.

REMEMBER

When you're more excited about the possibilities of your story than nervous about the workload required to explore those, you're probably ready to dive back in.

When you're ready to revise, don't just wing it. You need a plan. "Making things better" isn't a plan. Nor is "fixing everything." Problems identified are problems solved, so your plan should be to locate and deal with the many problems a first draft has, but in the most orderly way possible.

Here are a few ways to create a revision plan. Use one or more of them, as you are so moved.

Putting on your reader's cap

Take your writer's hat and throw it out the window. You're a reader now, and that's all you're going to do. You're not going to try to fix one darn thing yet. Follow these steps to start acting like a reader:

1. **Read the entire story from the first line to the last without pausing (if possible), taking notes, or fixing anything.**

   The goal is to see the entire thing as a complete whole versus the fragmented, convoluted mess it was during the act of creation. It may still read like a fragmented, convoluted mess, which is okay. First drafts are supposed to be a mess.

2. **Read the entire story again, this time slowly and carefully.**

   Make notes on a page-by-page, scene-by-scene, and chapter-by-chapter basis. Document everything that bugs you, confuses you, challenges you, or raises any questions. Mark gaps in logic, things that are missing, and things that are out of sequence. Note anything you wish were better.

TIP

   If you have two computer monitors going, you can have two files open at once and easily work with two documents. You may find it more effective to print out the story and make notes in the margin. Another option is to work with the story on your screen but take notes by hand on paper or in a notebook.

   Think more about character, plot, conflict, and setting aspects than small things you'll deal with later, such as sentence structure, grammar, or word choice. Focus on the big stuff here. Writers revise first and edit later.

   Resist the overwhelming urge to tweak, adjust, delete, and all that. This isn't yet the time!

3. **Put your writer's hat back on and work through each of your manuscript notes in order.**

   If you solicited the help of outside readers (more on this process in Chapter 23), incorporate their notes into yours and deal with them in the same way.

   Pay special attention to the cause-and-effect logic of plot, the motivations and actions of the characters, and all types of conflict.

Remaking the outline

On a wall, door, table, or whiteboard, create a visual chapter-by-chapter, scene-by-scene, or even a moment-by-moment outline. Yes, this is going to get big. In many ways, the bigger you make this outline, the more easily you'll notice problems.

TIP

We recommend using notecards or sticky notes, but go with whatever makes sense to you. Consider using colors to track story elements, such as blue being clues that move the main character closer to the solution of a mysterious magic crime or red being scenes that take place in a dreamworld.

Watch for imbalances and disconnects in terms of characters, conflicts, plot, and setting. Refer back to the outline as you're handling revisions so you don't lose track of important issues or fix one thing only to unfix something else.

Going high tech

No story exists or has ever existed that you can't lay out in a graph, chart, or spreadsheet. Mine your story for useful data. For instance:

>> Chart out how many scenes are in each chapter.

>> Mark what the per-chapter word count is.

>> Discover the frequency a villain or rival appears or is mentioned.

>> Find out the average sentence length and overall *lexile* (the reading difficulty rating of a text generated through the Lexile Framework for Reading). You want a relatively consistent rating or the writing will feel jarring since it's fluctuating between reading levels.

The data you've gathered will reveal gaps, imbalances, disconnections, and unintended consequences that go unnoticed when performing a more traditional read-through. Addressing these issues becomes your revision plan.

Going low tech

Using sticky notes doesn't get more low tech, but they're a versatile way to help manage revision. Purchase a few packs in a range of colors, sizes, and shapes. Play with them for a bit because you know you want to.

Then get serious about revision using one or more of the following ways to make the sticky notes work for you:

>> Read a physical copy of the story and mark each page with a color-coded note to indicate what type of revision is needed. For example, orange may be scene expansion, green may be adding more description, yellow may note a low-conflict scene, and so on. Afterward, go back and handle all of one color at a time, then repeat the process with the next color.

>> Read a physical copy of the story and mark each page with a color-coded sticky note to indicate which character has an important scene. You'll likely be shocked at how frequently this simple activity reveals that characters are more (or less!) important than you suspected by virtue of how many important scenes they're given. Adjust as needed.

>> Without going back to your story yet, write your main character's primary want and primary need on its own sticky note. Place those in clear sight of your work area so when you return to work on the story, you can't help but be reminded that every moment of the story should affect and be affected by those two things. Perhaps want/need notes for important secondary characters and antagonists might also prove useful?

>> Make notes about your story in the whirlwind of your day and smack them onto a wall, mirror, or whiteboard. (This one's great for super-busy people!) When you actually carve out to time to revise the story, address the issues, concerns, and thoughts one note at a time.

TIP

If you firmly pull a sticky note forward versus peel it backward to detach it from the pack, it'll remain flatter and stick better. Try it and see!

Answering first-draft questions

Every writer develops their own set of questions that get to the heart of what's not working in an early draft. Veronica Roth, the author of the massively successful *Divergent* trilogy, has blogged about her revision process, including revealing the questions she asks about her own story drafts. Mystery writer and *Writer's Digest* contributing editor Elizabeth Sims has detailed her revision process and questions she asks of her stories in her fine writing how-to book, *You've Got a Book in You.*

Ask the revision questions that these pros do, or use the following:

>> Where am I in this story? What makes it a story only I can tell?

>> Where does the *real* story begin? And where must it necessarily end?

>> What are the emotional stakes for the main character? For the other characters?

>> How much do the character arcs actually arc? Does the story clearly demonstrate character change?

>> What can I cut without losing meaning? ("If I had to pay $27 per word for each word in this draft, do I really want all those words in there?")

>> Which characters could most easily be combined into one?

>> Which scenes am I most excited about? Least excited about? Why?

>> Does every scene have conflict? Is the conflict strong enough?

>> Am I able to identify the purpose of every scene?

Your answers become a targeted revision plan. Act on it accordingly.

Using second opinions

Seeking an outside reader or two at any point in the revision process is acceptable, especially if you're unsure where to direct your efforts. Just realize that your story is likely a mess because creativity is messy, as are early story drafts. It's already asking a lot of someone to read any manuscript, but one that's going to be extremely flawed? That's a huge ask. Make sure the person knows what they're getting into and reward them appropriately.

Chapter 23 reveals how to find, work with, and thank outside readers.

Revising First, Editing Later

Both revision and editing require tools. Revision is bulldozers, cranes, and cement trucks. Editing is dental picks, brushes, and a polishing cloth. Read on for ideas on what happens in the revision process to move your story toward being audience-worthy.

Some people use the term "story development" to talk about revision and "copyediting" or just "editing" to refer to sentence-level fixes and general proofreading. So long as you do them in the correct order, we don't mind what you call them.

Figuring out who this story *really* is about

Revision time means everything gets reconsidered. That includes your protagonist. Again and again, we see student and client stories where the most dramatically interesting character is . . . the antagonist. Or a supporting character. Or simply someone who isn't the alleged protagonist.

REMEMBER

Stories are about a protagonist who deeply wants something, is willing to work hard to get it, and changes through their engagement with the forces of opposition that get in their way. Being interesting needs to be part of the whole package.

If that's the situation in your story, you have two options:

» Revise your protagonist into someone equally interesting.

» Admit that the story is really the antagonist's or supporting character's or whoever's story and pivot to embrace that fact. There's no shame in making the right choice a bit late in the process.

It's easy for us to just say "Change your main character!" because we don't have to do the hard work of making your story viable. Changing whose story it is represents a massive undertaking that has seismic repercussions throughout the whole manuscript. You may need to cut sections, add new ones, change point of view, and more. But if that shift moves you toward the best version of the story, do it right now. This is the second-best time to make big changes. (The first-best time is in the planning, prewriting, and outlining stage — before you write a single word of the actual story. Chapter 3 is where we talk at length about all the planning and plotting stories require.)

Discovering what this story *really* is about

Odds are that when you wrote the first sentence of the story, you were pretty sure the story was about one thing, like a wisecracking robot butler that becomes sentient. Now that you can see the entire thing after spending so much time with the story and creating it from beginning to end, no doubt you see it's potentially about cryogenics, the Fate Lords, black holes, and perhaps a dozen other things as well.

There's a huge difference between things that happen in your story and what your story is actually about. What a story is about is the thing that nonwriters are most attracted to when you describe your plot. That's The Cool Thing. The Hook. The Wow factor. It's the story aspect that will help you sell your story and earn a sizable audience.

Readers may mistake what simply happens in a story for theme. You need to guide them toward theme, and we talk in greater detail about that very thing in the next section.

If nonwriters don't consistently get attracted to a single thing, you may have problems. A story about too many things is just as problematic as having it meander without any particular focus. You're the writer. Every creative choice is yours, so make them. Decide what the story wants and needs to be about, and then deliver on all the promises and potential of that focus.

To zero in on what your story should be about, answer the following:

>> What do you most want audiences to take from the story?

>> What's the most important plot line?

>> What's a single image (or symbol) that characterizes the story?

>> What's a single word that characterizes the story?

>> What's the most meaningful way your protagonist changes?

>> What's the primary theme of your story?

After you're settled on what your story is about, revise with that agenda in mind. Tweak your protagonist's backstory and desire. Adjust plot to highlight the story's new focus. Scrutinize character arcs, the climax, and the ending. Also, layer in complexity and nuance as appropriate so your story isn't overly one-note about its focus.

Focusing on Theme — It Isn't Just for Eighth-Grade Book Reports

Writers can get evasive about theme. It's understandable because the idea of talking about theme feels awkwardly reductive, like the audience is tapping their feet, yawning, and checking the time as they whine, "Just bottom line it for me — what's this story about?"

Writers want their work to be read, appreciated, enjoyed, and reflected upon. They want any meanings to be the natural result of that multifaceted story experience. That's fine, but theme is inevitable, even in a story where the writer insists: "Aw, shucks! It's just a story!" Stories bring up questions, explore possibilities, present conflicts, and examine the consequences of character action. Given all that, there's simply no way for audiences *not* to find meaning in those words. Even if it were possible to write a meaningless story, who'd volunteer to experience such a thing?

TIP

Start with the larger, overall feel of the story before getting down to the nitty-gritty details. Writers can easily get lost in trying to perfect a single paragraph — or even a sentence! — and then may lose the heart of the story.

To make the most of themes in your story, you need to understand exactly what theme is. Then you need to find the themes that are already likely tucked away in your written pages before embarking on a plan to amp up those themes. The following sections guide you in those steps.

Understanding what theme is

General readers might call theme the meaning of a story. Literary critics consider theme the point of the work. As writers, we prefer to talk about theme as the core idea of a story: *Theme* typically reveals a truth about the human condition to audiences. A mother's love has limits. Always take your shot because regrets haunt you until you die. Absolute power corrupts everyone it touches.

As we mention in Chapter 2, theme isn't a statement that must hold true for all stories or even in real life. The theme need only be authentic to *this* story, given its unique characters, circumstances, conflicts, and choices. Theme deeply connects to and informs what your story is about.

REMEMBER

Given that, you can easily see how theme infuses a story with greater meaning. It also helps you plot a story by unifying its parts. Even though plot gives you the what, theme gives you the why. Knowing that will help you both write and revise.

For example, consider Thomas Harris's *The Silence of the Lambs*. The core thematic dilemma is this: *Is it worth dealing with one monster to catch another?* No matter what you do, you're dealing with at least one monster.

Finding an elusive theme

You may not know your theme, which is okay. Many writers focus on plot and character in the first draft because they're just figuring things out. The job of revising is to do big-picture work, and building up a potential theme is an effective big-picture way to improve your story fast.

REMEMBER

Here are places to look for the kernels of theme hiding in your manuscript:

>> **The logline:** If you're summarizing your story in a sentence, surely the theme is suggested because the story's key elements are — or should be! — present. Scrutinize nouns and verbs for clues to related themes. For example, if you use the word "school," then knowledge, maturation, justice, or revenge might be potential arenas for a theme.

>> **The conflict:** Yes, the theme must connect to the primary conflict, but it likely makes an appearance in other conflicts, too. Look for recurring threads that can be tied together to build, challenge, and finally demonstrate your story's theme.

>> **The character arc:** The challenges facing your protagonist as they grow and change offer a fine opportunity for the exploration of a theme. Think about the character's desires, fears, and flaws, too. Potential themes are tucked into those areas without a doubt. Chapter 2 discusses character arcs in greater detail.

>> **The ending:** Identify the takeaway you're creating for audiences in the climax and resolution That mood, idea, or the new norm for the protagonist's life is connected to the story's theme. Unpack it and you've got something to layer in all the way back to the start.

You may still be tweaking your theme well beyond the second draft. That's okay. Revision is like renovating an old mansion. You need to install, take down, or adjust all the walls, doors, and windows before you get down to decorating (in this analogy, that's the final editing).

You may wonder whether it's okay to have more than one theme. Of course, just like you can have more than one plot in a story. Remember that only a single option is the main one, however. Make sure it does the heaviest lifting.

REMEMBER

Themes don't have to be wildly unique in terms of the insight they offer. They often reveal a timeless truth, though your particular take on it should feel fresh, different, and relevant to the audience's real-life world at some level.

TIP

Avoid the temptation to outright state the theme so you're 100 percent sure audiences will get it. Themes are far more effective when audiences have to work a bit to suss things out. They're actually more interested in the subtle, nuanced layers of meaning related to your theme than anything pithy you can slap on a fortune cookie slip or bumper sticker. Plus, audiences hate speeches and words of wisdom masquerading as dialogue or exposition.

Revising for theme

When revising theme, think of it as a character. Think of all the things a character can do in a story: Advance the action. Generate tension. Become increasingly complex. Attack or be attacked. Suffer a glorious, terrible, or ironic fate. A theme can do all of that, too. So, let it. Chart out its own progress throughout the story. Does it experience meaningful change the same way you want characters to in small, medium, and large ways?

A character may also literally be a theme, or at least the theme personified. For example, the character of Frankenstein's monster in Mary Shelley's *Frankenstein* unmistakably represents the obligation of a creator to that which they create, which is related to larger concerns about the dangers of uncontrolled scientific progress. (Refer to Chapter 12 for more on the responsibility regarding the making of artificial lives.) What Frankenstein's monster does in response to being shunned by society is part of the story's comment on that obligation.

In terms of embodying a theme within one of your own stories, look for characters whose goal or dramatic situation is in alignment with your book's theme. Own that opportunity. Let their internal and external conflicts reveal the nuances inherent in your theme. Allow their character arc to mirror the development of theme in your story.

TIP

As early as possible in a story, have a character ask or think about a question related to the primary theme. Of course, you don't answer it yet, or if you do, the answer is insufficient or incorrect. The true answer necessarily comes from all that follows, as if the story is making an argument and needs to present all the evidence before a final judgment can be made.

Theme should be woven carefully throughout the story versus be lumped all together in the climax or at the very end. In fact, if you're dealing overtly with theme in the final scenes, you've probably done an insufficient job of developing it naturally in the previous scenes. You shouldn't need to hammer it home at the end.

Here are three of our favorite tips to help when you're revising for theme:

>> **Think small.** It's relatively easy to make your bar fistfight scene or screaming-at-McDonald's date-gone-wrong moment about the theme, because the theme is surely tied to the primary story question, so naturally all big conflicts relate back to it. Keep the theme persistent throughout the story by layering it in small ways in many scenes. Tweak the small conflicts and choices a character makes to connect with the theme in small ways. Those small moments will accrue meaning and end up being quite potent.

>> **Think drama.** Characters having intellectual debates about philosophical, political, psychological, or social ideas is a snore in most stories. Audiences want drama, so find ways to make theme come alive visually. Use descriptive language to establish mood and theme in these moments of action. Think about strong verbs and nouns more than just piling on the modifiers. Think about conflict. Make your theme earn its top billing over all the other potential and counter themes.

>> **Trust the audience.** Assume that the audience is smart and thoughtful. Trust that they'll figure out any key issues in play because you've done what we write about in this chapter and have layered theme appropriately throughout the story. Don't overcompensate at the end to ensure everyone gets it or you may get called out as being preachy. Have faith that audiences will get it without a booming "Hey, this is what I meant!" announcement or speech at the story's conclusion.

Buffing, Polishing, and Shining — The Final Edit

When every plot point is logical and well-placed, the characters are three-dimensional and properly motivated, the story world is ripe with character-revealing conflict, and theme flexes its well-earned muscles in a firm but not overly flashy manner, it's time for the buff, polish, and shine — the final edit.

Trusting your ears

Human brains are problem-solving machines. They're so adept at fixing things that they can correct the spelling or add in missing words before you notice the issue. Trust your ears instead. Read your story aloud — not silently in your head — at a normal pace, similar to the speed audiobooks are read on other professional formats. Your ears will pick up clunky language, awkwardness, and missing words that you'll miss if you read quietly to yourself.

Getting someone else to read it to you is even more effective. They may stumble over a line that you wouldn't have because you wrote it. If so, recheck that line for syntax, rhythm, and diction.

REMEMBER

An always-available option is one of the many free text-to-speech programs. Run these as many times as you need to guide your editing process.

If you can't get someone to read your entire story, ask them to read key scenes, like the first five pages, an important argument, or the story climax. If possible, bring in multiple readers to handle dialogue-heavy scenes so they can each take their own role like it's a play. Everyone has more fun this way, including you.

Editing your way to a better story

Your word-processing software has built-in grammar and spellcheckers, so use them. However, don't trust them blindly because they're not perfect. Ultimately, you need to figure out these things yourself, as all aspiring professional writers must.

We don't have the space to cover all the language and grammar skills you need to use in a final edit. So, we instead urge you to rely on these three sources:

>> **Grammar Girl:** This award-winning free online resource (www.quickanddirtytips.com/grammar-girl) is used by millions

because the advice is good, the explanations are practical, and the examples are funny. Much of her advice have been compiled into multiple books, if you prefer that format.

>> **Strunk and White's** *The Elements of Style:* This slim book has been a must-read for writers since it came out in the 1920s. It's been updated numerous times, which has only made it stronger. *Time* magazine even called this one of the 100 best and most influential books written in English since 1923.

>> **Roy Peter Clark's** *Writing Tools: 50 Essential Strategies for Every Writer:* He knows writing and story as well as anyone. This book is silly-good and extremely clear in the tips, advice, and examples.

It boils down to this: Strong language/grammar muscles of your own paired with spellcheckers and outside readers is a winning combination. For guidance on finding and using outside readers (which can include hiring a freelance proofreader), visit Chapter 23.

TIP

Many writers find it easier to narrow their editorial focus for a scene or chapter to one area versus try to fix everything. That's fine. Do a dialogue-only edit, description-only edit, action-only edit, and so forth, as you see fit.

REMEMBER

Don't try to master every one of your grammar hiccups at once. When you realize you're making a mistake — like the there/their/they're snafu — write the definitions on a notecard with clear examples that you fully understand and recognize. Tape that notecard cheat sheet next to your computer screen, and every time you encounter a story situation that involves that particular issue, check yourself. After some time, you'll internalize it. That's when it's time to tackle the next issue.

Chapter **23**

Getting Second Opinions: Editors, Experts, and Sensitivity Readers

At some point in the revision process, second opinions are necessary. You may want to use them to guide how you create draft two, to be the final set of eyes on the second-to-hopefully-final draft or to support you all throughout the entire process — that's up to you. Outside opinions let you know if your story works in all the ways it needs to.

Although writers are the first audience for their own stories, they're not the primary audience. Second opinions from outside sources help gauge the response of your intended audience. This chapter focuses on how you get feedback from second opinions on the story, authenticity advice from subject-area experts, and sensitivity reads from a qualified professional.

WARNING

The competition for publication or production is fierce. You may be tempted to skip this chapter and hurry ahead to all the how-to-submit information in Chapter 24. Second chances don't exist for a story when it comes to agents and editors. They're simply far too busy to look at revisions of something they passed on, so assume that any no they give is a no for good. With that mind, make sure they're considering the best possible version of your story.

Receiving Good Story Feedback

You may feel reluctant to share your work with others. "What if they don't get it? What if they get it but don't like it? What if they tell me to give up writing and go dig ditches? What if they steal my idea?" These fears are common, but the benefits of receiving feedback far outweigh potential negatives.

REMEMBER

In our combined half century of experience as writers, we personally haven't run across a single case of someone stealing a story. But if that still worries you, remember that your work is copyrighted from the moment it's written whether you include a copyright symbol © on the document or pay the increasingly expensive fees to officially register your work. Visit the U.S. Copyright Office for details on the whats, whys, and hows of registering creative work (www.copyright.gov), though look online for what writers, editors, and agents have said about this subject as well.

Feedback is an integral part of the storymaking process. For many writers, finding a regular source of quality responses to your work is the difference between reaching your publication goals or not. The following ideas can help you find or create a feedback situation that works for you.

Making the most of a critique group

Your goal is to partner with a group that's focused on supporting others and providing honest, actionable feedback designed to elevate every work-in-progress they review.

Here are a few suggestions:

>> **Social media platforms:** Facebook and GoodReads offer critique group options, though they vary widely in quality.

>> **Groups affiliated with industry organizations:** Locate groups that are affiliated with — or have members who are part of — industry organizations such as Science Fiction & Fantasy Writers of America (SFWA) or Horror Writers Association (HWA).

>> **Local libraries, bookstores, and coffeeshops:** They're common places for writers to host and promote critique groups.

TIP

There's nothing wrong with having a single critique partner. The benefit of a group, though, is that you'll receive multiple ideas on your story every time it's up for review. The magic sometimes happens best when people bounce ideas off each other in the live discussion portion of a meeting, which doesn't happen at the same level if it's just you and one other person.

Eyeing the characteristics of an effective critique group

Every critique group's goal must be to support each other as writers, to create accountability, and to offer informed, actionable opinions on what's working and not working in a story. How that happens can look quite different from group to group.

Some groups read things right on the spot whereas other groups read in advance and provide written feedback, for example. Some groups are super editorial whereas others are far more big-picture conceptual. However your group prefers to work is fine so long as the members are content with what they're doing and being asked to do, and that your writing is improving.

Here are clear signs that your group is a healthy one:

>> **"We follow our own rules."** The best groups have clear rules, such as all stories being turned in 24 hours before they meet, every story gets no more than 25 minutes of discussion, or they take turns with receiving critiques so everyone ends up going every other session. Make sure newcomers to a group know and agree to the existing rules in advance.

>> **"We do what we agree to do."** Quite simply, they don't flake out. They read what they agree to read, and they show up to the meetings as promised. They value the group enough to commit to it.

>> **"We're honest with each other."** Vague criticism or ephemeral praise isn't helpful. Successful groups agree to tell the truth. They share what's wrong, what's missing, what isn't clear, and what doesn't make sense. The writer listens and doesn't take the feedback personally.

>> **"We make sure to point out the positives."** For some, the word "critique" or "criticism" means something akin to "rip apart, tear down, and destroy . . . ideally with lots of sobbing." In contrast, quality feedback is generous, thoughtful, and specific, plus it's offered with respect. It should include questions and positive things versus just what's not working.

>> **"We listen to the writer."** Feedback on a story isn't a one-way street. Effective groups engage the writer to understand what weaknesses they perceive in their own work and the thoughts they have on how to overcome those. Most groups allow the writer to ask questions up front when sharing the story so that everyone knows to address them in the feedback.

>> **"I feel energized after we meet."** You should leave a session feeling hopeful and bursting with ideas that you feel confident will improve the story. Feeling confusion, sadness, or disempowerment is a clear sign of an unproductive critique session. If it happens once in a blue moon, just move on. If it's frequent, there's a pervasive problem with the group.

>> **"We celebrate each other's successes."** Writing isn't a zero-sum game. If a group member gets a publication offer, it's not one less publication opportunity in the world for you. It's just proof that people like you can succeed. Take it as a positive — a win. Steer clear of frustration, resentment, and jealousy in yourself or others.

>> **"We discuss the business of writing and publishing."** If the goal of every member is earning meaningful publication, sharing information is reasonable and useful. These groups set aside time in meetings to discuss industry changes, agents/editors, and the submission process, as well as their hopes, dreams, and fears related to their writing career. These conversations don't take the place of critique sessions but serve as a bonus add-on and a nice change of pace.

If you group is lacking in one or more of the preceding points, perhaps a candid discussion can change things for the better. If not, thank the group members for all their help and politely move on. Join a better-functioning group or start your own.

WARNING

Struggling writers aren't especially well-equipped to help other struggling writers. Typically, they offer unhelpful vagueness ("This doesn't work!") or equally unwelcome suggestions ("This is how I would do it!"). Ideally, a critique group has one or more members who've had writing and publishing success — they're likely well-trained to assess story problems and encourage effective writing. The model they provide helps others elevate their feedback ability, too.

Seeking input, not solutions

The purpose of peer feedback is not having other people fix things for you. If you want that, hire a professional editor. What you want from peers are their honest feelings, reactions, questions, and ideas. You want to be able to see your story through the viewpoint of others. You want honest insider information about what's working, what's wrong, what's missing, what isn't clear, and what just plain doesn't make sense.

You're plenty smart enough to figure out a solid solution of what to do next. After all, you know the characters and world of your story better than anyone else. Practically speaking, the buck stops with you because your name is on the piece. You're the one who has to fully believe in and be able to defend any choices you employ in the final draft.

WARNING

The more insecure or unqualified a responder feels, the more likely they are to lean on vague phrases such as "I liked the intro — it was really good!" or "I just don't like your protagonist!" or "The fight scene made me want to run out and kick some zombie butt!" What you want is specificity. Trust the power of *why*, *what*, and *how*:

>> Why are you responding so positively to the introduction?

>> What about the protagonist specifically irks you?

>> How did the writer create a fight scene so good that it made you want to leap into the undead fray?

Cultivate a golden reader

A *golden reader* is the perfect reader of your work. They're someone who gets your writing in all the ways that matter. These amazing people read your stories generously, thoughtfully, and carefully. Then they offer astute feedback that answers both the questions you have as well as those you didn't yet articulate. We call them *golden readers* because they're worth their weight in gold.

WARNING

A golden reader may not have the same range that you do. They may be dynamite at responding to high fantasy and body horror, yet they can't abide slashers or urban fantasy. Or maybe they don't like to read scripts, but they love a sprawling novel series. Recognize their limitations while valuing their strengths.

A golden reader doesn't need to be another writer. Any reader with a keen sense for story can serve in this role. In fact, you may have better luck with a golden reader who has zero aspirations for writing; writers are often too busy to spend their limited time and energy helping other people do the very thing they themselves yearn to do.

TIP

We're big believers in literary karma. If your golden reader doesn't need or want the thanks they deserve, pay it forward. Be someone else's golden reader, or at least a fervent supporter. Writing great stories is hard work. Help out your peers.

Hiring freelance editors

Language issues, grammatical gaffes, and story hiccups are relatively easy to spot in the writing of others. With your own work? It's incredibly difficult to identify because you know what you meant. This kind of blind spot is something all writers have at some level. Don't be ashamed — it's been our experience that even the strongest of writers run into this problem. If it weren't a real problem, there wouldn't be so many fulltime freelance editors thriving today.

You can save money by asking a friend to edit your story, enlisting the help of a bargain-basement freelancer, or hiring someone from a work-for-hire site. However we don't recommend these options because the quality is suspect. An editor who isn't properly trained can create as many new problems as those they fix.

They may mean well, but intentions aren't results. Ultimately, you tend to get what you pay for.

Not all editors are the same. Make sure you're hiring the right type of editor to address your story's needs:

>> **Developmental editor (DE):** The DE comes first in the editing process. This is the Big Stuff, like character relationships and plot points, but it also includes scene and chapter construction. Hiring just this type of editor may make the most sense before having an entire first draft, though a DE is able to help you more by seeing the scope of your vision via a full, complete draft.

>> **Line editor (LE):** The LE comes after developmental editing. Line editors often have several rounds of back-and-forth with the writer to get the point of view consistent, keep the language precise and fresh, and tighten scenes to make them more effective. They care about things like atmosphere, tone, pacing, narrative logic, and the emotional impact of the writing. Line editors *don't* scrutinize your manuscript for errors.

>> **Copyeditor (CE):** Copyediting comes after line editing. Because CEs are concerned with the mechanics of writing, they scrutinize your manuscript for errors. They care about correctness, readability, and adherence to the rules of a specific style guide. They'll also fix factual errors and inconsistencies in the text.

WARNING

A popular misconception is that in-house editors will fix your story after they buy it. If it has more than the occasional surface error, it may not get bought in the first place. Editors are limited in terms of how many titles they can acquire and how much time they can spend on each one. A problem-ridden manuscript doesn't hold a lot of appeal. The level of competition is so high that you can't afford to send in anything but well-edited, polished work. Many writers are hurting their chances of earning a "Yes!" by not getting professional-level input during one or more stages of revision.

HOW TO HIRE A PROOFREADER

After you've revised and edited everything to the best of your ability, you may opt to hire a freelance proofreader to look over the almost-final manuscript. Hiring a proofreader — even if you hired a professional editor — is smart because the proofreader can look over the manuscript after you've accepted or rejected the editor's edits. Here are the steps we recommend before signing someone up to handle the full project.

- **Read reviews.** On their website or in social media, professionals make sure that potential clients know about past great work. If you can't locate positive client feedback, assume there isn't any. Move on.

- **Find out if they specialize.** If they don't do sci-fi and your story is loaded with robots, blaster cannons, and warp drives, you probably should look elsewhere, even if they seem to be qualified at editing in general.

- **Request a sample.** Ask if they'll work on a few pages of your story — perhaps one chapter — to see if you're a good match. You may have to pay for this, but wouldn't you rather be out the cost of one hour of your proofreader's time than them doing the entire job at a lousy level and still insisting you pay their full rate?

- **Check their rates.** The Editorial Freelancers Association (https://the-efa.org) or the Chartered Institute of Editing and Publishing (https://ciep.uk) have rate information as well as robust directories of professionals. Trust these sites over places like Upwork (www.upwork.com), Fiverr (www.fiverr.com), or Freelancer (www.freelancer.com). You may find a well-priced professional at these three sites, but your odds of a successful interaction are higher with the EFA or CIEP.

Supporting Your Story with Expert Help

Creating a sense of believability to the characters and story world is a must for any story. Even though you're surely doing all you can to get things accurate, sometimes you need experts to confirm that things are correct.

Aspire for more than just factual correctness, however. Life is full of rich complexity and depth. It's appropriate for every type of story, genre or not, to use, value, and celebrate that fact.

TIP

As a writer, be kind, generous, and thoughtful about all people, cultures, and ideas — not just because it's a movement to be more diverse, inclusive, and fair, but because it's the right thing to do.

Depending on the story you're writing, using one or more of the following types of experts may push your story to the next level. For example, when creating a First Peoples Futurism story or alternate history based on projecting an existing culture into the future, having a sensitivity reader with a background in that area may help you avoid clichés and common misrepresentations — both problems can easily overshadow an otherwise well-written story. And if you're building a tech-heavy sci-fi tale, talking to someone at NASA, Stanford, or Apple might give you a wealth of authenticity and detail.

Talking to subject matter experts

We're going to share something potentially shocking here, so brace yourself. People *love* to talk about their work. How does that help you? Don't be afraid to directly ask questions of someone who works in the same field as one or more of the characters in your story, or for a job/industry relevant to the plot. If you do it in a manner that's respectful of their time, you can even approach people you don't know.

Here's an example of an email you can send that usually does the trick:

> Dear So and So,
>
> As part of the research to support my YA fantasy novel, I've been studying gemology. I recently ran across your website and found your blog posts on lab-created diamonds to be extremely helpful.
>
> Since gemology affects a sizable part of my story, I'd very much like to make sure I'm getting my facts correct. Are you open to answering a couple of questions via email, or perhaps speaking with me on the phone for twenty minutes at your convenience?
>
> Sincerely,
>
> You

We've used versions of this note with great success, earning chats with NASA scientists, Pulitzer-winning journalists, and city mayors. A 20-minute interview can easily turn into hours, and a two-question request might go on for weeks or months. Experts love to talk about what they've devoted their lives to. If you demonstrate a sincere interest, they're going to want to talk to you, especially if you're making a real effort to get the facts right.

REMEMBER

Keep the initial request small. Glancing at your watch at the 19-minute mark and saying, "Oh, I'm sorry, I promised to keep this to 20 minutes and we're nearly out of time!" often results in them suddenly discovering more time to talk about themselves and their work.

Tapping into the universe of universities

Another underutilized source for experts is colleges and universities. If the institutions are public, they have a state-sponsored commitment to bettering the community. If the institutions are private, the fact that they're teachers says they have a personal commitment to help.

If you're not sure who to reach out to, try department heads. They'll know the abilities and areas of expertise of their peers. Steer clear of administrators, though because they have a different agenda than do teachers.

In addition to reaching out directly to professors for information, many institutions have libraries, resources, and events that could be a story boon. At bigger research institutions, you'll find an equally compelling range of speakers in the sciences and other areas that may help with a current project but could also give you the idea and inspiration for future ones.

TIP

University professors know a lot of people in their field, be it other professors, researchers, or professionals who do the thing itself versus study it. Ask them this million-dollar research question: "Who else should I be talking to about this?" Odds are they'll not only have a few names of people who are perfect, and you'd never know about them otherwise, but the professors also likely will offer to make an introduction.

Using sensitivity readers

Author and sensitivity reader Patrice Williams Marks explains that sensitivity reading "is an emerging industry available to content creators who want to alleviate unintentional racism, bias, or misrepresentations in their books, in magazines, ad campaigns, television, film, gaming, app development, and more. Sensitivity readers point out any possible racism in projects' descriptions/actions of characters or story. They may also point out any possible stereotypes in descriptions/actions of characters or story, and suggest how to address the issue."

Marks reports that two frequent problem areas in manuscripts are character descriptions and dialogue. "Authors may only describe the Black characters by the color of their skin, perhaps even using a food metaphor," she says, "while describing non-Black characters using rich descriptives and characteristics. Some may also have the tendency to have all their Black characters living in 'the projects/ ghetto,' 'speaking slang/broken English,' or dealing drugs."

Another area of concern for sensitivity readers is issues around gender and sexuality. Beyond just running into the usual issues of writing outside of lived experience, writers can just as easily strike false notes even when actively trying to achieve political correctness. Identity is an increasingly important consideration in stories, especially in light of how genre audiences will see themselves in the characters you create. In sum, authenticity in character creation is more than just ticking boxes. It requires writers to have an honest curiosity and willingness to learn, as well as the ability to ask questions — and carefully listen to answers — when expert help is needed.

Fantasy writing, in particular, can suffer from issues of bias and insensitivity. For example, Marks asks, "Do the wizards have to be described as white or Black? Perhaps using descriptions, such as 'pure, light,' to convey the good guys and, 'ominous, retched, menacing,' etc. for the bad. But if that is not possible, and the writer wants to stick to the 'norms,' then they should make sure 'Black' is not a reference to their race or skin tone, but their soul, perhaps."

For more information on sensitivity reading, listen to Patrice's *Author Uncut* podcast (www.patricewilliamsmarks.com), which also has tips and information about screenwriting, novel writing, and being an indie author.

WARNING

Some people believe sensitivity readers are free-speech police or thought censors. That's a reductive, false way to examine the role they play in building better stories. Having a range of perspectives is valuable to any story's development.

AVOIDING OTHERING IN CHARACTER CREATION

To avoid othering or presenting unintentional bias or misrepresentations, Patrice Williams Marks recommends:

"Connect with people who are not like you and maybe step out of your comfort zone. Seek out activities where the people are diverse. That way you'll start to see people as they really are, and not treat everyone of a certain race as monolithic. Also, when creating characters and situations, think about switching the races. If your character were suddenly Caucasian, how different would that look? Would that change the dialogue, the attire, the neighborhood, their education, their job? That exercise would help you hone in on how you've created a character and could pinpoint stereotypes you may not have seen before."

Using cultural consultants

Related to sensitivity readers is the role of a *cultural consultant* — someone who has a deep, lived experience in a particular culture and is willing to share their expertise to ensure a writing project accurately portrays that culture. For example, if you're creating a role-playing game about Aswang, which are vampires from the Philippines, you may hire a Filipino cultural consultant to offer thoughts on how you present village life, the Tagalog language, and general Filipino ideas regarding the supernatural. Even if you spent a few summers in Manila when you were a kid, that's not enough. You'll have gaps in your knowledge, and the visitor and kid lenses through which you viewed that city surely missed key things.

If you're using real-world cultures in your story beyond your own lived experience, consider running your writing by a cultural consultant. It's shockingly easy to create harmful and upsetting misrepresentations of a group of people. Insensitivity and misrepresentation has real consequences — boycotts, social media fury, loss of sales, and scathing reviews. Plus, it's just a lousy way to treat people.

When in doubt, bring in an expert.

REMEMBER

Cultural consultants (and sensitivity readers) don't make corrections. Their job is to identify and explain issues, and, if needed, provide research links for your own follow-up. Similarly, they don't proofread or edit your manuscript unless you pay extra for that, and they're qualified to do so — it's an entirely separate service.

Looking beyond your own experiences

You may think the safest way to avoid inauthenticity or inappropriateness is to simply adhere to that old writer maxim: "Write what you know."

However, Marks doesn't agree, saying, "I think that is terrible advice. What a boring world that would be! Books, films, even commercials take you to places you've never been and people you may never meet. I'm not Hungarian, nor did I know anything about the Hungarian Revolution, but I wrote a screenplay with it as a backdrop. Research is the way to make that happen."

Research is so important that we devote Chapter 6 to it. Although including things you personally know in your stories to create that welcome authenticity is sound advice, doing so isn't enough. If it were, you'd probably just write an autobiography. This book is about writing science fiction, fantasy, and horror, after all, which means stories you (probably!) haven't lived.

So, you may wonder if you have permission to write about things beyond your experience.

Absolutely. As Marks says, it's all about research. Do the necessary work before you write, then do your best while knowing you'll likely still get things wrong. That's okay. The revision process exists not only to address story issues and weak writing, but also to overcome bias, insensitivity, and ignorance. Take the time to handle all your story's flaws and shortcomings.

Your obligation is to make sure that when the story is ready to be submitted for publication that it's full of integrity, nuance, and care, along with all the things that the audience wants from stories, such as character, conflict, change, and emotion. Take all the time you need to make that happen.

TIP

Make sure you examine your intentions for writing outside of your own lived experience. Writing authentically across differences is a charged topic. Don't do it without reflection and deep contemplation first. This is more than just a trend — it's the right, responsible thing to do.

LOOKING FOR MORE HELP

If you want more guidance in this area of challenging your own biases and embracing how diversity is more than a buzzword or being politically correct, consider the following sources:

- *The Anti-Racist Writing Workshop: How to Decolonize the Creative Classroom* by Felicia Rose Chavez (Haymarket Books)

- *Writing Diverse Characters for Fiction, TV or Film* by Lucy V. Hay (Creative Essentials)

- *Writing the Other: A Practical Approach* by Nisi Shawl and Cynthia Ward (Aqueduct Press)

Chapter **24**

The Three Ps: Publication, Pitching, and Promotion

When it's time, it's time — your story is the absolute best you can make it. Any work you're putting into the manuscript now feels superfluous versus making it better. Outsider readers verify that you have something good. You still believe in this story and honestly think it's on par with the things you've found at Barnes & Noble, on Amazon, seen on Hulu, or played at your local game store.

Great! That means it's time to get serious about sharing your story with the world. This chapter can steer you in the right direction.

Teaming Up: Agents, Editors, and Producers

If you aspire to see your work come out through mainstream media outlets, you need partners. In essence, you're asking for someone — many someones, really — to invest time, energy, and money on you. Any New York publishing house that chooses to publish a novel is investing a *minimum* of $50,000 in it, which has to cover printing, marketing, editing, art, the salary of all the publishing folks working on the novel, and the writer's advance. For TV and film, the number is far, far higher because so many more people are involved at every stage of the process.

Be honest. Is your story worth $50,000 at this point? If so, read on. If not, revisit Chapter 22 on revision and Chapter 23 on soliciting outside feedback to further improve your story. Follow the advice there until your manuscript is $50,000 good or better.

Recognizing what an agent does

A *literary agent* represents a writer and their work to media industries. They help shape material to make it salable, they handle contract negotiations, and they coach you all along the way. Some even find you paid writing opportunities between your own projects. The best agents also offer career guidance, brainstorm story ideas, and support you as a gentle friend or pushy taskmaster, depending on what you need.

In return, agents typically charge a 15 percent commission on all writing of yours that they sell. That means that you're in a success-based partnership. If the work doesn't sell, neither of you make money.

One big plus with agents is that they negotiate better terms for you when it's time to sign a contract. In fact, they should be able to earn you extra money that covers their 15 percent cut. Plus, they know what rights to keep and which to let go. They also know the gatekeepers who are most likely to want a story like yours.

After the deal is struck, the agent — for the most part — steps aside and lets an editor or producer take it from there. Editors and producers are going to have a lot of ideas about how to shape, develop, and fine-tune your story even further. Agents are available to step in and mediate the situation if creative differences slow or stop forward progress.

Figuring out whether you need an agent

An agent can do a lot for you, but the question might remain: "Do I *really* need an agent?" The answer is a resounding . . . maybe.

The type of media you're writing for may help you decide. For short stories, podcasts, tabletop games, video games, or immersive experiences, agents aren't really a thing. Having an agent just isn't the industry norm at the moment. For novels, films, TV, and plays? Agents are very much the norm.

Here are three extremely practical reasons that you may want an agent:

>> Most of the top media companies exclusively consider work submitted by reputable agencies.

>> Agents get responses to submissions far faster than you will on your own, and these responses often include feedback versus the "Dear Submitter(s) . . ." rejections non-agented writers mostly receive.

>> If an agent is handling all your business matters, you have more free time to actually write.

We know a few successful novelists and screenwriters who aren't represented by an agent. It's entirely possible for you to succeed without one, too. But if agents are the norm for your industry, they're the norm for a reason. Carefully consider what you believe you're gaining by not having an agent, or being actively in pursuit of one.

REMEMBER

Having a bad agent is worse than having no agent. "Bad" doesn't mean "villainous," but more like a bad fit for you. Common complaints about agents are that they don't return calls/emails promptly, give up on submissions too easily, have more excuses than answers, charge up-front or extra fees beyond the commission on sales, or insist on story changes you don't believe in.

TIP

If your agent isn't responsive, encouraging, and openly transparent, have an earnest conversation first and see if they're open to changing. An agent works for you, after all — you don't work for them. If things can't be mended, part ways without burning bridges. Although your agent might deserve a good blowing-up-at, doing so is never worth the fleeting moment of satisfaction. The fact that you're justifiably upset won't matter if you come across like a sociopathic barbarian. Leave all barbarians, sociopathic or otherwise, to the pages of your stories.

Landing an agent: The how and where

If you've ever dated, you have the skills required to get a literary agent. Do your research. Be picky. Realize it's about a strong match versus finding the perfect person. Make sure you have shared goals and expectations before making things official. Recognize that not all relationships last.

An agent is your representative to the publishing world. Are they making the right impression? Do they accurately represent what you are all about? In this way, they're more than just a private partner — their role is very public.

The nuts-and-bolts process for getting an agent is fairly straightforward. Locate an agent who represents and sells the type of story you have, then send them a polished, persuasive query letter, which we explore more in the next section. If agents like your query letter, they might ask to see some or all of the story. If they like that, they may offer to represent you.

If you're interesting in finding out more the world of agents, we suggest these resources:

>> **Publisher's Marketplace:** For about the same price of watching a movie in a cinema (with a small soda and a box of candy), you can purchase access for a month and find recent titles sold, deal specifics, industry trends, and specific agent contact information. Check out www.publishersmarketplace.com to see if that's something that can help you in your publication journey.

>> **Writer's Digest:** Another option is the annual marketplace guidebooks from *Writer's Digest* which have thousands of updated listings for publishers, magazines, contests, agents, and more. Buy print copies at your favorite local bookstore, or get free marketplace updates and spotlights at www.writersdigest.com.

>> **Manuscript Wishlist:** Although this option is less comprehensive, it's also a far more up-to-date resource with industry people linking to tweets and articles with comments like "Someone send me this YA novel right now!" Check out www.manuscriptwishlist.com.

>> **Writer's Guild of America West:** For agencies that specialize in scriptwriting, check out this free directory. Look up www.wga.org for details.

>> **In-person meeting and networking:** You can also meet film or TV agents in person at film festivals and scriptwriting conferences. Refer to the section "Making the most of conferences," later in this chapter for tips.

TIP

Although finding the names of agents is usually easy, their client lists often aren't public knowledge. One sneaky-good way to uncover the identity of a novelist's agent is to check the acknowledgments page of their books. Odds are, they'll thank their agent by name (just as we've done in this book).

TIP

Be sure to bypass a kneejerk "No!" by doing your homework before you submit. Submission guidelines for all industry people are easily found online. So are their specific story requirements in terms of genre, style, medium, and more. Follow those guidelines. Too many writers assume they're the exception and submit work that has zero chance of success for that particular industry person.

Pitching Like a Pro

At the heart of getting your work considered for production is pitching. Written or verbal, the *pitch* is your first chance to earn a "Yes!" from industry people who have the wherewithal to bring your story to the world.

Generally, small products like a short story or audio fiction don't require pitching — it makes more sense to just look at the thing itself. For anything larger, however, pitching is the primary way for someone to quickly assess whether it's worth their time to commit to examining the whole thing. The following sections explain just what you need to know about pitching.

Crafting the query

In nearly every media industry (novels, film, TV, and so forth), a written pitch is typically called a *query letter*, which comes from the word "inquire," meaning to ask a question. The question you're asking is some variation of this: "Has this one-page pitch hooked you enough for you to ask to see the rest of my story?"

Similarly, in all media industries, the query letter includes the same three parts, which are as follows:

>> **What I've got!** This is an exciting snapshot of your story idea, given as a one-liner or short paragraph. Also include a projected final word count or length as well as audience/marketing information. Here are a couple examples:

- "This will be an 80,000-word young adult urban fantasy novel set in Chicago during the Great Depression."

- "This proposed eight-episode miniseries is a space police procedural set on Pluto in the near future."

>> **Why you?** Because you're not sending willy-nilly to just anyone, share your specific reasons for sending to this industry person. Feeling chosen puts them in a far happier state of mind than any scattershot "Dear Occupant" letter will.

TIP

We suggest citing a recent sale they've made that sounds exciting or referencing one of their interviews or conference presentations that impressed you. Just to be safe, prove you're not offering false praise by offering something specific about it. (We discuss more about the power of writing conferences in the section, "Making the most of conferences," later in this chapter.)

>> **Why me?** What special experiences, training, or relationships do you have that inform or support this project? What previous publications, writing awards, or degrees make you ideally suited to write this particular story? If you don't have much to list other than enthusiasm, keep this part short. Like "John Doe is a writer who lives in the Seattle suburbs" short.

Even though you've spent weeks, months, or years on your story, too many writers dash off a query letter in an hour or an afternoon, so beware of this pitfall. This is your first chance to be rejected. Don't give them a reason to say "No!" by showing anything but your best writing.

TIP

Most fantasy and sci-fi novelists think big — a series. Don't try to sell more than the first book in the series. Just trust the power of this phrase: "This is a stand-alone story with series potential." Focus on selling one book. If it's a hit, trust us — they'll want more. If you really want to sell a massive series a single deal, write for TV.

Breaking down the three-floor elevator pitch

Whether you actually find yourself on a 25-second elevator ride with the head of a top publishing company, a world-famous director, or whomever, you need to be able to succinctly explain your story on demand, as needed. The goal of an *elevator pitch* is to communicate the main character, the primary conflict, the main force of antagonism, the setting, and the title. That's all you need at this point. You can share the later after you've hooked someone well enough to hear those three magic words: *Tell me more!*

REMEMBER

Here are elevator pitch best practices:

>> **Go short.** It's 30 seconds tops; 20 is even better. Time yourself to verify how long you're going. As with so many aspects of writing, the phrase "less is more" holds true here.

>> **Only give the basics.** There's not enough time to give everything. Why? See the previous bullet. Highlights are all you're giving here.

>> **Names don't matter.** It's too much to remember, and it can get confusing. Trust the power of the adjective + noun combo. A wisecracking space mercenary. A Bigfoot-hating psychic detective. A power-hungry witch queen.

>> **Get straight to the point.** Lose the filler phrases and words. Instead of "This is a story about this ex-detective who witnesses a spectacular alien abduction in one of those old-fashioned New Orleans cemeteries and after being unable to stop thinking about it, he wakes up one morning and decides to set out to learn if it was real or not" say "An ex-detective witnesses an alien abduction in a New Orleans cemetery and won't rest until he proves it's real."

>> **Practice, practice, practice.** You should be able to give your pitch at any time without cheater notecards or lots of "Oh yeah . . . and then there's this!" moments. If you're stumbling or misremembering, you don't yet know it well enough.

TIP

To practice, stand in front of a mirror with a timer and pitch again and again until you're comfortable with both the pitch and the art of pitching.

If your elevator pitch helps earn a deal, a version of it will become what your agent, editor, or producer will use later to sell this project to their team and others. Keep working at it until it sizzles.

Identifying the challenge before you

The volume of people submitting content is high. So high, in fact, that agents and other industry gatekeepers have to say no to stories and projects that are promising or even pretty darn good. You can't afford to aspire for anything but writing a great story. "Good enough" isn't good enough in an industry that aspires for massive success. Neither is hoping something will sell because that topic or type of story is trending. Trends don't last. Great stories do.

Being a pro in every step of the process can help you stand out because so many authors don't bother with professional standards like following directions.

REMEMBER

In the world of fiction, the industry standard for writing software is Microsoft Word. In the world of film and TV scripts, the industry standard is Final Draft. For podcasts, comics, and games, you have multiple acceptable options. If you refuse to go with the industry standard software, make sure what you're choosing to write with can accurately and easily convert your story into the industry standard formats.

Remember that turning in a manuscript is never a one-and-done thing. There's always some level of back-and-forth, which often takes place within the features of that industry standard software.

TRANSLATOR, PLEASE: DECIPHERING WRITING AND PUBLISHING JARGON

One barrier to getting your stories sold is understanding the jargon used by the writing and publishing industry. Here are a few key terms you'll see a lot:

- **Advance:** Money paid in advance of your story being published. It's a signing bonus, of sorts. You won't make additional money from the story until the advance is fully paid off via sales, which is when the story is said to have *earned out*. If your story doesn't earn out, you don't have to pay back the difference, though future publishers may be hesitant to buy your work if your track record shows multiple stories that don't earn out.

(continued)

(continued)

- **Comps:** Competitive or comparable titles. A good comp is something aimed at a similar audience that's published within the last five years. A comp doesn't have to be exactly like your book in style, tone, size, and medium, but it should be similar in noticeable ways.

- **Copyright:** The exclusive, legal right to reproduce or sell a creative work. You don't need to place a copyright notice © on your work for it to be copyrighted — it's copyrighted from the moment it's created. Few writers pay the money to register each work with the U.S. Copyright Office, though if you ever need to sue someone for using your work without permission, registering your work gives you the maximum amount of protection.

- **IP:** Intellectual property. These are the intangible creations of the human intellect. All original stories you solely create are your IP.

- **P&L:** Profit and loss statement. Companies will run a P&L using comps to estimate the profit potential of your project.

- **Royalties:** A calculated percentage of profits that an author receives for each copy of their story that's sold. Royalties are negotiated in the contract stage, so make sure you're happy with the terms, whatever they are. You can't change them after you sign a contract. Many royalty agreements have *escalator clauses,* which means the better your book does, the higher your rate of return becomes, such as you earning 10 percent on net sales for up to 10,000 copies sold, getting 12.5 percent on 10,001 to 25,000 copies sold, and maxing out at 15 percent for 25,001 and up.

- **Subsidiary rights:** All rights beyond the right to publish the story itself. These include film rights, TV rights, book club rights, translation rights, audio rights, and performance rights. Subsidiary rights also include licensing rights to make breakfast cereals, T-shirts, action figures, video games, and amusement park rides. (Lawyers often call these *derivative works.*)

Going It Alone: A Self-Publishing Success Plan

In the past, the only viable way to get a novel, movie, comic, or game out into the world used to be through established publishers and production companies. Now the technology used to produce and distribute those stories is easily and relatively cheaply available to everyone. That means you can do it yourself. But should you?

For certain kinds of projects, such as making a themed short story anthology or print-on-demand role-playing game, self-publishing has become a quick and efficient way to get those into the world. For other projects, the norm remains the more traditional routes like New York publishing for novels, Los Angeles production houses for TV, and so forth. Given that, what's the best option for you and your story?

Answering whether you can really do it all

You're a writer. Are you also a layout and design person? A cover artist? Can you handle publishing, marketing, and sales? If you can do all of those things, be honest — is your work truly at a professional level?

"Good enough" isn't good enough when writing a story, and the same holds true for all the related tasks in making and selling a novel, TV series, podcast, graphic novel, or story for other types of media. This isn't the time to overestimate your abilities or interest when wanting to self-publish.

Succeeding in self-publishing

Many self-published novels still have a stigma. The ease of technology to go from a Word file to Kindle Direct Publishing is too tempting for many, so they send out something that's simply not ready. People succumb to that same temptation in other story media, too, though in fewer numbers only because the production aspect is typically more demanding.

Regardless, stories that get launched into the world by through self-publishing often feature frequent problems. Here are ways to avoid those expected shortcomings:

>> **Commit to flawless editing.** A traditional media company uses a professional editor or two, so invest in one yourself regardless of how good your editing chops are. Visit Chapter 23 for more on working with editors.

>> **Get a great cover.** Unless you're good enough to have been paid money for your art many, many times, get someone else to do it. Avoid using templates or clip art, or getting a family member to create it (unless they've been paid money for their art many, many times). And trust an artist's input on images and style, too.

>> **Go for gorgeous design.** Writers don't think visually like artists and designers do. Bring in a professional. Layout designs such as typography, margins, and running headers matter far more than you'd think.

>> **Be ready to sell, sell, sell.** More than 2 million books are published a year. What's being done to alert people to the existence of yours? Have an actionable plan in place and start marketing well before the launch of your book, film, web series, or whatever form your story takes. Refer to the section, "Promoting You and Your Work — Making the Most of Marketing," later for more specifics.

TIP

Estimate the costs of all outsourced work so you know what you're getting into before you begin hiring people left and right. A budget can be your best friend.

Putting the crowd to work for you

One of the biggest changes in the world of self-publishing is the introduction of crowdfunding or crowdsourcing. Thanks to Kickstarter, Indiegogo, GoFundMe, and similar websites, people can directly invest in your project before you even have to create the actual thing. In return, investors earn perks related to their level of support, which you decide in advance.

Crowdfunding only works if the creator is making a product that's enticing, and they're willing to work hard to promote it before and during the campaign. Carefully examine the most well-funded campaigns of products similar to yours and borrow some of their strategies. Visual products like film, graphic novels, and video games often fare better in the crowdfunding world than text-only stories like a novel because the samples are multisensory.

Here are our tips for creating a successful crowdfunding campaign:

» **Stay realistic.** If you're a new writer or the scope of your project is relatively small, don't ask for $75,000. Choose a goal that's achievable and appropriate. Do your homework so you know your budget is reasonable. It'll also help in that you can clearly explain to contributors where the money will be going.

» **Have a clear production plan.** It's far better to deliver early than late. Before starting the campaign, secure manufacturers for your story and any rewards. If you need distribution, figure that out in advance, too.

» **Remember shipping.** It costs more to mail things than people realize, and it's far more expensive yet to mail overseas. Budget these factors in before arriving at your funding goal. And do you *really* think you're going to hand-mail 5,000 rewards yourself? If the answer is no, work with a production company that will also handle distribution. Remember that shipping can take more time than expected, so take that into account too before promising delivery.

» **Keep the campaign short.** Create urgency by keeping it short. Data shows that the most money is earned in the first and last week. Avoid that saggy middle by keeping it as brief as you can while still giving enough time to reach your goal.

» **Devise a Plan B.** What are you going to do if you've only hit 84 percent of your goal and the campaign is ticking out the final few hours? Crowdfunding is an all-or-nothing proposition at most sites. Have emergency money set aside to ensure you hit the goal if you're going to come up a wee bit short.

SEEKING OUT PATRONS

Another option for writers is based on the idea of patronage, where a wealthy individual or organization supports a creative, such as yourself. The website Patreon (www.patreon.com/) does this, allowing content creators like you to be paid by members via a monthly subscription fee. Patreon members don't have to offer any rewards, although the most successful Patreons offer at least two reward levels.

Popular reward options for writer accounts include access to early drafts, bonus unpublished material, acknowledgement in a published work, behind-the-scenes photos or videos, private Q&As, the use of a patron's name for a character in a story, and free downloadable stories (new or previously published).

If you want to see successful models, check out Seanan McGuire's Patreon (www.patreon.com/seananmcguire). Her rewards range from digital downloads to original poems to monthly hangouts. Author and interactive game designer Lena Nguyen (www.patreon.com/rinari) offers levels of rewards that include exclusive polls, Q&A sessions, a private Discord server, "secret plans," and more.

Remember: Don't get carried away with offering rewards. Providing content for Patreon supporters shouldn't interfere with your main writing goals. Patreon is more of a side income versus your real job. Let its community energize you and help you stay motivated . . . unless you start making huge bank, as a few members do. If that happens to you, go for it — if you want.

Promoting You and Your Work — Making the Most of Marketing

You can never start early enough promoting and marketing yourself as a professional writer. "But I'm just a beginner!" you may point out. "Is it fair? Legal? Appropriate?"

REMEMBER

No certificate, degree, or publication magically transforms you into a writer. You become one the moment you commit to writing the best stories you can. Own that truth. Embrace it. That's all the permission you need to call yourself a writer. Let the world know you're a writer, too.

Begin with free options, like actually telling people you're a writer both in person and on social media. Increasingly invest in marketing in new ways as your interests, needs, and career demands it. We recommend two paid options to get you started. Spend $20 at Got Print, Zazzle, or Vistaprint to get 500 or more nice-looking business cards. Go simple with just your name, contact info, and maybe "writer" as a title. Nothing fancy. Give these babies out like candy.

The other low-cost writing startup option we recommend is creating your own website. Get your name as the domain name if you can, or if it's taken, pick a reasonable alternative (try adding "writer" or "books"). Again, simple is the key. A one-page site with a well-written About section and a Contact Me area is a fine start. Update it as you see fit and your career grows.

TIP

If you choose to have a writer website, it must look professional. Keep it simple and polished. Anything less is more like anti-promotion.

Keep reading for more ways to promote yourself and your work.

Standing high on a platform

You became a writer to write, not to do marketing and branding. We get it. But the reality is, regardless of your target medium, a writer's platform matters.

A *platform* may seem to be social media because people use the term "platform" there in everyday conversation. That answer is partially correct, but a writer platform is more than just what social media you have. It's your cumulative visibility and influence as a writer, which translates into a certain number of story sales because audiences already like you. Basically, it's the number of people actively paying attention to what you do and say on online, in real life, and through your work, whatever that is.

If you're a celebrity, that's part of your platform. So is an Instagram following, being a frequent conference presenter, having your own radio/TV show, or putting out a monthly newsletter. Taken together, the combination of things such as these becomes your platform.

And here's a tough truth: Most writers don't have an effective one.

Well before your first story is out, consider building an effective writer platform from the ground up, starting with any of the following options.

Social networks

Even if you have a writer website, prospective agents, editors, or producers will also check you out on social media. Do you really want them poking through your zoo pictures, tequila recipes, and political posts? Choose one or two social media sites that you like and create writing-specific accounts for yourself. Keep the content there solely about writing and related matters. Post with whatever regularity you find comfortable.

You're building a brand as a writer. Proofread everything before you post, and always triple-check content for current or potential issues that may affect how it's received. The internet has plenty of people unofficially policing it — don't give them something to attack. Stay true to your brand in tone, style, and content. The followers you attract will then be more likely to purchase your stories if your public posts are in line with your writer brand.

Writing groups and organizations

Your fellow writers are a viable part of your platform. Not only are writers interested in the same things other writers are, but they like to raise up their peers and support one another.

Consider doing the following to build your brand:

>> **Join critique groups or reading clubs.** One of the best ways for people to get to know you as a writer is for them to hear you to talk about the stories of others.

>> **Seek out professional groups organizations.** For example, look into the Society of Children's Book Writers and Illustrators (SCBWI), which covers kidlit up to and including middle grade and young adult works. You don't even have to be published to join SCBWI.

With the Science Fiction and Fantasy Writers for America (SFWA), you do need some level of paid writing sales to join, whereas the Horror Writers Association (HWA) has various levels of membership, going from beginner to well-published pro.

Newsletters

We save the best for last. When you start to experience success as a writer, create a newsletter. Even if you're only sending out that newsletter once a month or even less frequently, delivering interesting free content deepens that bond. When it's time to announce that your next story is available for purchase, the folks who receive your newsletter will be interested.

Most writers have moved to e-newsletters since stamps get costly fast if your snail-mail list gets big. It's your call, however, on whether a print or digital news-letter best suits your writing brand. Just make sure that if you're emailing, you're sticking to a schedule to respect people's inbox.

REMEMBER

Newsletters aren't self-promotional sales pitches. That should be less than 10 percent of what you offer because constant "Buy my stuff!" pushiness will make your audience dwindle fast. Instead, offer things your audience will enjoy and appreciate: book/movie/game recommendations or reviews; short interviews with agents, editors, publishers, or fellow writers; links to how-to articles you found useful, and so on. If you run across things in your research that won't make it in your story but is still really cool, include that. You can also reveal a bit about you the person via an occasional pet photo or rose garden updates, but keep the primary focus on the world of writing.

Making the most of conferences

Going to a genre-specific or general writer's conference can pay off in many ways. Because writing is such a solitary act, surrounding yourself with people who get it creates a welcome sense of community and shared endeavor. Most likely, you'll come back energized and ready to dive deeply into your own writing and revising. You'll have a clearer sense of both what you and need to do, as well.

Conferences also deliver resources you can use for years to come, such as handouts, audio recordings, story recommendations, and more. You may discover about some publishing opportunities, contests, awards, trends, and new markets for your work. You may even be able to write it all off on your taxes — how's that!

REMEMBER

Don't think of writing peers as rivals or adversaries. It may feel that way sometime, but it's not a zero-sum game. Your friend, cousin, or neighbor selling a slasher novel doesn't mean they win, therefore you lose. Instead, consider it clear evidence that hard work, good writing, and a splash of luck can win the day. The pathway to publication is real — someone you know just proved it. That's very encouraging. In short, create and build relationships. Think long term, not transactionally.

TIP

One of the most popular benefits of a conference is the potential face time with industry people. Whether you're paying for a 15-minute critique session with an agent or just drinking a beer at a hotel bar with a Netflix producer, those moments are priceless. Even if you're not pitching something, just hearing these insiders talk in semi-casual moments can help you understand their role better and see what you need to do to win them over when you finally submit your work.

7

The Part of Tens

Chapter **25**

Ten Ways to Jump-Start a Stalled Story

Sometimes, the words don't come when you face a blank page. Sometimes you run dry when you've got a little, half, or most of a story written. No matter when it strikes, writer's block stinks.

There's hope, though.

To blast past writer's block, generate new ideas instead of continuing to struggle with what you already have on the screen or page . . . which is how you got stuck in the first place. Clearly, you didn't have enough ideas.

To unlock new possibilities, we recommend creating not just one fresh idea, but lots of them. If one doesn't work, no worries! Try another. Creating story ideas is a no-pressure, low-stakes act of discovery. Have fun with the process, and you'll soon be inspired to fill page after page with writing.

Sometimes a stalled story has nowhere to go. It's perfectly valid to put it aside and work on something new. Perhaps you can repurpose that stalled story — or part of it — into something new.

Use the following ideas in this chapter to create an endless supply of new story ideas. These techniques are equally useful for launching your next story or helping you break through a block on your current project.

TIP

Make sure you have a physical or digital way to keep track of all your ideas as they emerge. Use your brain to create, not to serve as a filing cabinet.

Extra, Extra — Reading Story Headlines

Look at newspaper, magazine, and website headlines for ideas. Don't read the stories themselves, just the headlines. What sparks a story idea for you? Try changing a word or two to come up with some new ideas.

TIP

Swap out the nouns in the headline to those particular to your story. Character names and geographic locations tend to summon all kinds of possibilities.

For example: "House Fire in Elmwood Park Leaves Two Hospitalized" to "Tavern Fire in Elmwood Park Leaves Two Elves Hospitalized" "Americans Overseas: Can Their Phones Be Hacked?" to "Soldier Bots Overseas: Can Their Brains Be Hacked?"

TIP

Don't limit yourself. Headlines in a gossip magazine might be as fruitful as *The New York Times*. Go ahead and check *The Huffington Post*, *The Onion*, and any favorite internet sites for source material. Just don't get caught up in reading the stories — it's all about the headlines!

Taking a Ride on the PPE Story Machine

For nearly a century, writers have been using variations on the *Person/Place/Event story machine*, also known as the *PPE story machine*. It works like this: Make a three-column list. At the top of column one, list ten types of people. At the top of column two, list ten places. At the top of column three, list ten events. Pick one thing from each column, combine them, and watch the story possibilities practically create themselves. Table 25-1 is an example of a PPE story machine.

TIP

Use characters from your story in the Person category and story settings for Places. Have fun with the Events category, too. Including unexpected options there will result in tons of surprising options for breaking past your story block.

For example, could you do something with librarians having a funeral at the town dump? Or an assassin at a formal dance aboard a flying zeppelin? What about a grave digger having an unexpected job interview inside an interstellar space leviathan?

TABLE 25-1   **Generating Ideas with the PPE Story Machine**

Person	Place	Event
banker	zeppelin	birthday party
assassin	mountain peak	funeral
librarian	town dump	formal dance
grave digger	ice prison	job interview
space pirate	belly of an interstellar leviathan	fistfight in the dark
And so on. . .	And so on. . .	And so on. . .

Roll dice to make unexpected pairings. For a whole new crop of ideas, swap out the words in one or more columns.

Writing to Free Up Your Blocks

Many writers love *freewriting*, which is the idea of writing as fast as you can about for a specific amount of time. Whether you use a prompt or not to get you going (like "write about forbidden places" or "write about dreams you never had"), don't hold back.

TIP

Try using a core phrase such as "I want to write about . . ." or "My character wants . . ." which you repeat in writing until something else emerges, which it will after you've written that phrase three or four times in a row. Follow whatever comes next. If you run out of creative energy, return to the core phrase and repeat it until something else sparks to life. Trust us. It will.

REMEMBER

Don't edit. Don't look back. Don't stop until the time's up. The goal is to outpace your brain with all its filters and limitations.

Noodling in Notebooks

Journaling is different than freewriting because you can journal in a notebook (or on your phone) anytime, anywhere, without rules or restriction. There's no time constraint or speed requirement. It can be leisurely, meandering, and roundabout.

What do you fill that notebook with? That's up to you!

Consider doing the following to jump-start your journaling:

>> Fill your notebook with any manner of story-related things in any type of media you choose (we especially enjoy sketches, collages, and mind-map charts). Eventually, those entries will cumulatively empower your creativity to discover a way through, over, or around the story block. Give it time to accrue power.

>> Jot down possible names for a vampire lord's lair (Tomb of the Gentle Spider? Ironvale Sanctum? Duskhorn Delves?). Make a fantasy city map. Doodle the layout of an underground moon base.

>> Journal in new environments, at different times, and with different writing tools (crayons, colored pencils, watercolor paint, and so on).

>> Keep your journal — physical or digital — nearby when you wake up. Dreams are a rich source of strange, interesting things that can fuel a new story.

Taking a Field Trip

In Julia Cameron's inspiring book on creativity, *The Artist's Way*, she recommends going on an artist's date. Essentially, the idea is to take a solo expedition to recharge your creativity by "wooing your consciousness." The venues don't have to be overly artsy to be effective — a museum, art gallery, public library, or craft store can all serve as good venues to spark some creativity.

TIP

Take the main character of your story with you on an artist's date. Ask yourself the following questions about your main character:

>> What inspires them about the venue?

>> What do they react to?

>> If they went on their own artist's date without you, where would they go? What might they do there?

>> In what ways might their own solo date nourish their soul?

>> Where might your story's plot allow an actual artist's date to fit?

Take along a notebook and jot down anything that strikes you, makes you curious, or tugs at your imagination. As often as not, you're discovering the kernels of story. Even when you're not feeling stuck, Cameron suggests going on a weekly artist's date to fire up the imagination and keep the inner well of inspiration filled.

For more on Cameron's idea of the artist's date, go to her website (www.juliacameronlive.com) for a free short video on that topic. She also wrote an ebook that shares 52 ideas on how to use the artist's date to "nourish your soul."

Figuring Out What the Story Is

With a friend or on your own, take any real-world stimulus — broken sunglasses on a park bench, a single blue rose on a highway, you name it — and postulate a possible story behind it. See how many different options you can create for each. Because genre stories have fewer limits than real-world ones, bring your creativity A-game to bear.

For example, you see a #2 pencil jammed into a wall, so you ask, "What's the story here?"

>> Idea 1: Just for a moment, gravity worked sideways in this room.

>> Idea 2: You just missed ninjas battling it out with school supplies.

>> Idea 3: The pencil is a lever that opens a secret hatch in the ceiling.

TIP

Incorporate a real-world "What's the story?" idea into your story. Or examine what's already in your story for unusual things that might be the way they are for reasons beyond the norm. Play "What's the story?" until you find reasons that creatively move you forward.

Answering the Great "What If?"

Playing the "What if?" game is a favorite of many writers, including the amazing genre writer, Neil Gaiman (see Chapter 9). He writes about this very thing (along with similar ideas and funny anecdotes) in his "Where Do You Get Your Ideas?" essay in the "Cool Stuff" section of his website (www.neilgaiman.com).

Shut your eyes, open your mind, and ask "What if?" Here are some suggestions to get your ideas flowing:

>> What if . . . my cat could talk?

>> What if . . . anything I drew with this pencil became real?

>> What if . . . mirrors were a magical gateway?

>> What if . . . World War II never happened?

>> What if . . . vampires were the dominant species on Earth?

TIP

Play the "What if?" game about various aspects of where you're stuck in your story, including the characters, setting, plot, and so on. Don't hold back! Let logic, reason, and commonsense drop away if they're keeping you from coming up with more ideas.

Blending, Stirring, and Mixing

Consider how introducing a character, conflict, or theme from another story would affect the blocked scene. Perhaps choose a purposefully unexpected or even bizarre choice to challenge your creativity to think anew. Small or large, any addition will spur numerous fresh story opportunities, whether you actually incorporate those new story elements into your story or not.

Whether Hollywood movies are actually sold via an "It's like [insert Story A] meets [insert Story B]!" pitch or not, it's easy to see how that tactic aptly describes some existing stories.

For example, isn't *Sharknado* just *Jaws* + *Twister*? And the story bible for *Stranger Things* literally says it's "a love letter to the golden age of Steven Spielberg and Stephen King." Yet another A + B formulation!

How might this look for genre stories that you could write? Maybe *Die Hard* meets *Star Wars*? *Lord of the Rings* . . . with robots? *Halloween* . . . on a generational star cruiser?

REMEMBER

This method isn't only about slamming two titles together. Mixing and matching characters or themes gets you somewhere potentially exciting as well. The goal isn't to plagiarize or covertly copy anything, but to get you thinking in original ways using elements you already know.

Beginning with an Idea

Instead of starting with a character, plot, or setting, begin with a premise, an idea that a story can explore. The most memorable are your beliefs that contradict what people commonly believe. For example:

>> Justice is always just a second crime.

>> Relationships don't survive on truth alone.

>> Love means always having to say you're sorry.

After you settle on a premise, think about characters, conflicts, and settings that would help get to the heart of the idea. Layer those until a story begins to take shape. Challenge and investigate that premise.

TIP

Add a second premise to your story. This one may directly relate to the primary premise, or it may be part of a subplot. How may this new premise interact with the existing premise? The characters? The plot? How does the introduction of this new premise give rise to solutions to bypass your block?

Using Someone Else's Words

You can use an epigraph to stoke your imagination and generate some ideas. Plenty of great novels include *epigraphs*, which are a quotation, phrase, poem, or song lyrics used at the beginning of a story, though you can find them at the start of acts, sections, or chapters as well. You can see them in games, comics, TV, and film, too.

TIP

Because plagiarism is a reasonable concern when dealing with words someone else wrote, always cite your sources. Include the original author and source in every epigraph you use, as you see in these examples from three genre works:

Haruki Murakami's *IQ84*

"It's a Barnum and Bailey world,

just as phony as it can be,

but it wouldn't be make-believe

if you believed in me."

—"It's Only a Paper Moon"

by Billy Rose and E.Y. "Yip" Harburg

Neil Gaiman's *Coraline*

"Fairy tales are more than true: not because they tell us that

dragon exist, but because they tell us dragons can be beaten."

—C.K. Chesterton

Kate Griffin's *A Madness of Angels*

"We be light, we be life, we be fire!

We sing electric flame, we rumble underground, we dance heaven!

Come be we and be free!

We be blue electric angels!"

—Anonymous spam mail, source unknown

Consider adding an epigraph at the start of a problematic chapter or section. Ask yourself the following questions for inspiration:

>> How does the epigraph inform what follows?

>> What layers, nuances, or tensions does it potentially create?

>> Would it be useful to add an overarching epigraph to the entire story?

>> What about including one at the start of every chapter or section?

Search online for "best epigraphs" or "best poetry lines" for options or locate them on your own through literary grazing at the local library or your own bookshelf. Whether you ultimately include the epigraph in your story or not doesn't matter, so long as you get inspired.

Chapter **26**

Ten Common Pitfalls in Writing Sci-Fi, Fantasy, and Horror

A udiences are smart — they won't react well if you're not delivering what they expect. Yet they're also dissatisfied when you give them exactly what they've seen before. Don't worry. There's a sweet spot in the middle, and this chapter is designed to help you stay right in that lane.

Whether you're just starting out or you're deep into your fifth draft, the following will be of use. These tips remind you of specific areas and ways that a genre story can fall short of what audiences want and need. Taken together with Chapters 2 (character), 3 (plot), and 22 (revision), this chapter can help hone your craft and sharpen up your ability to write compelling stories.

Perhaps equally important, the following are some of the most common things that merit an eyeroll or rejection from agents, editors, and producers. If you're serious about getting your work out to audiences beyond self-publishing, avoiding these pitfalls will absolutely help move you closer to that goal. Your future audiences will also really appreciate that you're avoiding these oh-so-common pitfalls, as well.

Putting Surface before Substance

Genre stories, including sci-fi, fantasy, and horror, often have an inherent spectacle that's compelling. But *spectacle* —the flashy, striking visual aspect of something — isn't what stays with audiences after The End. What audiences remember later are characters they can hope and fear for. They remember how a well-crafted story made them feel, not how many blaster fights happened.

REMEMBER

Don't be so enamored by your cool, genre-y things that you neglect story substance. No amount of deep space battles, vampire takeovers of the government, or CGI magic will overcome thin characterization, plot holes, or themes that resonate with emotion and truth.

Chapter 2 has what you need to make dynamic, interesting characters, and Chapter 3 can help you fill those plot holes.

Overrelying on Coincidence

In stories, a perfectly timed coincidence feels like a cheat. Up until that point, logic and cause-and-effect ran the show, but suddenly randomness now dictates plot? Audiences don't love when that happens.

REMEMBER

Yes, coincidences do happen in real life, so seeing one in a story isn't unreasonable. Just avoid them if you can. If you can't, then limit yourself to one coincidence per story and try not to make the story pivot as a result.

For example, you be able to get away with a gun jamming just before the fatal final shot or a rope breaking just as the hero reaches for it on the side of a cliff. Because this feels so stunningly convenient, audiences may rightly say, "Pffft! Yeah, right." They won't react that way when logic, commonsense, and cause-and-effect drive the story ahead.

For more on the importance of story logic and plot, flip to Chapter 3.

Worldbuilding with Endless Details

Although having the Second Robot Rebellion occurring in the Alpha Centauri system 3,700 years ago because of a single faulty organic neuroprocessor chip may be interesting, you don't want to create too much detail when worldbuilding.

After all, readers of your story really don't need that level of detail in order to understand, appreciate, and enjoy your story.

REMEMBER

You can research, create, and dream as much as you want. Just keep it to yourself unless it's actually necessary to include in the story.

For more on worldbuilding, revisit Part 2.

Not Reading Enough

This tip is so vital that it probably should've received top billing in this list. Reading widely, deeply, and thoughtfully is such a positive way to grow as a writer that doing so will likely help with nearly every other issue on this list.

TIP

We suggest you invest the time to experience great stories. Ideally, more than once. The first time is for pure audience enjoyment. Subsequent times are to carefully consider the craft choices the writer made.

Here are our other suggestions:

TIP

>> **Read award winners.** We urge you to read the prize-winning stories in your genre, like Hugo, Nebula, British Fantasy Award, and World Fantasy Award winners, as well as those that won Oscars, Tonys, Emmys, Pulitzers, or other industry-specific versus genre-specific awards.

If you don't have time to take in some of the noteworthy classic or contemporary stories in your specific medium, at least read what quality reviewers have written about them. Even better, read those reviews *and* put your own eyes on the original texts, even if it's just skimming.

>> **Check out the recommendations online.** To find gems beyond the critically acclaimed ones, trust the "Books You May Like" recommendations on Amazon when looking at other books in your genre. Libraries and bookstores often have special sections for staff-recommended titles, and those are often personal faves versus well-known classics. Netflix and other streaming sites recommend a host of new titles for you, as well.

>> **Trust writers.** We get some terrific horror books recommendations from following Stephen Graham Jones on social media. All genres and media have people like him who always seem to be in the know about great new writers and stories.

>> **Read outside of your specific genre and medium.** Good stories are good stories, no matter what genre they are or how you encounter them.

Refer to Chapter 6 to see how reading can play an important role in story research.

Reusing Aliens/Werewolves/Elves

If you're trusting your experiences with J.R.R. Tolkien's books or a secret love of cryptozoology to populate your story world, you're missing out. Readers have seen those exact creatures before and want something original, so keep your readers engaged and be careful about recycling creatures.

You have two options here with creatures:

» Invent entirely new ones, which might just be blending together aspects of existing creatures in interesting ways.

» Tweak existing creatures to transform them into your own brand of aliens, werewolves, or elves while retaining the archetypical features that audiences expect.

When tweaking, one or two noticeable ways should be enough. Perhaps your dwarves have all given up on mining and instead are deeply involved in a species-wide pyramid scheme versus humans. Maybe your werewolves only shift while asleep, so spells have been developed that allow wizards to control werewolves without waking them, thus creating an army of snoring lycanthropes.

WARNING

You know you've gone too far if your elves are ten-foot-tall barbarians with 50-year lifespans who live in makeshift villages atop the back of monstrous land turtles. Go ahead and use them, but just don't call them elves. Invent a new name for this warlike species.

For more on how to make creatures, consult Chapter 11 for aliens, Chapter 17 for fantasy story creatures, or Chapter 20 for horror story monsters.

Embracing a Richer Worldview

Most writing classes and how-to books are firmly rooted in Western storytelling traditions. It's no surprise then that many writers end up writing Western stories that are based on many explicit and implicit Western assumptions — often those of privileged white males. For more on this idea, refer to Chapter 23 on using sensitivity readers and cultural consultants. Don't fall into this same pitfall.

The world has a vibrant, rich range of storytelling modes and styles. You can and should consider cultural and historical contexts, and how gender, race, and sexuality affect lives. Those same things need to affect your stories, too, even if your story isn't in alignment with the culturally dominant population, whether that population is human Caucasians, space vampires, or lycanthropes of any ilk.

Following Trends Too Closely

You've been told to give audiences what they want, and from recent media successes, they want . . . found-footage horror. Or they want weather catastrophes that threaten life on Earth. Or they want steampunk fantasy. Or whatever new trend you discover in movie theaters, bookstores, and the world of gaming.

Following an active trend might feel like an ideal strategy, but by the time these stories hit the marketplace and you become aware of them, the industry has been working with them for years. Literally. Odds are, they've already bought years of fresh material in this same trend and are in the lengthy production process of putting all that out there. That means that the on-trend piece you're planning to submit is going to meet more competition than something considered off-trend.

Don't toss a story just because it's working within a trend. Just be aware the market might be oversaturated. You may have to shelf that particular story and work on something else until industry folks and audiences are once again ready for that kind of book.

Chapter 24 has more information about trends in relationship to the publishing industry.

Overusing Fantastic Language

Fantastic worlds need fantastic characters and fantastic plots. Shouldn't it need fantastic language, too? Not if it sacrifices clarity. That's not to say you can't pull character names from a Nordic word bank or that you can't create a cool name for the purple-leafed medicinal herbs that will cure your character's shadowland nightmares in the second act.

However, if you're writing *k'qqaffe* for coffee, you're making things unnecessarily hard for audiences. When in doubt, value clarity over potential confusion. If you miss these potential issues, asking outside readers (Chapter 23) for feedback on any potential sources of confusion often yields helpful results.

TIP

Another pitfall in the realm of naming characters is making them too similar to tell them apart. Readers sometimes look at the first letter of a character name and skip the rest of the letters, assuming they know who it is, so "Revnar the Bold" and "Ragar the Destroyer" becomes an issue. Just use a different initial letter for names and you should be fine.

Forgetting the Promise of the Genre

You can easily get so caught up in writing the story that you somehow neglect to make the horror scare, the fantasy fantastic, or the sci-fi amazing. Audiences like genre stories for a reason: They consistently deliver common elements and experiences. Although you don't have to give them every single thing they've seen before (note the next section), if you aren't fulfilling the promises of your genre, audiences will be disappointed, confused, or worse.

TIP

Peruse this book's Table of Contents and review specific chapters on your genre to remind yourself what audiences both want and need. Then rely on the genre conventions while bringing your creativity to bear to make yours unique. Industry folk sometimes call this the "same, but different" goal. Audiences want the same type of story as their favorites, but not *exactly* the same story.

To fully appreciate all that goes into each genre, we recommend reading Part 3 for science fiction, Part 4 for fantasy, and Part 5 for horror. That's a lot to read, we realize, but there's a lot to know about each genre.

Utilizing Clichés

At one time, writers came up with something interesting, memorable, and creative. Then audiences ran across the same things again and again to the point that these once-terrific things have nearly become a joke — enter the *cliché* — a phrase or expression whose effectiveness has been lost through overuse.

If you're doing any of the following in your stories, consider other options or find a different spin to make them feel fresh. Fast!

In sci-fi:

>> Evil aliens are ugly; good ones are attractive or have humanlike aspects/qualities.

>> Technical mumbo-jumbo covers plot holes.

>> Future Earth is always post-apocalyptic and dystopian.

>> Big Business wants to use a living creature as a weapon.

>> Humanity's problems are secretly caused by aliens.

>> Aliens/robots remark on the peculiar nature of humans (often to comic effect).

In fantasy:

>> Evil exists simply because writers need easy villains. (Dump the Dark Lords, or give them a believable reason to do bad things!)

>> Every group of gods (or godlike creatures) plays chess with humanity.

>> Damsels always need rescuing.

>> Villains insist on a midnight-black or blood-red wardrobe.

>> Professional soldiers are easily bested by untrained protagonists.

>> Mentors must be old, decrepit men.

In horror:

>> When being chased, characters lose the ability to open doors, climb a fence, or run without tripping.

>> Any grizzled old dude who correctly warns future victims is ignored or mocked.

>> Monsters are good for one final jump scare . . . even after everyone is sure the monsters have been defeated.

>> Authority figures are totally useless — especially (and ironically) police officers, security guards, and parents.

>> Characters are heroically self-sacrificing, saying things such as "Kill me . . . before I turn . . ." or "I'll hold off that zombie horde!"

>> In a dangerous situation, characters think the best course of action is always: "Let's split up!"

There are far more genre clichés than the ones listed here. Search online for lists — you can find lots of them out there — and check your story elements against them just to be safe.

Chapter **27**

Ten Popular Story Modes

*G*enre is a type of creative expression that has a common set of special characteristics, such as those we explain in this book regarding sci-fi, fantasy, and horror. But many writers, librarians, teachers, and academics like to push this concept further by using a related term, *subgenre.*

We understand that subgenre is widely used, but we don't love it. We much prefer the term *modes.* To us, it does a better job of suggesting a set of storytelling expectations that audiences have. These modes are a series of layers you can add to augment or expand a genre story (like sci-fi, fantasy, or horror). A mode connects or cuts across these genres and other modes in interesting, exciting ways.

Ultimately, knowing what audiences love about particular modes may help you empower your writing and guide your creative decisions to create truly great stories.

REMEMBER

You aren't limited to merely using one mode in a story. Pairing sci-fi with an adventure mode may equate to an effective tale, but you're allowed to do more if you want. A fantasy story can be both dark *and* epic, for example, just as a horror story can be apocalyptic, comic, and historical. In short, modes aren't mutually exclusive. Put a few in a blender and hit the puree button, if you think the outcome might be delicious . . . narratively speaking.

In this chapter, we select ten popular modes that match up well with sci-fi, fantasy, and horror. Other tried-and-true modes are available beyond these ten (such as thrillers, westerns, and spy stories, to name just a few), so feel free to investigate modes not on this list on your own and use as you see fit, though the ones we include here are real audience pleasers.

Danger at Every Step — The Adventure Story

In an adventure story, audiences follow your main character along a series of encounters that showcase derring-do, exploration, and discovery. These stories tend to be fast-paced and full of experiences well beyond the ordinary, which means dangerous situations pile up one atop another in relatively short order.

Adventure stories often

>> **Throw characters again and again into dangerous circumstances.** The result is a story full of thrills and near-misses because real danger is afoot from the start.

>> **Amp up the tension.** Whether it's a counting-down clock or increasingly challenging stakes, audiences keep guessing "What will happen next?" which is *the* question at the heart of great fiction.

>> **Offset the thrills with moments of lightness or humor.** It can't all be high-stakes action and conflict, so sprinkle in some comic relief or something that's not cranked to the max. The contrast will serve the story well.

>> **Use a picaresque/episodic story structure.** Because adventure stories include a lot of movement, the settings change as the main character moves from place to place. Whether these settings are exotic or mundane, the overall effect creates an episodic feel, even if the story is just a one-off tale versus a massive series, as so many adventure stories are.

TIP

To create dynamite adventure stories, make sure you have a driving plot (Chapter 3), a setting fraught with peril (Chapters 5 and 8), and a powerful antagonist (Chapter 2) fully committed to making things hard for your main character.

"It's the End!" — The Apocalyptic Story

Civil wars, world wars, environmental mayhem, biological/scientific disasters, alien invasions — although unwelcome in real life, these situations are the strength of a high-stakes, riveting apocalyptic story. Stories focused on the end of civilization may seem like they wouldn't be bestseller or big-box-office options for writers. Nothing could be further from the truth.

Apocalyptic stories often

>> **Showcase human resilience.** Audiences love to see humanity assert itself in the face of overwhelming large-scale adversity. Go, mankind!

>> **Magnify environmental/political/scientific threats.** The challenge to humanity doesn't come out of nowhere; these stories create a logical pathway of destruction that can shed new light on existing things that can easily get out of hand, if left unchecked.

>> **Reveal societal fragility.** People have so many local issues that few worry about civilization because everything is going fine . . . until it's not. And then it breaks at every possible stress point in dramatic, powerful ways that make for good stories.

>> **Examine the effects of resource depletion.** Few things push a character to the limit and force them to reveal their true selves as effectively as running out of ammo, fuel, food, or water. And toilet paper.

The richness of the setting is paramount, so let Chapters 5 and 8 deeply inform your story. Audiences must care about the world as much as the characters because the stakes for each should be existential. If the setting (or, gasp, the characters!) don't generate empathy from audiences, the story will fail.

TIP

Because apocalyptic stories deal with the destruction of billions of lives, let Chapter 23 offer ideas on how to be sensitive about that mind-boggling horror. Some writers treat the apocalypse like it's just a simple adventure like any other, which is a huge mistake.

Gags, Sketches, and Snark — The Comedy Story

Who doesn't love to laugh, right? Whether you're parodying a popular story, using irony, employing slapstick, including bumbling characters, or using a zinger-filled voice, humor can serve as a potent, welcome pause from high story tension. When done well, comedy transforms a sci-fi, fantasy, or horror story into something truly memorable.

Because humor writing requires serious study, we suggest reading a book like Scott Dikkers' *How to Write Funny* (Writer's Digest Books) in addition to scrutinizing the best humorous genre writing you can find to use as models and mentor texts. Examine stories that only occasionally use humor to good effect as well as those that aim for the guffaws all the way through.

Comedy stories often

>> **Use proven comedic moments.** Whether the entire piece is comedic or it's just a perfectly timed HA! in an otherwise serious story — the humor has to land. Don't just trust your own sense of what's giggle-worthy. Revise and tweak until your test audiences reacts in the right way.

>> **Use characters primed for humor.** Give them a terrific sense of humor, a keen sarcastic voice, or biases that go to a hilarious extreme. Everyday characters won't do the trick, unless they're the non-funny one (often referred to as the *straight man*) to contrast a humorous character or event.

>> **Turn conflict into comedy.** Try amplifying a problem into epic comic proportions. Examine near-endless ideas on how to do it from the pros who've been making this happen for decades — TV sitcom writers.

>> **Play off genre expectations.** Knowing what makes a fantasy (or any genre) story good allows you to undercut or overplay an element to comic effects. Subvert expectations to surprise your audience.

TIP

Because plot can set up comic outcomes, refer to Chapter 3 for ideas on how to make that happen. Another fun option is to check out the genre–writing pitfalls in Chapter 26 . . . and do them to the *nth* degree. Follow the pathway down the wrong routes to see if there's humor at the end of those tunnels. (Spoiler: We think there is.)

Capers, Cons, and Heists — The Crime Story

Whether your characters are the criminals or the ones chasing criminals, at the center of a crime story is — no surprise here — a crime and the subsequent investigation. Few story modes sell better than crime stories because the stakes are high, the action is fast, and the battle of good versus evil is embodied in the dogged pursuit of the criminal.

Crime stories often

>> **Vividly depict the crime.** Audiences are showing up for the crime. Let the tension crackle, and don't skimp on the magic, tech, and tools the criminals employ. Let audiences vicariously participate in the exciting moment, whether

it's rendered in rich in-the-moment scenes or strikingly described by someone in the final scenes of the story.

- » **Have a competent detective figure leading the chase.** Even if it's just an amateur detective, they should have the instincts, resources, and drive to really get after the criminals. If not, where's the tension?

- » **Share the clues the detective gets with the audience.** Audiences want to guess and predict alongside the forces of justice. Play fair with them. As the detective learns things about the crime, share them.

- » **Have ambiguous clues and multiple suspects.** Anything less than this and it's far too easy for audiences to figure out. If your audiences crack the case before the story's authorities do, they'll be disappointed.

- » **Utilize twists and tricks.** A detective may play dumb to coax a suspect into revealing more than they intended, or a con artist may generate misdirection to steal the elven crown.

TIP

To keep crime stories from merely being about a crime, let Chapter 2 help you create satisfying ones to give depth to the criminals and those who seek to imprison them. Chapter 23 gives ideas on how to enlist expert help — from lawyers and police, perhaps? — to raise the level of authenticity in your story.

Doom and Gloom — The Dark Story

Even though horror is already intrinsically dark, sci-fi and fantasy stories can benefit from layering in horror, menace, mystery, or a general feeling of unease. In short, a dark story is genre with an edge. The magic is more potent and costly, the setting is just plain nastier, and the general story has a toughness to it that might make audiences squirm.

Dark stories often

- » **Happen in a dark world.** Not necessarily literal darkness, but the setting should be thick with history, atmosphere, magic, technology, or potential conflicts that aren't upbeat. Set a somber mood. Think gritty. Think nasty.

- » **Embrace the middle ground.** No white-hat/black-hat morality here. Everyone and everything — from characters to governments to religion to magic systems — is nuanced and complex, with a hard lean toward the dark side of things. It all exists in the murky gray.

- » **Don't end well . . . for anyone.** If you want happy endings, look elsewhere. The heroes don't always win in a dark story, and even if they do, the cost is tragically high. (Remember that audiences have to care about the characters, though, or the story doesn't mean anything, whether those characters win, lose, or draw.)

>> **Force audiences to confront uncomfortable things.** The lines between good and evil are so blurred that a character audiences love might well do something horrendous. Audiences will have to deal with fears, unknowns, and uncertainties that are at the oozy center of dark stories.

TIP

When creating a dark version of a genre story, make sure the setting (see Chapter 8) and the monsters and minions (see Chapters 17 and 21) have teeth, real or figurative. The sharper the better! Plus, you want to use flawed characters (see Chapter 2) — there are no shiny, rainbow-farting unicorns or squeaky-clean heroes in dark stories!

The Grandest of Scales — The Epic Story

Epics are big, and we mean *big*. For books, that usually means a trilogy or more. In terms of narrative timespan, epic stories can cover years, decades, or centuries. Equally common is how epics are built upon a sizable backstory or setting well beyond the norm of most stories.

Clearly, creating an epic requires a lot of planning because of the sheer amount of characters, settings, and plot points, but that's what readers love about epics — the deep, sometimes near-fathomless dive into a riveting world that goes on and on and on as well as the bigger-than-life struggles that take place there.

Epic stories often

>> **Unfold over a long period of time and/or geographic space.** Your story is big, after all, so make sure that the time or space covered is proportionate. A common strategy is to start small and snowball into the vastness that is your story.

>> **Have intricate plots.** And subplots, too. The epic has room to explore narrative options, so deliver on those possibilities with conflict-rich plots and scenes.

>> **Include lots of characters.** Having many characters gives you lots of point of view options, puts more people at risk, and allows for complex, multilayered conflict. Put those characters to work for the story.

>> **Require big stakes, big problems, and big solutions.** The size and scopes of epics let writers dream up big wonders, present huge scenes, and allow the story to operate on a magnificent, grand scale.

TIP

To create audience-pleasing epics, invest extra time into building a rich world that's ripe with the potential for conflict (Chapters 5 and 8), and populate it with characters with enough complexity to carry story and after story (Chapter 2). And go big with the word count of your stories — like *really* big.

The Power of the Past — The Historical Story

As opposed to worlds built mostly or entirely from the imagination, historical stories are set in a specific, recognizable period of human history (generally more than 50 years in the past) like the Victorian period, the Old West, or ancient Rome.

Audiences love history-based stories because the story is like a literary time machine — they're transported to the past in a compelling, meaningful way. They get to witness historical events unfold, and certain times, places, and situations from the recent and deep past hold ongoing appeal. Equally important, the literary experience of engaging with the past can help audiences appreciate and understand the present, too.

Historical stories often

>> **Are based on deep research.** Of all the modes in this chapter, this one may require the most planning and research. We're not just talking using Google, either. Visit your library and perhaps even reach out to real-world experts. Research is more than just dates and places; it's also how people thought, where they went for fun, and what they feared.

>> **Weave history into the plot.** History isn't just a backdrop. Connect it to the happenings in your story. You've picked this specific moment of history for a reason — make it more than just scenery.

>> **Blend imagination and fact.** Let "What if?" questions guide you to blend the exciting aspects of your genre with the most interesting parts of this particular place and time in history.

>> **Privilege readability over era-authentic dialogue.** Too many writers want dialogue to sound real, so characters speak in nearly indecipherable languages or dialects. Avoid that temptation. Drop in a hint or a word now and then to remind your readers, but write it in clear, understandable English. Aim for authenticity, not accuracy.

REMEMBER

The challenge of writing a historical story is that you both start with and stick with Earth for nearly all of your creative choices (see Chapter 6 for guidance on mixing reality and imagination).

Fighting on the Frontlines — The Military Story

A team of dwarven sappers taking out a castle. A troop of Martian ant warriors besieging a smuggler's space port. A horde of werewolves raging across the battlefields of World War II. Audiences are drawn to these kinds of moments because so many interesting things happen at once: bravery versus cowardice, justice versus injustice, order versus chaos, and so much more.

Military stories often

>> **Acknowledge that soldiers have flaws.** Having military training gives them a specific area of expertise. That doesn't mean they're a ninja-deathlord-killing machine. They likely don't know how to use weapons beyond the one they were trained on. And they'll have flaws like any other character. Lean into those shortcomings and flaws to keep them relatable.

>> **Often include an ensemble cast.** Soldiers don't go it alone, so include the squad, team, or troop. If audiences don't know anything about the other soldiers, they're just nameless meat shields or anonymous fodder for a body count.

>> **Forefront the soldier's experience.** They put you in the smoke-filled dungeon trenches, in the cockpit of the interplanetary gunship, in the ancient city now overrun by winged horrors. Or they follow battles from a commander's vantage point, seeing things from that high-level, high-stakes perspective.

>> **Center on believable strategy and tactics.** Battles aren't just two sides mindlessly slamming headlong into each other. There are calculated ebbs and flows, pushes and counter pushes. A smart leader works hard to discover a way to outfox an enemy and snare the upper hand.

>> **Acknowledge the aftermath and trauma of battle.** Whether your soldiers are humans, dwarven sappers, or five-armed Drugmits from the Solar Maelstrom, killing as a profession takes a toll. And what about those who are forced into the ranks of the military? How do they cope with the violence and death?

TIP

Refer to Chapter 23 to see how to work with a sensitivity reader to properly handle a tough topic like war, which goes hand-in-hand with trauma, pain, and violence. Good readers can also help ensure you're not lapsing into clichés, military or otherwise.

Sleuthing Out the Truth — The Mystery Story

Almost every story is better with some mystery in it, and at the center of any mystery is a great unknown. Yes, a mystery can be a crime, but that's merely one type of mystery — they can just as easily be an eerie occurrence, a missing android, or an unsolvable mystical puzzle. Audiences love filling in the gaps of suspicious circumstances and following the clues, which make the best mysteries almost like an interactive story experience.

Mystery stories often

» **Include the whodunnit? question.** In mysteries, the goal is to figure out who did it, and why — thus, the vital whodunnit? question. Often, the culprit is someone the audience met long before and has been hiding in plain sight ever since.

» **Have secrets that explode when discovered.** Withholding is a powerful way to create tension and suspense, so long as it doesn't feel like a cheat. Make sure that your secret relates to the main conflict and is reasonable to be kept hidden for most of the story. If the main character doesn't know the secret, it's fair for audiences not to know either. But teasing/taunting your audiences with it may generate suspense!

» **Share all need-to-know and common information.** Withholding things in this way feels like a cheat. It's too much like being excluded from a private joke that others are laughing at. No one likes feeling excluded or manipulated for no good reason. Keep an even playing field.

» **Thoughtfully reveal pieces of the puzzle.** The clues — the puzzle pieces — have to be strategic. Audiences need to sense that they're making progress toward the aha moment without letting them get there before the story is primed and ready for that reveal. (Bonus points if it's a shocker that, in retrospect, feels absolutely believable.)

TIP

One of the biggest hiccups in a mystery is handling how to release the clues at the right pace. Chapter 22 offers tips on how to supercharge your story and ensure the clues become a strength versus a liability. And because mystery thrives in a world/ setting built for conflict, let Chapter 5 help you design the ideal one for your mystery.

The Heart of the Matter — The Romance Story

A romance story presents the struggles and challenges two people face as they pursue romantic love with each other. Because this story mode is first and foremost about love, this type tends to have an optimistic, aspirational quality to it that audiences appreciate. The romance mode plays especially well with nearly every genre and mode.

Romance stories often

>> **Focus on courtship.** A romance story can have other plots and subplots, but the budding romance must be central or it's just a minor romantic subplot versus an actual romance.

>> **Know the difference between sexual attraction and love.** The love-at-first-sight thing is hard to buy. Sure, it exists, but it's usually far more rewarding for audiences to watch a meaningful relationship grow from a spark.

>> **Let misunderstandings and surprise build tension.** Audiences want that happy ending, so anything that gets in the way is frustrating (in a good way). So, delay, delay, delay. Use whatever tactics you can to throw that happy outcome into question and hold off that final resolution.

>> **Embrace the idea that goodness is rewarded.** Good people tend to come out on top in a romance, even if they encounter incredible opposition and face tremendous obstacles. This affirmation of the power and value of goodness plays into the warm, fuzzy feelings audiences often have about romances of any type.

>> **Have a happily ever after.** That optimistic ending the audience knows is coming fills them with hope and a sense of emotional justice — after all, love is a fundamental element of the human experience. To see it fulfilled is endlessly satisfying.

TIP

To make a romance story work, you must create characters that audiences deeply connect with whether those characters are humans, robots, sentient mice, or ooze creatures. Chapter 2 can help with that. And Chapter 22 has advice on how to revise to enhance your theme to ensure it'll resonate with your audience.

Index

A

academic databases, 101

accuracy, striving for, 99–100

actions, bringing world to life with, 107–108

activating weapons of war, 152–154

Adams, Douglas (author)
The Hitchhiker's Guide to the Galaxy, 148

adaptation, from Earth, 94–98

adding variety to scenes, 57–58

adorable aliens, 167–168

advance, 349

adventure stories, 376

adversary, as a supporting character, 28

agents, for publishing, 344–346

agents of chaos, 121

Aickman, Robert
"The Hospice," 268

Alien (film), 143, 161–162, 278, 295–296

alien biology, 159

alien society, 159–160

alien technology, 160

aliens
about, 157–158, 295–296
adorable, 167–168
as allies, 164
audiences and, 160–162, 168–169
creating your own, 169
differences between, 158–160
dramatics, 162–165
emotions, 166–169
as enemies, 163
grotesque, 166–167
metaphors, 158–162
as mysteries, 164–165
as obstacles, 165

power fantasy, 167
as protagonists, 163–164
reusing, 370
as rivals, 164
sublime, 166
uncanny, 167

allies, aliens as, 164

'alone in the night,' for spaceship crew, 142

alternate histories, 186–187

alternate presents, 187–188

alternate timelines, 191–192

aMazing element, in MMMaM Index of Wonder, 204, 216

American Gods (Gaiman), 216

anachronisms, primary sources and, 103

animalistic character trait, of monsters, 290

animals, aliens as, 161–162

answering
first-draft questions, 321
"what if?" questions, 131–138

antagonists
about, 25–26
in horror stories, 274–275

Anticipation element, in formula for fear, 259, 260

antigravity, 148–149

The Anti-Racist Writing Workshop: How to Demonstrate the Creative Classroom (Chavez), 342

apocalyptic stories, 376–377

appearance
of characters, 34
as a monster characteristic, 247

Aristotle, 260

armor, 154–155

Arneson, Dave, 224–226

Arrival (film), 162

captivating character trait, of monsters, 292

Carroll, Noël (author)

The Philosophy of Horror, 276, 288, 289

Carter, Angela (author)

The Bloody Chamber, 215

The Castle of Otranto (Walpole), 305

catharsis, in horror stories, 260, 280

cause and effect, 47–48

Cavendish, Margaret (author)

The Description of a New World, Called The Blazing-World, 133

central figures. *See* protagonists

Chaing, Ted (author), 174

change, creating, 121

change/transformation arc, 24

chaos, agents of, 121

character arcs

about, 51–52

theme and, 325

character interiority, 66

character traits

giving to artificial life, 173

magic items as, 238

of monsters, 246–249

characters

answering questions with, 134–135

antagonists, 25–26

appearance of, 34

choosing a point of view, 29–33

conflicts and, 11

creating, 11, 19–40

creating from conflict, 89

creepy/creeped-out, 273–276

disagreements between, 88

focusing on their wants, 20–22

giving revelatory actions to, 112

growth of, 24–25

hiding, 90–91

in horror stories, 271–276

introducing the cast of, 22–29

magic items as, 239

from Middle Earth, 219–220

monsters as, 243–244

multiple POV, 223

narrative expositions and, 108

protagonists, 23–25

psychology of, 34–35

reacting to, 118

rotating point of view of, 110

showing, 89–90

supporting, 26–29

telling details, 33–36

as a tool for horror story writers, 256–257

treating artificial life as, 178–181

using dialogue, 36–40

what's important to, 88

worlds as, 117–127

Chartered Institute of Editing and Publishing (website), 337

Chavez, Felicia Rose (author)

The Anti-Racist Writing Workshop: How to Demonstrate the Creative Classroom, 342

Cheat Sheet (website), 4

Childhood's End, 162

choosing

fantastical points of view, 208–211

point of view (POV), 29–33

The Chronicles of Narnia: The Lion, the Witch, and the Wardrobe (Lewis), 66

Circe (Miller), 215

citations, following, 101

Cixin, Liu (author)

The Three-Body Problem, 190

Clark, Roy Peter (author)

Writing Tools: 50 Essential Strategies for Every Writer, 329

Clasen, Mathias (scholar)

Why Horror Seduces, 256

clichés, 372–373

cliffhangers, 71

climax

defined, 63

in Freytag's Pyramid, 46, 47

in horror stories, 260, 280

fiction, using research to balance science and, 98–103

fictive novum, 135

field research, 102

field trips, 362–363

film, writing for, 69–71

films

  Alien, 143, 161–162, 278, 295–296

  Arrival, 162

  Blade Runner, 174

  The Blob, 295–296

  Close Encounters of the Third Kind, 162

  The Creature from the Black Lagoon, 296

  Eraserhead, 280

  E.T. the Extra-Terrestrial, 167–168

  The Exorcist, 279

  The Fly, 297

  Forbidden Planet, 175

  Halloween, 279

  Hannibal, 299

  Henry: Portrait of a Serial Killer, 301

  The Mandalorian, 167–168

  Misery, 299

  The Mummy, 296

  The Night of the Living Dead, 268

  Psycho, 299

  Rosemary's Baby, 279

  Seven, 279

  The Silence of the Lambs, 325

  The Thing, 298

  The Wicker Man, 268

final edit, 328–329

finding themes, 325–326

fine nuances

  story spaces and, 127

  storytelling and, 114

first impressions, making, 106

first person

  about, 30

  in horror stories, 272

  point of view (POV) and, 110

first-draft questions, answering, 321

first-person plural, 30

The First Fossil Hunters: Dinosaurs, Mammoths, and Myth in Greek and Roman Times (Mayor), 245

Fiverr (website), 337

flash fiction. *See* short stories

flash forward scenes, 58

flashback scenes, 58

The Fly (film), 297

focus character, 55

"fog of war," 123

foil, as a supporting character, 28

fold space travel, 148

following citations, 101

footloose adventures, for spaceship crew, 142

forbidden houses, 310

Forbidden Planet (film), 175

forced confines, for spaceship crew, 142

foreboding environments, for horror stories, 307–308

Forester, C. S. (author), 140

found family, for spaceship crew, 142

framing stories, 43

Frankenstein (Shelley), 176, 187, 326

freelance editors, 335–336

Freelancer (website), 337

Freytag, Gustav (writer), 46

Freytag's Pyramid, 46–48, 51, 60–62

future

  far, 189–190

  looming, 188–189

future tech, 153–154

G

Gabaldon, Diana (author)

  Outlander, 66

Gaiman, Neil (author)

  American Gods, 216

  "Where Do You Get Your Ideas?" essay, 363–364

Y

About the Authors

Rick Dakan's first publication was *Dark Kingdom of Jade* in 1995, a tabletop role-playing game book about ghosts. He went on to write more than two dozen horror, fantasy, and science fiction role-playing books from 1995 to 2000, including *The First Line: Starfleet Intelligence Handbook* for the Star Trek game, *Atlas of Earth Alliance Wars* for the Babylon 5 Wars game, *Fantastic Four Roster Book* and *Rise of the Titans* for Wizards of the Coast, and the award-winning *All Flesh Must be Eaten* and *Enter the Zombie* for Eden Studios.

In 2000 he co-founded Cryptic Studios and was lead designer and writer for the hit superhero online computer game *City of Heroes*, as well as writer for the monthly *City of Heroes* comic book. Rick is the author of the Geek Mafia Trilogy of techno-thrillers set in the world of hackers and geek culture (*Geek Mafia*, *Geek Mafia: Mile Zero*, and *Geek Mafia: Black Hat Blues*). In 2011, after earning his MFA from the Rainier Writers Workshop at Pacific Lutheran University, his horror novel *The Cthulhu Cult: A Novel of Obsession* was published.

After several years as lead writer for Blue Mammoth Games (now a division of Ubisoft), Rick began teaching Creative Writing at the Ringling College of Art and Design in 2015.

In addition to his regular writing for newspapers and magazines and occasional short stories, Rick continues to publish in the tabletop game industry and is the organizer for the Anyone's Game Conference at Ringling College.

Visit him at www.rickdakan.com.

Beyond running the Creating Writing major at Ringling College of Art and Design, **Ryan G. Van Cleave** is an author, writing coach, and keynote speaker on creativity, writing, and publishing. For well more than 20 years, he's taught about these very subjects at Clemson University, Eckerd College, Florida State University, George Washington University, the University of Wisconsin-Green Bay, and the University of Wisconsin-Madison.

Ryan has more than 20 books with his own name on the spine, such as *Memoir Writing For Dummies*, *The Weekend Book Proposal: How to Write a Winning Proposal in 48 Hours and Sell Your Book*, and *Visual Storytelling: An Illustrated Reader*. As a ghost-writer, book doctor, and coach, he's been involved in dozens of other books and projects. His most recent writing plus teaching venture is serving as The Picture Book Whisperer, where he specializes in helping celebrity and executive clients create kidlit projects of all types.

Ryan's first professional publication was a short story about a dragon that appeared in Marion Zimmer Bradley's *Fantasy Magazine*. He's been making a lot of dragon, robot, and zombie stories ever since.

Visit him at `www.ryangvancleave.com` or `www.thepicturebookwhisperer.com`.

Dedication

To all the students we've ever had in classes, workshops, and coaching sessions — you brought out the best in us. We created this book for writers just like you.

Authors' Acknowledgments

Great books come from great teams, and although more people influenced this book than we can ever discretely note, special thanks are due to the following wonderful people:

Elizabeth Harding, literary agent extraordinaire, for her guidance, encouragement, and indefatigable spirit.

At John Wiley & Sons, Inc., Lindsay Lefevere, executive editor; Vicki Adang, learning design specialist; Chad Sievers, editor; and Ann VanderMeer, technical editor. Talk about an All-Star lineup!

Patrice Williams Marks for her wonderful guidance regarding outside readers and editors.

Our terrific families, who gave us the time and space to have so many Zoom sessions that were (mostly) about this manuscript.

Our colleagues at Ringling College of Art and Design who model the best of classroom instruction, writing practices, and creativity.

Publisher's Acknowledgments

Executive Editor: Lindsay Sandman Lefevere

Project Editor: Chad R. Sievers

Technical Editor: Ann VanderMeer

Proofreader: Debbye Butler

Production Editor: Tamilmani Varadharaj

Cover Image: © Greg Brave/Shutterstock

Take dummies with you everywhere you go!

Whether you are excited about e-books, want more from the web, must have your mobile apps, or are swept up in social media, dummies makes everything easier.

Find us online!

dummies.com

dummies
A Wiley Brand

Leverage the power

Dummies is the global leader in the reference category and one of the most trusted and highly regarded brands in the world. No longer just focused on books, customers now have access to the dummies content they need in the format they want. Together we'll craft a solution that engages your customers, stands out from the competition, and helps you meet your goals.

Advertising & Sponsorships

Connect with an engaged audience on a powerful multimedia site, and position your message alongside expert how-to content. Dummies.com is a one-stop shop for free, online information and know-how curated by a team of experts.

- Targeted ads
- Video
- Email Marketing

- Microsites
- Sweepstakes sponsorship

20 MILLION PAGE VIEWS EVERY SINGLE MONTH

15 MILLION UNIQUE VISITORS PER MONTH

43% OF ALL VISITORS ACCESS THE SITE VIA THEIR MOBILE DEVICES

700,000 NEWSLETTER SUBSCRIPTIONS TO THE INBOXES OF

300,000 UNIQUE INDIVIDUALS EVERY WEEK

# of dummies

Custom Publishing

Reach a global audience in any language by creating a solution that will differentiate you from competitors, amplify your message, and encourage customers to make a buying decision.

- Apps
- Books
- eBooks
- Video
- Audio
- Webinars

Brand Licensing & Content

Leverage the strength of the world's most popular reference brand to reach new audiences and channels of distribution.

For more information, visit dummies.com/biz

PERSONAL ENRICHMENT

Staying Sharp
9781119187790
USA $26.00
CAN $31.99
UK £19.99

Facebook
9781119179030
USA $21.99
CAN $25.99
UK £16.99

Guitar
9781119293354
USA $24.99
CAN $29.99
UK £17.99

Investing
9781119293347
USA $22.99
CAN $27.99
UK £16.99

Beekeeping
9781119310068
USA $22.99
CAN $27.99
UK £16.99

Digital Photography
9781119235606
USA $24.99
CAN $29.99
UK £17.99

Meditation
9781119251163
USA $24.99
CAN $29.99
UK £17.99

Pregnancy
9781119235491
USA $26.99
CAN $31.99
UK £19.99

Samsung Galaxy S7
9781119279952
USA $24.99
CAN $29.99
UK £17.99

iPhone
9781119283133
USA $24.99
CAN $29.99
UK £17.99

Crocheting
9781119287117
USA $24.99
CAN $29.99
UK £16.99

Nutrition
9781119130246
USA $22.99
CAN $27.99
UK £16.99

PROFESSIONAL DEVELOPMENT

Windows 10
9781119311041
USA $24.99
CAN $29.99
UK £17.99

AutoCAD
9781119255796
USA $39.99
CAN $47.99
UK £27.99

Excel 2016
9781119293439
USA $26.99
CAN $31.99
UK £19.99

QuickBooks 2017
9781119281467
USA $26.99
CAN $31.99
UK £19.99

macOS Sierra
9781119280651
USA $29.99
CAN $35.99
UK £21.99

LinkedIn
9781119251132
USA $24.99
CAN $29.99
UK £17.99

Windows 10
9781119310563
USA $34.00
CAN $41.99
UK £24.99

SharePoint 2016
9781119181705
USA $29.99
CAN $35.99
UK £21.99

Fundamental Analysis
9781119263593
USA $26.99
CAN $31.99
UK £19.99

Networking
9781119257769
USA $29.99
CAN $35.99
UK £21.99

Office 2016
9781119293477
USA $26.99
CAN $31.99
UK £19.99

Office 365
9781119265313
USA $24.99
CAN $29.99
UK £17.99

Salesforce.com
9781119239314
USA $29.99
CAN $35.99
UK £21.99

Coding
9781119293323
USA $29.99
CAN $35.99
UK £21.99

Learning Made Easy

ACADEMIC

9781119293576
USA $19.99
CAN $23.99
UK £15.99

9781119293637
USA $19.99
CAN $23.99
UK £15.99

9781119293491
USA $19.99
CAN $23.99
UK £15.99

9781119293460
USA $19.99
CAN $23.99
UK £15.99

9781119293590
USA $19.99
CAN $23.99
UK £15.99

9781119215844
USA $26.99
CAN $31.99
UK £19.99

9781119293378
USA $22.99
CAN $27.99
UK £16.99

9781119293521
USA $19.99
CAN $23.99
UK £15.99

9781119239178
USA $18.99
CAN $22.99
UK £14.99

9781119263883
USA $26.99
CAN $31.99
UK £19.99

Available Everywhere Books Are Sold

dummies.com

dummies
A Wiley Brand

Small books for big imaginations

9781119177173
USA $9.99
CAN $9.99
UK £8.99

9781119177272
USA $9.99
CAN $9.99
UK £8.99

9781119177241
USA $9.99
CAN $9.99
UK £8.99

9781119177210
USA $9.99
CAN $9.99
UK £8.99

9781119262657
USA $9.99
CAN $9.99
UK £6.99

9781119291336
USA $9.99
CAN $9.99
UK £6.99

9781119233527
USA $9.99
CAN $9.99
UK £6.99

9781119291220
USA $9.99
CAN $9.99
UK £6.99

9781119177302
USA $9.99
CAN $9.99
UK £8.99

Unleash Their Creativity

dummies.com

dummies®
A Wiley Brand